Yves Congar's Theology of the Holy Spirit

Recent Titles in
AMERICAN ACADEMY OF RELIGION
ACADEMY SERIES

SERIES EDITOR
Kimberly Rae Connor, University of San Francisco

A Publication Series of
The American Academy of Religion
and Oxford University Press

AMERICAN ACADEMY OF RELIGION

Yves Congar's Theology of the Holy Spirit

ELIZABETH TERESA GROPPE

UNIVERSITY PRESS

2004

OXFORD

UNIVERSITY PRESS

Oxford   New York
Auckland   Bangkok   Buenos Aires   Cape Town   Chennai
Dar es Salaam   Delhi   Hong Kong   Istanbul   Karachi   Kolkata
Kuala Lumpur   Madrid   Melbourne   Mexico City   Mumbai   Nairobi
São Paulo   Shanghai   Taipei   Tokyo   Toronto

Copyright © 2004 by The American Academy of Religion

Published by Oxford University Press, Inc.
198 Madison Avenue, New York, New York 10016
www.oup.com

Oxford is a registered trademark of Oxford University Press

Library of Congress Cataloging-in-Publication Data

Groppe, Elizabeth Teresa, 1963–
Yves Congar's theology of the Holy Spirit / Elizabeth Teresa Groppe.
p. cm.—(American Academy of Religion academy series)
Includes bibliographical references.
ISBN 0-19-516642-6
1. Holy Spirit—History of doctrines—20th century. 2. Congar, Yves, 1904–
I. Title. II. Series.
BT121.3.G76 2003
231'.3'092—dc21   2003000516

9 8 7 6 5 4 3 2 1

Printed in the United States of America
on acid-free paper

Dedicated to
Catherine Mowry LaCugna (1953–1997)
in gratitude for her life in the Spirit.

Acknowledgments

This study of Yves Congar's theology of the Holy Spirit required many solitary hours in library stacks and study carrels, but it could never have been written without the support of many people. God created us, Congar emphasized, not as isolated individuals but as persons in communion, and there are many persons without whom this book would not have been possible. The book began as my doctoral dissertation at the University of Notre Dame, and I would like to express my debt of gratitude to the many persons who enriched my years of graduate study—my student colleagues and the faculty and staff of the theology department. I am particularly grateful to my dissertation directors and committee. Catherine Mowry LaCugna was the original director of the dissertation, and her work in trinitarian theology was a great inspiration to me, both spiritually and intellectually. The grace and courage with which she continued to teach even as she faced her illness and endured excruciating suffering are a testimony to the truth of her words: "The mystery of God is revealed in Christ and the Spirit as the mystery of love, the mystery of persons in communion who embrace death, sin, and all forms of alienation for the sake of life" (*God for Us*, p. 1). This book is dedicated to her.

Mary Catherine Hilkert, O.P. graciously assumed the directorship of the dissertation after LaCugna's death, and she too was a superb mentor and a great personal inspiration. I am forever grateful for her generous help and guidance. I also had an excellent dissertation committee in the persons of Robert Krieg, Richard McBrien, and Thomas O'Meara, O.P. My work benefited greatly in structure, style and content from the comments and assistance of my entire dissertation board. I am particularly grateful to Thomas O'Meara for loaning me many of his personal Congar files and books. I would also like to express my gratitude to the late Dolores Zohrab Liebmann and to the Liebmann Trustees for the award of the Dolores Zohrab Liebmann fellowship which supported the final years of my graduate study. Thanks are due as well to the Sisters of the Holy Cross at the Church of Loretto in South Bend for their liturgical hospitality. Congar professed that he learned half of his theology through liturgy, and I have no doubt that my appreciation for Congar's work was enhanced by the fact that I was able to worship as a graduate student in a place where liturgy was celebrated with such commitment, conviction, beauty, and grace, in a community of women dedicated to putting the Gospel into practice in the world.

I am deeply grateful as well to my husband John for his love and support, and to my most formative teachers, my parents John and Rose Marie. They helped keep a roof over our heads as John and I completed our graduate studies together, and my mother Rose Marie was such a superb proofreader that one of the faculty on my dissertation board remarked on the quality of her work. She also made time to proofread the manuscript for this book with my father on stand-by as editorial consultant.

In the course of the preparation of the dissertation, portions of several chapters were presented at the systematic theology section of the American Academy of Religion and the contemporary theologies section of the College Theology Society. I would like to thank the following persons for helpful comments made on these occasions: Bernard Cooke, Dennis Doyle, Bradford Hinze, and Miroslav Volf. Condensed portions of the dissertation were published in an article in *Theological Studies*, and I am grateful to Michael Fahey, S.J., for his assistance with that article and for permission to use this material in book form. I would also like to thank all my new colleagues in the theology department at Xavier University for their exceptional collegiality and support. I thank as well Ramiro Pellitero for sharing his bibliography of recent European secondary literature on Congar. This arrived too late to be incorporated into my own bibliography, but if others doing Congar research are interested in this resource, Professor Pellitero is graciously willing to share his work. You may contact him at the Faculty of Theology, University of Navarra, 31080-Pamplona, Spain.

Finally, I am grateful to Kim Connor of the University of San Francisco, editor of the American Academy of Religion Academy Series; Cynthia Read, Executive Editor at Oxford; production editors Stacey Hamilton and Rebecca Johns-Danes; copyeditor Jerilyn Famighetti; and two anonymous reviewers for all their time and contributions. The limitations of the book that remain are, of course, my own.

Contents

Yves Congar's Theology
of the Holy Spirit

Introduction

*The Contribution of Yves Congar's Theology
of the Holy Spirit*

The Spirit of God, wrote the French Dominican Yves Congar, is the
Spirit of Wisdom—"intelligent, holy, unique, manifold, subtle, mobile, clear, unpolluted, distinct, invulnerable, loving the good, keen,
irresistible, beneficent, humane, steadfast, sure, free from anxiety,
all-powerful, overseeing all, and penetrating through all spirits that
are intelligent, pure, and altogether subtle" (Wis 7:22–23).[1] How
does one write "academic" works of theology about the subtle and
the holy? How does one speak of one of whom it is said "she is a
breath of the power of God, and a pure emanation of the glory of
the Almighty" (Wis 7:25)?

Congar was well aware of pneumatology's intrinsic difficulty. He
emphasized that it is more important to live in the Spirit than to try
to explain the Spirit's mystery, and that our theologies of the Spirit
will inevitably be inadequate.[2] At the same time, Congar believed
that we must not underestimate the value of theological efforts.[3] The
priority of what he called a "living pneumatology" did not abrogate
his sense of the need for serious theological reflection but rather demanded close attention to the presence of the Spirit in human
hearts and in creation and history. "The Gospel and the Spirit," he
wrote in 1984, "are constantly rising again in hundreds, even
thousands of springs from an underground source of water below
the contemporary desert of France."[4]

Congar's interest in the theology of the Holy Spirit was inseparable from his lifelong work in the discipline of Roman Catholic ecclesiology, for which he is most well known. His manifold contributions to a renewed theology of the church earned him recognition as

the most important Roman Catholic ecclesiologist of the twentieth century. The theology of the Holy Spirit was always a component of his ecclesiology, but in the last decades of his life his research and writing concentrated in a more focused and intensive way on pneumatology. Between 1967 and 1985, he published more than fifteen articles on the theology of the Holy Spirit, the three-volume *I Believe in the Holy Spirit* (1979–1980), and the monographs *Esprit de l'homme, Esprit de Dieu* (1983), and *The Word and the Spirit* (1984). In these works, Congar made more manifest an insight that had been present in at least an incipient way in some of his earlier writings: the need to integrate reflection on the indwelling of the Holy Spirit in the human person (*une anthropologie pneumatologique*) with reflection on the activity of the Holy Spirit in the church (*une ecclésiologie pneumatologique*). This insight, I submit, is Congar's distinctive contribution to a contemporary Roman Catholic theology of the Holy Spirit, and its implications are broadly ecumenical in scope.

The magnitude of Congar's contribution stands out with particular force when his theology of the Holy Spirit is read in contrast to the pneumatology of his immediate predecessors within the Roman Catholic tradition. It is commonly said that Western Christianity has forgotten or neglected the Spirit, and it is certainly true that the Eastern Church—with its distinctive theology of the procession of the Spirit, its liturgy, and its mystagogy—has a vital pneumatology from which the West has much to learn. And yet, it would be improper to charge Western Christianity indiscriminately with a neglect of pneumatology. The dominant Roman Catholic theology of Congar's youth did in fact include attention to the Holy Spirit. This attention, however, was limited primarily to reflection on the indwelling of the Spirit in the human soul. In neoscholastic theological manuals and in popular works of spirituality, theologians discussed the indwelling of the Spirit and the consequent bestowal of spiritual gifts and fruits, while professional theological journals carried on extensive deliberations about the divine indwelling and the theology of appropriations.[5] At the same time, however, there was little or no reflection on the ecclesiological consequences of the indwelling of the Spirit. In many of the *De Ecclesia* treatises that were standard seminary fare during this period, Congar observed, "the Holy Spirit is not even mentioned."[6] Those treatises that did mention the Spirit typically did so only in a limited way, appealing to the Holy Spirit in order to affirm the authenticity of the Catholic tradition and the infallibility of the magisterium.[7] "[I]n the domain of the thematized, systematized thought," Congar commented, "there was not a pneumatological ecclesiology."[8] Pneumatology was restricted almost exclusively to a theology of the Spirit's indwelling of the human person, and this spiritual anthropology was divorced from systematic ecclesiological reflection. Both theological anthropology and ecclesiology suffered as a consequence.

This disjunction of spiritual anthropology and ecclesiology was characteristic of much of post-Reformation Roman Catholic theology. Congar considered Robert Bellarmine (1542–1621) the dominant Catholic ecclesiologist of this era and noted that his theology of the church was not pneumatologically developed. Dionysius Petavius (1587–1652), meanwhile, was "famous for his theology of the personal relationship between the righteous soul and the Holy Spirit, but this theology lacks an ecclesiological extension."⁹ Johann Adam Möhler (1796–1838) and Matthias Joseph Scheeben (1835–1888) were important exceptions to the general practice of disjoining spiritual anthropology and ecclesiology in the centuries that span the period between the Reformation and the twentieth century. Their approach, however, was not reflected in the dominant theology of the seminary manuals in which aspiring priests and theologians of Congar's youth were trained.

In these manuals, a *De Ecclesia* treatise that made little or no reference to the Holy Spirit was typically accompanied by treatises on grace that discussed at some length the indwelling of the Holy Spirit in the human person. In the widely used *Brevior synopsis theologiae dogmaticae*, by Adolphe Tanquerey, for example, the treatise on grace (*De Gratia*) explains that the Spirit is poured forth and inheres in the hearts of the justified, regenerates and renovates the soul, makes us adopted children of God and temples of the Holy Spirit, is present to different degrees in different persons, bestows the gifts of the Spirit, and illumines the intellect.¹⁰ In Tanquerey's manual, this theology of the indwelling Spirit has little bearing on the preceding treatise, "On the Church of Christ," which mentions the Holy Spirit only four times: twice in the subsection "On the Infallibility of the Apostolic College and the Gathered Episcopacy"; once under the heading "The Infallibility of Peter and the Roman Pontiff"; and once in the article "On the Exceptional Holiness and Inexhaustible Fecundity of the Catholic Church," which discusses the superiority of the Roman Catholic Church to the Orthodox and Protestant communities.¹¹ Whereas the treatise on grace addresses the Spirit's transformation of every member of the church, the treatise "On the Church of Christ" mentions the Spirit only with respect to papal and episcopal infallibility and to the Roman Catholic Church's preeminence over other Christian denominations.

This separation of a theology of personal indwelling from systematic ecclesiology is characteristic not only of neoscholastic theological manuals but also of more popular spiritual writings of this era. Britain's Cardinal Henry Edward Manning, known for his devotion to the Holy Spirit, wrote in the *Internal Mission of the Holy Ghost* (1895):

> Now God the Holy Ghost has the office of our sanctification; and the office of the Sanctifier is twofold. There is the work of the Holy Ghost in every individual soul from the beginning of the world; and that work of sanctification in each individual soul will continue to the end of the world. There is also the work of the Holy Ghost in the Mystical Body of Christ, that is His Church, which office began

from the day of Pentecost, and will continue to the second advent of the Son of God.[12]

In the *Internal Mission of the Holy Ghost*, Manning's purpose was to speak not of the second or corporate office of the Spirit but only of his operation "in the souls of men, one by one."[13] He hence undertook a lengthy exposition of the Spirit as source of grace and of the virtues of faith, hope, and charity; of the bequest of divine filiation; of the seven gifts of fear, piety, fortitude, knowledge, counsel, understanding, and wisdom; of the fruits celebrated by Paul in Gal 5:22; and of the perfection of the beatitudes. True to his intent to consider only the work of the Spirit in the souls of individual persons, Manning did not explicate the ecclesiological implications of the Spirit's graces, gifts and fruits. He reserved his discussion of the Spirit in the church for *The Temporal Mission of the Holy Ghost*, where he described the Spirit as the sanctifier of the church and the guarantor that the church can "never err in enunciating or declaring the revealed knowledge which it possesses."[14] Manning did not draw upon his analysis of the work of the Spirit in the human soul to elaborate a more comprehensive, pneumatologically informed ecclesiology.

Manning's work, in Congar's judgment, "does not constitute a pneumatology."[15] His approach, nonetheless, was representative of most Roman Catholic theology of the Spirit in the decades prior to the Second Vatican Council.[16] The elaboration of a detailed account of the indwelling of the Spirit in the human soul divorced from a systematic ecclesiology is characteristic not only of Manning's *Internal Mission of the Holy Ghost* but also of other popular spiritual writings of this period. Barthélemy Froget's *De l'inhabitation du S. Esprit dans les âmes justes* (1890) is another case in point. This popular work, which draws heavily on Thomas Aquinas, went through numerous editions in French and was also translated into English.[17] The emphasis throughout Froget's work is the activity of the Spirit in the individual soul; like Manning, Froget addresses issues of grace, divine filiation, the infused virtues, and the gifts and fruits of the Spirit. There are references to the sacraments, and heaven is described as a feast; an ecclesial context is thus clearly presumed. Nonetheless, as the title of Froget's work suggests, his concern is the indwelling of the Spirit in the individual souls of the just, and it is assumed that this indwelling has no major implications for the organization and mission of the church. This presumption is also characteristic of writings by subsequent authors such as Hugh Francis Blunt, *Life with the Holy Ghost: Thoughts on the Gifts of the Holy Ghost* (1943); James Carroll, *God the Holy Ghost* (1940); George Frederick Holden, *The Holy Ghost the Comforter* (1907); Edward Leen, *The Holy Ghost and His Work in Souls* (1937); and *El Espiritu Santo* by Luis M. Martínez (1939).[18]

"Spiritual anthropology," Congar lamented, "now seems to have been drawn off from ecclesiology; the legal structure is all-sufficient with its guaranteed administrative charisms."[19] Searching for an alternative approach, Congar found spiritual and theological nourishment at the Saulchoir, the famous Dominican house of prayer and study. Utilizing a method of positive theology, Congar surveyed God's revelation as manifest in the testimonies of Scripture, liturgy, and tradition, reflecting on what the Saulchoir's Ambroise Gardeil, O.P., had termed God's *donné*. Congar also engaged in ongoing dialogue with Protestant and Orthodox theologians and was actively involved in the life of his own Roman Catholic Church. Through theological *ressourcement*, ecumenical dialogue, and participation in ecclesial life, Congar developed a theology of the Holy Spirit that includes both a spiritual anthropology and a theology of the church—both *une anthropologie pneumatologique* and *une ecclésiologie pneumatologique*.

Congar's theology of the Holy Spirit is in many respects a recovery of ancient traditions. In biblical writings, as Congar himself observed, there is no divorce between a theology of personal indwelling of the Spirit and a theology of the church. "In St. Paul's thought there is no opposition, no systematic and exclusive priority as between the Church and the individual believer. Each needs the other and in them both the Holy Spirit is the principle of life."[20] In Paul's letters, each person, as well as the church as a whole, is a temple of the Holy Spirit (1 Cor 3:16–17; 6:19; 2 Cor 6:16; Rom 8:9; Eph 2:19–22).

In like vein, Congar's historical research uncovered no separation of spiritual anthropology and ecclesiology in the patristic period. He reflected:

> Perhaps the greatest difference between ancient patristic ecclesiology
> and modern ecclesiology is that the former included anthropology,
> while the latter is merely the theory of a system, a book of public
> law; one may ask if the system requires men of a certain quality, or
> if it considers them interchangeable. The anthropology of patristic
> ecclesiology is that of a human communion, which finds its full au-
> thenticity in and through that communion, because in this way it
> rediscovers a resemblance to God. This is the meeting place of the
> anthropology and the ecclesiology, and it is this "communicating hu-
> manity" which is the subject of the Church's actions and attributes.
> A tradition exists on this question that should one day be restored
> and infused with new life.[21]

This synthetic quality of patristic theology is also characteristic of the work of Thomas Aquinas. Aquinas, Congar surmised as early in his own career as 1939, acted deliberately when he wrote no separate treatise on the church in his *Summa Theologiae*, for his ecclesiology is constituted precisely by his pneumatological anthropology and his Christology.[22] Aquinas's pneumatology is not a theology of the third person per se but rather "a certain dimension of ecclesiology in so far as this calls for or assumes a certain anthropology."[23]

The seamless character of ecclesiology, theological anthropology, and pneumatology that had been neglected by the Roman Catholic tradition was not forgotten by the Eastern Orthodox. In October 1963, as the schema on the church was being prepared at the Second Vatican Council, Congar dined with the Orthodox theologians Nikos Nissiotis and Alexander Schmemann. "If we were to prepare a treatise *De Ecclesia*," they commented in the context of a discussion on the Council proceedings, "we would draft a chapter on the Holy Spirit, to which we would add a second chapter on Christian anthropology, and that would be all."[24] Congar was quite struck by this comment and repeatedly recounted the story of this conversation.[25]

Congar's ecumenical outreach and theological research provided him with an alternative vision to the dominant forms of late-nineteenth and early-twentieth-century Roman Catholic pneumatology. In the theological manuals used in seminaries and in more popular works of spirituality, spiritual anthropology and ecclesiology had been disjoined. In Congar's ecumenical dialogue and historical scholarship, in contrast, he discovered a tradition in which pneumatology was at once a theological anthropology and a theology of the church. Congar firmly believed that this was a theological legacy that "should one day be restored and infused with new life."[26] Congar himself, I argue in this book, brought new life to this tradition. Congar's theology of the Holy Spirit transcended Roman Catholicism's separation of ecclesiology from spiritual anthropology, and this accomplishment makes an indispensable contribution both to Roman Catholic theology and the discipline of pneumatology at large.

My analysis of Congar's contribution proceeds in five chapters. Chapter 1 provides an introduction to Congar's remarkable life and work. The chapter recounts some of his childhood experiences in the French Ardennes, his discernment of his Dominican vocation, and his passionate commitment to the renewal of the Catholic Church, the reunification of a divided Christianity, and the service of a suffering humanity. The chapter describes the theological method Congar learned at the Saulchoir and discusses some of the primary influences on his theology of the Holy Spirit: the legacy of Thomas Aquinas, the work of the German theologian Johann Adam Möhler, ecumenical dialogue with the Protestants and with the Orthodox, and the event of the Second Vatican Council. In addition, the chapter presents in very schematic fashion a survey of Congar's vast corpus of writings, noting his intensified attention to the theology of the Holy Spirit in the last decades of his life.

Chapter 2 outlines the trinitarian theology that served as the overarching framework for Congar's theology of the Holy Spirit. Congar affirmed that God created the cosmos out of love and destined creation to share in divine communion. Through the missions of the Word and the Spirit, the cosmos is fashioned, and human creatures bear the divine image of knowledge and love. We fall into sin, and yet humanity is called to conversion and invited into redemptive communion with God—a communion that intensifies as the economy of salvation progresses to the Incarnation of the Word and the gift of the Holy Spirit. In the 1970s and 1980s, Congar emphasized the inseparability and the nonduality of the missions of the Word and the Spirit. He advocated a pneumatological Christology, emphasizing that Jesus of Nazareth is not simply proclaimed but constituted to be the Messiah through the activity of the Holy Spirit in his baptism, life, death, and resurrection. In the eschatological era initiated by the resurrection, the Word and the Spirit act inseparably to carry creation forward toward that day when "God will be all in all" (1 Cor 15: 28). The glorified Lord has become a "life-giving Spirit" (1 Cor 14:45), and the Spirit is the Spirit of the glorified Lord.

Chapter 3 describes Congar's pneumatological anthropology (*anthropologie pneumatologique*) and his pneumatological ecclesiology (*ecclésiologie pneumatologique*). Just as the Holy Spirit transforms the humanity hypostatically united to the eternal Word from the *forma servi* to the *forma Dei*, so, too, the Spirit transforms human creatures made in the image of God into members of the body of Christ; we are assimilated to Christ in a profound manner that is not simply juridical, or moral, or imitative, but we *are* in fact "truly sons in the true Son."[27] The indwelling of the Holy Spirit in the human person is a mystery of deification that elevates humanity to a new level of participation in divine life. This divine indwelling does not eclipse our human capacities for knowledge, love, and freedom but rather calls us to cooperate in synergy with the Spirit, who is the principle of our deification. In the Spirit of Christ, we know and love one another not simply with human knowledge and love but also with the knowledge and love of God; we exercise not only human freedom but also the true liberty of the conformity of our will with the will of God; and we live not only in relations of human sociality but also in communion with God and all creation. The indwelling of the Spirit is not foreign or antithetical to our created nature but rather fulfills our deepest human desires in a manner that could never be attained by purely earthly means, and this bears fruit in the theological virtues of faith, hope, and charity, in the gifts of the Spirit and the beatitudes, and in the praise and adoration of God. This indwelling of the Holy Spirit, Congar emphasized, is inseparable from the mystery of the church. The Holy Spirit is simultaneously the deifying principle of the human person and the co-institutor and life principle of the church. Through the Spirit, Jesus Christ laid the foundations of the church during his earthly life, and the Spirit of the glorified Lord carries the church forward throughout human history, preserving it in apostolicity until it reaches its eschatological destiny. The church is constituted by the sacraments, which are completely dependent on the Spirit's activity for their efficacy and fruitfulness, and the life of the church is entirely epicletic. The Spirit invoked in liturgical celebration fosters charisms in all the church's members, elevating natural gifts in the service of God such that the church is not a homogeneous uniformity but rather a communion of unique persons with a rich diversity of gifts and talents that express a true catholicity. As Congar's pneumatology developed, he critiqued aspects of his own earlier ecclesiology, including his portrayal of the hierarchy as a quasi-autonomous entity existing above and apart from the church's members, and he emphasized that the ordained ministries of the church exist only within the communion of the faithful, dependent on the epiclesis of the Spirit of God. In both his anthropology and his ecclesiology, Congar emphasized that the gift of the Spirit is the foretaste of our eschatological participation in God's eternal life.

Chapter 4 examines the integration of Congar's spiritual anthropology and ecclesiology by analyzing these two dimensions of his thought through the lens of three biblical themes that permeate his theology: the mystical body of Christ, the people of God, and the temple of the Holy Spirit. In Congar's work, each of these themes serves to varying degrees as a point of synthesis of the anthropological, the ecclesiological, and the pneumatological. The chapter also offers some sense of the genesis of Congar's theology as each of these biblical themes emerges with intensity at different points in Congar's career. The theology of the mystical body, which Congar developed in the 1940s and 1950s, offers a rich sacramental spirituality that reaffirms the anthropological and pneumatological dimensions of ecclesiology. Yet, as the Congar scholar Joseph Famerée has noted, there is a certain autonomization of the church in Congar's early theology of the mystical body insofar as the hierarchical apostolic body exercises a formal causality upon the church's members. This weakens the integration of pneumatological anthropology and pneumatological ecclesiology in Congar's work of this period. In the 1960s, the theology of the people of God became a central theme in Congar's writings. One of the merits of this biblical theology, as Congar himself noted, is precisely the strong anthropological emphasis that this paradigm brings to ecclesiology. The church consists of the *people* of God—the faithful women, men, and children who carry out the church's mission and advance the destiny of the human race. In the 1970s and 1980s, Congar's focus turned increasingly to the theology of the Holy Spirit, and he advocated the construction of a synthetic theology in which pneumatology, theological anthropology, and ecclesiology would be inseparable. This is evident in his reflection on both the human person and the church as a temple of the Holy Spirit.

Chapter 5 concludes my study with some reflections on the significance of Congar's theology of the Holy Spirit. The framework Congar has provided— his integration of an *anthropologie pneumatologique* and an *ecclésiologie pneumatologique*—is a paradigm that can stimulate constructive theological reflection in a variety of areas, including ecclesiology, sacramental theology, spirituality, theological anthropology, ecumenism, and ethics. Congar himself did not fully develop his theology of the Holy Spirit as comprehensively or as systematically as he might have done, in part because of the many demands on his time and talents but also because of his theological temperament. "Congar was not a systematic theologian," comments Hervé Legrand, O.P., a former student of Congar and now himself a prominent French ecclesiologist. "But he was a genius. He was a *sourcier*: he could point you towards a well of living water."[28] Chapter 5 examines the significance of Congar's theology of the Holy Spirit for some of the ongoing conversations in contemporary systematic theology.

The first section of chapter 5 addresses the continuing discussion as to whether the Catholic Church should be a hierarchy or a democracy. Congar's theology brings a pneumatological perspective to bear on this debate, a perspective that can help clarify some of the issues involved and help us to appreciate the truths championed by both sides of the discussion. From the perspective of a theology of the Holy Spirit that is at once an *anthropologie pneumatologique* and an *ecclésiologie pneumatologique*, the church is not a hierarchy in the sense of a society of superiors and subordinates, for the indwelling of the Holy Spirit is common to all. In this sense, the advocates of ecclesial democracy are right to critique ecclesial frameworks that subordinate some persons to others. At the same time, however, the church is not a democracy in the Jeffersonian sense of a society with "power inherent in the people," for the church originates not in the people per se but rather in the Spirit of God, the Spirit of Christ. Its origins and foundations are not democratic in the precise sense of this term. Rather, the church exists as church by virtue of its origin in God, a sacred origin—which is one etymological meaning of the term *hier-archē*. Congar's approach, in sum, can help members of different schools of thought in contemporary Catholicism to find some common ground. This section of chapter 5, moreover, examines some of the developments and changes in Congar's own ecclesiology, demonstrating that, as his pneumatology developed, he amended his own theology of church structure and ministry to better reflect an integration of his *anthropologie pneumatologique* and his *ecclésiologie pneumatologique*.

The second section of chapter 5 considers how Congar's theology of the Holy Spirit might contribute to the construction of a theological discourse in which contemporary reflection on theological anthropology and ecclesiology can proceed. Reflection on the human person and the church often ensues within the framework of the discourse of the "individual and the community," and I propose that the alternate paradigm of "persons in communion" is better suited to the integration of pneumatological anthropology and pneumatological ecclesiology that Congar advocates. Although some do view "individual" and "person" as synonymous and interchangeable terms, there is sound basis in contemporary personalist philosophy, Thomism, spirituality, and trinitarian theology to distinguish the communitarian and relational term "person" from the term "individual." In like vein, the term "communion" has theological connotations that a sociology of human community does not adequately convey. This section of chapter 5 concludes with reflections on the trinitarian,

analogical, and apophatic character of Christian theological language support-
ing the use of "persons in communion" as an apt discourse for theological
reflection that aims to integrate a theology of the personal indwelling of the
Holy Spirit with a theology of the church.

Finally, chapter 5 inquires into the significance of Congar's theology of the
Holy Spirit for contemporary discussions about the difficult topic of the personhood of the Holy Spirit and the theology of appropriations. In the decades
of the 1940s and 1950s, there was an ongoing debate as to whether the indwelling of the Holy Spirit in the human person is proper to the Holy Spirit
in a technical trinitarian sense—that is, in a way distinctive to the Holy Spirit—
or whether the divine indwelling is in fact the indwelling of the triune God
that is simply appropriated to the Spirit. Congar has transformed the framework in which that discussion takes place. Both those theologians who advocated a proper indwelling of the Spirit and those who endorsed an appropriated
indwelling limited their reflection to consideration of the divine indwelling in
the just soul abstracted from interpersonal or ecclesial relationships. Congar's
wedding of an *anthropologie pneumatologique* and an *ecclésiologie pneumatologique* provides a more relational and sacramental context from which to consider the mystery of indwelling and suggests new possibilities for describing
the Spirit's *proprium*. This concluding section of chapter 5 also observes that
the theology of appropriations has itself fallen into disuse in much of contemporary pneumatology. Congar's continuing adherence to a methodology of appropriations is instructive in that his use of this tradition was grounded in his
conviction of the absolute communion of the Holy Spirit with God and Jesus
Christ, a principle that contemporary pneumatology must preserve, even if the
discourse of appropriations itself is not revived.

Cardinal Yves Congar will be remembered as a great ecumenist who awakened the Roman Catholic Church to the ecumenical movement, impelled by
his desire "that they may be one" (Jn 17:11). He will be remembered as a Celt
from the French Ardennes who was inspired to become a priest in order to
preach conversion to a world that had embroiled itself in the First World War,
which he endured as a young boy, and he will be honored as a man who lived
with courage and determination as a German prisoner during the Second
World War. He will be known as an exemplary Dominican priest and prolific
scholar, an ecclesiologist who served his church with love and steadfastness in
spite of rebuke and exile. And he will be memorialized as a premier contributor
to the Second Vatican Council—"one of a handful of scholars," Peter Steinfels
eulogizes, "who utterly changed Roman Catholicism."[29] Yves Congar should
also be remembered as a theologian of the Holy Spirit, a man who gave new
life to a neglected tradition in which pneumatology, theological anthropology,
and ecclesiology had been seamlessly united. We can learn much from Congar's approach, and his legacy can bear fruit in the contemporary renewal of
pneumatology and in the life of the church at large. "I would like, then," Congar

mused, "to be an Aeolian harp and let the breath of God make the strings vibrate and sing. Let me stretch and tune the strings—that will be the austere task of research. And then let the Spirit make them sing a clear and tuneful song of prayer and life!"[30] The pages that follow are my attempt to listen to the song of prayer and life of this French Dominican friar and scholar.

I

Yves Congar—Theologian of the Holy Spirit

"Each one has his vocation," Yves Congar wrote, commenting on John 3:28–30, "and that is the one which is most beautiful. . . . Yes, each one's is the finest for him . . . the Holy Spirit leads toward a goal and brings everything together."[1] Congar found his own vocation in theological service, as the biographical sketch that begins this chapter describes. A general overview of Congar's theological method and prolific publications follows. The chapter then continues with a discussion of major influences on Congar's theology of the Holy Spirit: Thomas Aquinas, Johann Adam Möhler, Protestant and Orthodox theology, and the Second Vatican Council and its aftermath. This discussion of Congar's life, theological method, and sources of theological inspiration provides background and context for the discussion of Congar's pneumatology that follows in subsequent chapters.

A Life in the Spirit

Lucie Desoye Congar and Georges Congar announced the birth of Yves, their fourth child, on May 13, 1904. The Congar family, originally of Celtic origin, resided in Sedan, France, a village nestled in the Ardennes just miles from Belgium. Congar and his brothers and sister—Robert, Pierre, and Marie-Louise—grew to adulthood in the picturesque beauty of the countryside where pristine forests swept the horizon and deer and wild boar roamed freely. "We live in a 'setting' like a fish in the water," mused Congar, "but the setting also penetrates us, its woof is entangled in the web of our lives."[2]

Congar's setting included not only the natural beauty of the Ardennes but also the rich history of French Catholicism. The land once known as Gaul had been home to Irenaeus, Hilary of Poitiers, and Martin of Tours. In 496, the baptism of the Frankish king Clovis cemented Frankish rule of the region and began the assimilation of the Germanic peoples to Christianity, earning France the title the "eldest daughter of the church." The centuries to come brought Joan of Arc, Prosper of Aquitaine, Teresa of Jésus, Bernard of Clairvaux, Francis de Sales, Vincent de Paul, and so many other inspirational men and women. Monasticism flourished at Cluny, Cîteaux, and Clairvaux, and theology prospered at the University of Paris. Gothic cathedrals testified to God's beauty at Chartres, Notre Dame, Amiens, and Reims.

The grandeur of the cathedrals stood in contrast to the transgressions of French Catholicism—acts of ecclesiastical inquisition and violence that contributed to the antichurch hostilities of the French Revolution of 1789. Signs of these hostilities persisted into Congar's day. In 1904, the year of Congar's birth, the Paris city council was persuaded by the French section of the International Free Thought Federation to erect a statue of the Chevalier de la Barre outside the Basilica of the Sacred Heart. In 1766, the horseman whom the statue commemorated had been mutilated and burned at the stake by ecclesiastical authorities for the alleged crime of knocking a cross from the bridge of Abbeville into the river below. He had been eulogized by both Victor Hugo and Voltaire, and his memory was a disturbing reminder of the church's transgressions.[3]

The young Congar, however, knew only the nurturing church that he would later refer to as a "maternal hearth."[4] This maternal metaphor, he explained, is not an expression of mere sentimental attachment but rather suggests "something beyond formulation in clear ideas, something involving a vital incorporation of our deepest self, something pre-reflective and yet charged with truth—something that began before us, is beyond us, yet surrounds us and supports us in all we do."[5] The maternity of the church was one of the primary themes of Humbert Clérissac's *Le Mystère de l'Église*, a book Congar found in his mother's library that impressed him with its poetic ecclesial vision. Congar's use of maternal terms to describe his ecclesial experience may also have been shaped by his mother, Lucie, who had a strong influence on his religious upbringing and sensibilities. Congar described her as a saintly presence and a mystic, and he remembered sitting beside her in the evenings with his brothers and sister while she read from *The Imitation of Christ* by Thomas à Kempis. On Saturdays, as dusk fell on the village of Sedan, she also read from the Gospel text the family would hear once again at church on Sunday morning. "Childhood," Congar later reflected, is an age "that lives entirely from faith."[6]

The pastor of Sedan's small Catholic church made a deep impression on the young Congar. A man of the old French clergy, he wore a black rabbat, and his sermons were often commentaries on the catechism, the creed, or church history. Jewish and Protestant friends and neighbors enriched Congar's religious upbringing. The princes of Sedan had been Protestant in the sixteenth century, but they had respected the Catholics, and the Catholics in turn accommodated the Protestants when Sedan became Catholic through annexation to France in 1642.[7] Sedan thus had a more ecumenical flavor than most European cities of Congar's period, a circumstance that would prove to be important in his later ecumenical commitments. "I knew then," Congar stated as he reminisced about the shared life of Catholics, Protestants, and Jews in Sedan, "an awakening to the sense of the Church."[8]

Congar also had an awakening of another sort—a young introduction to the brutality of war. He was only ten years old when World War I began, in the summer of 1914. Lucie Congar had asked her children to keep a journal during their summer vacation, and young Yves' *Journal des vacances* soon became instead his *Journal de la guerre: 1914–1918*. "Here," he wrote in his notebook on August 25, 1914, "begins a tragic history."[9] He recounted the tragedy he had witnessed in daily journal entries and graphic drawings that vividly portrayed the desolation around him. Sedan lay in the direct path of the German offensive, and soldiers besieged the city, razed the Catholic church, deported Congar's father to Lithuania, and forced emaciated prisoners to march through the city streets. With colored pencils, Congar drew scenes of homes brimming with life juxtaposed with pictures of the charred skeletal remains of houses—scenes he captioned "before the war" and "after the invasion."[10]

Indeed, World War I was a turning point in Congar's life, a marker of time that separated the "before" and the "after." The war, he later recalled, "marked me profoundly."[11] As a young boy, Congar had originally aspired to be a doctor, and he had requested a microscope as a first communion gift. Wartime austerity, however, made his request impossible to grant, and by the time the war finally ended he had a new vocation. Yves Congar knew that he wanted to be a priest. He recalled:

> At the beginning of 1918—perhaps already at the end of 1917—I went through a very difficult period. I was invaded by a sort of incertitude; a very sad emptiness, with the feeling of no longer knowing anything, of no longer having perspective. And it was in this darkness that I perceived for the first time in an extremely clear manner, a call. The call to preach.[12]

Congar knew nothing at this time of St. Dominic or the Order of Preachers, but he was deeply moved by the "spectacle of misery, of the immense misery into which we had been plunged."[13] He determined, "I wanted to preach conversion to men. I wanted to convert France."[14]

During this period, Congar made the fortuitous acquaintance of Father Daniel Lallement, who would later join the faculty at the Institut Catholique, in Paris. Lallement encouraged Congar's aspiration to the priesthood and personally inspired him. "His exigent, rigorous, even austere vision of Catholicism and spiritual life, of the sacerdotal vocation," Congar recalled, "marked me profoundly."[15] Lallement introduced Congar to the works of Thomas Aquinas and to Jacques Maritain and Maritain's select circle of friends. He also counseled Congar to enter the minor seminary at Reims, where Congar studied from 1919 to 1921. Congar continued his training at the university seminary Les Carmes from 1921 to 1924, and military service followed. Stationed in Germany beside the Rhine, his vocation was confirmed "far from all influence . . . in the solitude of my thoughts."[16]

In 1925, Congar presented himself to the Order of Preachers. After a year of novitiate he was sent to the Dominican House of Studies on Mt. St. Aubert, in Kain-la-Tombe, Belgium. This house of study had been established by the Dominican Province of Paris, in Flavigny, in 1865; expelled from France in 1903, it moved to Belgium, where it was renamed Le Saulchoir. Congar was enamored by the fraternal spirit, the intellectual vitality, and the liturgical rhythm of life at the Saulchoir, where he completed four years of theological studies. On July 25, 1930, the feast of St. James, he was ordained. He prepared for his ordination by studying the gospel of John with the aid of the commentaries of Aquinas and of Réginald Garrigou-Lagrange. He also studied the theology of the eucharistic sacrifice, particularly Eugene Masure's Le Sacrifice du chef.[17] His ordination card pictured St. Dominic at the foot of the cross and featured these words, which Congar thought to be from Tennyson: "But none of the ransomed ever knew / How deep were the waters crossed."[18]

During Easter preparations in the spring preceding his scheduled July ordination, Congar had been asked to perform the Sermo Domini, a Dominican Holy Thursday tradition. On the eve of the commemoration of the passion, Congar chanted John 13–17, chapters that include this verse:

> That they may all be one, as you, Father, are in me and I am in you, may they also be in us, so that the world may believe that you have sent me. The glory that you have given me I have given them, so that they may be one, as we are one, I in them and you in me, that they may become completely one. (Jn 17:22–23)

These words had profound resonance. "It was while meditating upon the seventeenth chapter of St. John's Gospel," Congar later explained, "that I clearly recognized my vocation to work for the unity of all who believe in Jesus Christ."[19] Even though there were other events in his life that prepared the way for his ecumenism, Congar affirmed that "it was entirely this study of John 17 that set my course."[20] Congar had come to realize not only his affinity to the Dominicans but also his own particular charism within the Order of Preachers. He would devote his life to the service of the unity of the church.[21]

Congar realized immediately that this ecumenical vision was not simply a matter of unifying Catholics, Protestants, and the Orthodox—the vision would require a fundamental renewal of the Catholic Church itself. Indeed, he would later speak of his encounter with John 17 as a double revelation, a disclosure of a mission inseparably ecumenical and ecclesiological.[22] Following his ordination, Congar traveled to the Dominican house in Düsseldorf, Germany, where he penned an entreaty expressing his distress at the Roman Catholic Church's attitude of condemnation and censure. This handwritten prayer to God bears quoting at length:

> My God, why does your Church always condemn? True, she must above all guard the "deposit of faith"; but is there no other means than condemnation, especially condemning so quickly? . . . My God, you know how I love your Church; but I see clearly that only concerted action has force: I know that your admirable Church once played an immense and splendid part in civil affairs and in the whole of human life and that now she plays hardly any part at all. My God, if only your Church were more encouraging, more comprehensive; all the same!
>
> My God, your Church is so Latin and so centralized. True the pope is the "sweet Christian on earth"; and we only live by Christ by remaining attached to him. But Rome is not the world and Latin civilization is not the whole of humanity. . . . My God, enlarge our hearts! Grant that men may understand us and we may understand men, all men!
>
> My God, I am only a wretched child (*adolescentulus et contemptus*); but you can dilate and enlarge my heart in proportion to the immense needs of the world. . . . Time presses—there is much work to be done! My God, make my mind consonant with your Church; your mother Church is all-embracing and all-wise, rich and discreet, immense and prudent. My God, let there be nothing more that is trite and commonplace. There is no time to waste on such things. My God, there is so much work; give us leaders, give me the soul of a leader. The union of the Churches! My God, why has your Church, which is holy and is one, unique, holy and true, why has she so often such an austere and forbidding face when in reality she is full of youth and life?
>
> In reality, we are the Church's face; it is we who make her visible; my God, make of us a truly living face for your Church! I long so much to help my brothers to see her true countenance. . . .
>
> My God, so many great things, a task too heavy for human shoulders; help us.
>
> Enlarge, purify, enlighten, organize, inflame, make wise and stir up our poor hearts![23]

These poignant reflections were written on September 17, 1930. Some of the concerns expressed in these private remarks are also evident in "The Reasons for the Unbelief of Our Time," an essay Congar published in 1935 that identified the church's shortcomings as one of the causes of atheism.[24] Congar longed for the conversion of humanity and for what he spoke of at this time as the "return of the separated Christians" to Christian unity, but he also had a wrenching awareness of the Catholic Church's failings and a passionate desire to restore its true countenance.

Upon his return to France, Congar dedicated himself wholly to this ecumenical and reformist mission. After six more months of study, his life became a flurry of research, writing, teaching at the Saulchoir, preaching, and ecumenical meetings. We can imagine him, as Thomas O'Meara writes, "an energetic figure, striking in his white monastic habit, with a face of conviction and intelligence."[25] Congar clearly understood his mission in scholarly terms and collaborated closely with his Saulchoir colleagues Marie-Dominique Chenu and Henri-Marie Féret. This Dominican trio believed that the revitalization of the church required a study of history that would recover critical dimensions of ecclesiology lost during the period they identified as the era of "baroque theology." Congar, Chenu, and Féret used this term loosely to refer to the defensive theologies of the post-Reformation period that limited theology to a deductive logical exercise, reduced faith to submission to authority, and envisioned the church as a hierarchical pyramid.[26] In the Saulchoir's library, Congar read Irenaeus, Augustine, Bonaventure, Thomas Aquinas, and other patristic and medieval authors in his determined historical *ressourcement*. This return to the sources, Congar believed, should not be limited to the most renowned aspects of the tradition but should include the entirety of the theological heritage insofar as it can nourish and stimulate contemporary faith and theological reflection.[27] According to the French church historian Étienne Fouilloux, Congar had assiduous work habits, an impatience with wasted time, and a proclivity to accumulate great piles of materials and notes. Fouilloux traces these traits of character—like Congar's sometimes brusque temperament—to his Breton lineage and to his roots in the French Ardennes.[28]

Congar's efforts bore fruit in numerous ways. In 1937, he founded *Unam Sanctam*, an ecclesiological series intended to restore forgotten themes of the Catholic heritage.[29] For years, Congar served as the editor of this highly significant collection. He had hoped to publish a new French translation of Johann Adam Möhler's *Die Einheit in der Kirche* (1825) as the first volume of the series, but delays with the translation obliged him to find an alternative, and his own *Divided Christendom* was *Unam Sanctam*'s first volume. The *Unam Sanctam* series grew over the years to include seventy-seven volumes and became a theological collection of great import in the life of the twentieth-century church. "It would be difficult to exaggerate the role this series has played," comments Jean-Pierre Jossua, and Fouilloux reiterates that *Unam Sanctam* represented a "genuine ecclesiological breakthrough" for French Catholicism.[30] Congar also wrote prolifically for a wide variety of theological journals, including *Vie spirituelle, Vie intellectuelle, Irénikon, Oecumenica, The Eastern Churches Quarterly, Catholica,* and *Geistige Arbeit.* For ten years he served as the editor of the Saulchoir's *Revue des sciences philosophiques et théologiques.* Beginning in 1932, he taught the standard treatise *De Ecclesia* at the Saulchoir and led workshops for interested Dominican students on the theme of catholicity.

Congar's fervent work did not proceed without interruption. Although *Divided Christendom* was hailed by many as a landmark in Roman Catholic ecumenism, the Vatican greeted the book with suspicion. After the publication of the original French edition in 1937, Congar's superior Father Gillet was called to Rome, and an article against Congar appeared in *L'Observatore Romano.* Henceforth, Congar had to work for ecumenism in a more indirect way.[31] Shortly thereafter, Europe returned to war. The Saulchoir had just relocated from Belgium to Étiolles, France, but Congar was there a mere eight days before leaving to serve as a reserve officer in the French army. He was stationed at a fuel station, and in the spring of 1940 he was captured by German forces and taken into captivity. In the various camps through which he passed, he gave talks critical of national socialism and tried on several occasions to escape. Labeled a *Deutschfeindlicher* (enemy of Germany), he was sent to the high-security prisons of Colditz and Lübeck, where he remained until 1945. At both Colditz and Lübeck, he continued to lecture on liberty and to preach against Nazism, and he took sustenance from the courage and resistance of his fellow prisoners. Congar later referred to his wartime friendships as one of the great graces of his life.[32] At the same time, Congar was gravely disheartened by the war's ethos of terror that was inimical both to the Christian unity he longed to serve and to his own spirit. "The walls of Colditz," he later reflected, "the atmosphere of the little active wars of Colditz and Lübeck worked deeply in me and made me more closed, more hostile, more defiant."[33] He was also distraught by the interruption of his work. At the Saulchoir he had labored from seven every morning until ten each evening, carefully husbanding every minute of his time. In captivity, he agonized over the loss of not only hours or days but entire years—years that should have been among his most fruitful and productive. In the spring of 1942, he had even further cause for discouragement: "completely dumbfounded," he learned that Chenu had been removed from his post as Regent of the Saulchoir and his book *Le Saulchoir* placed on the Index.[34]

In 1945, after five years of captivity, Congar finally celebrated the war's end. France was decimated; yet his spirit gladdened as he returned home to witness the reestablishment of ecumenical contacts and the undertaking of new ecclesial initiatives by Catholics. Scholarly efforts of *ressourcement* had borne fruit, and under their aegis the biblical and liturgical renewal was well under way.[35] A variety of youth groups and adult organizations were active in the church, efforts were being made to help war refugees, and priests in work-ing-class blue were joining the ranks of the factory laborers.[36] Congar remem-bered the years 1946 and 1947 as "one of the finest moments in the life of the Church."[37] He reflected, "We rediscovered freedom, breathed again, took ini-tiatives."[38] Chenu echoed: *Quelle période passionnante!*[39] Although the climate at the Saulchoir was decidedly different without Chenu as Regent, Congar once again committed himself to an intense schedule of research, writing, teaching, and speaking. He returned to projects interrupted by the war, seasoned with intensified concern and sympathy for humanity. "I will never again," he wrote in a letter to himself composed in prison, "be able to work as if men did not suffer and certain forms of academic work will be henceforth impossible for me."[40] In the first year of the war's aftermath, Congar reflected, "It is necessary to write in a manner that can be understood by the conscience of all men."[41] He replied to all the invitations and requests for collaboration that he received and became, in Fouilloux's terms, a "theologian of service."[42] When reproached for working too hard, he said simply, "I cannot refuse them. . . . St. Dominic would not have, either."[43] Moreover, Jean-Marie Le Guillou notes, Congar con-sidered himself indebted to the service of others because he had received the opportunity to study.[44] He set himself to the task of probing the principles of the unfolding ecclesial reform that he perceived as the beginning of the renewal of the church, and these reflections were published in 1950 as *Vraie et fausse réforme dans l'Église*, a tome that some consider to be Congar's most important book.[45] This volume does not represent his most mature reflections and differs in some notable ways from the books he would write in the 1970s and 1980s, but, historically speaking, it is arguably a most influential publication. A copy of *Vraie et fausse réforme* reached the hands of the man who served as papal nuncio to Paris from 1944 to 1953: Cardinal Angelo Roncalli. According to a missionary who visited Roncalli and browsed through his host's edition of *Vraie et fausse réforme*, the Cardinal who would one day become Pope John XXIII wrote in the margin of Congar's book, "A reform of the church—is it possible?"[46]

Cardinal Roncalli's pensive response not withstanding, Rome received *Vraie et fausse réforme* with mistrust, a response that must have been distressing to Congar, for this was precisely the reaction that he had worked hard to avoid. Well aware of the tensions between church authorities and popular movements that existed in this period, Congar was concerned that *Vraie et fausse réforme* could be misinterpreted, and before publishing the manuscript he asked sev-eral friends for advice and rewrote the book according to their recommenda-tions.[47] Despite these careful efforts, the announcement of an Italian transla-tion of *Vraie et fausse réforme* provoked the prohibition of any translations or a new edition.[48]

This was not the first time Congar's work had been subjected to Vatican scrutiny, nor would it be the last. In 1947, Congar had been refused permission to publish an article on Catholic ecumenism, and subsequently he was denied approval for publication of a revised edition of *Divided Christendom*. By 1952, he was required to send all of his manuscripts to Rome for editing, down to the smallest review. "[F]rom the beginning of 1947 to the end of 1956," he recalled, "I knew nothing from that quarter [Rome] but an uninterrupted series of denunciations, warnings, restrictive or discriminatory measures and mistrustful interventions."[49] In a letter written on December 4, 1946, to a Dominican brother in Rome, Congar stated that he welcomed "objective criticisms of a scientific and theological character" but not shadowy "whispered criticisms."[50] He put together a folder of documents for his defense and entitled the collection *La tarasque*. A *tarasque*, he explained to Jean Puyo, is an "animal that is very dangerous—but imaginary!"[51] Congar never had the opportunity to use this material to formally defend his work, and he grew disheartened by the censorship, denunciations, and rumors.

Finally, in what has been called the 1954 "Raid on the Dominicans," Congar was told to stop teaching and was prevailed upon to leave France together with Chenu, Féret, and Pierre Boisselot (editor of Éditions du Cerf).[52] Vatican officials were displeased with much of the direction of French Catholicism—the priest-worker movement was one of the new developments that disturbed them, and its flourishing was closely connected with the Dominicans. Congar himself had some connections with priests involved in this movement and had written an article entitled "L'Avenir des prêtres-ouvriers" (The Future of the Worker-Priests).[53] He had not penned the title of the article, which was likely an affront to the Apostolic See, which had recently condemned the movement. In the essay, Congar spoke of the plight of the poor and commented that one can critique the worker-priests if they represent a false solution to a social problem but that one must nonetheless address the problem that remains. To satisfy the growing Roman reproach and to prevent entire French Dominican seminaries from being closed, the Dominican Master General Emmanuel Suárez traveled to France in 1954 to attempt to moderate the situation. Congar, Chenu, Féret, and Boisselot were all exiled from Paris.[54]

Congar had just been offered a chair at the *Hautes Études*. Instead of assuming this post, he began a nomadic journey that took him first to Jerusalem, in 1954, and then to Rome, from November of 1954 through February of 1955. There, representatives of the Holy See explained that there was general concern with the overall direction of his theology. Congar accepted the disciplinary exile imposed on him with an interior resistance, for he believed that the theology endorsed by the magisterium was that of a single theological school, rather than the only legitimate manner of theological reflection.[55] Congar's expatriation continued, in 1956, in Cambridge, where his activities were very limited. At the end of 1956, Bishop Weber, of Strasbourg, invited Congar to his diocese, where at least he was able to live his vocation as a preacher.

A misunderstood scholar, Congar had been unjustifiably reproached and separated from his friends and homeland. Remarkably, however, his love and commitment did not waver. Rather, he intensified his resignation to the cross as he reflected on suffering, patience, and hope:

> Anyone who is acquainted with me knows that I am impatient in little things. I am incapable of waiting for a bus! I believe, however, that in big things I am patient in an active way about which I would like to say a word here. This is something quite different from merely marking time. It is a quality of mind, or better of the heart, which is rooted in the profound, existential conviction, firstly that God is in charge and accomplishes his gracious design through us, and secondly that, in all great things, delay is necessary for their maturation. One can only escape the servitude of time in a time which is not void but in which something is happening, something the seeds of which have been confided to the earth and are ripening there. It is the profound patience of the sower who knows that "something will spring up" (cf. Zechariah 3:8; 6:12). . . . If this patience is that of the sower, it is necessarily accompanied by a cross. "Those who sow in sorrow, reap in shouts of joy" (Psalm 126:5), but sometimes they do not reap at all, for "one sows and another reaps" (John 4:37). The cross is a condition of every holy work. God himself is at work in what to us seems a cross. Only by its means do our lives acquire a certain genuineness and depth. Nothing is meant wholly seriously unless we are prepared to pay the price it demands.[56]

"When the Lord restored the fortunes of Zion," begins the psalm Congar cited in the preceding quotation, "we were like those who dream" (Ps 126). In July 1960, when Pope John XXIII invited Congar to serve on the preparatory theological commission of the Second Vatican Council, Congar indeed may have felt like a dreaming man. This council, unimaginable to him when he was in exile in Jerusalem, would ultimately bring to fruition his long years of patience and labor.

Pope John XXIII charged the Council with two primary missions—*aggiornamento* within the Catholic Church and progress toward ecumenical union—goals that had been the twin pillars of Congar's own theological work. Congar nonetheless responded hesitantly to the papal invitation to participate in a council that he feared would simply reiterate the reigning neoscholastic ecclesiology, and he was uneasy at the prospect of sitting on committees with men who had condemned his writings. Indeed, initially Congar was hardly consulted. He did not become deeply involved in conciliar activities until the worldwide council of bishops rejected the prepared treatise, *De Ecclesia*, and called for a new theology of the church. Jean Daniélou initially took up the task of redrafting the schema on the church, and when he turned to Congar (among others) for assistance, Congar threw himself wholeheartedly into the task. He approached the ensuing discussions and disagreements with both enthusiasm and a spirit of realism, accepting formulations that proved to be the most satisfying or the least disagreeable if nonetheless imperfect.[57] As the Council progressed, Congar would make critical contributions not only to *Lumen gentium* (which replaced the rejected schema *De Ecclesia*) but also to *Unitatis redintegratio, Nostra aetate, Dei verbum, Dignitatis humanae, Ad gentes divinitus, Presbyterorum ordinis,* and *Gaudium et spes.*[58] "Beyond a shadow of a doubt," writes Fouilloux, "Congar seemed to everyone to have been the one who contributed the most to the drafting of the conciliar documents. . . . Congar became *the* theologian of Vatican II *par excellence.*"[59] Congar himself was simply delighted at the Council's achievement. "I was filled to overflowing," he remembered warmly.[60] The very event of the Council was "absolutely fantastic!"[61]

Once a suspect, mistrusted, and exiled theologian, Congar suddenly enjoyed a different form of distinction. On March 13, 1963, Congar was called to appear before the Dominican Master General Aniceto Fernandez and was surprised to learn that the purpose of the summons was simply an expression of goodwill. This was "the first time in my life," Congar commented, "that a superior summoned me for such a thing."[62] Congar was in high demand at conferences around the world and was received graciously and respected wherever he traveled. "I am confounded," he confessed, "by the insane credit that I have everywhere. . . . I hardly dare to say my name, for doing so sets off protestations of affection and veneration."[63] Undistracted by his fame, he committed himself to working toward the realization of the Council's mission of *aggiornamento,* for he saw Vatican II not as an end in itself but as the beginning of the church to come.[64] "Congar in no way," Jean-Pierre Jossua observes, "remained fixed within the advances or the limits of the Council. From the very first broad reception of Vatican II there was a lively openness to rapid changes in ideas and praxis."[65] The Council, as Congar himself explained to Jean Puyo in 1975, had done very good work, but in numerous regards it had gone only half-way, and "it would be absurd to think that things should remain as they were at the end of the Council on December 8, 1965."[66] Congar continued his intense routine of research, writing, and speaking, addressing a wide array of topics. He served on the editorial board of *Concilium* from the journal's inception, although he did not always agree with the views of the contributing writers.[67] He continued to read avidly, to learn, and even to reformulate his ideas. In an article published in 1971, when Congar was sixty-seven years old, he offered a critical assessment of his own theology of ministry and outlined an alternative approach.[68] "I have not ceased learning," he professed, "and still learn new things each day, beginning afresh to glimpse or lay hold of the most elementary matters."[69] Congar never ceased to plead for a better reception of Vatican II; yet, at the same time, Fouilloux notes, "he did not set himself up as a guardian of the conciliar temple. . . . [H]e maintained a critical solidarity with all those in the heart of the Catholic Church who wish that the reformatory movement of Vatican II does not become a new norm stifling all creativity."[70]

In November 1994, Congar's lifelong dedication to the church was formally recognized by his appointment to the College of Cardinals. Fouilloux postulates that Paul VI wanted to give Congar this distinction shortly after the Council. In 1969, however, *Concilium* published a declaration concerning the "freedom of theologians and of theology in the service of the Church," and Congar agreed to sign the statement—despite reservations about its wording—because of the importance of the issue at hand. The title of cardinal went instead to Daniélou, who had refused to sign the declaration.[71] When Congar was finally made a cardinal at the age of ninety, his niece Dominique Congar celebrated the honor but lamented that it had come too late.[72] Her uncle, she explained, was too old and too ill to serve the church in the manner he would have done had the distinction been awarded earlier.

Indeed, by 1994, Congar's activities were very limited. In 1936, while preaching in Paris during January's unity octave, Congar had experienced the first symptoms of a neurological illness that causes a form of sclerosis. For decades, the disease had been in remission, but in 1960 the illness resurfaced, and as the years passed it became increasingly severe, restricting his range of motion. Congar carried a cane during the Council and subsequently relied upon a wheelchair. In 1972, he moved from the Saulchoir to the Couvent Saint-Jacques, in Paris, and in 1984, as the illness became more painful and paralysis progressed, Congar was forced to take up residence at the Hôpital des Invalides, where he could receive the appropriate medical attention. He bade farewell to his room at Saint-Jacques where shelves, tables, and even beds and chairs creaked beneath the weight of books, notes, correspondence, and files. Thomas O'Meara visited Congar shortly before he entered the hospital and noted that "the special light was still in his eyes, a light which mirrors the energy, honesty and courage in his life."[73] O'Meara remarked to Congar on the tremendous impact of his life's work, but Congar preferred to speak of how inspired he was by the many activities of the church in the world, particularly in the area of social action.[74]

Infirmity, Congar reflected, separates us from the normal teeming of daily life but can be an invitation to pass to another level of communion with the mystical body of Christ. Through prayer, psalmody, and *lectio divina*, Congar sought to join himself to all the prisoners, the poor, and the Lazareths of the world, "so many of whom enjoy neither the care nor the aid with which we are provided."[75] He reflected:

> Withdrawn from active life, I am united to the mystical body of the Lord Jesus of which I have often spoken. I am united to it, day and night, by the prayer of one who has also known his share of suffering. I have a keen awareness of the vast dimensions of the mystical

body. By and in the Holy Spirit I am present to its members, known (to me) and unknown.[76]

Sclerosis gradually paralyzed Congar's entire right side. Van Vliet observed, however, that "the rigidity of his body stood in contrast to the vitality of his spirit."[77]

Congar died on June 22, 1995. His funeral was concelebrated by three hundred priests, twenty-five bishops, and three cardinals and attended by representatives from the Orthodox, Protestant, and Anglican Churches, as well as by many veterans of World War II.[78] At the conclusion of the funeral liturgy, Congar was buried in the Dominican cemetery beside his confrère Marie-Dominique Chenu. In "Nunc et in hora mortis nostrae," an article Congar wrote in 1935, when he was only thirty-one years old, Congar contrasted pagan and Christian views of death. For the pagan, he explained, death is either the end of life or a passage to immortality, understood as a prolongation of life as known on earth. The Christian, in contrast, lives earthly life in continual relation with *another* life, true life, the life of God, life of another order. Death is then the passage to full communion with this life, the realization of the totality of our life and *Life* itself. As we approach this fulfillment, we must be ceaselessly oriented to God like a flower following the sun through the course of the day. The only time of preparation for death is now, each instant of our lives, for Christian life has not only an end but a goal: participation in the eternal life of God. "Alors nous serons fixés dans la joie, sous son regard, pour toujours" [Then we shall be established in joy, below the gaze of God, forever].[79]

Congar's Theological Method

Congar's life of dedicated scholarship was rooted in his passion for knowledge and truth. The motto of the Dominican order is *Veritas,* and Congar often prefaced the handwritten drafts of his essays and books with the heading *Veritas domina mea.*[80] "I have loved the truth," he professed, "as one loves a person."[81] For Congar, the quest for truth was necessarily a theological pursuit, and he described theology as "the form that faith takes when it is received by an intelligence in scientific activity, in the activity of research."[82] His theological method was formatively influenced by Ambroise Gardeil, who served as Regent of Studies at the Saulchoir from 1894 to 1911. By the time Congar himself entered the Dominican house of study, Gardeil had retired from this post, but his book *Le Donné révélé et la théologie* continued to serve, in Congar's words, as the Saulchoir's breviary.[83] In contrast to a neoscholastic method that prioritized logical deduction, Gardeil's approach accorded primacy to God's *donné*— the biblical and historical testimony of revelation. Marie-Dominique Chenu succeeded Gardeil as Regent of Studies at the Saulchoir, and he continued in

Gardeil's vein.[84] Congar wrote of Chenu: "What a teacher, what an extraordinary intellectual inspiration was Father Chenu."[85] According to Jean-Pierre Torrell, Chenu himself learned as much from Congar as Congar did from Chenu. "It is thanks to Congar that Chenu abandoned his conception of theology as a deductive science (*science des conclusions*) and embraced the truly Thomist conception of a theological wisdom entirely centered on the knowledge of its 'subject,' God himself."[86]

Following Gardeil and Chenu, Congar divided theology into positive and speculative dimensions. The positive theologian's task is to become as conscious as possible of the Christian mysteries through study of the ensemble of testimonies of God's revelation and to rigorously elaborate upon this testimony with the available instruments of knowledge. This elaboration nourishes faith by developing the properly historical intelligibility of revelation and serves systematic theology by providing the systematician with resources and texts.[87] Speculative theology draws upon positive theology and systematically explicates its coherence; additionally, it can serve as a preamble to reflection on the testimonies of God's action in history through consideration of the consonance of revelation with human nature and reason.[88] Congar considered himself a positive theologian, both because of his training and also because of his own natural predilection for history—that "great teacher of truth."[89] He emphasized, however, that the positive theologian is not a historian in the strict sense of the word, for the theologian reads history with the eyes of faith and undertakes historical scholarship with doctrinal commitments.[90] "I am a firm believer in history," he wrote, "and I practice it, but I am a dogmatician, not a historian."[91]

Congar believed that both positive and speculative theology must have an ecclesial locus, and he offered a criteriology of the sources available to the theologian in the practice of the theological craft. In *La Foi et la théologie* and *Tradition and Traditions*, Congar outlined a criteriology of *loci theologici* that distinguished two fundamental kinds of theological sources: constitutive *loci* and declarative *loci*. Constitutive *loci* preserve the heritage of the apostles, while declarative *loci* help us to understand the meaning of the constitutive tradition. Scripture and the unwritten apostolic traditions of the church make up the constitutive *loci*, while the declarative *loci* include, in descending order of importance, the teachings of the magisterium, the liturgy, the writings of the fathers and doctors of the church, ecclesial life and church canons, and, finally, theologians and the use of reason.[92]

Congar gave primacy to theology's constitutive *loci* and described the apostolic age as a qualitatively unique period in the life of the church.[93] The Scriptures that are the written testament of this period are the soul of all theology and the forecourt of the kingdom of God.[94] Through the Scriptures, God speaks to us and communicates that which we need to know in order to respond to God's plan.[95] Congar drew heavily on scriptural sources in all of his theological writings, and scriptural meditation was also a foundational component of his own spiritual life.[96] The psalms "mean so much to me," he wrote. "They are the daily bread that nurtures my hope, they give voice to my service of God and my love of him. Would that I could penetrate all the wealth they contain as my lips shape their words."[97]

The scriptural testaments of the church's constitutive era are always in need of interpretation, and, in the twentieth century, Catholic scholars appropriated the historical-critical methods of scriptural study originally developed by Protestants. Congar welcomed the contribution that philology, archeology, geographical study, cultural history, and literary analysis could make to a better appreciation of the biblical heritage. *Dei verbum*, he reflected approvingly, responded to attacks against critical biblical scholarship by "stating clearly that the use of scientific means together with a critically enlightened reading is a way of pinpointing what the author of a given scriptural passage—and God through him—intended to convey. It follows that the sound, honest, balanced and unpretentious use of biblical science is demanded by the object and sheer purpose of exegesis."[98] Congar believed that the fruits of this research, shared in books and articles and notes to the new translations of the Bible, offered a "real feast of understanding."[99] He did warn, however, that new scientific approaches carried the danger that the human element of Scripture might eclipse the divine, and he was disconcerted about the lack of consensus among biblical scholars with respect to the origin and interpretation of biblical texts.[100] He also expressed concern about the growing separation of technical biblical scholarship from systematic theology, and he urged a closer and more mutually enriching relationship between Scripture scholars and systematicians.[101] To remedy the fragmentation that can result from a purely critical analysis of Scripture, Congar recommended a focus on the core of the Christian mystery nurtured by study of the church fathers and by immersion in the liturgy.[102] The Christian's ultimate goal, he insisted, is a spiritual reading of Scripture carried out through the Holy Spirit and leading to conversion. "We must therefore beg the help of the Holy Spirit. Indeed reading the Scriptures, like any other Christian act, calls for an invocation of the Holy Spirit. As a result the Word enshrined in the dead letter becomes a spiritual experience and a communication of life."[103]

Scripture, then, is a constitutive *locus* of theology, but its interpretation is inseparable from use of theology's declarative *loci*. The first declarative *locus* is the ordinary and extraordinary magisterium, which Congar described as the teaching church.[104] He used this term to encompass both the ecumenical councils held throughout the church's history and the teaching office as exercised in the Catholic Church today, and he believed that the magisterium was established by God to preserve the church in truth through the promised Holy Spirit.[105]

The liturgy, the second major declarative source of theology, is also the domain of the Holy Spirit's activity. "It is in the liturgy," wrote Congar, citing Guéranger, "that the Spirit who inspired the Scriptures still speaks to us; the liturgy is tradition itself, at its highest degree of power and solemnity."[106] Congar believed that liturgical action ritually and symbolically synthesizes the fullness of a mystery that can be fragmented in other forms of the Christian tradition, and he considered liturgical immersion absolutely critical to theological activity. "I owe to the liturgy," he remarked, "to the celebration of the Christian mysteries half of what I have learned in theology."[107] He emphasized, furthermore, that the purpose of theological knowledge is ultimately liturgical in character. Theology culminates in praise, doxology, and the celebration of the mysteries of communion and love.[108]

Congar's third *locus theologicus* is the corpus of the writings of the fathers and the doctors of the church. Congar accorded patristic authors a distinct theological significance because they contributed decisive elements to the church's life during a formative period. "One maintains," he explained, "the feeling of a creative inspirational moment on which subsequent centuries will always be dependent."[109] Congar believed the church fathers acted under the guidance and inspiration of the Holy Spirit, and he considered them exemplary models of Christian existence, for they lived *in sinu Ecclesiae* and integrated prayer, asceticism, study, and ecclesial service.[110]

The fourth *locus* includes the exemplary lives of all Christians throughout Christian history: the events of birth, death, love, and service that shape the ordinary setting of daily existence and the exercise of saintliness.[111] The entire church throughout the ages was for Congar a *lieu théologique*. "One can not exaggerate the novelty and importance of this perspective in 1937," comments Joseph Famerée. "A new ecclesiology and a new theology are in gestation: not only do the acts and events of the church speak of God, but God speaks and acts through them, God's Spirit animates the daily life of the faithful."[112] In Congar's own life, both his ecumenical work and his meetings with the youth of the J.O.C. (*Jeunesse ouvrière chrétienne*) were important encounters with church life beyond the lakeside school of the Saulchoir. Chenu regularly invited the J.O.C. leadership to the Saulchoir, and Congar recalled, "I owe much to these young men. They revealed to me the sense of insertion of the Gospel in humanity."[113] Congar also believed that his contacts with the worker-priests greatly enriched him, and the elder Congar stressed that the very event of the Second Vatican Council was of critical significance to the church and the discipline of theology.[114] "Pneumatology," he reflected, "like ecclesiology and theology as a whole, can only develop fully on the basis of what is experienced and realized in the life of the Church. In this sphere, theory is to a great extent dependent on praxis."[115] As Congar's sclerosis progressed, he regretted that the illness hindered him from more active ecclesial engagement. As a result of his confinement, he also felt he had difficulty understanding the questions and concerns of younger generations.[116]

Congar's schema of declarative *loci*, as outlined in *Tradition and Traditions*, concludes with a discussion of theologians and the use of reason. Theologians draw from the theological tradition and also employ the forms and instruments of knowledge available in their own day. Philosophy has been a particularly important theological tool, but Congar considered many forms of modern philosophy limited in their theological applicability because they cast doubt over the referentiality of language and sense perception. He did believe, however, that phenomenology and existentialism offered good resources for thinking about faith in terms of personal relationships.[117] Congar regretted his own lack of instruction in modern philosophy, preparation that he believed would have enabled him to be a more speculative theologian. He had received a poor formation in contemporary philosophy at the Institut Catholique, and, at the Saulchoir, his mentor Chenu "belonged to a Dominican generation closely linked to the study of St. Thomas which he enlarged with the study of history and with apostolic experience, but with rather little contact with other philosophical schools of thought."[118] Van Vliet observes that contemporary thinkers such as Henri Bergson, Maurice Blondel, Gabriel Marcel, and Max Scheler exercised very little influence on Congar during his studies at the Saulchoir.[119] "I would not have been a philosopher," Congar commented, looking back on the gaps in his education, "but I would have acquired perspectives, manners of approaching questions and even a language that would have enriched my theological thought."[120]

Had Congar schematized his *loci theologici* in his later years, he would likely have also included in his inventory of theological sources the importance of attentiveness to the questions and difficulties of the world at large. Subsequent to the Second Vatican Council, he observed that theologians had become more aware of their social and global responsibility. "Theologians have taken consciousness not only of the real state of the world from the point of view of faith but of their role with regard to this situation."[121] This awareness, Congar continued, should not simply lead to the insertion of a new paragraph into existing theological treatises but should generate a new orientation to all of theology. The new epistemology of Vatican II departs "not only from the *donné* of revelation and tradition but from the facts and questions received from the world and from history."[122] Congar warned against a horizontalism that focused exclusively on the secular and human to the exclusion of the supernatural, but he saluted in principle the "transfer of attention from the pure 'in-itself' of supernatural realities to the relationship they have with men, with the world, with the problems and the affirmations of those who, for us, are the *Others*."[123]

Overview of Congar's Theological Works

Through Congar's exercise of positive theology and his engagement with Scripture, the teachings of the magisterium, the liturgy, the church fathers, church
life, other theologians, and the modern world, he produced a daunting corpus
of publications. During the Second Vatican Council, one of the bishops in
attendance reportedly said to Congar upon meeting him for the first time, "Ah,
you are Congar, the French theologian who has written so much. I have one
question: Have you yourself also *read* all these books?"[124] A glance at the Congar
bibliographies compiled by Pietro Quattrocchi and Aidan Nichols confirms the
perception that Congar's corpus is unbelievably vast: the bibliographies, prepared for the years 1924–1987, number 1,790 entries.[125] These include fifty-
two books and collections of essays, multitudinous scholarly articles and en-
cyclopedia entries, and hundreds of book reviews and popular columns for
French newspapers. In addition to publishing prolifically, Congar also preached
actively throughout his life.[126]

O'Meara remarks that Congar's work in the thirty years prior to Vatican II
contains so many creative ideas for the renewal of theology that Congar was
arguably the most important Roman Catholic theologian in the decades that
preceded the Council.[127] Yet Congar's corpus is not only monumental in size
and scope but also unsystematic in character. Although Congar originally
dreamed of writing a new, synthetic *De Ecclesia* treatise, he never had the opportunity to realize this vision. Le Guillou believes that Congar's constant commitment to the concrete service of the church hindered the realization of his
De Ecclesia dream. Congar himself commented, "I never had a plan. I've tried
to respond to appeals, requests, circumstances."[128] Most of Congar's monographs are prefaced with remarks that advise the reader of the incomplete
character of his work. He noted in the introduction to *Lay People in the Church*,
for example, that the book offers "only a patchwork,"[129] and his introduction
to the three-volume *I Believe in the Holy Spirit* states, "I have no carefully pre-
conceived and detailed plan, but rather a project and an intention."[130]

Le Guillou considers the unsystematic character of Congar's writings and
his lack of the kind of training that would have enabled him to develop the
speculative dimension of his theology in dialogue with current philosophical
trends to be the major weakness of his writings. Le Guillou postulates that the
crisis in theology of the late 1960s could have been prevented had Congar
further developed his speculative thought.[131] Van Vliet agrees that Congar's
strength was not in the area of speculative penetration and grand schemati-
zation; yet he believes that, before 1959 and even into the 1960s, "the state of
ecclesiology was not ripe for a synthesis. Too many questions were still open
or in flux. The process of the return to the sources and the rebirth of forgotten

ecclesiological insights was still in full swing. Ecclesiology of that period required historical-theological work on particular themes."[132]

Given the character of Congar's writings, other scholars have tried to synthesize his prolific publications. Aidan Nichols and Timothy MacDonald have
identified some of the key themes that structure Congar's thought.[133] Others
give cohesiveness to Congar's vast corpus of works by analyzing his work di-
achronically, identifying some of the defining features of his theology at different stages of his career. Ramiro Pellitero, for example, distinguishes five
phases in Congar's theology of the laity.[134] The most comprehensive analytical
studies of Congar are, without question, the excellent works of Joseph Famerée
and Cornelis van Vliet.[135] Famerée's *L'Ecclésiologie d'Yves Congar avant Vatican
II: Histoire et Église. Analyse et reprise critique* (1992) uses Congar's preconciliar
works as the axis of his historical and systematic study, while van Vliet provides
a diachronic framework for the study of Congar's entire corpus of scholarly
writings in his *Communio sacramentalis: Das Kirchenverständis von Yves Congar—genetisch und systematisch betrachtet* (1995). Van Vliet's framework serves
as the outline for the following very broad overview of Congar's work. He
identifies four major periods of Congar's scholarly life: 1931–1944, 1944–1959,
1959–1968, and 1969–1991. Within each period, he discusses the development
of Congar's thought and identifies major themes and guiding concepts. These
are summarized in the following sections, with particular attention to their
significance for Congar's theology of the Holy Spirit.

1931–1944

These early years between Congar's first teaching assignment at the Saulchoir
and the Second World War are the period of *Chrétiens désunis: Principes d'un
"oecuménisme" catholique* (1937); *Esquisses du Mystère de l'Église* (1941); Congar's
monumental "Theology" essay for the *Dictionnaire de théologie catholique*
(1946); and numerous journal articles. According to van Vliet, the fundamental
ecclesiological concept underlying Congar's work in this period is that of the
mystical body of Christ.[136] Famerée, for his part, finds in *Esquisses* in particular
several indications of the importance Congar accords the pneumatological dimension of the church—the Holy Spirit is the soul of the mystical body and
the principle of new life in Christ.[137] Famerée believes, however, that Congar's
theological framework as a whole is pneumatologically underdeveloped in
these early works.[138]

1944–1959

In this period between Congar's release from German prison camps and John
XXIII's announcement of the Second Vatican Council, Congar published

widely, despite the restrictions and limitations imposed on him by Rome. The many books of this era include *Vraie et fausse réforme dans l'Église* (1950); *Le Christ, Marie et l'Église* (1952); *L'Église catholique devant la question raciale* (1953); *Jalons pour une théologie du laïcat* (1953); *Neuf cents ans après. Notes sur le "Schisme oriental"* (1954); *La Pentecôte—Chartres 1956* (1956); and *Le Mystère du Temple ou l'Économie de la Présence de Dieu à sa creature de la Genèse à l'Apocalypse* (1958). Van Vliet identifies Congar's central concerns during this period as the reform of the church, the promotion of an active laity, and reflection on the church's essence. Congar's foundational ecclesiological concepts at this time include his distinction between the church's structure and life and his emphasis on the church as both hierarchy and communion.[139] Within these ecclesiological frameworks, van Vliet believes that Congar portrayed the Spirit as secondary to Jesus Christ, for the Spirit comes only to animate a church that Jesus Christ has instituted.[140]

1959–1968

In these ebullient conciliar years, Congar published prolifically. Books of this period include *La Tradition et les traditions. Essai historique* (1960); *La Foi et la théologie* (1962); *Les Voies du Dieu vivant. Théologie et vie spirituelle* (1962); *Sacerdoce et laïcat devant leurs tâches d'évangélisation et de civilisation* (1962); *Pour une Église servante et pauvre* (1963); *Sainte Église. Études et approches ecclésiologiques* (1963); *La Tradition et la vie de l'Église* (1963); *La Tradition et les traditions. Essai théologique* (1963); *Jésus-Christ, notre Médiateur et notre Seigneur* (1965); *Le Sacerdoce chrétien des laïcs et des prêtres* (1967); *Situation et tâches présentes de la théologie* (1967); and *Cette Église que j'aime* (1968). Predominant themes in these works include conciliarity, collegiality, and primacy, the relationship between the church and the world, and the meaning of tradition. According to van Vliet, the foundational ecclesiological concepts that structure Congar's thought in this period are the church as the people of God and as a sacrament of salvation.[141]

1969–1991

Despite his worsening illness, the last quarter of Congar's life was very fruitful. Among his many books of this period are *L'Église. De saint Augustin à l'époque moderne* (1970); *L'Église, une, sainte, catholique et apostolique* (1970); *Ministères et communion ecclésiale* (1971); *Un peuple messianique. L'Église, sacrament du salut. Salut et libération* (1975); *Diversités et communion. Dossier historique et conclusion théologique* (1982); *Esprit de l'homme, Esprit de Dieu* (1983); *La Parole et le Souffle* (1984); *Le Concile de Vatican II. Son Église, peuple de Dieu et corps du Christ* (1984); and *Appelés à la vie* (1985). During this period, van Vliet comments, Congar grew increasingly interested in pneumatology as a consequence of the inner logic of his own mature ecclesiology, the influence of the Orthodox tradition, and the charismatic movement. The best-known book of this period is the three-volume *Je crois en l'Esprit Saint* (1979–1980), and, in van Vliet's analysis, the underlying themes and dominant ecclesiological concepts of Congar's other works of this period are also pneumatological—Congar described the church as a *communio spiritualis structurata* and a *templum Sancti Spiritus*.[142] Famerée, for his part, believes that in the postconciliar period Congar attained a theology of the Spirit and an ecclesiology that is qualitatively different from that of his earlier writings. Earlier works were predominantly christocentric, despite discussion of the Spirit. Now, Congar described the Spirit not simply as the animator of the church of Christ but also as the church's co-institutor.[143]

Important Influences on Congar's Theology of the Holy Spirit

Congar's career spans five decades, and his prolific work drew from a wide variety of theological sources. The most significant influences on Congar's pneumatology include his study of the theology of Thomas Aquinas and Johann Adam Möhler, his ecumenical engagement with Protestants and the Orthodox, and his experience of the event of the Second Vatican Council. From Aquinas Congar adopted central theological principles that shaped his own theology of the Holy Spirit—the inseparability of Christ and the Spirit, the *Filioque*, the theology of appropriations, and the theology of the Spirit as the love of God and the new law of the Gospel. In Möhler, Congar found inspiration for a truly theological—rather than simply juridical—approach to ecclesiology. Luther and Calvin impressed him with their theocentrism, and the Orthodox inspired him with their strong pneumatological tradition. Aquinas, Möhler, and the Orthodox stimulated his thinking about the need to integrate pneumatological anthropology with ecclesiology, and the experience of the Second Vatican Council contributed to his increased attention to the theology of the Holy Spirit in the last decades of his life.

Thomas Aquinas

Congar entered the theological world on the crest of the revival of the theology of Thomas Aquinas that followed a period of theological experimentation. In the nineteenth century, Catholic scholars throughout Europe, such as Joseph de Maistre, Georg Hermes, Johann Sebastian von Drey, Anton Günther, Vincenzo Gioberti, and Antonio Rosmini, had turned to Romanticism, Kantian philosophy, and post-Kantian idealism to develop epistemological and ontological alternatives to rationalist systems of thought.[144] By the end of the century, however, church leadership grew critical of these new theological developments and was concerned about incoherence in seminary curriculums. In 1879, Leo XIII's *Aeterni Patris* determined that the most cogent response to modernity would come not by appropriating post-Cartesian philosophy but by drawing on the philosophy and theology of the Angelic Doctor, Thomas Aquinas. Neo-Thomism became official and would dominate Catholic thought and seminary education into the middle of the twentieth century.

As a seminary student first at Reims and later at Carmes, Congar studied standard scholastic fare. But, beyond the seminary walls, neo-Thomism was by no means a monolithic enterprise. There were different schools of neo-Thomism and different traditions and emphases within different religious orders. Efforts to bring Aquinas into dialogue with modern intellectual currents also produced different neo-Thomist strands, ranging from the post-Kantian transcendental Thomism of Pierre Rousselot, Joseph Maréchal, and Karl Rahner to the aesthetic and political writings of Jacques Maritain.[145]

Congar was introduced to Aquinas by Daniel Lallement, who was first a diocesan priest in Sedan and later a professor at the Institut Catholique. In Sedan, Lallement held meetings for boys destined for the seminary, and together they read Aquinas and Cajetan.[146] At the Institut Catholique, Congar took formal courses from Lallement and other Thomists, including Jacques Maritain. He also became a member of Maritain's elite circle of French intellectuals. Congar's decision to join the Dominicans, however, led him away from Maritain and into the distinct tradition of Dominican Thomism—indeed, the Thomism of the Dominican's Paris Province. As was required of all Dominican students, Congar read the original works of Aquinas rather than relying only on secondary commentaries, and, as a student and later a faculty member at the Saulchoir, Congar was influenced by the Saulchoir's distinctive Thomist tradition. Both Ambroise Gardeil, the Saulchoir's Regent of Studies from 1904 to 1911, and Gardeil's successor, Marie-Dominique Chenu, emphasized an historical approach to the study of Aquinas. At the Saulchoir, Congar recalled, "the *Summa* of St. Thomas was our manual. We commented on it article by article." But, he continued, "St. Thomas was placed in his historical context. We did not consider his word as an oracle."[147] Congar never became a medieval specialist, but Jean-Pierre Torrell is nonetheless impressed with Congar's use of the historical resources that were available to him and with his perspicacious reading of Aquinas.[148]

Aquinas was not only Congar's theological mentor but also an important spiritual influence. "Two loves," Congar once said, "that have occupied a large place in my life are Thomas and the Church."[149] Congar found in Aquinas a model of poverty, purity, and fidelity; he admired his dissociation from worldly power and wealth and also the poverty of spirit manifest in his attitude of self-surrender and petition. Congar was also struck by the probing character and constancy of Aquinas's work and prayer, his great attention to detail, his all-encompassing breadth of vision, and his respect for truth.[150] In the course of

Congar's own career, he repeatedly returned to the study of the *Summa Theologiae*, as well as Aquinas's commentaries on John and Paul, his *Quaestiones Disputatae*, and other works.[151] Congar wrote numerous essays on Aquinas and made reference to him in all of his major theological writings.

CONGAR'S INTERPRETATION OF AQUINAS'S PNEUMATOLOGY. Aquinas influenced all aspects of Congar's theological work, including his theology of the Holy Spirit. Congar's interpretation of Aquinas's pneumatology emphasizes the pivotal character of the missions of Christ and the Spirit, the inseparability of Christ and the Spirit, the procession of the Spirit from the Father and the Son, the appropriation of grace to the Holy Spirit, the Holy Spirit as the "New Law" of the Gospel, and the inseparability of pneumatology, ecclesiology, and theological anthropology.[152]

The Pivotal Character and Inseparability of the Missions of Christ and the Spirit. Congar believed that the very structure of the *Summa Theologiae* revealed the critical significance of the missions of Christ and the Spirit in Aquinas's theology. Aquinas strategically placed *ST* I[a] q. 43 on the missions of the divine persons between *ST* I[a] qq. 1–42 on God and *ST* I[a] qq. 44–119 on the free *egressus* of creation.[153] The divine missions are the linkage between God and creaturely beings. In the sending of the Son and the Holy Spirit, Congar explained, "God in a certain sense goes out of himself to exist within the relative and the historic and lead it back to Him."[154] This is an eschatological activity, particularly in its pneumatological dimension.[155]

The Inseparability of Christ and the Spirit. "Whatever is done by the Holy Spirit," said Aquinas, "is also done by Christ."[156] The missions of Christ and the Spirit are absolutely inseparable. Aquinas's theology of the church, for example, is an ecclesiology that is grounded in Christology and encompassed [*couronné*] by pneumatology.[157] The church is the body of Christ and the Spirit is the church's soul, and Congar emphasized that this description of the Spirit as the soul of the body of Christ was not just a flowery metaphor but "a powerful technical factor in [Aquinas's] theological thought."[158]

The Procession of the Spirit from the Father and the Son (Filioque) as Love. According to Aquinas, the Spirit proceeds eternally *a Patre et Filio tanquam ab uno principio*. This affirmation of the Spirit's procession from the Father and the Son had been included in the creeds of Western churches since the Council of Toledo in 579, and Aquinas grounded his own account of the *Filioque* in both scriptural texts and his own theology of divine personhood, divine relations, and the emanation of divine intellect and will or love.[159] The Word and the Spirit proceed eternally as God's knowledge (Word) and love (Spirit) of God's own goodness. Congar observed that Aquinas accepted the traditional theology of the Holy Spirit as the mutual love of the Father and the Son, but he did not make this "the principle by which the mystery of the holy Triad should be understood *theologically* or that on which a *theological* construction should be erected. The principle that he prefers is the structure of the spirit itself, which includes knowledge and love of itself."[160]

The Appropriation of Grace to the Holy Spirit. In Aquinas's theology, the Spirit has a crucial role in the economy of salvation. Aquinas attributed to the Spirit the movement of creation's return to God,[161] the communication of properly divine life,[162] the efficacy of the sacraments,[163] and the operations of love and gift.[164] These divine activities carry humanity into a destiny that totally transcends their creaturely capacities, enabling them to be children of God. At the same time, Congar qualified, "The Holy Ghost, according to Thomas at any rate, has, in the giving of grace and the work of our likening to God's image, no kind of proper and particular causality but appears as the object only of an 'appropriation.' "[165] The work of grace and sanctification is not proper to the Holy Spirit as a person in a technical trinitarian sense—it does not distinguish the Spirit from the Father and the Son. Grace is the work of God, but it can be fittingly appropriated to the Spirit.

The Holy Spirit as the New Law of the Gospel. Congar repeatedly made reference to Aquinas's striking discussion of the New Law in ST II^a-II^{ae} qq. 106–108. Here, Aquinas elaborated a position that was in keeping with Paul and Augustine but that was nonetheless undeveloped by other medieval theologians.[166] Countering those who described the New Law as a written law, Aquinas argued that "the New Law is chiefly the grace of the Holy Spirit, which is given through faith in Christ."[167] For Congar the ecclesiologist, this was a fundamental point. The Holy Spirit—not ecclesiastical canons or even the written texts of the Scriptures—constitutes the new stage of the divine economy in which we become ontologically members of Christ.[168] This New Law cannot be carved in stone; it is dynamic faith active through love, a living, interior, and personal reality.[169] The canons of the church and the biblical texts do, of course, have their place; the New Law is principally the grace of the Holy Spirit, but it is secondarily those things that dispose us to receive the grace of the Spirit or those things that pertain to the use of this grace.[170] Scriptures, sacraments, and precepts ordering human affection and action are all part of the new dispensation. They themselves, however, are not the New Law but rather serve as *dispositiva ad gratiam Spiritus Sancti.*[171]

Pneumatology as Inseparable from Ecclesiology and Theological Anthropology. Congar believed that in Aquinas's writings, the theology of the Holy Spirit cannot be separated from ecclesiology and theological anthropology. For Aquinas, he observed, pneumatology is not a theology of the third person per se but rather that dimension of ecclesiology that requires a pneumatological anthropology.[172] This approach to ecclesiology distinguished Aquinas from some of his medieval contemporaries. "It is probably true," Congar commented, "that . . . [Aquinas] can be said to be more original in his pneumatologico-moral notion of the Church than in his christological."[173] Already in 1939, Congar stressed the importance of this dimension of Aquinas's legacy. In response to those who argued that there was no treatise on the church in the *Summa Theologiae*, Congar insisted:

> In reality everything in the thought of St. Thomas has an ecclesio-logical phase, and the author of an essay on his theology of the Mys-tical Body has gone so far as to say that this doctrine is the heart of his theology. The reason is that the Church is not a separate reality, something outside the Christian-Trinitarian mystery, outside the an-thropologic, christologic, sacramental thing which is the subject of theology. So much is this true that I am forced to ask myself if it be not a deliberate act on St. Thomas' part that he has refused to write a *separate* treatise *De Ecclesia*, seeing that the Church pervaded his theology in all its parts. I am inclined, personally, to think so.[174]

For Aquinas, the church is "the whole economy of the return towards God, *motus rationalis creaturae in Deum*, in short, the *Secunda Pars* of his *Summa Theologiae*."[175] The *Secunda Pars* is the locus of discussion of Christian action, the gifts and fruits of the Spirit, merit, and the theological virtues of faith, hope, and charity. There, Aquinas explains that the Holy Spirit elevates our human will, intentions, passions, and habits—an orientation of human life to God that occurs within the context of ecclesial communion in the body of Christ. The Spirit gathers us in love as the power, agent, principle, and dyna-mism of our return to God.

CONGAR'S APPROPRIATION OF AQUINAS'S PNEUMATOLOGY. In many ways, Congar's pneumatology bears the stamp of his great Dominican predecessor. Congar emphasized the centrality of the missions of Christ and the Spirit in the divine economy. He upheld the validity of the theology of the *Filioque* even as he grew in appreciation of the Orthodox alternative. He appropriated grace and sanctification to the Spirit, and he described the Spirit as the New Law of the Gospel. A passing observation that Congar made in 1939 about Aquinas's synthesis of pneumatology, anthropology, and ecclesiology was an insight that would come to fruition in Congar's later works when he himself articulated the importance of the integration of an *anthropologie pneumatologique* with an *ecclésiologie pneumatologique*.

As Congar's own thought developed, he did find some limitations in Aqui-nas's approach. "Although I am a grateful and faithful follower of Thomas Aquinas," he reflected toward the end of his career, "I have had occasion grad-ually to extend my vision."[176] Ecumenism, the study of history, and contem-porary thought led him beyond an exclusively Thomist or scholastic perspec-tive. "The scholastics were too encapsulated in their own certainties," he explained, "and in a Church which was closed to any doubts about itself. Surely our boundaries have become more diffuse!"[177] Aquinas was in many ways an incomparable and exemplary teacher, but he also has his limits, and perhaps even his dangers. I do not regret that I was formed in his school: he gave me both an order and an overture. But, having arrived at the autumn of my life, after having worked much and learned a bit, I understand that scholasticism can be a prison of the spirit and that in my Church it has diminished the reception of certain truths. For a long time I have been, and I am still in part a prisoner of a systematic ideal due to my scholastic formation.[178]

As Congar's horizons broadened, his pneumatology developed in some ways that distinguished his own theology from that of his medieval mentor. Congar observed, for example, that Aquinas's discussion of ecclesial unity tended toward a centralizing universalism that did not give adequate expression to the church as a communion of local and particular churches. Orthodox pneumatology, in Congar's judgment, was more suited to the expression of an ecclesial communion that was an ensemble of the gifts of the Spirit, a communion in diversity.[179] Jean-Pierre Torrell finds Congar's critique of Aquinas on this point rather anachronistic, even as Torrell observes that it is indeed regrettable that for such a long time the great weight of Aquinas's authority discouraged other theologians from differing with him on this issue.[180]

Aquinas, in any case, always remained Congar's most fundamental theological mentor. Even as Congar learned from other theological sources and Christian traditions, he continued to find in Aquinas's writings a compelling clarity, precision, and rigor of thought, and he always admired his incessant quest for foundational principles and causes. Congar believed that the brilliant thirteenth-century Dominican should continue to be an important source for contemporary theology because of the spiritual structure of his work, his genius for order, and his sense of openness and dialogue.[181]

Johann Adam Möhler

Congar found inspiration not only in the theology of Aquinas but also in the work of Johann Adam Möhler (1796–1838). Möhler, the son of an innkeeper in the German village of Ingersheim, was ordained a priest in 1819 and became one of the greatest theologians of Germany's Tübingen school. A student of Johann Sebastian Drey, Möhler forged his own theology in the ethos of nineteenth-century German romanticism and idealism in conversation with Schelling, Schleiermacher, and Hegel.[182]

When only twenty-nine years of age, Möhler wrote *Unity in the Church, or the Principle of Catholicism Presented in the Spirit of the Church Fathers of the First Three Centuries.*[183] This influential book went through several editions and translations, although Möhler later disavowed much of what he had written in this youthful volume. "Much that is in it I can no longer hold to," he told

Johann Weber in 1837. "It is not all properly digested or convincingly presented."[184] Seven years later, Möhler published *Symbolism, or Exposition of the Doctrinal Differences between Catholics and Protestants as Evidenced by Their Symbolical Writings*, another book that went through multiple editions.[185] Notably, these publications share some themes with Congar's work written a century later: an interest in historical scholarship as a basis for the renewal of the church and distress over a denominationally divided Christianity. By the end of the nineteenth century, however, Möhler's works were no longer in circulation.

When Chenu gave Congar a copy of *Unity in the Church* in 1928, Möhler's theology came back to life.[186] Möhler now had a new advocate, and Congar a new source of inspiration. In Möhler, Congar reflected, "I discovered a source, the source that I needed."[187] He described Möhler's thought as synthetic, vital, and communitarian and classified Möhler with Pascal, Racine, and other intellectually inexhaustible authors.[188] Indeed, Congar accorded such significance to Möhler that he hoped to open the *Unam Sanctam* series in 1937 with the publication of a new French edition of Möhler's *Unity in the Church*, a work that Congar thought "represented remarkably well the character and the spirit of the sort of material I hoped to supply."[189] As has been noted, difficulties with the translation thwarted Congar's plans for the inaugural volume of *Unam Sanctam*, but Möhler's work did appear in 1938 as *Unam Sanctam*'s second book. Congar also published a series of articles on Möhler's theology in 1938, the one-hundredth anniversary of the Tübingen theologian's death.[190] These are among Congar's earliest works, but, in Sicouly's assessment, Congar remained in dialogue with Möhler throughout his entire life.[191] Indeed, in 1975, Congar acknowledged, "Yet today, Möhler remains a reference."[192] Möhler's inspiration took many avenues: *Unity in the Church* and *Symbolism* influenced Congar's methodology, his ecclesiology, his ecumenical work, his theology of tradition, and his pneumatology.

MÖHLER'S *UNITY IN THE CHURCH* AND *SYMBOLISM*. In Congar's estimation, *Unity in the Church, or the Principle of Catholicism Presented in the Spirit of the Church Fathers of the First Three Centuries* was a masterpiece.[193] Möhler expounded patristic ecclesiology with an emphasis on pneumatology, working under the influence of German romanticism, which emphasized the organic, the communitarian, and the vital. Since Pentecost, Möhler explained in Part I of *Unity in the Church*, the Spirit has been present in the church as the new life principle (*das neuen Lebensprinzips*), a principle of unity, totality, and wholeness.[149] From generation to generation, each new member of the church is begotten of this same Spirit, and the church is consequently a unitary community (*Gemeinheit*) that shares a common life (*gemeinschaftlichen Leben*).[195] The interior mystical unity wrought by the Spirit is a vital force that seeks outward expression in the form of Scripture, doctrines, and liturgical practices.

These exteriorizations of the Spirit are organically related; just as a seed yields a plant bearing homogeneous fruits, so the Spirit yields consonant concretizations, and the Christian church has a stable identity throughout successive generations. Part II of *Unity in the Church* explains that this organic unity is concretized not only in doctrine and liturgy but also in the very structure of the ecclesial body. The bishop of each diocese personifies the love of each community and serves as the community's center. The bishops of nearby dioceses join to form a metropolitan association, and ultimately unity is manifest in the episcopate and papal primacy.[196]

Whereas *Unity in the Church* draws heavily on Ireneaus, Origen, and other patristic sources, Möhler's *Symbolism, or Exposition of the Doctrinal Differences between Catholics and Protestants as Evidenced by their Symbolical Writings* explores sixteenth- and seventeenth-century conflicts that persisted into Möhler's own era. In Möhler's analysis, these Reformation controversies concerned the condition of primeval humanity, the degree of indemnification wrought by original sin, and the character of justification and sanctification. Roman Catholic theology held that Adam's sin had disordered—not destroyed—humanity's spiritual nature such that humanity was capable of responding freely and collaboratively with the gracious redemption offered through Jesus Christ. "By the mutual interworking of the Holy Spirit," Möhler explained, "and of the creature freely co-operating justification really commences."[197] Luther, Calvin, and Zwingli, in contrast, believed that Adam's sin had completely ravaged the prelapsarian means of humanity's communion with God—the human faculty of will and the created capacity for knowledge of God. Justification and sanctification are consequently an entirely divine work, human participation is impossible, and "the Holy Spirit is exclusively active."[198] Möhler acknowledges some merit in Protestant theology, but his overall assessment is critical: this theology is inconsistent, illogical, individualistic, and divisive.[199] *Symbolism* complemented *Unity in the Church* with its insistence on the Catholic theology of the theandric (*gottmenschliches*) activity of the Holy Spirit and the human person. As a whole, however, *Symbolism* has an orientation different from that of Möhler's earlier work; it places less emphasis on the Spirit as the dynamic interior principle of ecclesial unity and much more importance on Jesus Christ and his established legacy.[200] Möhler identifies Jesus Christ as the divine founder of the church and describes the church as a "permanent incarnation."[201] In contrast to *Unity in the Church*, Congar explained, "the visible institution, the body of the Church is no longer only a means of expressing the interior Spirit; it is a means of its production . . . a divinely instituted means of transmission, realization, and development."[202] Congar attributed this change in Möhler's thought to his critical engagement with Protestant ecclesiology.

CONGAR'S ASSESSMENT OF MÖHLER'S PNEUMATOLOGY. For Congar, the "astonishingly rich and vibrant thought" of the young nineteenth-century Tübingen theologian was highly significant, his theology "of great profundity and beauty."[203] *Unity in the Church* recovered a theology of the church; Möhler demonstrated that the church is not simply a *societas inaequalis*, as juridical ecclesiologies presumed, but a people enlivened by the Holy Spirit, who is the principle of the church's life and interior mystery. "This restored," Congar reflected, "a radical primacy of supernatural ontology above the church's structures."[204] He believed that Möhler had recovered the pneumatological dimension of the mystical body theology and an anthropology of communion.[205] This inspired Congar's own ecclesiological efforts and was also foundational to his work on the theology of tradition. Whereas many Roman Catholic theologians had assumed that tradition was timeless, static, exhaustively codifiable in texts, and the exclusive prerogative of the papal magisterium, Congar drew upon Möhler to speak instead of a living tradition and an interior tradition—a "vital, spiritual force, which we inherit from our fathers and which is perpetuated in the Church."[206] Tradition in this vital sense is not something simply written in magisterial documents; rather, it is the organic life of the Spirit in the entire ecclesial body, a spiritual event in the consciousness of each believer. For Möhler and the Tübingen school, Congar explained, "the whole ecclesial community is the organ of Tradition."[207]

Congar held Möhler in great esteem and learned much from this Tübingen theologian, but he also found limitations in his approach. In his judgment, "the pneumatological construction of *Unity in the Church* was unsatisfactory."[208] Congar believed that Möhler himself had recognized this deficiency, for *Symbolism* took a corrective, christological view and emphasized that the structures of the church emerged not solely from an organic spiritual development but also from the divine institution of Jesus Christ. Congar defended Möhler against those who claimed that the christological and institutional element was completely lacking in *Unity in the Church*, but in Congar's assessment this dimension was indeed secondary and underdeveloped.[209] He repeatedly upheld Möhler's theological evolution as an example of the need to properly balance pneumatology and Christology.[210] In a 1970 reflection, Congar noted other limitations in Möhler's theology of the Spirit: he had remained on a functional level of analysis and scarcely reflected on the person of the Holy Spirit; he was a prisoner of the idea of the *Volksgeist*; his organic-vitalist pneumatology was subject to hierarchical appropriations that were incongruent with his intentions; he hardly reflected on the broad context of the economy of salvation; he offered little discussion of the charisms of the Spirit.[211] Möhler's theology, Congar concluded, is not a paradigm for contemporary pneumatology. Together with the entire Tübingen school, however, Möhler did offer an overture and an ethos. He was "an awakener," Congar said with deep appreciation and respect. "That is what he was for me more than forty years ago."[212]

Ecumenical Influences on Congar's Pneumatology

While Johann Adam Möhler was deeply troubled by Christianity's denomina-tional fragmentation, he did not believe that ecclesial reunion was possible in the 1800s. Even in the 1920s, when ecumenical initiatives had germinated among Protestants and the Orthodox, most Roman Catholics remained leery of the burgeoning ecumenical movement.[213] When Congar was granted per-mission to take courses with a Protestant faculty of theology in Paris, a fellow Dominican exclaimed to their provincial superior, "You have thrown him into the arms of apostasy!"[214] Even Chenu, who had spoken to his students at the Saulchoir about the 1927 ecumenical conference in Lausanne, expressed be-wilderment when Congar confided his desire to pursue an ecumenical voca-tion.[215] Yet Congar was undeterred, and his resolute efforts ultimately trans-formed Roman Catholic attitudes about ecumenism. Indeed, his work was so significant that some spoke of Catholic ecumenism "before" and "after" the publication of Congar's *Divided Christendom*, a book based on a series of lec-tures Congar delivered during the Christian unity octave in Paris, in 1936.[216] Appreciative readers told Congar that *Divided Christendom* had awakened them to the cause of ecumenism or given them a broader sense of the church.[217]

Congar not only transformed Roman Catholic attitudes about the ecu-menical movement but also changed Orthodox and Protestant perceptions of Roman Catholicism. The Orthodox theologian Léon Zander, of the Institut Saint-Serge, in Paris, described Congar as a living icon of St. Dominic in whom "we come nearer to Catholicism, we see the spiritual riches that it has and that it can reveal in its faithful . . . we have many things to learn, to imitate, to discover, which completely change our attitude toward this Church."[218] Oscar Cullmann has stated that Congar played a major role in bridging relations between Catholics and Protestants, and the Reformed Pastor J. J. von Allmen attests, "What we Protestant theologians owe to [Congar] is that, like no one else, he has destroyed the equivalence which (since the national synod at Gap in 1603) we have been accustomed to establish between the bishop of Rome and the anti-Christ, between Roman Catholicism and the adversary of the Gos-pel."[219]

Congar himself was personally affected by his ecumenical encounters. "Every experience of this kind," he reminisced, "leaves one to some extent a new person. Things appear in a different light and one can never think or speak again in exactly the same way as one did before."[220] Ecumenism touched Congar's heart—and his theology of the Holy Spirit. He reflected:

> Ecumenism has certainly been, and remains, a favorable terrain
> and, better still, a fertile soil for the development of pneumatology.
> Is it not itself quickened by the Holy Spirit? Do not our Orthodox

and Protestant brethren constantly stimulate and practically provoke us to emulate them in the domain of pneumatology?[221]

Ecumenical engagement, Congar was convinced, fostered "greater fervor, a deeper understanding of Christianity and . . . 'peace and joy in the Holy Spirit' (Rom 14:17)."[222]

PROTESTANT ENCOUNTERS AND CONTRIBUTIONS. The seeds of Congar's commitment to ecumenism were sown in his childhood village of Sedan, where Protestants and Catholics lived together respectfully. Interdenominational cooperation was particularly pronounced during World War I. When the Germans burned Sedan's Catholic church in 1914, the Calvinist pastor graciously offered the Catholics use of his own building, where the Catholic congregation worshiped until 1920. "I cannot believe that my vocation to ecumenism has no connection with these circumstances," Congar reflected. "I was often fired with a desire to make some return to the Protestants for all I had received from them."[223] Indeed, Congar originally understood his ecumenical vocation as a mission to seek reunion specifically between Roman Catholics and Protestants.

Martin Luther quickly became a key figure in this pursuit. Shortly after Congar was ordained, he traveled to the Dominican house in Düsseldorf, Germany, where he discovered the Lutheran journal *Die Hochkirche* in the Dominican library. "[I]ts pages," he recalled, ". . . opened my eyes to a new world. . . . I realized that there were depths in Luther which demanded investigation and understanding."[224] Fascinated, Congar returned to Germany the following summer and visited Luther's birthplace and browsed through Lutheran archives in Wartburg, Erfurt, and Wittenberg. Upon returning to France in 1932, he took courses with Auguste Lecerf and André Jundt, of the Protestant Faculty of Theology, in Paris. He also read Kierkegaard and studied Barth.[225] When Barth came to Paris in 1934 for a series of lectures, Congar invited him to Juvisy for a symposium with Étienne Gilson, Jacques Maritain, Gabriel Marcel, and other scholars.[226]

Through these encounters, Congar quickly realized that Catholics had been laboring under some misconceptions about the Reformation traditions. In 1935, he undertook the regular publication of "Cahiers pour le protestantisme" in *Vie intellectuelle*, a series designed to allay misunderstandings and to introduce Catholics to the Protestant sensibility.[227] According to Fouilloux, these "*Cahiers* played a decisive role in the ecumenical career of Father Congar; they either brought him credit—or rendered him suspect—in different places; their appearance multiplied the demands for his collaboration."[228] The series continued until interrupted by World War II. Meanwhile, Congar himself continued to read Protestant theology regularly. Luther in particular was a perennial resource. Congar called Luther "one of the greatest religious geniuses in all of history" and placed him on the same level with Augustine, Aquinas, and Pascal.[229] "There is scarcely a month," Congar commented, "in which I do not return to his writings."[230] Luther's avid opposition to scholastic methodologies made this Protestant reformer an unlikely source of inspiration for a Dominican schooled in Thomism, and methodological differences did indeed affect Congar's interpretation of Luther's writings.[231] Over the years, Congar grew in his understanding of Luther's theology and softened and nuanced some of his earlier critiques. In the Preface to the second edition of *Vraie et fausse réforme* (1968), for example, Congar noted that the long, critical exposition of the Protestant Reformation in Part III of the 1950 original edition was incomplete and failed to convey the richness of the Protestant tradition.[232] In a 1982 reflection entitled "Nouveaux regards sur le christologie de Luther," Congar also modified the position he had taken with respect to Luther's Christology in a 1954 publication.[233]

Martin Luther as well as other Protestant theologians surely exerted a positive influence on Congar's theology of the Holy Spirit through their strong emphasis on the primacy of grace and the sovereign initiative of God. "Luther," Congar observed, "gives an absolute primacy to the point of view *of God*, to God's initiative."[234] For Karl Barth, in like vein, all is "*of God*. God is the active subject of all that is done."[235] Congar was appreciative of this decisive theological and hence implicitly pneumatological dimension of Protestant theology.[236] On the other hand, Congar believed Luther's account of the radical difference between God and all that is human, sinful, and creaturely inevitably denied the vocation and the capacity of the human person to actively cooperate with the indwelling Spirit.[237] He was critical of Luther's theology of nature and grace and also of the pneumatological deficit of his ecclesiology—or, rather, what Congar perceived as Luther's lack of any proper ecclesiology. Congar believed that the resounding emphasis on justification *pro me* and Luther's characterization of the church as an entirely human institution betrayed theology's properly ecclesial dimension.[238] For Luther, as Congar read him, the church is simply the congregation of those individuals who have accepted God's promises, not a divine institution imbued with the theandric power of the Incarnation and the gift of the Spirit.[239] "Protestantism," he commented in 1937, with reference to Luther, Calvin, and Barth, "has stopped short with John the Baptist and still awaits the fulfilment of the baptism of water and of the Spirit."[240] Years later, in *I Believe in the Holy Spirit*, Congar was not as dismissive of the role of the Spirit in Luther's theology. According to Luther, he noted, the Spirit brings people to faith when the Gospel is preached and causes them to cling to the Word.[241] Congar remained concerned, nonetheless, that Luther's theology so emphasized Christ the Word that it was not fully pneumatological.[242]

ORTHODOX ENCOUNTERS AND CONTRIBUTIONS. Although Congar's ecumenical mission was originally oriented to Protestants, he grew increasingly interested in the relation between Roman Catholics and the Eastern Orthodox, officially separated since 1054. Through his encounters with the Eastern tradition, Congar grew enamored of the Orthodox ethos—the ambiance of mysticism, symbolism, and sacramentality—and of Orthodoxy's great appreciation for liturgy. "I admit to love Orthodoxy very much," he told Puyo in 1975, "and to feel vividly its attraction."[243] Congar had various opportunities for fruitful contact with Eastern worship and theology as a young Dominican at the Saulchoir. St. Basil's Russian Seminary had been established nearby in Lille (France) at the injunction of Pius XI, who had hoped to support the development of the Russian Uniate Church. St. Basil's eventually evolved into the Centre Istina under the administration of Dominican Christophe Dumont, and Congar remained in close contact with Dumont throughout his life and collaborated in the Centre's work. During Congar's work with the Protestant faculty in Paris, in 1932, he also made contact with Russians who had emigrated to France after the 1907 Revolution. In the French-Russian Circle, Congar grew acquainted with Nicholas Berdyaev, Fr. Serge Bulgakov, and Fr. Lev Gillet, the latter a Roman Catholic priest converted to Orthodoxy. At Paris's Institut Catholique, Congar also befriended Fr. Albert Gratieux, who taught courses on Aleksei Stephanovich Khomiakov and the Slavophile movement. Khomiakov was an Orthodox lay theologian who had developed the theology of *sobornost* in the nineteenth century, and Congar believed that Khomiakov, like Möhler, had constructed an ecclesiology "out of precisely the elements which the Counter-Reformation left in the shadows: the pneumatological element and the anthropological element: interior action of the Holy Spirit and the active part of the body of the faithful."[244] Gratieux became Congar's first Russian teacher, and Congar later invited him to contribute to the ecclesiological series *Unam Sanctam.*[245] During the summer of 1932, Congar also traveled from Paris to Belgium to visit Dom Lambert Beauduin, founder of the monastery of Amay, where worship proceeded simultaneously in both the Latin and Russian Byzantine rites in order to spiritually anticipate the union of East and West. Over the years, Congar remained in close contact with the monastery (which moved to Chevetogne in 1939) and contributed to its journal *Irénikon.*

Famerée believes that, of all Congar's ecumenical contacts, "The Orthodox especially had a strong influence on him, much more perhaps than he has indicated in his writings."[246] Famerée traces Congar's conception of collegiality to Khomiakov's *sobornost* theology; he believes that the discussion in *Divided Christendom* of the church as a theandric reality comes from Soloviev, even though Soloviev is not explicitly mentioned in this text; and he finds signs of Florovsky's ecclesiology in Congar's *Christ, Our Lady and the Church.*[247] Famerée also finds evidence of Orthodox influence in Congar's theology of ecumenism and his rediscovery of the importance of the episcopate and the local church.[248]

Certainly the Orthodox influenced Congar's pneumatology. The Eastern tradition is well known for its emphasis on the Holy Spirit, and Congar spoke of the Holy Spirit as the "great unresolved issue between Eastern Orthodoxy and us."[249] Congar defended the West against the Eastern critique of christomonism, but he did acknowledge the East's challenge to a Western christocentrism.[250] Congar's own theology evolved from a dominant christocentrism to a more fully trinitarian approach, and surely the Orthodox contributed to this development in his thought. Of notable significance for the focus of this study, the Orthodox also inspired Congar's efforts to develop a pneumatology that would overcome Roman Catholicism's separation of spiritual anthropology and ecclesiology. As has been noted in the Introduction, Congar was quite taken with a comment made by Nikos Nissiotis and Alexander Schmemann over lunch during one of the sessions of Vatican II. "If we were to prepare a treatise *De Ecclesia*," they commented in the context of a discussion on the Council proceedings, "we would draft a chapter on the Holy Spirit, to which we would add a second chapter on Christian anthropology, and that would be all."[251] The expression *une anthropologie pneumatologique*, which later appears in Congar's writings, comes, Congar himself noted, from Nissiotis.[252]

The Second Vatican Council

Congar's provocative luncheon conversation with Nissiotis and Schmemann was only one encounter in the course of his intense engagement with the Second Vatican Council. Congar was so influential in Rome from 1962 to 1965 that, according to Avery Dulles, "Vatican II could almost be called Congar's Council."[253] The Council to which Congar contributed so much influenced, in turn, Congar himself. He believed that ecclesial events can be sources of theological reflection, and the Vatican Council was a *lieu théologique* par excellence, a religious event of singular importance in the twentieth century. The Council convoked more than 2,600 bishops from all over the world and welcomed observers from Protestant and Orthodox denominations. At Vatican II, Congar reflected:

> The facts preceded and set ideas in motion. . . . One might wonder how the idea of collegiality, so absent from people's minds before 1962, was able to win favor so rapidly. The reason is that in St. Peter's the college was assembled. It was not necessary to prove its existence. It was there.[254]

The influence of the Council on Congar's pneumatology is more difficult to delineate than the influence of theologians such as Aquinas and Möhler, who leave their marks on Congar's books and articles in the form of footnotes and citations. But it is surely no coincidence that Famerée finds a qualitative change in Congar's pneumatology in the postconciliar period.[255]

After the Council, Congar was free from censorship and enjoyed renewed opportunities to write, speak, and publish. His growing interest in the theology of the Holy Spirit during this period was influenced by his own experience of life in the postconciliar church. The liturgical reforms initiated by *Sacrosanctum concilium*—which included the addition to the sacramentary of three Eucharistic prayers that (unlike the Roman Canon) did include an explicit epiclesis of the Spirit—undoubtedly influenced Congar's theology.[256] Congar was also clearly affected by the dramatic increase of lay participation in liturgical worship and myriad forms of ministry. As he witnessed lay people taking initiatives in the church and striving to live out their faith convictions, he reflected that biblical, liturgical, patristic, and ecumenical renewals all have led us to "consider the Church less as the 'Establishment' than as a community of believers and thus to reintroduce anthropology into ecclesiology. This meant the reintroduction of pneumatology, for it is the Spirit who makes Christ dwell within men, prompts consciences and suggests initiatives."[257] The rapid growth of the charismatic movement in the 1970s also contributed to Congar's increasing interest in the theology of the Holy Spirit.

The Second Vatican Council transformed not only the liturgical and pastoral practice of the church but also the theological climate. Congar contrasted the postconciliar period with the years subsequent to the Second World War (1947–1950), when Catholic theological and pastoral research had proceeded within a well-established framework. Whereas the period 1947–1950 had been a period of adaptation in which theologians and pastoral leaders strove to enrich and renew existing theological systems and ecclesiological structures, the postconciliar era required theologians to rethink and reformulate the very foundations of Christian faith in response to the intellectual, cultural, and social currents of a world to which the church had opened its doors and committed its evangelical service. Pope John XXIII had reached out to all people of goodwill and dismantled the fortress mentality that had separated the Catholic Church from the modern world. In this spirit of openness, the theology of the postconciliar period was no longer simply a theology of adaptation but rather a theology of foundational reformulation.[258] "It is astonishing," Congar noted in a letter to Thomas O'Meara, "how the postconciliar period has so little to do with the Council. . . . The postconciliar questions are new and radical."[259] Theologians like Rahner, Schillebeeckx, and Gutiérrez responded to these questions through sustained dialogue with modern philosophy, hermeneutics, critical theory, and political and social analysis. Congar's training had not equipped him for these types of engagement, but he had his own form of response to the new theological climate. It is notable that Congar's most important book from the years 1947–1950 is *Vraie et fausse réforme*, a study of the principles of ecclesial reform in the service of ecclesiological adaptation. In the postconciliar period, in contrast, Congar's best-known book addresses a topic at the very foundations of Christian faith. This book, according to van Vliet, is the three-volume *I Believe in the Holy Spirit* (1979–1980).[260]

2

Spirit of God, Spirit of Christ

The Trinitarian Foundations of Congar's
Pneumatology

Trinitarian theology is the distinctively Christian way of speaking
about God, the cornerstone of systematic theology, and the necessary
framework for a theology of the Holy Spirit. In recent decades, there
has been a resurgence of interest in the doctrine of the Trinity and a
growing concern that Christian theology has neglected its trinitarian
foundations. "From all sides, in recent times," Congar commented,
"people have denounced the inadequacy of a notion of God that is in
reality pre-trinitarian."[1] Congar linked this pre-trinitarianism to the
predominance of patriarchal and masculine theologies in Christianity.[2] He also observed, at the pastoral level, that the trinitarian tradition often had no relation to the lived spirituality of Catholics; a survey of Belgium's Catholic schools conducted in 1970 reported that 65
percent of the school's youth believed that the doctrine of the Trinity
had no consequences for daily life.[3] Neglect of theology's properly
trinitarian character was also evident in the disjunction of the doctrine of the Trinity from other dimensions of systematic theology,
such as ecclesiology, sacramental theology, and theological anthropology, and in the pervasiveness of a form of christocentrism that under-
stated theology's trinitarian context. Yet, even as Congar saw signs of
the neglect of the trinitarian tradition, he also witnessed a renewal of
trinitarian spirituality, which he attributed to a growing recognition of
the foundational character of the doctrine of the Trinity, the influence
of patristic *ressourcement*, and ecumenical dialogue (particularly with
the Orthodox). He believed that this trinitarian revival paved the way
for both the trinitarianism of the Second Vatican Council and the renewal of pneumatology.[4]

Congar himself consistently worked with a trinitarian intention. His early *Divided Christendom* (1937) spoke of the *Ecclesia de Trinitate*, and his mature *I Believe in the Holy Spirit* (1979–1980) included a survey of trinitarian theology's historical development. "I am more concerned with pneumatology," Congar wrote, in 1980, "but this is, of course, inseparable from the mystery of the Tri-unity of God himself."[5] This chapter explores key components of Congar's trinitarian theology: his account of the economy of salvation, trinitarian ontology, the distinction of the economic and eternal Trinity, the relation between the Word and the Holy Spirit, and the Holy Spirit as person of the Trinity.

The Economy of Salvation

God, St. Paul wrote to the Ephesians, has "made known to us the mystery of his will, according to his good pleasure that he set forth in Christ, as a plan (*oikonomia*) for the fullness of time, to gather up all things in him" (Eph 1: 9–10). Congar upheld both the chapter from Ephesians from which this passage is extracted and Romans 8:18–30 as exemplary summaries of the history of salvation.[6] Following the methodology of Gardeil in which he had been trained, Congar practiced theology as a reflection on God's *donné*, God's self-manifestation in the economy (*oikonomia*) of creation and redemption. "All of the revelation of the Holy Trinity is . . . economic; the divine persons are revealed in their relation with redeemed humanity and the work of the redemptor Christ."[7]

Congar believed that God's revelation culminated in the life, death, and resurrection of Jesus Christ and the apostolic era of the Christian church—the events that together form the constitutive period of Christianity.[8] Congar held that revelation was, in some sense, complete at the close of this era; he opposed, for example, the dogmatic definition of the bodily assumption of Mary, "since historically the ancient evidence is very sparse and we can no longer accept that the present faith of the church has a revelatory value, even if one can draw certain consequences from divine motherhood."[9] Yet, even if present faith is not revelatory in the technical sense of this term, it nonetheless participates in the continuation of the divine economy and the manifestation of the divine presence in history. "[T]he economy of salvation continues after the constitutive period. All epochs have their leaders and their prophets—ours just as all the others."[10] Indeed, the divine economy is coextensive with the entire history of the world.[11] Congar carefully qualified this assertion to avoid an identification of salvation history with the created order itself. He was determined to avoid both horizontalism (the identification of human history and salvation history) and extrinsicism (a juxtaposition of human history and salvation history in which the two are discontinuous). He carefully distinguished what he termed "temporal history"—that is, creation operating through its own proper energies—from the gratuitous interventions of God that constitute the history of salvation. The world of itself is "a natural, nonsacred world. But the transcendent and living God intervenes in a sovereign and free manner. . . . Thus are combined God's utter transcendence and his utter immanence."[12] If the transcendent God were ever to offer a total self-disclosure, this would put a stop to history, for in our creaturely state we cannot yet receive God's fullness.[13] Yet, within our current limits, God is truly present. Congar differentiated two dimensions of this economy of salvation: (1) the secret action of God that begins with creation, and (2) the public and visible economy that begins with the revelation to Abraham and culminates in the Incarnation and the church. The former is the general history of salvation/revelation and the latter, the special history of salvation/revelation.[14]

In broad terms, temporal history can be easily distinguished from general and special salvation history, but in practice these dimensions of history are much harder to differentiate amid the ambiguities of our actual existence. Congar compared our human vantage point to that of the weaver of a Gobelins tapestry who works from the back side of a loom such that the shape and design of the fabric are not immediately visible and the weaver sees only a mass of colorful threads. In like vein, we cannot see the full shape and design of God's economy on this side of the eschaton, and yet we "must build as best we can, interweaving the threads known to God."[15] We are guided in this endeavor by the proleptic vision of God's design that we have by virtue of the public revelation made originally to Abraham and consummated in the Incarnation of the Word of God and the gift of the Spirit. Although we cannot see the entire pattern of salvation history, we do know that God intends to be in communion with human creatures in an "ever more generous, ever deeper Presence."[16] Indeed, Congar mused, the mystery of God's presence "is the 'golden string' that runs through all God's purposes."[17] Communion with God intensifies at each stage of the economy of salvation: creation, the Covenant with Israel, the Christian dispensation, and the eschaton.

Creation

God is a God of effusive love who desires to live not in eternal aseity but rather in communion with creation:

> No Absolute exists which is not also Love, no mighty God who is
> not the loving God, God turned towards us, God for us. There is no
> "I am," no *Ens a se*, no Aseity, that does not contain within itself, not
> only the possibility, but also the positive desire to be "I will be (for
> your sake, moving towards you, acting with you)."[18]

God's creation is an act of love.[19] God's Word is eternally uttered in love, and God's Spirit proceeds inseparably with the Word as the term of the substantial communication within God. With supreme liberality, the Spirit continues this movement of love outside God such that creation commences. The Spirit is (by appropriation) the "principle of generosity through which God extends his family to his creatures."[20] This act of generosity occurs outside God not in the sense of spatial separation, for strictly speaking God has no outside whatsoever. Rather, Congar's terminology is intended to express that creatures are distinct from God and have a creaturely being that is not the same as the being of God.[21]

Like Aquinas, Congar distinguished God's eternal and necessary generation of the Word from the temporal and voluntary creation of the cosmos.[22] At the same time, Congar believed that the Word is eternally generated by the Father precisely with creation in view, for in God the necessary and the free are unopposed.[23] "In God . . . his freedom and his essence are *really* identical."[24] According to St. Paul, Congar observed, there is an identity between the preexistent Word and the incarnate Son, and Congar himself spoke not only of an eternal generation of the Word but also of the Word's eternal assumption of human nature.[25] "[L]et us remember," he urged, "that the Logos is, in the eternal present of God, conceived *incarnandus, primogenitus in multis fratribus, crucifigendus . . . primogenitus omnis creaturae, glorificandus*" (to be incarnate, the firstborn of many brethren, to be crucified . . . the firstborn of all creation, to be glorified).[26] The Word eternally proceeds from God with creation and redemption in view, and creation in turn is brought into existence to receive the Incarnation and eternal life. God's initial creation is "more a kind of sketch, a very precarious sketch in expectation of something else, which is redemption or . . . salvation."[27]

The Covenant with Israel

God's incarnational intention is prepared and prefigured in the Covenant with Israel, which Congar typically referred to as the "old dispensation."[28] This language is no longer standard in Catholic theology, which has begun a process of repentance and reform for the manner in which it has denigrated Judaism over the centuries. But in Congar's day, this terminology was common, and it parallels the use of the term "Old Testament" to refer to the Hebrew Scriptures. As these scriptures recount, God established a people and covenanted with them, and Sarah and Abraham and their descendants knew and worshiped the one God. Revelation became public and palpable in the ark of the Covenant, the stories of exodus and liberation, and the splendor of the Temple of Solomon. The Hebrew people professed that they had been created through the *rûach* (Spirit, breath) of God (Gn 1:2) apart from which all life would cease (Jb 34:15). They testified that the *rûach* of Moses had been passed to Joshua and the seventy elders (Nm 11:29 and 27:18), and that God's *rûach* had stirred

Othniel and Gideon and the other judges who provided leadership in the land of Canaan (Jgs 3:10, 6:34, 11:29, 13:25, 14:6, 14:19). They believed that when Samuel anointed David king of Israel, the *rûach* of God had come mightily upon him (1 Sm 16:13), and they knew that when Israel was in exile God had promised the prophet Ezekiel that God's *rûach* would be poured out on the house of Israel to bring life to their dry, dying bones (Ez 36 and 37). They remembered that Isaiah, too, had prophesied that God would "pour my *rûach* upon your descendants" (Is 63:11–14) and that this commitment had been reiterated by Haggai, Zechariah, and Nahum (Hg 2:5; Zec 4:6, 12:10; Neh 9: 20). The sages of Israel spoke of God's Wisdom as the *rûach* that held the entire cosmos together (Wis 1:6–7), a *rûach* that is "intelligent, holy, unique, manifold, subtle, mobile, clear, unpolluted, distinct, invulnerable, loving the good, keen, irresistible, beneficent, humane, steadfast, sure, free from anxiety, all-powerful, overseeing all and penetrating" (Wis 7:22–25).[29] In sum, Congar concluded after surveying the meaning of *rûach* in the Old Testament, the Spirit does whatever is necessary to guarantee that God's plan for Israel and for all creation will be carried forward.[30] In this dispensation, the Spirit is a power that accomplishes the work of God.[31]

At the same time, Congar believed that the presence of God's *rûach* in the period recounted in the Old Testament was qualified and limited. God periodically intervened in the history of the chosen people but did not dwell permanently, intimately, and personally among them. Congar was aware that this position put him at odds with the majority of theologians in the Western tradition, most of whom affirmed a personal and substantial indwelling of the Holy Spirit in the souls of the righteous men and women of the Old Testament by virtue of their implicit faith in the Christ who was to come. Augustine, Leo the Great, Thomas Aquinas, and Thomists such as Franzelin, Pesch, and Galtier are among those who held that there was a personal indwelling of the Spirit in the righteous men and women of this period, and this was also the position taken in Pope Leo XIII's *Divinum illud munus* and in Pius XII's *Mystici Corporis*.[32] Yet the Greek tradition has made a distinction—indeed, Congar noted, almost an opposition—between the old and the new dispensations that reserves the personal indwelling of the Spirit for the time of Christ. In Congar's judgment, the Greek approach was closer to the biblical testimony than the Western tradition, and more in keeping with the historical character of the economy of salvation.[33] In 1954, some of Congar's fellow Dominicans critiqued his approach to this issue, but Congar maintained his position.[34] He described the presence of the Spirit in the Old Testament period as consecratory rather than sanctificatory, for the Spirit protectively guided the Hebrew people in accordance with God's plan but did not indwell the souls of persons so as to communicate an inner moral sanctity, holiness, or perfection.[35] Congar explained:

> There was never any question of the Holy Spirit or of God taking up
> his dwelling in souls as persons who are his temple. His presence is
> a collective one and is conferred on his people as such. It is not so
> much an indwelling of souls as a presence which guides men and
> strengthens them so that they may implement a plan which is
> God's. . . . This is the root of the matter. God does not dwell fully
> and perfectly among his people because he is not yet fully given or
> communicated to them.[36]

There were, however, signs and promises in the Hebrew tradition of the fuller
presence of the Spirit yet to come. The awaited Messiah was described as the
one to be anointed by the Spirit of God. "There shall come forth a shoot from
the stump of Jesse," Isaiah prophesied, "and a branch shall grow out of his
roots. And the Spirit of the Lord shall come upon him" (Is 11:1ff). Centuries
later, in about 350–340 B.C.E., the prophet Joel foretold an eschatological outpouring of the Spirit upon all flesh (Jl 3:1–2). On the day of Pentecost, Congar
noted, Peter proclaimed that this outpouring had come to pass.[37]

The Christian Dispensation

Congar was convinced that the Incarnation of the Word of God, the paschal
events of Jesus Christ's death and resurrection, and the sending of the Holy
Spirit had wrought something radically new in the economy of salvation and
had deepened God's communion with humanity in a profound way.[38] Since
the dawn of creation, God had been present to humankind as the causal principle of created existence, and in the Covenant with the people of Israel God
had become the object of humanity's knowledge and love. Now, in the hypostatic union of the Word of God with the human nature of Jesus Christ, God
has overcome the separation and duality between God and creature "in so far
as this is possible without a meaningless confusion of beings or pantheism."[39]
The divine immanence in creation is now "total, ontological," and the divine/
human communion consummate in Jesus Christ is extended to all humanity
through the gift of the Holy Spirit.[40] It is now appropriate to speak not simply
of God's providential presence in history but also of "an *indwelling* of God in
the faithful."[41] The economy has progressed "from things to persons, from
fleeting moments of God's Presence to a Presence that is lasting, from the
simple presence of his action to a vital gift, inward communication and the joy
and peace of communion."[42]

Congar emphasized—particularly in his later writings—that the mission
of the Spirit in the new dispensation is just as important as that of the Word.
The Spirit conceived Jesus in Mary's womb (Lk 1:35), and from this moment
the Word of God was hypostatically and ontologically united with the humanity
of Jesus of Nazareth. The subsequent life of Jesus was not simply a manifes-

tation of this mystery of hypostatic union, as Aquinas's Christology seemed to imply. Rather, through the activity of the Holy Spirit in the historical events of Jesus Christ's life, death, and resurrection, Christ was *constituted* the messianic Son of God *for us*.[43] "[N]ot from the point of view of his hypostatic quality or from that of his ontology as the incarnate Word," Congar explained, "but from that of God's offer of grace and the successive moments in the history of salvation."[44] In the waters of the Jordan, the Holy Spirit came upon Jesus, and he became the anointed one—*ho christos*—the Christ (e.g., Acts 10:38).[45] Jesus' baptism was a new communication of the Spirit beyond that of his conception that constituted him as Messiah and Servant.[46] Immediately after baptism in the Jordan, the Holy Spirit led Jesus into the desert to confront the temptations of power and evil, and Jesus rebuked Satan and was empowered to announce and make manifest the Kingdom of God—he healed the sick, cast out demons, and declared, in the words of the prophet Isaiah, "The Spirit of the Lord is upon me, because he has anointed me to bring good tidings to the afflicted" (Lk 4:21).[47] Throughout his life, Jesus Christ grew in understanding and increased in wisdom and favor with God (Lk 2:52).[48] He manifested God's mercy and salvation, and finally offered himself—through the eternal Spirit (Heb 9: 14)—even unto death. The Christ, the anointed one, became the Crucified. He took the sins of humanity upon himself and offered himself as our ransom (*goel*).[49] Through the Holy Spirit of God, Jesus Christ was then raised and exalted—"designated Son of God in power according to the Spirit of holiness by his resurrection from the dead" (Rom 1:3–4).[50] His victory over the temptor in the desert was completed by this definitive triumph over evil, and the resurrected Christ is so completely penetrated by the Spirit that "the Lord is the Spirit" (2 Cor 3:17).[51] The Spirit who wrought the *kenōsis* of Incarnation, baptism, and death is also the Spirit of Christ's glorification—a glorification not of domination but of communion. Jesus Christ exercises his divine Sonship precisely by giving the Spirit to others such that they, too, may become sons and daughters of God. "Receive the Holy Spirit," the risen Christ said when he appeared to the apostles who had locked themselves away in fear after the crucifixion (Jn 20:22). "[I]t is the Spirit," Congar commented, "who places the life of Christ in us, who makes us sons in the divine Son and who dedicates us to resurrection after him (See Rom 8:9–11 and 14–17; Gal 4:6; 1 Cor 12: 13)."[52]

Congar distinguished the gift of the Spirit to the fearful apostles recounted in John 20:22 from the gift of the Paraclete (*Paraklētos*) promised in John 14–16. In John 20:22, "[t]he Spirit is not given personally (there is no article preceding *pneuma hagion*), but as a force that corresponds to the mission that is communicated."[53] The promised Paraclete is given on the day of Pentecost, a Jewish harvest festival and celebration of the Torah observed fifty days after Passover. According to the book of Acts, the apostles had gathered in Jerusalem for the feast immediately after the ascension of Jesus Christ, and tongues like fire descended upon them and "all of them were filled with the Holy Spirit" (Acts 2:4). They discovered that they could speak and understand all languages—a reversal of the division of tongues and the scattering of peoples that occurred at Babel—and they were empowered to proclaim the gospel, heal the sick, establish communities, welcome the gentiles into the nascent church, and baptize.[54] These activities of the apostolic church were a continuation of the activity of Jesus Christ in his glorified state. Just as the Spirit conceived Jesus in Mary's womb at the beginning of the Gospel of Luke, so, too, the Spirit of Jesus Christ brought the church into the world at the beginning of the book of Acts.[55] "The Spirit does not invent or introduce a new and different economy. He gives life to the flesh and words of *Jesus* (Jn 6:63). He recalls those words to mind and penetrates the whole truth."[56] This is evident, Congar explained, in a close analysis of the Gospel of John, which describes the activity of Christ and the Spirit in the same terms.[57] The gift of the Spirit is not a replacement of Jesus Christ but a communication and transmission of Christ's ongoing presence and power—the power to remake humanity in the image of the Son such that all may be reborn from above (*anōthen*) as sons and daughters of God.[58] "The Spirit is therefore the Spirit of *Christ* in the economy of grace through which the *Unigenitus* becomes *primogenitus in multis fratribus*."[59]

Congar considered the apostolic period foundational to the life of the church and the Christian tradition, and he made a qualitative distinction between the apostolic era and the subsequent centuries of Christian history. The first century is of paramount importance because in this period Jesus Christ acted in the Spirit to institute the means of salvation: the faith, the sacraments, and the apostolic ministry of the church.[60] Yet the presence of the Spirit is ongoing throughout the entire Christian dispensation.[61] The Spirit guided the work and writing of the church fathers, inspired conciliar decisions and the formulation of Christian doctrine, assisted the magisterium, acted in the sacraments, preserved the church in holiness, and wrought conversions in the lives of saints—holy men and women such as Augustine, Francis Xavier, Thérèse Martin, and Blaise Pascal.[62] The Spirit also brought about renewal in the church's life, kindling the proliferation of new religious orders that occurred in the twelfth century and inspiring the ecumenical movement that flourished in the twentieth. "The Holy Spirit," Congar pondered, "is active in history and causes new and sometimes very confusing things to take place in it."[63] Indeed, Congar believed that the Holy Spirit is active in all of human history—in the Incarnation, God became *human* and embraced all the joy and pain of human life.[64] Yet, at the same time, Congar was reluctant to designate any nonbiblical event as a definitive component of salvation history. Was the fall of Rome, or the Reformation, or the death of Innocent IV an intended part of God's plan? Congar believed one would need a prophetic charism to answer such questions, a charism that no theologian or historian is assured.[65] We can attest to the ultimate triumph of God's salvific love as manifest in the resurrection of Jesus

Christ and the gift of the Holy Spirit, but we still stand on the back side of a Gobelins tapestry in a jumble of tangled threads and raw edges, and God alone knows how the full pattern of salvation history will appear on the other side of the veil.

The Eschaton

Our current experience of the Spirit is only the *arrha* (pledge) of the full, eternal communion with God to which creation is destined (Eph 1:14). We live, as St. Paul suggested, like a woman in labor, groaning in pain.[66] The Spirit, Congar assured, is in labor with us—with Christian believers and all peoples—bringing the new creation to birth.[67] This new creation has already begun, for the Spirit *is* given, and through this gift we live in "the messianic era, which is the last epoch of time and will not be followed by anything substantially better or new."[68] Yet at the same time—as Congar knew so well through his own personal experience of war, exile, and illness—we are still a people on pilgrimage, following Jesus Christ, who is the forerunner of a procession en route to what Congar called the "true country."[69]

In this eschatological journey, the Spirit of Christ sustains us and inspires within us an ardent desire for the fullness of life to come.[70] The ongoing gift of the Holy Spirit is our assurance that we will someday reach the new Jerusalem, the city of pure gold that "has no need of sun or moon to shine on it, for the glory of God is its light" (Rv 2:18 and 23). All of creation will ultimately participate in this redemptive mystery, Congar explained, noting that the Lenten lectionary begins with the first chapter of Genesis—a story that is also recounted at the beginning of the Easter vigil—so as to suggest the participation of all creatures in Christ's redemption. "The Catholic idea of salvation takes in all creation."[71] This new creation is brought forth from the old; the Spirit embraces and completes all things, carrying creation forward toward that full communion in which God will be all in all (1 Cor 15:28).[72] Even now, we participate incipiently in this reality of communion, although it eludes attempts at description. Congar reflected:

> I often also think of eternal life. I think that one has it now. That is spelt out in St. John, but I think of it in an existential, real way. Like everyone else, I know that this eternal life now must emerge, after death, in some kind of exaltation towards God, in whose presence it will be completely revealed. But one cannot imagine it, any more than one can imagine how a chrysalis will become a butterfly, or [how a] cherry blossom, so beautiful in April, will become fruit. I often think about it, but each time I end up with a mystery which I cannot see clearly.[73]

We cannot clearly envision the end of the economy; yet Congar was confident that the promised eternal life will be nothing less than the deification of the creature and the eternal praise and adoration of God.[74]

Trinitarian Ontology

Congar's conviction that theology must be rooted in the scriptural accounts of God's economy did not preclude him from embracing the ontological terms and categories that theologians employed to elaborate trinitarian doctrine over the course of Christian history. Contrasting his position to that of Martin Luther who prescinded from theological reflection on God *in natura et maiestate sua* because he believed it sufficient to know God in Jesus Christ, Congar maintained that it is necessary to progress from the scriptural narrative of the economy to trinitarian ontology.[75] "Economy," he explained, is the "historical account of what God has done for our salvation, the historical realization of his plan of grace."[76] This account is functional in character. Ontology, in contrast, concerns knowledge of a reality (in this case, God) in itself. When theology moves from economy to ontology, it "applies itself to contemplate and to define, with revelation as a point of departure, the in-itself [*l'en-soi*] of God and of Christ, that is to say that which they are in themselves [*ce qu'ils sont en eux-mêmes*]."[77]

It is generally acknowledged that the Hebrew Scriptures are not preoccupied with ontological questions.[78] Indeed, according to Dupuy and Chenu, the entire Bible is concerned with the destiny—not the essence—of creation and God.[79] Congar believed, nonetheless, that the Greek idea of truth as that which things are in themselves—an idea that shaped patristic and medieval theology—was not completely foreign to the biblical worldview, even as it was not exhaustive of the rich meaning of truth in biblical tradition.[80] Scripture "ignores or surpasses the opposition between the *for-us* and the *in-itself*, and certain of its functional statements spill over into the ontological."[81] On the basis of what God has done in the economy, we do truly know something of that which God is.[82] Congar maintained, moreover, that it is the very law of our God-given intellectual spirit to inquire into the *ce que sont* of realities, and he insisted that the theological problems of the second and third centuries are an historical illustration of the need for an adequately elaborated theological ontology.[83] In the patristic period, it became evident that a purely functional approach to trinitarian theology ran the risk of modalism.[84] "History has shown and Barth has admitted that the true and full meaning of the economy can only be preserved if we also include the theology, and the true and full meaning of Jesus Christ only if the eternal Word, the Son, is affirmed."[85] The theology of God *en soi* must be unequivocally grounded in the economy of salvation, but fidelity to this very economy requires ontological exposition.

Congar began his work in trinitarian theology in the aftermath of conversations generated by Theodore de Régnon's *Études de théologie positive sur la Sainte Trinité* (1892–1898).[86] De Régnon's book gave new impetus to the study of trinitarian doctrine and drew sustained attention to foundational differences between Eastern and Western approaches. In both East and West, trinitarian theology has been shaped by what G. L. Prestige terms the "Cappadocian settlement," the formulation that God exists as the persons (*hypostases*) of Father, Son, and Holy Spirit, who share a common divine nature (*ousia*).[87] In the West, de Régnon argued, Augustine and his successors elaborated a dogmatic structure that emphasized the divine essence over the triune persons and unity over trinity. Conversely, the East emphasized the triune persons over the divine essence and trinity over unity. De Régnon's *Études* were widely cited, and his characterization of the differences between East and West became commonplace. Congar observed that Orthodox theologians in particular have appropriated his clear-cut formulas as they stand.[88]

Congar himself believed that de Régnon had demonstrated that East and West share the same faith and yet approach the trinitarian mystery with different theological constructions.[89] In Congar's understanding, the East affirmed the coequal divinity of the Son and the Spirit on the basis of their common origin in God the Father. Greek theologians then differentiated the Son and the Spirit according to their distinct modes of coming to be—begetting in the case of the Son and procession in the case of the Spirit. In John Damascene's classic explanation, all three divine hypostases have everything in common except for the hypostatic properties *agennētos*, *gennētos*, and *ekporeuomenon*. Greek theologians rely on Scripture to make these distinctions, particularly John 15:26. They do not seek to analyze this further, for the modes of coming to be of the divine persons are ineffable.[90] In contrast, Congar continued, the West has postulated that the begetting of the Son and the spiration of the Spirit produce four relations of origin (Father→Son, Son→Father, Father & Son→Spirit, Spirit→Father & Son) that differentiate the three divine persons who in all other respects hold everything in common. This approach is foreign to the Greek view, for in the East "[t]he relationships are not what define the persons—they follow and are constituted by the persons, like inseparable properties."[91] For the Orthodox, Vladimir Lossky explains, "the relations only serve to *express* the hypostatic diversity of the Three; they are not the basis of it."[92] A further difference between East and West, Congar observed, is that the Orthodox point of departure

> is a difference between the essence or substance and the hypostases of a kind that enables them to speak in two different ways about the

divine Persons, according to whether they are regarded as hypostases or are seen in their relationship to the divine essence. In Latin dogmatic theology, on the other hand, the hypostases are really identical with the divine essence.[93]

The Greeks seem to think of hypostatic being as "an autonomous and absolute value," and Congar expressed appreciation for their "lively sense of the originality of the person" that enabled them to speak of hypostasis without speaking of substance.[94]

Yet, even as Congar acknowledged these differences in the trinitarian ontologies of East and West, he maintained that de Régnon's characterization of Eastern and Western theology was oversimplified and even a misleading caricature.[95] It would be unfair to Augustine to claim that he prioritized the divine essence over the divine persons, and futile to try to determine whether Richard of St. Victor's speculative triadology affirms person over essence or essence over person.[96] Any attempt, moreover, to present Thomas Aquinas as an essentialist would "betray the balance of his theology."[97] Congar's own trinitarian theology illustrates the limitations of de Régnon's contrast of East and West, for Congar gave equal emphasis to both the divine persons and the divine essence. Central features of Congar's trinitarian theology include his emphasis on the monarchy of God the Father, a divine ontology of charity, the circumincession and being-towards-another of the divine persons, the identity of God's substance (*essentia*) and God's to-be (*esse*), and the doxological character of theology.

The Monarchy of God the Father

"The first insight into the mystery of the Trinity," Congar wrote, "is that concerning its origin in the monarchy of the Father."[98] God the Father is the unoriginate and invisible source (*archē*) of all that is.[99] The Son is begotten by the Father, the Spirit proceeds from the Father and the Son, and the cosmos is created by the Father through the Son in the Spirit. "[E]verything comes from God, that is, from the Father."[100] In a 1980 reflection, Congar recounted the efforts of theologians in both the East and the West to speak of the mystery of the Father's monarchy: the Father is *pēgē tēs theotētos, pēgaia theotēs, tēs theotētos archē, anarchos, agennētos, plenitudo fontalis, auctor, auctoritas processionis, esse principium, fons et origo divinitatis.*[101]

Congar observed that important differences in the Greek and Latin languages have shaped efforts to express the Father's monarchy, and this has influenced the way in which theologians speak of the procession of the Holy Spirit in East and West. The Greek terms *ekporeuesthai, aitia,* and *archē* that are central to reflection on the Father's monarchy were translated into Latin as *procedere, causa,* and *principium.* The Latin terms lack the subtlety of the Greek, as the Orthodox have often remarked.[102] In Greek, the term *ekporeuomai* that is used with reference to the procession of the Spirit—"the Spirit of truth who comes from (*ekporeuomai*) the Father" (Jn 15:26)—connotes procession from an *original* source and hence can be used only with respect to God the Father. In theological Latin, however, *procedere* has the more general sense of "coming from another." This other need not be the originating source, and thus the term *procedere* is used by the West to describe not only the Spirit's procession from the Father but also the Spirit's relation to the Son. Similarly, the Greek *aitia* and *archē* express first origin (that is, origin from God the Father), while the Latin *causa* and *principium* have a more general meaning.[103] The Western theology of the Spirit's spiration from both the Father and the Son (*Filioque*) drew support from these linguistic differences and further contributed to an attenuated emphasis on the monarchy of the Father in the Western tradition. Aquinas and others who used the *Filioque* theology were careful to affirm that, while the Son was a principle of the Spirit's spiration, the Spirit came *principaliter* from God the Father, and yet the very structure of Latin thought gives less emphasis to the Father's monarchy. "The Latins were therefore careful to preserve the full truth of the monarchy of the Father," Congar observed. But "they did not make it the axis of their theological construction, as the Greeks did in their triadology."[104] Indeed, Congar believed that some Western theologians (such as Anselm) treated the Father's monarchy in a manner quite different from that of the Orthodox, and he also expressed concern about potential neglect of the Father's monarchy in the christocentric theologies of some of his own contemporaries.[105] "[I]f the Holy Spirit has sometimes been overlooked in the past, today the Father risks being equally overlooked; an exclusive centering on Christ, though justifiable and fortunate in itself, may result in what P. A. Manaranche calls *'jesuism.'* "[106]

Reasserting the monarchy of the person of the Father, Congar reiterated Rahner's reminder that the term *theos* in the New Testament refers in all but six instances not to the Trinity generically or to the divine essence but to God, who is *Pater*.[107] We must, Congar urged, eradicate our false image of a divine nature that is anterior to God the Father, Son, and Holy Spirit.[108] The divine essence does not act or exist prior to or independent of the Father or any of the divine Persons:

> The nature, essence or being may be common to the Three, but not in the sense of being a common stock that is somehow prior—even logically prior—to the Persons. Their common essence or existence is situated only in the mutual communication of the processions and being of the Persons (their circumincession or circuminsession).[109]

This mutual communication begins with God the Father, the unbegotten source of everything that is. God is God *because* God is Father, Congar clarified, and "he is certainly God by being Father, and not according to something anterior to this quality."[110]

A Divine Ontology of Love

God the Father is "love flowing like a source, love initiating being and life."[111] God is the unoriginate origin (*archē*) of all that is—not the first link in a mechanistic chain of cause and effect—but abundant, generous love. The Incarnation, Congar wrote, reveals "that the Absolute does not exist only in and for itself but that it is self-giving Love, that is, *Agapē*. 'God is Love' (John 4:8 and 16)." We can presume to speak of God's being or essence only because of God's act of revelation, and in the Incarnation and the gift of the Holy Spirit God is made known as love itself. This must be the foundation for all reflection on trinitarian ontology and should also shape our efforts to think in ontological terms about the created order. "For if the Being *a se* is *Caritas*, this must have repercussions in the ontology of his whole creation and especially in that of those created beings whom he made in his own image."[112] In the revelation of the supreme Being, something is revealed about the character of all being. This is an insight that Congar never developed systematically, although he did remark that his proposed general ontology of charity should be qualified by Blondel's recovery of Augustine's *esse vere esse* in terms of the distinction of degrees of being.[113]

The Circumincession and Being-Toward-Another of the Divine Persons

The revelation of God as Love challenges us to think of God the Father in such a way that the Father is never conceived of alone—even in his quality as the unoriginate origin (*archē*) of the Son, the Spirit, and creation. This, Congar observed, is difficult for the Cartesian intellect to grasp:

> A Cartesian or geometric spirit tends to conceive of the Person of the Father as *totally constituted before* the actual generation of the Son, and in like manner the person of the Son *before* the spiration of the Spirit, but there is a simultaneity in the same existence; the Persons don't exist without each other but one with another. They mutually condition each other in the womb of the processions from the Father.[114]

The divine persons exist in circumincession—in a being-toward (*être-à*) one another, in mutual exchange and reciprocity.[115] The Father unoriginately begets the Son and is eternally Father. The Son is ceaselessly begotten and is eternally Son. Together, the Father and the Son eternally spirate the Holy Spirit and exist in a communion of love that has no beginning and no end.

The eternal divine relations of begetting and spiration define Father, Son, and Spirit as persons. Congar used the term "person" in his trinitarian theology without hesitation, despite the term's post-Enlightenment connotations of individual self-consciousness. These connotations prompted Rahner and Barth to speak of Father, Son, and Spirit as *Subsistenzweisen* or *Seinsweisen*, rather than as divine persons, but Congar was disinclined to dispense with traditional trinitarian terminology.[116] Instead, he appropriated Aquinas's understanding of a divine person as a subsisting relation and distinguished the persons of Father, Son, and Spirit from one another on the basis of the *relationis oppositio* (opposition of relation) that results from the acts of generation and spiration:[117]

Father↔Son (relation of paternity/relation of filiation)
Father & Son↔Spirit (relation of spiration/relation of procession)

"The Persons . . . consist in a relation to another person."[118] Father, Son, and Spirit are not three self-conscious individuals. Rather, they are one God, consubstantial and alike in all things, with the exception of the *relationis oppositio* that demarcates them as persons. As Anselm implied, in his *De processione Spiritus Sancti: in Deo omnia sunt unum ubi non obviat relationis oppositio.*[119] Aquinas incorporated this principle into his own theology, and it was formally promulgated by the Council of Florence (1442). Congar described it as "not strictly speaking a dogma" in the West but "nonetheless more than a theologoumenon."[120] The Orthodox, he noted, do not speak in these terms and frequently misinterpret this aspect of Western theology. Paul Evdokimov, for example, assumes that Western trinitarian theology implies a separation of the divine persons, which he contrasts with the Orthodox emphasis on trinitarian mutuality, reciprocity, and communion.[121] Congar insisted that Evdokimov's portrayal of Western theology was indicative of a serious misunderstanding.[122]

The Identity of God's Substance (essentia) and God's To-Be (esse)

Relation was one of only two categories that Congar believed could be applied to God without detriment to the divine simplicity.[123] The second category is that of substance, and Congar grounded the circumincession of Father, Son, and Spirit in the "unity and identity of substance between the three [persons]."[124] Congar's position that the common essence of God is the basis for trinitarian communion may at first glance appear inconsistent with his insistence that God's essence is not in any way prior to Father, Son, and Spirit; it may also strike one as incompatible with his statements that identify divine personhood as the ground of circumincession.[125] After all, Congar had insisted that the divine essence itself exists only through the trinitarian circumincession of the divine persons.[126]

Congar's various statements about person, essence, and circumincession are in fact quite coherent within the Thomistic context that shaped his trinitarian reflection. For Aquinas, God's essence (*essentia*) is identical with God's *esse* (God's to be), and God's *esse* is an eternal, dynamic act of knowledge and love—an act of Father, Son, and Spirit.[127] "Everything active in God," Congar explained, "was, for Thomas, done by Persons (*actiones sunt suppositorum*)."[128] The essence of God must not be approached in a reified sense. Rather, the divine *essentia* is identical with the divine *esse*, the eternal love and knowledge of God the Father, Son, and Holy Spirit. Congar could thus write without contradiction that the divine substance *is* love and that love is a hypostatic mark of God the Father.[129] God's essence, God's *esse* (to-be), and God's personhood are ultimately one in the unspeakable divine simplicity that surpasses the comprehension of the finite human mind. God is fully present to creation only when God is present personally—when God is united *personnellement* to humanity in the event of the Incarnation and when, in the gift of the Spirit at Pentecost, God has "come in person instead of sending only his gifts."[130] Yet, Congar wrote elsewhere, in these mysteries, we touch God's "own living Substance."[131] In the Christian dispensation, the Holy Spirit is not simply revealed to humankind but now "dwells substantially."[132] For Congar, in sum, Christianity is rooted in the "personal and substantial" coming of God.[133] It is a coming of God as love.

The Doxological Character of Theology

Even as Congar stressed the importance of moving from the scriptural narrative of salvation history to ontological reflection on God's essential being, he cautioned that God transcends all of our limited human expressions.[134] Theology aims not to circumscribe God in our finite conceptual systems but rather to serve the creature's movement toward the destined end of divine union. Congar cited with approbation Aquinas's definition of an article of faith: *Perceptio divinae veritatis tendens in ipsam*.[135] We tend toward God's truth, Congar commented, although we cannot grasp it conceptually. "Person," "essence," and all of our theological concepts inevitably fall short of the reality of the supremely gracious and ineffable God. When we express belief in God, we do not define God but rather "express a movement or thrust of faith by which we are taken up."[136]

Theological truth is ultimately expressed by lives taken up into the glory, lives lived in service of others and in praise of God. Congar observed that the trinitarian theology of many of the ante-Nicene Fathers was by current standards imprecise, but Justin, Ignatius, and others nonetheless gave their lives for their faith. Revelation, Congar echoed Geffré, is not a "reified truth but a dynamic truth, a truth that happens, a practical truth in St. John's sense."[137] We express this truth through acts of love and the praise of God. "I still consider the highest mode of theology to be doxology," Congar wrote, "it is content to refer, in praise and adoration, to the Reality who is 'light beyond all light.' It anticipates the eschatological communion in which there will be only praise."[138]

The Economic and Eternal Trinity

Even as Congar emphasized the importance of reflection on God *en soi*, God's created order and economy of salvation were never far removed from his attention. He moved readily from remarks about the profundity of God's supreme Love to musings about the need to understand all creation through a general ontology of charity.[139] His thought easily progressed from reflection on the eternal begetting of the Son to speculation that the Son is ceaselessly begotten *incarnandus* (to become incarnate)—or even begotten eternally as the Word made flesh.[140] "Perhaps the greatest misfortune of modern Catholicism," Congar cautioned, "is to have turned towards the in-itself of God and religion in theology and catechesis without ceaselessly joining to this the importance of all this *for humanity*."[141] Theology's emphasis on God *en soi* contributed to the spread of atheism; humanity responded to a theology of God without the world by postulating a world without God.[142]

"[W]e shall reach the eternal Trinity," Congar wrote, "only by way of the economic Trinity."[143] By virtue of God's assumption of human nature in Jesus Christ, human history is taken up into the eternal life of God and this mystery must inform our reflections on divine ontology, for the history of salvation is not extrinsic to God's eternal being even as it remains distinct from God. This suggests, Congar continued, that within the eternal being of God there is a desire for communion with creation. He explained:

> If there exists such a profound link between "theo-logy" and the Economy, if God reveals the *in-itself* (*l'en-soi*) of his mystery in the *for-us* (*pour-nous*) of the covenant of grace and Incarnation—all that which was and is done for us, including Incarnation—is it not known, despite its absolute liberty, by that which God is *en soi*? And is there not in the mystery of his in-itself (*en-soi*) a presence, a call "for us" including humanization?[144]

Congar distinguished his own theology from philosophies such as that of G. F. Hegel or Maurice Merleau-Ponty, which so identified God and world history that God's transcendence over history was abrogated.[145] Congar's intention was not to reduce God to historical process but rather to take seriously the mystery of God's incarnation in history even as he affirmed God's eternal distinction from creation. "From a biblical and Christian perspective, one may even speak here of the historicity of God: not in himself, evidently, because he is the simultaneous presence of all himself to himself (eternally), but in us and in the world. . . . In Jesus Christ in a direct and personal manner and in us in a mediated manner, God is the subject of a history, of a becoming."[146] God, strictly speaking, is not dependent on human history or subsumed in historical determinacy, but through Christ and the Spirit God embraces and assumes the history of the cosmos, and creation in turn participates in the suprahistorical life of God.[147]

Congar's views on the relationship between salvation history and the eternal Trinity are further clarified in his response to Karl Rahner's trinitarian *Grundaxiom*. In 1967, Rahner offered the following formulation as a corrective to neoscholasticism's disjunction of trinitarian theology and soteriology: "the 'economic' Trinity *is* the 'immanent' Trinity and the 'immanent' Trinity is the 'economic' Trinity."[148] Congar heartily affirmed the first clause of the axiom, for the economy is our only basis for knowledge of the mystery of God.[149] At the same time, he questioned Rahner's concomitant position that the immanent Trinity is the economic Trinity. Congar had three fundamental objections: (1) This later clause of the axiom confused the free mystery of the economy with the necessary existence of the triune God. Even were there no Incarnation or Pentecost, the processions of the Word and Spirit would nonetheless take place eternally. The immanent Trinity is thus not necessarily the economic Trinity.[150] (2) God's economic self-communication as we now experience it is incomplete and kenotic, for the missions of the Word and the Spirit occur in conditions of abasement and suffering that are not connatural to the divine Persons.[151] The full self-communication of God will take place only at the end of time in the beatific vision. The immanent Trinity is thus not yet fully revealed in the economic Trinity.[152] (3) Rahner's position that the " 'immanent' Trinity is the 'economic' Trinity" does not adequately account for the unknowability of God.[153] Congar insisted that we must preserve the unspeakable distance between what God is in God's self (*en lui-même*) and what is communicated in the economy, and he believed that Rahner's axiom could jeopardize this necessary distinction.[154]

The first point of Congar's critique is not self-evidently compatible with statements Congar made elsewhere about the ultimate identity of freedom and necessity in God.[155] At any rate, nonetheless, in both Congar's response to Rahner's *Grundaxiom* and his own theological reflections, he manifested a concern to preserve simultaneously two fundamental truths: (1) God is indeed personally and substantially present in the economy of salvation. Indeed, in light of God's assumption of human nature in Jesus Christ, we affirm that God desires communion with creation and has assumed a human historicity. This mystery should inform all reflection on God *en soi*. (2) At the same time, God is ultimately transcendent of human history. God is not dependent upon history, nor is God exhaustively revealed or fully knowable within human space and time. The eternal Trinity is in this sense suprahistorical.

The Word and the Spirit

Congar's conviction that trinitarian theology must begin with God's revelation in history shaped his approach to the various theological issues that surround the relation of the Word and the Spirit. How are these two divine processions distinguished from each other? What is the mission of the Incarnate Word in the economy of salvation, and what is the mission of the Spirit? What do they have in common, and how are they distinct? How are they related to each other? Over the course of Congar's career, there were important changes in his conceptualization of this relationship. In the 1950s and 1960s, Congar portrayed the Holy Spirit as ancillary to the Word incarnate in Jesus Christ, while in writings from the 1970s and 1980s he emphasized the inseparability and nonduality of the missions of the Word and the Spirit. These developments in Congar's thought influenced his ultimate position on the *Filioque*, the Western theology of the Spirit's procession from the Father and the Son that the East has always found objectionable.

Jesus Christ and the Holy Spirit in Congar's Writings of the 1950s and 1960s

Congar's two-volume *Tradition and Traditions* (French edition, 1960 and 1963) directed readers who were particularly interested in the relation of Jesus Christ and the Holy Spirit to two of Congar's previously published essays, a referral indicative of the importance of these two essays as representative of Congar's thought at this time.[156] These essays are "The Holy Spirit and the Apostolic Body: Continuators of the Work of Christ" (1952–1953) and "The Church and Pentecost" (1956).[157] In these reflections, Congar emphasized that the Holy Spirit comes to us as a consequence of Jesus Christ's passion and resurrection to continue and complete his work. The mission of the Spirit is to animate the ecclesial structures established by Christ and to interiorize subjectively the objective redemption Christ has wrought. At the same time, the Spirit also retains a certain freedom and autonomy with respect to ecclesial institutions.

THE GIFT OF THE HOLY SPIRIT FOLLOWS CHRIST'S PASSION AND RESURRECTION. In "The Holy Spirit and the Apostolic Body" and "The Church and Pentecost," Congar described the gift of the Holy Spirit as a consequence of Jesus Christ's passion and glorification. Through death and resurrection, Jesus Christ has merited the Holy Spirit for us.[158] The effusion of water from the pierced side of the crucified Christ was the moment at which the outpouring of the Holy Spirit began, an outpouring that continued throughout Easter and culminated on Pentecost.[159] Pentecost, strictly speaking, is not a feast day of the Holy Spirit but rather a celebration of the Incarnation of the Word of God in human flesh and a fulfillment of the paschal mystery.[160] Congar explained:

> The Spirit relates himself wholly to Christ and comes from him. In fact, Pentecost is the final mystery of the Christological cycle: there is no cycle proper to the Holy Spirit. It is the completion of Easter, that is of the work of the Incarnate Word, but brought about by a new Person sent by the Father and the Son.[161]

The fiftieth day of Easter simply brought the *acta et passa Christi* to their fullness.

Congar's emphasis on the gift of the Spirit as the completion of the mission of Jesus Christ is evident in the very title of his essay "The Holy Spirit and the Apostolic Body, Continuators of the Work of *Christ*," which portrayed both the Spirit and the apostolic body as agents of Christ's mission.[162] Each continues Christ's work in a distinct manner: the Spirit "indeed continues and accomplishes the work of Christ, but as linked with Christ's coming and his life in the flesh in a very different way from the apostles. The mission of the Holy Spirit is certainly presented as *a* continuation of Christ's, but not precisely as *its* continuation."[163] In the Christian tradition, the apostolic body has been referred to as the vicar of Christ, a designation that some (such as Tertullian) have also accorded to the Holy Spirit. Congar did not categorically reject this usage, but he cautioned that the Holy Spirit, unlike the apostles, "is not merely a vicar, he does not simply exercise a 'ministry' of the Incarnate Word, he is not an 'instrument.' "[164] Once the apostles have discharged the mandate given them by Christ, their soteriological task will be complete, but the Holy Spirit will always retain a role in our salvation.

Yet, even as the Spirit is not a mere transitory instrument of Jesus Christ, it is clear in Congar's essay that the Spirit is Christ's agent, sent to complete the incorporation of all humanity into his mystical body. Christ builds up his church "by means of *his* apostles and *his* Spirit."[165] The Spirit "makes no innovations, he does not create anything that bears no relation to the work of Christ."[166] Although the church grows and develops in the period of time between the Incarnation and the eschaton, this development is simply an extension and expansion of what has already been accomplished, for the eschatological fulfillment "will be found to contain nothing which is not derived from the initial stage."[167] Congar concluded: "In short, if, as regards us, the Spirit is creative ('Veni Creator Spiritus'), he is simply completing what was established by Christ."[168]

THE HOLY SPIRIT ANIMATES THE ECCLESIAL STRUCTURES ESTABLISHED BY CHRIST. Congar's designation of the Holy Spirit as the continuator of the work of Jesus Christ may lead one to wonder whether the Spirit has a proper mission of its own. In fact, Congar affirmed that the Spirit is "a Person distinct from Christ and one sent on a new mission which cannot be equated with that of the Incarnate Word."[169] There is indeed a proper mission of the Spirit, but it differs from the mission of the Word not in content or purpose but rather in manner of execution. Whereas Jesus Christ provided the means for human salvation by instituting the essential structures of the church (the deposit of faith, the sacraments, and the apostolic ministry), it is the mission of the Holy Spirit to infuse these structures with life. Christ established the form of salvation, and the Spirit animates this form with life and power.[170] "[A]s regards the body of Christ, we can distinguish two moments, so to speak: that of its realization and, as it were, its structuration, and that of its sanctification and animation."[171] The growth of the church that is Christ's body follows the general law of God's action—God formed Adam and then filled him with breath (Gn 2:7), and God fashioned a skeletal structure from Ezekiel's dry bones and then gave them new life (Ez 37). Likewise, "Christ redeemed us and established his mystical body, *then* he communicated to it life through his Spirit."[172]

THE HOLY SPIRIT IS THE SUBJECTIVE AND INTERIOR DIMENSION OF CHRIST'S OBJECTIVE REDEMPTION. Congar's account of the Spirit as the animator of the ecclesial forms established by Jesus Christ shaped his conviction that it is the particular mission of the Spirit not only to animate the church but also to contribute a subjective dimension to the redemption that Jesus Christ objectively accomplished.[173] Jesus Christ definitively redeemed humanity through his life, death, and resurrection, and the Holy Spirit subsequently brings the grace of this redemption to fruition within human hearts over the course of Christian history. While Jesus Christ acted *for us*, the Holy Spirit acts *within us*.[174] The Spirit penetrates the inner depths of the human soul such that redemption becomes wholly interior and personal.[175] Our divine filiation was secured objectively by the *acta et passa* of Jesus Christ, but it is the Holy Spirit who touches our hearts such that we do indeed exclaim "Abba!" (Gal 4:6)

THE HOLY SPIRIT RETAINS A CERTAIN FREEDOM AND AUTONOMY. Congar's essays of this period also spoke of "a sort of liberty or autonomy" of the Spirit.[176] He certainly did not mean by this that the Spirit was free or autonomous with respect to Jesus Christ or that the Spirit could institute a qualitatively new era of salvation history such as that postulated by Joachim of Fiore.[177] But Congar did believe that the Spirit is autonomous with respect to the church that Jesus Christ established. Jesus Christ gave the Spirit to the church to animate and sanctify it; yet the Spirit "remains transcendent to the Church he dwells in; he is not just a divine force giving supernatural efficacy both to the ministry and to the sacraments, but a Person sovereignly active and free."[178] The Spirit operates, for example, not only through the instituted forms of ministry and sacraments but also through a variety of charismata, direct interventions, or unexpected events.[179] There is a "kind of free sector" of the Spirit's activity—an idea that Congar thought was comparable to a position Walter Kasper held at this time, although other theologians expressed disagreement with this approach.[180] The ministry and sacraments of the church are indeed animated by the Holy Spirit, but the Holy Spirit is not exclusively bound to the institutions of the church.

Jesus Christ and the Holy Spirit in Congar's Writings of the 1970s and 1980s

Congar's *Tradition and Traditions* (1960–1963) was shaped by the pneumatology and Christology of the two essays just discussed—"The Holy Spirit and the Apostolic Body" and "The Church and Pentecost." Decades later, in *I Believe in the Holy Spirit* (1979–1980), Congar looked backed critically at his earlier work; in *Tradition and Traditions*, he commented, "the pneumatological aspect, although it is very important, has been rather overshadowed by the Christological aspect."[181] Indeed, Congar's writings from the 1970s and 1980s evidence some important changes in his understanding of the relation of Christ and the Spirit. Famerée comments that there is no dramatic Copernican turn in Congar's theology but nonetheless an evident progression in which the *christocentrisme* or *incarnationnisme* of his preconciliar work is recontextualized in new ways.[182] Whereas Congar had earlier designated the Spirit as the one who continues the work of Christ, his books and essays of the 1970s and 1980s emphasize that the Word and the Spirit together do the work of *God*. The Holy Spirit is not simply sent by the risen Christ but constitutes Jesus Christ as the Messiah. The church is co-instituted by Christ and the Spirit, and Jesus Christ and the Holy Spirit exist in inseparable communion.

THE WORD AND THE SPIRIT TOGETHER DO THE WORK OF GOD. Congar's 1952–1953 essay "The Holy Spirit and the Apostolic Body, Continuators of the Work of Christ" was aptly titled and serves as a point of contrast with a chapter heading in Congar's 1984 monograph *The Word and the Spirit*: "The Word and the Spirit Do *God's* Work Together."[183] Famerée draws attention to this important titular shift, which he believes is indicative of a qualitative change in Congar's theology.[184] Congar's thought is now oriented more explicitly towards God the Father and has become more fully trinitarian, less christomonistic. "Christ is the centre and indeed the culmination of our life as Christians," Congar explained, "but he is not the end. . . . He is everything *ad Patrem, pros ton Patera*—towards the Father and for him."[185] The idea that Christ exists *pros ton Patera* is by no means a completely new theme in Congar's work, but it appears now with a new emphasis and recasts his discussion of the relation of Christ and the Spirit. While Congar continued to portray the mission of the Spirit as

the continuation and completion of the work of Jesus Christ, he also emphasized that Jesus Christ himself acts in the Spirit and that Christ and the Spirit
together do the work of *God*.[186] Congar drew up tables of biblical references in
parallel columns headed "The Paraclete and Jesus" or "Pneuma and Christ" to
illustrate that the Holy Spirit and Jesus Christ are described in the Scriptures
in parallel terms, and both act inseparably to carry forward the divine plan.[187]
"[I]n the economy," Congar wrote in 1985, "the Son Jesus Christ and the Spirit
are inseparable. They are the two means and manners of the self-revelation
and self-communication of God."[188]

THE HOLY SPIRIT CONSTITUTES JESUS CHRIST AS MESSIAH. Whereas Congar's
earlier writings portrayed the Spirit as the fruit of Christ's passion and glorification, a gift poured forth from Christ's crucified side to continue his mission,
Congar's publications of the 1970s and 1980s highlighted the important role
of the Holy Spirit in the very life of Jesus Christ himself. The glorified Christ
does send the Spirit; yet it was originally the Spirit who conceived Jesus in
Mary's womb. It was the Spirit who anointed Jesus in the Jordan and constituted him as Messiah, the Spirit who guided Jesus Christ throughout his ministry, and the Spirit who raised him from the dead. If we take salvation history
seriously, Congar insisted, it becomes apparent that Jesus Christ is not simply
revealed as a preexistent Messiah but becomes the savior for us through the
events of his life, death, and resurrection. Jesus is the *Christ* through the power
of the Holy Spirit.[189] Christology must account for this crucial role of the Spirit
in the messianic life and glorification of Jesus Christ—it must be a pneumatological Christology. This, Congar, explained, is a Christology shaped by "the
perception of the role of the Spirit in the messianic life of Jesus, in his resurrection, and in the glorification that have made him Lord and caused the humanity hypostatically united to the eternal Son to pass from the *forma servi* to
the *forma Dei*."[190]

THE CHURCH IS CO-INSTITUTED BY CHRIST AND THE SPIRIT. Congar's articulation of a pneumatological Christology recasts his discussion of the Spirit's
ecclesial mission. In the 1950s and 1960s, Congar had portrayed the Spirit as
the animator of the ecclesial forms established by Jesus Christ and the agent
of our subjective appropriation of Christ's objective acts of redemption. In this
view, the Spirit's ecclesial mission succeeds that of Jesus Christ—first Jesus
Christ institutes the church, and then the Spirit fills the church with life. In
Congar's work of the 1970s and 1980s, in contrast, the Spirit who constitutes
Jesus Christ as Messiah does not simply animate but also *constitutes* Christ's
church. "The Church is Made by the Spirit," proclaims the heading of chapter
1 of volume 2 of *I Believe in the Holy Spirit* (French edition, 1979–1980).[191] In
a 1982 article, moreover, Congar remarked that he now understands the Spirit's
role in the institution of the church in an even ampler sense than that sug-

gested in his three-volume pneumatology.[192] "[T]he Holy Spirit or Christ pneu-
matized and in glory is here and now co-institutor of the church of the incarnate Word."[193]

JESUS CHRIST AND THE SPIRIT EXIST IN INSEPARABLE COMMUNION. In his
essays of the 1950s and 1960s, Congar reserved an autonomous free sector for
the Spirit's activity; this enabled him to account for the gift of charismata and
other interventions that go beyond an animation of the structures established
by Jesus Christ. In the 1970s and 1980s, when Congar identified both Christ
and the Spirit as co-institutors of the church, it was no longer fitting to distinguish the Spirit's autonomous acts from those more directly tied to the dominical institution. "I still think," Congar wrote in 1980, "that what I called,
perhaps rather awkwardly, a free sector is something that really exists."[194] But,
he went on to explain, this is a freedom of both the Spirit *and* Jesus Christ
with respect to the instituted church. In 1984, Congar clarified:

> It is a mistake to think, as I did in 1953 [in *The Mystery of the
> Church*] that a kind of "free sector" reserved for the Holy Spirit ex-
> ists alongside the operation of the instituted structures and means
> of grace. The whole of Christian history bears witness to the fact
> that this freedom really exists, but it is the freedom of the living and
> glorified Lord Jesus together with his Spirit.[195]

Conjointly, continuously, and freely, Jesus Christ and the Spirit constitute the
church, sustaining its foundational structures and inspiring new initiatives.
Strictly speaking, these new initiatives are not a manifestation of the free sector
of the Spirit but a manifestation of the free activity of the Spirit of Jesus
Christ—and the activity of Christ who lives in the Spirit.

For St. Paul, Congar observed, the glorified Lord has become a "life-giving
Spirit" (1 Cor 15:45), and the Spirit is the Spirit of the glorified Lord.[196] The
Word is entirely permeated by the Spirit, and at the same time the Spirit is
entirely permeated by the Word.[197] Both are inseparable, and both proceed from
the Father. Congar regretted that his desire to give proper attention to the Spirit
in earlier writings had precluded his full appreciation of the communion of
Christ and the Spirit. "My mistake," he reflected, in *I Believe in the Holy Spirit*
(1979–1980),

> was that I followed Acts more closely than the Pauline epistles and I
> wanted to give the Holy Spirit his full worth. As a result I was not
> sufficiently conscious of the unity that exists between the activity of
> the Spirit and that of the *glorified Christ*, since "the Lord is the Spirit
> and where the Spirit of the Lord is, there is freedom" (2 Cor 3:17).
> According to Paul, the glorified Lord and the Spirit may be different
> in God, but they are functionally so united that we experience them

together and are able to accept the one for the other: "Christ in us,"
"the Spirit in our hearts," "(we) in Christ," "in the Spirit"—all of
these are interchangeable. The Lord became a "life-giving spirit"
(1 Cor 15:45).[198]

Congar here expressed a new appreciation for the nonduality of the glorified
Lord and the Spirit. He no longer portrayed the Spirit as a discrete agent of
Jesus Christ, sent afield like a commissioned apostle. Rather, in Congar's writings from the 1970s and 1980s, the inseparability and the communion of Jesus
Christ and the Holy Spirit are much more pronounced, and Christology and
pneumatology are indivisibly bound together. "If I were to draw but one conclusion from the whole of my work on the Holy Spirit," Congar reflected in
1984, "I would express it in these words: no Christology without pneumatology
and no pneumatology without Christology."[199]

As Congar's understanding of the communion of Christ and the Spirit
intensified, his account of their activity broadened:

There is no separation of the activity of the Spirit from the work of
Christ in a full pneumatology. Everything that I have said so far
points to the impossibility of making such a division. A pneumatology of this kind, however, goes beyond simply making present the
structures set up by Christ; it is the actuality of what the glorified
Lord and his Spirit do in the life of the Church, in all the variety of
forms that this activity has assumed in time and space.[200]

The ongoing activity of the Holy Spirit *is* the ongoing activity of Jesus Christ,
and the ongoing activity of the glorified Christ *is* the work of the Spirit. The
conjoint activity of the glorified Lord and the Spirit is more than the continuation and animation of the ecclesial structures instituted by the earthly Christ.
"It is the source of a new element in history."[201]

The Filioque

As Congar's discussion of the relation of Jesus Christ and the Holy Spirit
developed new nuances and emphases, so did his approach to the *Filioque*.
Western theology has traditionally professed that the Spirit proceeds from the
Father and the Son (*Filioque*).[202] Meanwhile, the East has insisted that the Spirit
proceeds from the Father alone (*ek monou tou patros*).[203] In the sixth century,
the churches of Gaul and Spain added a *Filioque* clause to the Nicene-
Constantinopolitan creed in an effort to guard against Arianism, and the East
protested vigorously. This conflict intensified in the ninth century when Patri-
arch Photius clashed with Carolingian theologians over the *Filioque*, and in
1054 the *Filioque* dispute contributed to the official separation of the Eastern
and Western churches.[204] Today, the *Filioque* theology continues to spark dis-

cussion as East and West strive for reconciliation. The Orthodox theologian Vladimir Lossky has argued that the *Filioque* is the origin of all the differences between the Greek Orthodox and the Roman Catholic Churches, an insurmountable obstacle to communion, and the root cause of Roman Catholic juridicism.[205] Congar told Lossky repeatedly that he disagreed with this adamant stance.[206] Nonetheless, Congar considered the procession of the Holy Spirit to be the most serious dogmatic difference between Eastern and Western theology.[207] While he disputed Lossky's position that the *Filioque* was responsible for Roman juridicism, he admitted that in other respects there is "a certain influence or at least a coherence" between the *Filioque* and Western ecclesiology.[208] Congar himself pointed out to Lossky that Aquinas had linked the *Filioque* with papal primacy in *Contra Errores Graecorum*.[209]

Congar was trained in the *Filioque* tradition, and he never altered his view that the Holy Spirit proceeds from the Father and the Son. At the same time, his study of the Orthodox tradition, as well as developments in his own theology of the relation of Christ and the Spirit, helped him to appreciate the validity of the Eastern approach. Congar's writings of the 1970s and 1980s discuss the complementarity of Eastern and Western theologies, the advisability of recension of the *Filioque* clause from the Nicene-Constantinopolitan creed, and the ontological issues implicit in the *Filioque* debate.

THE COMPLEMENTARITY OF EASTERN AND WESTERN THEOLOGIES. Greek theologians have consistently rejected the West's theology of the procession of the Holy Spirit from the Father and the Son (*Filioque*). Yet Epiphanius, a fourth-century bishop of Salamis, did maintain that the Paraclete proceeds from the Father and receives from the Son.[210] And Cyril of Alexandria believed that the Spirit is proper (*idion*) to the Son, comes from (*ek*) the Son, and even proceeds (*proienai* or *procheitai*) from the Son or from the two (*ex amphoin*—that is, Father and Son) or from the Father through the Son.[211] In a 1957 essay, Congar highlighted this Orthodox tradition and suggested that it was fundamentally equivalent to the Latin *Filioque* theology.[212] In later writings, in contrast, he emphasized the complex differences that separate Eastern and Western trinitarian theology. He critiqued Anselm and the Council of Florence for their presumption that the Eastern "through the Son" was equivalent to the Latin *Filioque*, for he now believed that such an attempt to assimilate Eastern and Western theology failed to recognize the different shades of meaning expressed by different theological traditions.[213]

Congar's survey of the historical development of trinitarian theology in East and West led him to the conclusion that Eastern and Western traditions each proceed within a distinct theological framework. Consequently, a theological formulation of the procession of the Holy Spirit that is coherent in one tradition is not necessarily transferable to the other. Western theologians who use the intradivine *relationis oppositio* (Father↔Son; Father & Son↔Spirit) to distinguish the consubstantial divine persons must affirm that the Spirit proceeds from the Father and the Son. In this framework, the Spirit cannot proceed from God strictly as Father, for the Spirit would then be another Son or the same as the Son—there would be no *relationis oppositio* to distinguish the Spirit's person. Aquinas, for example, wrote that "we must hold that the Holy Spirit proceeds from the Son; if he did not, he could in no way be a person distinct from the Son."[214] Within this tradition, furthermore, the *Filioque* is necessary to affirm the Son's divine consubstantiality, which requires that the Son have everything in common with the Father except for fatherhood, the pole of the Son's *relationis oppositio*. The Son thus shares in the Father's spiration of the Spirit, for, technically speaking, the Spirit does not proceed from God as Father (that is, in a *relationis oppositio* to the Father), but rather the Spirit proceeds from God who is Father (because of the Father's relation to the Son).

Meanwhile, however, the Orthodox—who do not use the trinitarian theology of *relationis oppositio* to distinguish the divine persons—insist, to the contrary, that if the Spirit indeed comes from both the Father and the Son (*Filioque*), the Spirit must proceed either from the divine essence or from two originating principles. They consider either of these possibilities absurd. Congar believed that the Orthodox interpretation of the Western *Filioque* is perfectly "justified within the perspective of Eastern triadology," although the West has often perceived it as pure obstinacy.[215] For centuries, East and West have thus talked past each other. Each has read the other's theology in terms of its own presuppositions and has misunderstood the other's approach. Congar urged East and West to recognize that they rely on "two theological constructions of the same mystery, each of which has an inner consistency, but a different point of departure."[216] Eastern and Western theologies of the procession of the Holy Spirit, Congar concluded, are complementary.[217] He used this term in a variety of ways; sometimes he spoke of Eastern and Western formulations as complementary in the sense of equivalent,[218] while elsewhere he stressed that Eastern and Western theologies express different aspects of the mystery of God but yet are complementary in the sense that they do not challenge the fundamental unity of the faith.[219] In any case, Congar clearly believed that each theology was coherent in its own terms and that neither was erroneous; yet the two approaches could not be superimposed.[220] Both traditions must be accepted, for the mystery of God surpasses any given theological construction, and therefore several different trinitarian theologies can exist, even several different dogmatic formulae.[221]

THE RECENSION OF THE *FILIOQUE* CLAUSE FROM THE NICENE-CONSTANTINOPOLITAN CREED. Congar's appreciation for the different theological frameworks that have shaped Eastern and Western pneumatology led him to reconsider the West's inclusion of the *Filioque* clause in the Nicene-Constantinopolitan creed. Reversing an earlier position, Congar urged the recension of the *Filioque* clause as a gesture of Roman humility and brother-hood.[222] The Orthodox, he noted, had insisted at Ferrara-Florence in 1428–1429 that the *Filioque* must be rescinded from the creed and "the question is still with us, and its importance should not be underestimated."[223] Even as Congar called for removal of the offending clause, however, he emphasized that the recension of the *Filioque* need not be a repudiation of Latin pneuma-tology itself. The *Filioque* is an undeniable part of the Roman Catholic expres-sion of faith and is cogent within its own context and in its own terms.[224] When Pope Leo III received the envoys sent by Charlemagne to campaign for the universal inclusion of the *Filioque* in the creed, the Pope made a distinction between the teaching itself (which he affirmed) and its inclusion in a formula or creed (which he refused to require).[225] Following this precedent, Congar believed that the removal of the *Filioque* from the creed should be accompanied with the avowal that it is a nonheretical formula complementary to the Eastern formulation of the procession of the Holy Spirit from the Father through the Son.[226]

THE ONTOLOGICAL SIGNIFICANCE OF THE *FILIOQUE*. Congar affirmed the validity of the *Filioque* clause even as he called for its removal from the creed, for he believed it communicated an important truth. The *Filioque* rightfully highlighted that the Son has a role not only in the economic sending of the Spirit but also in the Spirit's eternal existence. Augustine and Aquinas con-cluded from scriptural passages such as Romans 8:29, John 15:26, John 16:14–15, and John 20:22—passages that state that the Son gives us the Spirit—that the Spirit must proceed eternally from the Son.[227] The West has insisted, Con-gar explained, on the ontological continuity between the economy of salvation and the eternal life of God. In patristic literature, he found indications that the Greek fathers too believed that the Son played a part in the eternal being of the Spirit, although this dependence was not of a causal kind.[228] Congar con-sidered Epiphanius and Cyril of Alexandria the most important Eastern theo-logians in this regard. He also found evidence for this position in Gregory of Nyssa and in John Damascene.[229] These Greek patristic texts speak of (a) pro-cession of the Spirit from the Father through the Son; (b) procession of the Spirit from the Father receiving from the Son; (c) procession of the Spirit from the Father resting on the Son. Contemporary Orthodox theologians interpret such formulas with reference not to the Son's origin but rather to his mani-festation. Congar wondered, however, whether such patristic texts might in fact call for an affirmation of the Son's part in the Spirit's hypostatic existence. "I am not alone to think that they [do], although it is difficult to say exactly to what extent and in what sense. Probably not in the sense of *a Patre Filioque tanquam ab uno principio*."[230]

In any case, it was Congar's understanding that the theology of his Eastern ecumenical partners presumed a distinction "between the economy, in which

Christ gives the Spirit causally, and theology."²³¹ The Orthodox might respond that it is the Western tradition that has in fact breached economy and theology by its failure to consider the ontological implications of the constitutive role of the Spirit in the life of Jesus Christ. In the economy, Christ surely sends the Spirit, but the Spirit conceives, anoints, guides, resurrects, and glorifies the Son—as Congar himself emphasized in his later writings. The Orthodox theologian Paul Evdokimov thus suggested that the Son is eternally begotten *ex Patre Spirituque*.²³² Congar initially expressed reservations about Evdokimov's formulation.²³³ In 1984, however, Congar agreed that insofar as the Son is eternally begotten *incarnandum*,

> the Word proceeds *a Patre Spirituque*, from the Father and the Spirit, since the latter intervenes in all the acts or moments in the history of the Word *incarnate*. If all the *acta et passa* of the divine economy are traced back to the eternal begetting of the Word, then the Spirit has to be situated at that point.²³⁴

If the economy of salvation is the basis for the affirmation of the procession of the Spirit from the Father and the Son *(a Patre Filioque)*, then a corresponding affirmation must be made of the procession of the Word from the Father and the Spirit *(a Patre Spirituque)*.

The Person of the Holy Spirit

Congar wrote at great length about the historical development of the theology of the Holy Spirit in East and West, the *Filioque* dispute, the relationship of Christology and pneumatology, and the work of the Spirit in the church. He published the major three-volume work *I Believe in the Holy Spirit* (1979–1980), as well as *The Word and the Spirit* (1984) and numerous articles specifically devoted to pneumatology. Like all theologians, however, Congar found that the person of the Holy Spirit eludes definition. "[R]evelation and knowledge of the Spirit," he cautioned, "are affected by a certain lack of conceptual mediation."²³⁵ In contrast to the Father and the Son, whose very names reveal their mutual relation and the unique character of their persons, the terms "holy" and "spirit" do not belong strictly to the person of the Spirit, for the Father and Son also are holy, and both are spirit. Furthermore, the words "Father" and "Son" connote the common human experience of relation between parent and offspring, whereas the terms "holy" and "spirit" do not have any such readily apparent human associations.²³⁶ The Spirit, Congar echoed von Balthasar, is the "Unknown One beyond the Word."²³⁷ Congar surmised:

> it has been suggested that the Holy Spirit empties himself, in a kind of kenosis, of his own personality in order to be in a relationship, on

the one hand, with "God" and Christ and, on the other, with men, who are called to realize the image of God and his Son. "In order to reveal himself, he did not, like Yahweh in the Old Testament and Jesus in the New, use the personal pronoun 'I.'" The Holy Spirit is revealed to us and known to us not in himself, or at least not directly in himself, but through what he brings about in us.[238]

Yet even our knowledge of what the Spirit brings about in us is limited. Invisible and ineffable, the Spirit moves through history in a way that is impossible to retrace, and the theologian can only identify "certain particularly meaningful aspects of the knowledge that has been gained and expressed of the Spirit."[239] Congar struggled to find ways to write of the Holy Spirit in a manner respectful of this divine ineffability. He described the Spirit as the Love of God and the principle and term of divine communion, the divine person to whom grace is appropriated, and God's ecstatic Gift.

The Spirit as the Love of God and the Principle and Term of Divine Communion

The Holy Spirit is the Breath of God who proceeds ineffably from God as God speaks the eternal Word. "[T]he Holy Spirit is, as his name indicates, a going out, an impulse, an 'ecstasy.'"[240] Just as our human locutions are inseparably accompanied by an expellation of breath, so, too, the Breath of God proceeds indivisibly with the divine Word.[241] The terms "Breath" and "Spirit," Congar noted, suggest divine motion and power. This *virtus Spiritus Sancti* is the ecstasy of divine generosity and love.[242]

In the West, there are two primary forms of theological reflection on the Spirit as love. In the first version of this theology, the Word and the Spirit proceed eternally as God's knowledge (the Word) and God's love (the Spirit) of God's own goodness. This theology underlies Aquinas's account of love as a personal name of the Spirit in *ST* I[a], q. 37. "When anyone understands and loves himself he is in himself," Aquinas explained, "not only by real identity, but also as the object understood is in the one who understands, and the thing loved is in the lover."[243] In the case of God, the conception of the object understood is the Word, who proceeds by way of the divine intellect, and the impression of the thing loved is the Spirit, who is "love proceeding" (as differentiated from God's essential love) by way of the divine will. A second trajectory in the Western tradition portrays the Spirit as the mutual love of the Father and the Son. Augustine spoke of the Spirit as the sweetness of the Begetter and the Begotten and the enjoyment (*perfruitione*), charity, and joy of their inexpressible embrace (*complexus*).[244] The theme of the Spirit as the mutual love of the Father and Son also appears in the writings of Anselm, William of Saint-Thierry, Richard of St. Victor, Alexander of Hales, Bonaventure, and other theologians.[245] Congar himself affirmed: "The Father and the Son are for each other, they are relative to each other. The Spirit is the one in whom they are united, in whom they receive each other, in whom they communicate with one another, and in whom they rest."[246] At the same time, Congar highlighted Dodaine's caution that a theology of the Spirit as mutual love risks an anthropomorphic trinitarianism insofar as it suggests that Father and Son are two friends or two beloved persons in the human sense of these terms.[247] Congar shared Dodaine's concern and found evidence of anthropomorphism in Yves Raguin's use of the mutual love tradition.[248] Aquinas, Congar concluded, had rightly prioritized a theology of the Word and Spirit as the knowledge and love that proceed eternally from God's self-knowledge and will, and only once this foundation was established did Aquinas also incorporate into his theology the tradition of the Spirit as mutual love.[249]

The theology of the Spirit as the mutual love of Father and Son is rare in the East.[250] Instead, Orthodox pneumatology is shaped by the doxological formula Greek patristic theologians appropriated from scriptural and liturgical sources: "from the Father, through the Son, in the Spirit"—*ek Patros, di' Huiou, en Pneumati*—a doxology that of course is also common in the West.[251] Congar believed that this trinitarian formulation—like the Western theology of the Spirit as love proceeding—aptly expresses the dynamism of the divine life. He considered this Greek formulation akin to the Western theology of the Spirit as mutual love, since it portrays the Spirit as the one in whom the divine communion is perfected and completed, the one in whom Father and Son are sealed.[252]

The Spirit Is the Divine Person to Whom Grace Is Appropriated

The Spirit is uniquely God's love proceeding. At the same time, the attributes we commonly predicate of the Spirit—holiness, goodness, power, wisdom, and even love—are attributes not only of the Spirit but also of the Father and the Son, and the Western tradition has typically qualified statements such as "the Spirit is holy" with the proviso "by appropriation." The theology of appropriations developed in the West in order to reconcile the consubstantiality of the triune God with scriptural and liturgical language that speaks of Father, Son, and Spirit in distinct terms—"the Son is wisdom" or "the Spirit is holy." Technically, only what Aquinas termed the "personal notions" can be constitutively predicated of each of the divine persons: paternity, which is proper to the Father; filiation, which is proper to the Son; and procession, which is proper to the Spirit.[253] All essential divine attributes, in contrast, are common to Father, Son, and Spirit and are appropriated to a divine person only by virtue of a resemblance of this attribute to a personal property. Aquinas defined appropriation as a "manifestation of the divine persons by the use of the essential attributes."[254] Congar remarked, "There is really something in that Person to justify the appropriation, but we cannot clarify it or say with certainty that there is an attribute peculiar to that one Person that would exclude the other Persons from what is appropriated to the one."[255] The theology of appropriations has been used not only with reference to the divine attributes but also with respect to divine activity in the economy of salvation. "In the West at least," Congar explained, "the fact that every action performed by God is common to all three Persons of the Trinity has given rise to the idea that an activity in creatures can only be *appropriated* to one Person, but is not peculiar to him, or his own."[256]

In recent decades, the theology of appropriations has been subject to critique. Heribert Mühlen found it contrary to Scripture, while Karl Rahner believed that it precludes a theological affirmation of the economic communication of each of the divine person's own uniqueness and particularity.[257] The Incarnation, Rahner maintained, is a dogmatically clear instance of an economic relation that is proper (that is, not appropriated) to a divine person, for it is the Logos—not the Father or the Spirit—who enters into hypostatic union.[258] Congar himself acknowledged that the theology of appropriation has limitations and leaves some dissatisfied.[259] The very terminology of this tradition "does not . . . succeed in understanding or in making understood the reality contained in this conceptualization, nor in indicating that this same conceptualization corresponds to the directions of Holy Scripture."[260] He seemed to share Rahner's concern about the need for theological expression of the distinct missions of the Word and Spirit. "Our theology," Congar stated, "is strictly a theology of appropriation and does not see enough that the mission of the Spirit is proper and original."[261]

At the same time, Congar was reluctant to dispense entirely with the theology of appropriations and continued to employ this approach even as he noted its limitations.[262] He believed that the doctrine of appropriations has a strong basis in Scripture, liturgy, and tradition.[263] And, although he concurred with Rahner's position that the Incarnation was proper (not simply appropriated) to the Son, Congar did not believe that a similar judgment could be made about the mission of the Spirit.[264] The Son—not the Spirit—entered into a hypostatic union with a human nature, and thus the person of the Son has a proper (nonappropriated) activity and causality in the economy in a way that the Spirit does not. "There is a mission but not a hypostatic incarnation of the Holy Spirit. So he is not personally manifest."[265] In the 1950s, 1960s, and early 1970s, Congar made extensive use of the theology of appropriations in his reflections on the Holy Spirit. Congar appropriated to the Spirit the efficacy of the sacraments and solemn definitions of faith, our union with God, and our sanctification.[266] He spoke explicitly of appropriation less frequently in *I Believe in the Holy Spirit, The Word and the Spirit,* and other publications of the late 1970s and 1980s. But he never entirely abandoned this approach. "By appropriation," he wrote in *I Believe in the Holy Spirit* (1979–1980), ". . . the Holy Spirit is the subject who brings about everything that depends on grace."[267]

Yet, even as Congar maintained his position that the Holy Spirit does not have a personally proper (nonappropriated) activity in the economy of salvation, he affirmed that the uniqueness of the Spirit's person is truly communicated in salvation history. In the Greek tradition, Congar noted, the *taxis* of the immanent trinitarian processions (from the Father, through the Son, in the Spirit) is identical with the *taxis* of the missions in the economy (from the Father, through the Son, in the Spirit). Hence, the eternally unique properties of Father, Son, and Spirit manifest in the immanent processions are communicated to creatures through the divine missions. God the Father creates the cosmos through the Son and in the Spirit such that the hypostatic marks of the Son and the Spirit are manifest in creation, even though creation is an act of efficient causality. God redeems and divinizes the cosmos through the Son and in the Spirit, an act of quasi-formal causality in which the uniqueness of each of the divine persons is present to humanity in an even more profound manner.[268] "[T]here are two missions and each of these, in a way that we cannot describe in words, bears the hypostatic mark of the Person sent."[269]

The Spirit Is God's Ecstatic Gift

The hypostatic mark of the person of the Spirit as manifest in the economy cannot be described in words. Scripture and tradition have nonetheless used many different images to try to speak of the Spirit's mystery: the Spirit is called wind (Gn 1:2), living water (Is 44:3–4; Jn 4:10; 7:3–39), dove (Mk 1:9–11), chrism (Is 61:1, Lk 4:18), fire (Acts 2:3; Is 6:6), and peace (Jn 20:19, 21).[270] Of all the terms used of the Spirit, Congar believed that the word that most aptly expresses the Spirit's unique hypostatic mark both in the economy of salvation and in God's eternity is Gift.[271] As Hilary of Poitiers wrote, in the third century, "He (the Christ) commanded (his disciples) to baptize in the name of the Father and the Son and the Holy Spirit, that is, by confessing the Author, the only Son and the Gift (*Doni*)."[272] Augustine, too, identified the personal name of the Spirit as *Donum* or *Munus*.[273] Peter Lombard continued this pneumatological tradition, and Aquinas identified "Gift" as one of the Spirit's two personal names (the other is "Love.")[274] The name "Gift," Congar explained, is appropriate to the person of the Spirit, for, like the names Father and Son, it expresses a *relationis oppositio*—the Gift is relative to the Giver, namely the Father and Son.[275] Although the theology of the Spirit as Gift is uncommon in the East, it is not entirely unknown. Moreover, the dynamic trinitarian pattern *ek Patros, di'Huiou, en Pneumati* that is common in Greek theology is suggestive of the Spirit's ecstatic character.[276]

Congar maintained that the person of the Holy Spirit can be appropriately named as the divine Gift apart from the created order in which the Spirit is actually given, for the Spirit proceeds eternally as "giveable."[277] Yet God does in fact desire to continue the divine ecstasis outside of God, and the Spirit is not only the eternal Gift of the Father and the Son but also God's Gift to creation—divine love, generosity, and grace.[278] In Scripture, the Spirit is called *dōrea*, which means "formal donation."[279] On Pentecost, Peter promised that all who repented and were baptized would "receive the gift (*dōrea*) of the Holy Spirit" (Acts 2:38). And Luke recounted that in Caesarea "the gift (*dōrea*) of the Holy Spirit was poured out even on the gentiles"(Acts 10:45).[280] Furthermore, scriptural references to the Spirit frequently occur as the complement of various forms of the verbs *didōmi* (to give) and *lambanō* (to receive). Paul wrote to the Corinthians, for example, that God "has given (*didōmi*) us his Spirit in our hearts as a guarantee."[281] Indeed, Congar believed that in Scripture, the Holy Spirit is the gift of God par excellence—the gift of the fulfillment and renewal of creation, salvation, and eternal life. The Spirit is the fulfillment of the promises of God—the eschatological *arrha* and agent of the achievement of God's purpose.[282] The Spirit "is implored as riches and as Gift, in the name of what is wretched and lacking. We ask him to come to us in the sequence *Veni, Sancte Spiritus.*"[283]

3

Congar's Pneumatological Anthropology and Pneumatological Ecclesiology

"Come, true light! Come, eternal life! Come, hidden mystery!"[1] With
these words, Simeon the New Theologian entreated God to send the
Holy Spirit among us. Congar considered Simeon to be one of the
greatest of the Byzantine mystics, and like Simeon he believed that
theology culminates in the praise of God and the exercise of the
spiritual life. The theology of the Holy Spirit, Congar emphasized, is
not simply an account of the third person of the Trinity but concerns the mystery of God's transformation of human life—the mystery of our deification in Christ and our communion with God and
one another.[2] A theology of the Holy Spirit requires what Congar
termed in the 1970s and 1980s *une anthropologie pneumatologique*
and *une ecclésiologie pneumatologique*—a pneumatological anthropology and a pneumatological ecclesiology.[3] Congar's insight into the
need to develop and integrate these two dimensions of pneumatology is his distinctive contribution to a contemporary Roman Catholic theology of the Holy Spirit. In much of post-Reformation Catholicism and certainly during the late nineteenth and early twentieth
centuries, theology and spirituality addressed the indwelling of the
Spirit in the human soul but gave very little attention to the pneumatological foundations of the church. As I have described in the
Introduction, neoscholastic theological manuals typically discussed
the indwelling of the Holy Spirit in the treatise *De Gratia*, describing the Spirit's conferral of divine filiation, the theological virtues,
and spiritual gifts and fruits. In the same manual, the treatise *De
Ecclesia* would make only minimal reference to the Holy Spirit, or
perhaps not even mention the Holy Spirit at all.[4] These theological

manuals were primarily seminary fare, but even in popular works of spirituality reflection on the indwelling of the Spirit in the human person proceeded with the assumption that this indwelling had no major implications for the structure or mission of the church. Congar discerned that this divorce of spiritual anthropology from ecclesiology was inconsistent with biblical and patristic theology, the theology of Thomas Aquinas, and the Eastern Orthodox tradition. In the library of the Saulchoir and in his ecumenical engagements, he discovered a tradition that integrated ecclesiology with spiritual anthropology, and he believed that this was a tradition that must be given new life in contemporary Catholicism. Congar never had the opportunity to develop this insight in a comprehensive and systematic way. Sifting through the pages of his books and articles, however, one can find the elements in his own work of both an *anthropologie pneumatologique* and an *ecclésiologie pneumatologique*.

Congar's Pneumatological Anthropology

Congar is known primarily for his ecclesiological contributions, rather than for work in the area of theological anthropology. Unlike his German contemporary Karl Rahner, who undertook a systematic reconceptualization of Roman Catholic theological anthropology in light of the modern turn to the subject, Congar, in his research, teaching, and writings, focused on ecclesiology. When Congar did engage in anthropological reflection of an explicit character, his thought was influenced by his formation in Thomism, which shaped his theology of the human person and his reflections on the relation of nature and grace. For Congar, another entrée into the realm of theological anthropology was his reading of Scripture. As Congar read, studied, and prayed the Scriptures, he was struck by the fact that in biblical literature God and humanity are inseparable. "The Bible does not talk about God without talking about man, and vice versa. It is indivisibly theology for man and anthropology for God."[5] For centuries, Congar believed, Christian theology had neglected this biblical truth and contributed inadvertently to modern atheism, much of which was rooted in an affirmation of humanity, rather than a determined disavowal of God. Christianity had failed to convey to modern men and women that the God whom Christians worship was a God absolutely committed to humanity, not a God who could be served by an eclipse of the human.[6] Quoting Irenaeus's maxim "It is God's glory that man lives," Congar called for a contemporary theology that would communicate that humankind is inseparable from God to such a degree that no anthropology or humanism can provide an adequate account of human existence unless it proceeds with a theological orientation.[7] "The most important work today," he stated emphatically, "is to show the unity between theology and anthropology. . . . [Y]ou cannot separate God and man."[8] Congar distinguished his advocacy of a unified theology and anthropology from anthropocentrism, against which he cautioned.[9] His intention was not to reduce theology to anthropology but rather to do justice to the mystery that humankind is made in the image of God and destined to share in God's eternity. Congar's anthropology emphasized the creation of human persons in this divine image, the fracture of the divine image occasioned by human sin, and the healing and deification of humanity wrought through Jesus Christ in the Holy Spirit.

The Creation of Human Persons in the Image of God

On the sixth day of creation, according to the book of Genesis, God declared, "Let us make humankind (*'ādām*) in our image, according to our likeness" (Gn 1:26). This Genesis passage became the foundation of a long tradition of *imago Dei* anthropology in the Christian tradition, and over the centuries it has been subject to a variety of interpretations. In the West, theologians have often used Augustine's discussion of the similarity and difference between the triune God and the tripartite character of the human soul—a soul with memory, understanding, and will—to develop a so-called psychological doctrine of the Trinity and a corresponding theological anthropology.[10] In recent decades, others, such as William Hasker and Jürgen Moltmann, have advocated a social trinitarianism that locates the *imago Dei* in human social relationships.[11] Congar recognized truth in both approaches. He found the *imago Dei* in the human soul; yet, at the same time, he did not think the *imago Dei* can be limited to the psychic structure of the individual human person. "The human being is made in the image of the triunity of God, not only in psychological structure but also in the reality of existing in society and communion."[12]

Congar carefully qualified his position that the divine image can be found in human social relations, for, although human society manifests the image of God, it is not an appropriate image *of* God. God is triune, but God is not a plurality of persons in the manner of a human community. Both Augustine and Aquinas opposed the suggestion that the image of God is to be found in the primordial human family of Adam, Eve, and Seth, and in 1215 the Lateran Council rejected Joachim of Fiore's attempt to use human society as a basis for a conception of the Trinity.[13] We cannot, Congar emphasized, project forms of human sociality upon God. Nonetheless, a converse theological movement can be made: the mystery of God can illumine the mystery of human social relationships. We "can clarify the human condition in light of who God is: a communion of persons."[14] In this light, Congar explained that human persons are gifted with knowledge and love so as to exist in relation with God and one another. Human persons are active, free historical subjects; we share a common human nature, which each person instantiates in a unique way; and we serve as a cosmic microcosm.

HUMAN PERSONS ARE GIFTED WITH KNOWLEDGE AND LOVE. Congar believed, as Aquinas had maintained, that the image of the triune God can be found in the procession of the word in the human intellect and the procession of love in the human will.[15] This anthropology stands in the trajectory of Augustine's supposed psychological trinitarian theology, which critics fault for its individualism. Yet Congar's Thomistic anthropology is by no means individualistic. The human intellect and will through which we image God lead us *beyond* the self toward knowledge and love of another. We are created with the capacity to speak to another, to strive to know another, to love one another, and to receive one another in love. There is within us "an overture to other persons and [the human being] only realizes himself [or herself] in communion with them. The human being is made to live in relations of exchange with others, in a situation and an exercise of 'co-humanity.' "[16] Above all, our vocation to knowledge and love is indicative of our capacity to be called by God.[17] We are created in the divine image for the purpose of receiving God's call and responding to God with trust, fidelity, and love.

Even as we respond in love to God and others, human relationality is not an identical reflection of the communion of the triune God in whose image humanity is made. The divine persons are subsisting relations whereas each created person is an autonomous substance.[18] Yet, despite this fundamental difference between divine and human persons, relation to others is inscribed at the very heart of the human vocation. We find our truth, Congar insisted, in being *with*, *through*, and *for* (*avec, par,* et *pour*) one another in trinitarian *circumincessio*.[19] He reflected:

> [T]his giving and sharing . . . are of the order of being itself, and
> they suffer at the touch of any individual, self-interested holding
> back. It is the order of friendship; an order of intimacy because the
> persons themselves share together and so do not remain wholly ex-
> ternal one to the other. Here, so far from being interchangeable, the
> persons are part of the relations, of the mutual exchange, of that
> which is put in common; and the putting in common means not to
> lose but to find oneself and to achieve one's best.[20]

To live in the *imago Dei* is to live in relation to others.[21]

Congar contrasted his emphasis on the human vocation to love and relationality with both secular individualism and some strands of Christian theology. He critiqued forms of Christian spirituality such as that of Peter Nicole (d. 1695), who professed: "A man is created to live alone with God for ever."[22] Congar also faulted Protestantism and classic Roman Catholic theological ethics for individualistic tendencies.[23] He opposed the existentialism of Jean-Paul Sartre and Albert Camus, for in his view their philosophy of human autonomy and individual liberty failed to account for humanity's creaturely

dependence and transcendent openness toward God.[24] Congar likewise contested what he termed a *"mystique* of sincerity" in Rousseau and Gide, as well
as Descartes's reduction of the person to self-consciousness. For Congar, these
philosophies were fraudulent mysticisms that destroyed what is noblest in the
human person: responsibility, obligation, and relation to others.[25]

HUMAN PERSONS ARE ACTIVE AND FREE HISTORICAL SUBJECTS. Aquinas's
discussion of the *imago Dei* emphasized not only the procession of knowledge
and love from the human intellect and will but also the profoundly active
character of human creatures made in the image of a God who is pure act.[26]
The human person, Aquinas wrote, "is said to be made to God's image, in so
far as the image implies an intelligent being endowed with free-will and self-
movement . . . man . . . is the principle of his actions."[27] In Congar's own
terms, human beings are personal subjects (*sujets personnels*).[28] The modern
term "subject" does have connotations that differ in some respects from those
of the language of Aquinas; as Congar noted, the modern emphasis on the
human subject is in some sense in continuity with the theology of Aquinas
and Augustine, but in another sense *il s'agit d'autre chose encore.*[29] Congar believed that modern philosophers such as Descartes and Locke exalted individual subjectivity and self-consciousness in a manner inconsistent with the
Christian tradition, and he described human persons as subjects not in order
to endorse modern individualism but rather to affirm that *relation* with other
persons and with God requires the recognition of human capacity for active
initiative. The secret of true relationship is respect for others as "subjects,
persons, centers of emotion and projects."[30] Congar opposed all anthropologies
that reduce the human person to an object of determinism, Marxist collectiv-
ism, or the social forces of modern technological and industrial society.[31] He
acknowledged that human persons are indeed shaped by societal structures,
but he noted that persons also create and transform these structures through
their work and their cultural and social lives.[32]

As human subjects, we are free. This freedom is manifest in part in our
capacity for active judgment and choice.[33] There are many limitations to the
exercise of choice that often force us to submit to circumstances, but nonetheless "our freedom is real if choice be considered as the total meaning we give
to the whole fact of our existence."[34] Even God respects this freedom of choice
and tailors revelation accordingly, veiling the fullness of the divine goodness and beauty such that God's grandeur does not overwhelm our human
faculties and we truly can say "No" to God.[35] Congar explained:

> God does not of necessity present himself for our free choice with
> face unveiled. He even cannot do so, for it would be to constrain our
> freedom of choice: so glorious would be his beauty, so over-

whelming the evidence that here is absolute Good, that it would not be possible to refuse him. That freedom of choice of ours requires that God should be as it were disguised.[36]

Yet, at the same time, human autonomy and choice do not exhaust the meaning of freedom and do not have an absolute value. "The truth is that man could never be more free than were he, by some blessed impossibility, to reach the state of being unable to sin. . . . The highest degree of freedom is not to govern oneself, but to be wholly governed by God."[37] Freedom is ultimately not a mere autonomy of choice but rather freedom for relationships of mutuality and communion grounded in communion with God. It is found in the exercise of our capacity to know and to love others and to receive love from them in mutual invitation and reception that "flows from one liberty and addresses itself to another liberty."[38]

The capacity of human subjects to exercise true freedom is expressed in our human historicity, "the becoming of civilization . . . all the efforts made by man in society to make the world a dignified habitation."[39] Modern thought has given new emphasis to this dimension of human existence, and there has been a new appreciation for the human capacity to transform human society and culture over the course of time. Indeed, Congar observed, some now talk of human "becoming," rather than human "being." He found important overtures toward historicity in the work of Aquinas, but in the modern era "historicity has become a category of thought, an existential of the human condition."[40] While Congar affirmed this development of modern historical consciousness, he also believed that our sense of historicity must remain grounded in its ancient biblical roots. Scripture affirms that the truth of things is found not simply in their becoming but in their *destiny;* the meaning of Genesis is complete only in the book of Revelation.[41] Only in the eschatological era, as Tennyson reminds us, will we truly be able to proclaim "It is finish'd. Man is made."[42] Human historicity must thus be viewed in the context of God's intention and purpose for creation, and Congar critiqued Camus's insistence that one must invent one's own path and create one's own future.[43] He believed that the homogeneity of spiritual experience through the ages confirms the existence of an objective religious reality that can guide human becoming toward its intended end and prevent historicity from sliding into relativity.[44] Humanity exists not simply in an existential state of becoming but also in the state of vocation.[45]

HUMANITY SHARES A COMMON HUMAN NATURE THAT EACH PERSON INSTANTIATES IN A UNIQUE WAY. The divine image that is manifest in our existence as free, historical subjects capable of knowledge and love defines our common human nature, which Congar described as "that structuring principle that permits one to identify as 'human' all those individuals thus designated: a principle received through generation at birth."[46] In Gregory of Nyssa's exegesis of Genesis, the passage "God created humankind (*'ādām*) in his image" (Gn 1: 27) refers not to God's primordial creation of a single human person but rather to God's creation of a universal human nature that is shared by all human beings and that binds us to one another.[47] Congar himself believed that the "ontological unity of the genus *humanum* is the common basis for the quest of unity which men propose and for the most fundamental dogmas of Christianity."[48] In the words of Pascal: "The whole succession of men should be seen as one and the same man, continuing always to exist and to learn."[49]

Congar believed not only that humanity has a common nature and a common destiny but also that every person "has a destiny of his own, that he cannot relinquish to anybody else."[50] The *imago Dei* is not a mold that casts human persons identically from a single prototype. Rather, every human person bears the divine image in a unique and incommunicable way, for God loves all persons in themselves and calls each by his or her own name.[51] Human corporeality, furthermore, instantiates each human person as a particular man or woman at a particular time or place.[52] We are each unique persons who share a common nature, and as such we manifest the image of the triune God;[53] in both humankind and in God, there is a person-nature dialectic in which nature is a principle of commonality and person is a principle of uniqueness and distinction.[54] In the triune God, this dialectic is manifest differently than among human creatures, for "Father, Son, and Spirit are one sole substance, numerically one," whereas corporeal human persons such as Peter and Paul are individuated in matter as two men, not *a* man.[55] Our common humanity is the basis of a collective unity, rather than a substantial unity such as that of the triune God.[56] Nonetheless, the corporeality that individuates us should not separate us from one another but rather should serve as an important mode of our relationality. Indeed, Congar emphasized, it is through our bodiliness that we encounter and relate to one another.[57]

HUMAN PERSONS SERVE AS A COSMIC MICROCOSM. Our bodiliness also relates us to the entire created order. God creates us, Congar believed, with historical, cosmic, and social dependence, and therefore "God creates us *through* [these cosmic and social relations]."[58] The cosmos provides the matter through which humans are formed, and humans in turn use their gifts of self-consciousness, speech, and knowledge to bring the speechless universe to spiritual expression. In the words of patristic and medieval theology, humanity is the microcosm of the universe. We are

> the epitome that sums up and completes the vast world with which
> we have community of material substance and of general destiny.
> . . . It is on this very ground and in this way that we, immortal souls
> animating a body taken from the dust of the earth, are the first-

fruits of the world. My destiny is not that of an isolated soul; taken integrally, it is that of the world of which I am part, which acts on me and on which I act.[59]

The universe, Congar concluded, is fundamentally interrelated, and it is the human vocation to give expression to this cosmic communion. Congar called not only for a pneumatological anthropology but also for a "pneumatological cosmism"—a theology that would articulate the cosmic role of the Holy Spirit.[60]

Human Sinfulness: The Divine Image Fractured

God had a clear purpose and intention for creation. In supreme generosity, God created the cosmos through the Word and the Spirit and gave to human creatures the special responsibility of bearing the divine image—the image of knowledge and love. Human beings were intended to use this gift to receive and respond to the call of God and other persons. We were created to use our active freedom to love God in liberty, to live in harmony with one another, and to construct societies that would lead history to its intended destiny. Our common human nature was designed to unify us, and human consciousness and speech were intended to enable us to give spiritual expression to the entire cosmos.

In Adam, however, humanity repudiated God. The root of sin is our rejection of the God in whose very image we are made. To sin is "[t]o hinder God being God in us, for us and, through us."[61] The divine image is never entirely lost to humanity, for God continues to love us even as we turn away. But the *imago Dei* necessarily fades as a consequence of human infidelity, for we have removed ourselves from the divine *exemplar*, and the created order is fundamentally disordered. The common human nature that was to be a basis of our unity has become instead the vehicle of original sin, and our relations with others are breached by conflict, contradiction, and separation.[62] Men are divided from women, Germans from French, and each person from others such that "other people are hell."[63] We abuse our capacities for active initiative and freedom such that history becomes a succession of wars and injustice where the power of evil holds sway. Satan finds modern allies in "Money, Power, Public Opinion and its instruments, the Party, the Race, the Nation, and in Progress, Comfort, Production, and so on and so on."[64] Our misdeeds are concretized in collective structures that thwart true liberty and deny our personal uniqueness, and our corporeality becomes a means of separation from one another. Our lives are clouded and opaque, and things are divorced from their true meaning.[65] This tragedy is ongoing. "When we look at Jesus on his cross, we become conscious of how really sin banishes God from the world."[66]

The Grace of God: The Divine Image Healed and Deified

The cross is a symbol of humanity's banishment of God, but it is also a sign of God's embrace of sinful humanity. On the cross, God responded to our infidelity with the offer of atonement and reconciliation. The incarnate Word of God has taken up the sins of humankind and given his life as a ransom for the many (Mk 10:45).[67] This theology of atonement was not the primary focus of Congar's Christology; Congar emphasized that the Incarnation of the Word occurred as a fulfillment of the plan of God and an expression of God's desire to lead creation to its intended end of divine communion. Even had humanity never sinned, Congar believed, God would have sent the Word and the Spirit to us.[68] In the context of a disordered cosmos, however, the mission of the Word and the Spirit includes the atonement of our sin and the vanquishing of the power of evil in the world, a power so great that it cannot be overcome without an act of divine redemption. Congar's ordination card, as I noted earlier, pictured St. Dominic at the foot of the cross and bore these lines, which Congar thought to be from Tennyson:

> But none of the ransomed ever knew
> How deep were the waters crossed.[69]

Congar pondered the meaning of these words even as he cautioned that the atonement is a mystery that cannot be explained. "I am aware that I am stammering," he told Bernard Lauret, in a 1987 interview, when this topic arose, "and stammering very badly; theology is too profound a mystery."[70] In response to death and sinfulness, God has offered life, reconciliation, and communion.[71]

God not only redeems us from sin but also invites us to partake of a divine life that exceeds all the capacities of human nature even in its most pristine form. In Jesus of Nazareth, the eternal Word who is *the* Image of God has become incarnate, and through incorporation into the body of Christ we too may become God's very sons and daughters. This invitation to divine filiation is not foreign to our created nature, for we are made in the divine image and there is within us a longing for divine communion.[72] Yet this longing cannot be satisfied solely by virtue of our created capacities for knowledge and love, and it is grace that "sweeps on to [human nature's] perfection, a perfection beyond its intrinsic possibilities but not beyond its inefficacious desire."[73] Grace elevates human knowledge and love to a new level of communion with God.

Congar's theology of nature and grace challenged post-Tridentine scholastic theologies that distinguished the natural and supernatural orders in an extrinsic fashion and denied a natural desire for union with God. Congar attributed this extrinsicism to a poor interpretation of Aquinas under the influence of Cajetan and Suarez, and he joined Henri de Lubac, Karl Rahner, and others in offering an alternative to this approach.[74] Divine grace, Congar believed, is a gift that was envisioned from the very moment of our creation in God's image.[75] Drawing from Blondel and Rahner, he maintained that the human person is structured to be open, receptive, and responsive to a divine call.[76] We are created with a divine destiny and can find definitive fulfillment only in God.[77] We reach this destiny through conversion, forgiveness, and the indwelling of the Holy Spirit. This indwelling requires our active cooperation, leads to deification, and will not be consummated until the eschatological era.

CONVERSION AND FORGIVENESS. "Today as ever," Congar reflected, "and more than in many other epochs, lives are changed by the action of the Spirit."[78] This transformation begins with a recognition of our sinfulness. Before human nature can be elevated in grace, it must first be healed, and the Spirit of Truth invisibly confronts us and makes us conscious of our selfishness and fault.[79] The promised Paraclete "will prove the world wrong about sin" (Jn 16:8).[80] Simultaneously, the Spirit envelops us with forgiveness and dissolves our mechanisms of self-justification, for the Paraclete is not only our prosecutor but also our pardoner (Jn 20:21–23; Acts 2:38).[81] The Holy Spirit

> begins the movement of conversion which he continues by stirring up in us a conviction of sin, a rooted feeling of the need to change our life and to be truly converted. The Holy Spirit, too, makes us hear in the heart, as if directly and actually spoken to us, the calls of the scriptural witness: "If you hear his voice speaking to you this day, do not harden your hearts" (Heb 3:7).[82]

Our transformation in grace begins with repentance, conversion, and forgiveness.

THE INDWELLING OF THE HOLY SPIRIT. When we repent of our sin, the Holy Spirit dwells (*oikei, katoikēsai*—1 Cor 3:16; Eph 3:17) or remains and abides (*menei*—Jn 14:16–17) within us. "Do you not know," Paul questioned, "that you are God's temple and that God's Spirit dwells in you (*oikei en humin*)?" (1 Cor 3:16).[83] As God lives in us, so we in turn live in Christ and in the Spirit (e.g., 2 Cor 5:17; Gal 3:28; Eph 2:13; Eph 2:18). These biblical accounts of indwelling, Congar clarified, are not intended in a spatial sense. Rather, Paul used the language of dwelling and abiding as an expression of our elevation to a new level of communion in the life of God. Subsequent to the Incarnation and the gift of the Spirit, "it is no longer a *presence* that is involved, but an *indwelling* of God in the faithful."[84] Paul's discussions of our life in Christ and the Spirit employ *en* (in) not as a preposition of place but rather as a referent to the christic and pneumatic principles of life and action that shape Christian existence in the state of grace.[85]

Congar's reflection on the indwelling Spirit as a transformative principle of human life was informed by the theology of Aquinas, who had described the entire cosmos as ordered in divine wisdom such that all creatures are endowed with active principles proportionate to the ends they are created to achieve. The proper principles of human nature are knowledge and will, and these principles serve the properly human end of knowing and loving God.[86] The indwelling of the Holy Spirit, in contrast, is a supernatural gift that transcends the created order—a divine principle proportionate to a suprahuman end. In assenting to matters of faith, Aquinas explained, the human person is raised above nature and this elevation "must needs accrue to him from some supernatural principle moving him inwardly; and this is God."[87] God "draws the rational creature above the condition of its nature to a participation of the Divine good," for God desires for us "the eternal good, which is Himself."[88] In Christ and the Spirit, we not only live through the proper capacities of our created human nature but also share a divine principle of life and action that is commensurate with our new divine destiny; we know and love with the very knowledge (the Word) and love (the Spirit) of God. In the state of grace, we know and love God actually and habitually, and in the state of glory we will know and love God perfectly.[89] Congar's discussion of the indwelling Spirit presumed this Thomistic theology. Through the indwelling of the Spirit, our lives are elevated by a divine principle of life and action. In prayer, Congar wrote citing J.-C. Sagne, " 'the Holy Spirit is the desire of God in God himself and also the desire of God in us.' "[90] In the Spirit, we love God with *God's* own love. Congar quoted John of the Cross:

> The soul loves God not through itself, but through God himself, because it loves in this way through the Holy Spirit, as the Father and the Son love each other and according to what the Son himself says in the gospel of John: "that the love with which thou hast loved me may be in them, and I in them" (Jn 17:26).[91]

Other mystics, such as William of Saint-Thierry, St. Theresa of the Infant Jesus, and Maximus Confessor, testify to a similar experience.[92] This experience of divine love is inseparable from love for God's creatures, with whom we are united in charity.[93] All of this is possible not by virtue of any human prowess but rather because God has sent the Holy Spirit, and "he dwells with you and he will be in you" (Jn 14:17).

HUMAN COOPERATION WITH GRACE.   In the Spirit of Christ, we participate in the very holiness, desire, and love of God. At the same time, the indwelling Spirit does not eclipse the activity of our own human faculties. Because we are created in the *imago Dei*, grace coincides with our deepest human desires and elevates but does not negate our human knowledge, love, and freedom. "When we cry, 'Abba! Father,' " St. Paul wrote, "it is the Spirit of God bearing witness with our spirit that we are children of God" (Rom 8:15). And yet, Congar commented, "it is *we* who cry."[94] With the exception of the absolutely miraculous,

> the action of God passes totally and entirely through *our* mental, psychological and corporeal resources. It is even necessary to avoid imagining that our part is just about 75% and that where this stops, divine intervention takes over. All is of us, all is of God. God is and acts within us; he remains transcendent in this very immanence.[95]

The Spirit is given in our hearts with such subtlety, intimacy, and interiority that the action of the Spirit is almost indistinguishable from our own.[96] God "is so deeply within us, because he has been sent 'into our hearts' and, as the Holy Spirit, he is so pure, subtle and penetrating (Wis 7:22) that he is able to be in all of us and in each one of us without doing violence to the person, indiscernible in his spontaneous movement."[97] Certainly our sinful deeds are not the work of the Holy Spirit, but, if our actions are truly rooted in goodness and love, they are acts of both our human faculties and the indwelling Spirit of God. With Aquinas (and contra Peter Lombard), Congar believed that a created *habitus* or principle of action always accompanies the uncreated charity that is the Spirit of God.[98] The East has traditionally spoken of this human cooperation with grace as synergy, the principle that "we make ourselves through our actions, and it is the work of God (see Gal 4:7)."[99] The Orthodox combine a strong sense of God's initiative with an equally strong emphasis on human freedom, and Congar was convinced that Roman Catholic theology was really not very different from the East in this regard despite century-spanning Western debates on the relationship between grace and free will.[100]

Human cooperation with grace does not mean that God and creature operate on the same level or that we earn our own salvation. Congar heartily agreed with Aquinas that human beings can merit salvation only insofar as the Holy Spirit is operative in us, for "merit only exists because of grace and assumes that the Spirit is 'sent.' "[101] Our human faculties—even when exercised rightly—are incommensurate with our destiny to share in the eternal life of God. Thus, "the Holy Spirit as uncreated grace takes the initiative and provides the dynamism until the ultimate victory is reached in which God is merely crowning his own gifts when he awards us a crown for our 'merits.' "[102] We can never earn salvation of our own accord.

We can, however, impede our salvation and grieve the Holy Spirit by our refusal to cooperate with grace.[103] Congar thus emphasized the importance of spiritual practices that cultivate an openness to God. " 'The real aim of our Christian life is that we should be overcome by the divine Spirit,' " he echoed Seraphim of Sarov, and this requires prayer, fasting, almsgiving, charity, and other good works undertaken in the name of Christ.[104] Congar cited Bonhoeffer: "If you search for liberty, learn first discipline."[105] He recommended a nondualistic asceticism that affirmed the goodness of the human body but that also recognized that it is impossible to have a serious spiritual life if one cedes to the body's every desire.[106] He highlighted the need for constant prayer and for the elimination of noise and distraction.[107] He stressed the importance of a spiritual reading of Scripture and of an active sacramental life, and he counseled his readers to seek ardently for the will of God:

> [A]ny programme for holy living in the world presupposes an attempt on our part to learn what God wants: for the world in general, for us in particular. . . . We can thus come to know exactly what work and calling has been assigned to us individually, what responsibility to the Father has been entrusted to us, after we have "died" to worldliness.[108]

Congar urged commitment to virtuous practices and an active engagement with the world carried forth with simultaneous dedication and detachment so as to live in the world, but not of it.[109] "No one," Simeon the New Theologian cautioned, "will leave the darkness of the soul and contemplate the light of the most Holy Spirit without trials, efforts, sweat, violence and tribulation."[110] As Seraphim of Sarov advised, constant effort is necessary in order to attain the measure of Christ.[111]

THE MYSTERY OF DEIFICATION. The Christian life requires constant effort, but Congar also believed—as St. Seraphim himself had testified—that the labors of the Spirit fill our soul with sweetness, happiness, joy, and inexpressible delights.[112] In the waters of baptism we are deified, an Eastern expression used to describe the depths of God's grace.[113] Congar believed that the West's theology of the divine missions communicates the same profound mystery of human transformation that the Eastern language of deification professes. He did wonder, however, whether

> our theological talk about the divine missions and created grace suffice to do justice to the terms in which the mystics and the spiritual writers have spoken about the transforming union—iron which becomes fire in contact with a source of intense heat, air which glows when the sun penetrates it, and so on.[114]

In his own work, Congar tried to do justice to the mystics' experience of intense communion with God through a theology of divine filiation and an emphasis on uncreated grace.

Through the Incarnation of the Word of God and our incorporation into Christ's mystical body, we become adoptive sons and daughters of God. This divine filiation "is not simply a legal status" but "a real state."[115] Congar affirmed the abiding difference between the eternal Word who is Son of God by nature and we who are children of God by grace; yet he also believed that we "form with the Son one single being as sons."[116] As Paul exclaimed continually, Christ is in us and we are in Christ (Rom 8:1; Rom 8:2; Rom 8:39; Rom 16:7; 2 Cor 5:17; 2 Cor 13:5; Eph 2:13). We rejoice in Christ (Phil 3:3), hope in Christ (1 Cor 15:19), speak the truth in Christ (Rom 9:1), and triumph in Christ (2 Cor 2:14). Paul coined numerous verbs with the prefix *sun-* to express our intimate association and coaction with Christ; we are crucified with Christ (Col 2:20), die with Christ (Col 2:20), and rise with Christ (Col 3:1).[117] Throughout the centuries, Congar noted, great mystics like John of the Cross, Jean-Jacques Olier, Teresa of Avila, Marie de l'Incarnation, and Elizabeth of the Trinity have borne witness to this mystery with their testimony that "I no longer live" but it is "Christ who lives in me" (Gal 2:20).[118] Like Paul, they speak of a sovereign power of God that comes to take possession of the soul "in order to become one with it."[119]

The mission of Christ is inseparable from the mission of the Spirit in whom we are united to Christ and through Christ to God. The indwelling Holy Spirit *is* the uncreated grace of God. "Catholic theologians speak of 'grace,'" Congar observed. "In so doing, they run the risk of objectivizing it and separating it from the activity of the Spirit, who is uncreated grace and from whom it cannot be separated."[120] Congar shared Rahner's concern that Catholic theology's emphasis on created grace had eclipsed the mystery of our vocation to participate in the uncreated life of God.[121] Rahner had reasserted the primacy of uncreated grace by describing the indwelling of the Spirit in terms of quasi-formal causality, an expression he used to try to communicate that the uncreated Spirit really does transform and deify the human person but does not become part of our physical composition.[122] Congar believed this theology had roots in Basil, Cyril of Alexandria, Bonaventure, and Aquinas and was also implicit in the Patristic description of the Holy Spirit as a seal.[123] Just as a seal leaves its mark on molten wax, so, too, the Spirit of God impresses a divine form upon our soul.

LIFE IN THE SPIRIT. The Spirit of Christ sealed upon our soul acts in synergy with our natural human capacities for knowledge, love, and freedom to transform human lives. This new life is manifest in a multitude of ways. In the Spirit, we are enabled to exercise the theological virtues of faith, hope, and charity. According to Aquinas, God creates in the soul a habitual availability or *habitus* to enable us to practice the virtues *supra modum humanum* by means of an impulse received *ab altiori principio*.[124] Our exercise of the virtues is enabled by habitual grace and enhanced by the gifts of the Spirit—wisdom, understanding, counsel, might, knowledge and fear of the Lord (Is 11:1–2)—which perfect the practice of the virtues.[125] Spiritual fruits flower from this practice, and we experience love, joy, peace, patience, generosity, faithfulness, gentleness, and self-control (Gal 5:22). We are gifted with goodness, righteousness, godliness, steadfastness, gentleness, purity, forbearance, and kindness.[126] We become, Congar reflected, men and women given up to God and others— "free, truthful, demanding, merciful, recollected, and open to all."[127]

Congar's account of our transformation in the Spirit emphasized that the Spirit makes us truly free. "Now the Lord," wrote St. Paul, "is the Spirit, and where the Spirit of the Lord is, there is freedom" (2 Cor 3:17; cf. Gal 5:13, 18; Rom 8:2,14). The Spirit heals our dispersion and superficiality such that our lives truly have a center (un dedans).[128] The resulting perfect liberty is neither license nor mere conformity to an external law but what Congar termed "interiority"—the total coincidence of our own desire and will with the love of God. The new law of the Gospel is, as Aquinas stated, the very Holy Spirit of God who "is so much the weight or inclination of our love that he is our spontaneity intimately related to what is good."[129] In this perfect liberty, even the most difficult and burdensome tasks become exigencies of love.[130] We become capable of true apostolic freedom: openness, availability, and confidence (parrēsia) even to the point of martyrdom.[131]

Interior freedom is manifest in a life of Christian communion. "The Holy Spirit," Congar wrote, "is that active presence of the Absolute in us who, at the same time, deepens our interior life by rendering it alive and passionate and brings us into relation and communion with others."[132] It is natural for human creatures made in God's image to exist in relation to others, but in the Spirit of Christ our love for one another is elevated to a suprahuman level. We love one another with the very love of God, and we are bound to one another in the unity of the body of Christ. We are "members of one another."[133] This communion is not a fusion of existences, for the Spirit deepens our own unique personhood at the same time as the Spirit unites us in charity to one another in a manner both sublime and concrete.[134] Communion in the Spirit is evident in the time- and space-defying mystery of the communion of saints, and also in the charitable execution of the very ordinary requirements of common daily life. In the Spirit, we must live together with a love that is patient and kind—a love that is not jealous nor boastful, arrogant, rude, irritable, or resentful (1 Cor 13:4–5).[135]

Our transformation in the Spirit of Christ culminates in the adoration of God. In response to God's gift of the Spirit, we must glorify God with our entire lives, offering our very existence to God as a spiritual sacrifice in the manner of Jesus Christ (Jn 4:24), Paul (Rom 12:1), and Peter (1 Pt 2:5).[136] We voice our thanksgiving and adoration in hymns of grateful praise, and yet even this very gratitude comes from the Holy Spirit. "Beyond all that we know consciously and all thoughts that we can form or formulate, the Spirit who dwells in our hearts is there himself as prayer, supplication and praise."[137] We who are the microcosm of the cosmos express the doxology of the entire universe in liturgical adulation.[138]

THE SPIRIT AS ESCHATOLOGICAL *ARRHA*. The Incarnation of the Word and the gift of the Spirit that we celebrate with liturgical praise are the culmination of God's salvific economy. Yet Congar was acutely aware that we live in the tension of the already and the not yet, a period in which all creation is still groaning (Rom 8:22). In this era, the Spirit strengthens us in our tribulations and consoles us in the sufferings we share with Jesus Christ, the crucified One.[139] In the midst of our distress, Paul assures us that there is often "a true *spiritual* joy (Rom 11:17; Gal 5:22)."[140] This joy is a foretaste of the promised kingdom of God for which we have a passionate longing.[141] When the bonds of sin and death are finally wholly overcome, there will be a new communication of the Spirit—God's gift of the Spirit will bear its ultimate and definitive fruit.[142] In this eschatological era, we will enjoy "spiritual glory in our vision of God and bodily glory through the resurrection."[143] In the interim, the Spirit is our pledge (*arrha*) and promise that creation will be set free from bondage and decay. The Spirit is our hope that God *will* be "all in all" (1 Cor 15:28) and that "we will be like him, for we will see him as he is" (1 Jn 3:2).[144]

Congar's Pneumatological Ecclesiology

The eschatological mystery of deification is inseparable from the mystery of the church. Ecclesial life is both an expression of our new life in the Spirit and a means toward our transfiguration; our fulfillment as creatures made in the divine image can be found only in communion with God and with others. Congar noted that, in both the Gospel of John and the epistles of Paul, the Spirit is promised and given to the church.[145] "The Father will give *you* [plural] the Spirit" (Jn 14 and 16), Jesus promised, while Paul proclaimed that "the love of God is poured forth in *our* hearts through the Holy Spirit who is given to *us*" (Rom 5:1–11).[146] For St. Paul, it is the community of Christians that is a temple of the Holy Spirit (1 Cor 3:16–17; 6:19; 2 Cor 6:16; Rom 8:9; Eph 2:19–22). In patristic theology, Congar continued, pneumatology and ecclesiology were inseparable. Ireneaus proclaimed that "where the Church (*ecclesia*) is, there is also the Spirit of God and where the Spirit of God is, there are also the Church and all grace."[147] Augustine always linked the church and the Holy Spirit, and so did creeds and confessions of faith.[148] Congar was particularly struck by the fact that the First Council of Constantinople (381) enhanced Nicaea's "We believe in the Holy Spirit" with the addition of a clause enumerating what would become known as the four ecclesial marks [*notae*] of the church: "We believe in the Holy Spirit, the Lord, the giver of life. . . . We believe in one holy, catholic, and apostolic church."[149] For Congar, a pneumatological anthropology was inconceivable apart from a pneumatological ecclesiology—an account of the action of the Spirit in the ecclesial communion.

And yet, as I have described, there was scant development of pneumato-logical ecclesiology in the nineteenth-and early-twentieth-century Roman Cath-olic theology that Congar inherited. Neoscholastic theological manuals, popular works of spirituality, and papal encyclicals such as Leo XIII's *Divinum illud munus* did offer reflections on the gifts of the Spirit, the charity of the Spirit, and the indwelling of the Spirit in the souls of the righteous. Yet, "when the Spirit *in the Church* was discussed," Congar noted, "he was mainly presented as the firm guarantee given to the institution and to its magisterium."[150] In-deed, some purely juridical ecclesiologies failed to even mention the Holy Spirit at all.[151] In sum, Congar observed:

> The spiritual and personal aspects of the Holy Spirit were treated of
> in "Spirituality," in an atmosphere of what would now be called "pri-
> vatization." The indwelling of the Holy Spirit as systematized by
> Saint Thomas was thoroughly and lengthily discussed. But this had
> little influence in ecclesiology because the anthropology of the
> Christian sprang from the latter, and this was often excessively jurid-
> ical.[152]

Congar believed that this privatized theology of the indwelling of the Spirit did not constitute a viable pneumatology. An authentic theology of the Holy Spirit must integrate a theology of personal indwelling with a theology of the church:

> By pneumatology, I mean something other than a simple dogmatic
> theology of the third Person. I also mean something more than, and
> in this sense different from, a profound analysis of the indwelling of
> the Holy Spirit in individual souls and his sanctifying activity there.
> Pneumatology should, I believe, describe the impact, in the context
> of a vision of the Church, of the fact that the Spirit distributes his
> gifts as he wills and in this way builds up the Church. A study of
> this kind involves not simply a consideration of those gifts or char-
> isms, but a theology of the Church.[153]

As we have seen, Congar never wrote the comprehensive, systematic theology of the church that he had envisioned as a young man. Had he realized this lifelong dream in the last decades of his life, his theology of the church would have surely been the *ecclésiologie pneumatologique* he ultimately advocated. In his books and articles of the 1970s and 1980s, one finds the elements of this ecclesiology. Congar emphasized that the Spirit co-institutes the church, em-powers the sacraments and inspires the praise of God, structures the church with charisms, effects ecclesial communion, makes the church holy and cath-olic, preserves the church in apostolicity, and kindles the church's eschatolog-ical mission.

The Holy Spirit Co-institutes the Church

Congar's pneumatological ecclesiology was grounded in the affirmation that the church is made by the two inseparable divine missions of the Word and the Spirit. As I have described in chapter 2, Congar gradually moved from his portrayal of the Spirit as the animator of the ecclesial structures established by Jesus Christ to the position that the Spirit is not simply the animator but also the co-institutor of the church. Congar's conviction that the church is made by the Spirit was a consequence of his growing emphasis on the nonduality of Jesus Christ and the Spirit and a component of his pneumatological Christology. He wrote:

> A pneumatological ecclesiology presupposes a pneumatological
> Christology, that is to say an appreciation of the role of the Spirit in
> the messianic life of Jesus, in the resurrection and glorification that
> have made him Lord and have caused the humanity hypostatically
> united to the eternal Son to pass from the *forma servi* to the *forma
> Dei*.[154]

In the Spirit, Jesus Christ laid the foundations of the church both during his earthly life and in his glorified state. Christ and the Spirit act inseparably to establish what Congar typically called the ecclesial "means of grace"—the Word, the sacraments, and the apostolic ministry. The institution of these essential ecclesial elements occurred gradually throughout the apostolic era. "Together with many other contemporary theologians," Congar wrote, in 1982, "I recognize that Jesus put in place the foundations but that the full institution of the Church was the work of the apostles after Pentecost."[155] Jesus Christ gave a sacramental signification to certain events—baptism in the Jordan, the sharing of bread on Passover—but the sacramental rites of baptism and Eucharist developed throughout ecclesial history.[156] Likewise, Christ chose twelve apostles and thereby instituted the apostolic body, but the practice of apostolic succession in the form of an ecclesial episcopacy occurred after Pentecost.[157] Jesus Christ is thus not simply the founder of the church but, more broadly, the church's foundation.[158] Upon this foundation, the church is edified over the course of Christian history through the inspiration and assistance of the Spirit of the glorified Lord and the cooperation of the Christian faithful.[159] A pneumatological Christology implies that "there is not only Christ the historical founder of the church, but also the Christ who is the church's foundation through the faith of the believers of which the church is the 'we'; there is the glorified Christ acting without cease as Spirit to form his Body, and sending his Spirit."[160]

    Congar's affirmation that the church is made by the Spirit was intended to counter not only exclusively christological accounts of ecclesial institution but also those ecclesiologies that portrayed the ecclesial institution in humanly self-sufficient terms. In Congar's estimation, the conception of the church as a well-oiled machine that operated smoothly of its own accord without God's active initiative was all too common in Roman Catholicism.[161] Too often, it was presumed that, once Jesus Christ had instituted the hierarchy and the sacraments, divine initiative in the church was no longer necessary. Congar recalled that, during the course of the Second Vatican Council, a theologian of repute said to one of the *periti*, "You speak of the Holy Spirit, but that is for the Protestants. *We* have the teaching authority."[162] Congar countered such presumptions with his repeated reminder that it is God who established, sustains, and builds up the church through Jesus Christ and the Spirit. "It is *God* who calls us (Rom 1:6. People of *God*, Church of *God*: 1 Cor 1:1; 2 Cor 1:1); it is *God* who distributes the gifts of service (1 Cor 12:4–11); it is *God* who makes things grow (1 Cor 3:6)."[163] This divine activity is not a one-time event. The church is not a prefabricated, ready-made institution but rather a living organism, "always in the process of being built, or rather being built by God."[164] This theocentric emphasis is the cornerstone of Congar's pneumatological ecclesiology.

The Church Lives by the Sacramental Epiclesis of the Spirit and the Praise and Glorification of God

The ongoing divine activity that builds up the church is preeminently evident in the church's sacramental and liturgical life. In the liturgy, Jesus Christ's redemptive actions become not simply historical deeds but, presently, efficacious events.[165] In the sacraments, mortal human persons and earthly material elements are transformed by the deifying power of God and taken up into God's eternal life. This is possible, Congar insisted, not by virtue of earthly means or by the power of the ecclesial institution but by the epiclesis and intervention of the Holy Spirit:

> What we have here is an absolutely supernatural work that is both divine and deifying. The Church can be sure that God works in it, but, because it is God and not the Church that is the principle of this holy activity, the Church has to pray earnestly for his intervention as a grace. . . . [T]he Church does not in itself have any assurance that it is doing work that will "well up to eternal life"; it has to pray for the grace of the one who is uncreated Grace, that is, the absolute Gift, the Breath of the Father and the Word. . . . "I believe the holy Church" is conditioned by the absolute "I believe in the Holy Spirit." This dogma means that the life and activity of the Church can be seen totally as an epiclesis.[166]

The epicletic character of ecclesial life is evident in all the church's sacraments. Baptism is given in the name of the Father, the Son, and the Holy Spirit by immersion or sprinkling with water that the Spirit has sanctified, and through the power of the Spirit we die to sin and are reborn as members of Christ's body.[167] Confirmation completes and fulfills baptism through an anointing of the Spirit that seals our Christian commitment.[168] The sacrament of penance and the power of the keys are "entirely under the sign of the Holy Spirit," Congar wrote, noting that the Spirit is mentioned more than twenty times in the *Praenotanda* of the new penitential rite of 1973.[169] And in the sacrament of ordination, the Spirit is communicated through the laying on of hands and an epicletic prayer that calls upon the Spirit to strengthen and renew the candidates for the deaconate, presbyterate, and episcopacy.[170] Congar also believed that there is an epicletic character to the sacrament of marriage, although this is more pronounced in the Orthodox rite than in the Latin Catholic West.[171] Finally, the sacrament of the Eucharist that culminates the Christian life is entirely dependent on the activity of the Holy Spirit. Congar believed that the Eucharistic mystery is contiguous with the mystery of the Incarnation—just as the Word became flesh through the Spirit of God, so, too, the conversion of bread and wine into the body and blood of Christ takes place through the power of the Holy Spirit.[172] The consecration of the elements requires not only the properly intentioned recitation of the words of institution but also the prayer of epiclesis.[173] The Spirit, furthermore, must touch the hearts of those who receive the Eucharist if the sacrament is to bear fruit in their lives—if the sacrament is to be taken not simply *sacramentaliter* but also *spiritualiter*.[174]

The church implores the Spirit of Christ with earnest hearts in the prayer of epiclesis, and in response to God's gift the church voices its praise and thanksgiving. Ecclesial life is both entirely dependent upon the Spirit and wholly orientated to the glorification and adoration of God. Praise is offered to God, through Jesus Christ, in the Holy Spirit. All the Eucharistic prayers in today's Roman rite, Congar noted, end with the doxology "Through him, with him, in him, *in the unity of the Holy Spirit*, all glory and honour is yours, almighty Father, for ever and ever."[175] Congar commented that he himself prayed these words daily with great intensity and understood them to indicate that:

> The Holy Spirit, who fills the universe and who holds all things in unity, knows everything that is said and gathers together everything that, in this world, is for and tending towards God (*pros ton Patera*). He ties the sheaf together in a hymn of cosmic praise through, with and in Christ, in whom everything is firmly established (Col 1:15–20).[176]

In the Spirit who is God's ecstatic Gift to us, we return to God our grateful praise.

The Charisms of the Spirit Are a Structuring Principle of the Church

The church grows and thrives through the charisms of the Spirit given to the members of the ecclesial body. Charisms, Congar explained, are gifts of nature and of grace given for the fulfillment of the mission of the church.[177] He was critical of the charismatic movement's limitation of the term "charism" to refer to extraordinary gifts such as speaking in tongues.[178] The Spirit awakens natural human talents—gifts for teaching, healing, advocacy for justice, reconciliation, music, and so forth—and elevates them to a new level of orientation toward God in the love and service of others. Charisms are given to all the members of the church and take many different forms. "The Church receives the fullness of the Spirit only in the totality of the gifts made by all Her members," Congar wrote. "She is not a pyramid whose passive base receives everything from the apex."[179]

In the decades prior to Vatican II, charisms played little or no role in Roman Catholic ecclesiology.[180] If theologians mentioned them at all, Congar noted, they were considered only in terms of their contribution to personal spirituality and were attributed no ecclesiological importance or value; they "were seen in the sense of the personal vocation without structural value for the Church."[181] Pius XII did discuss the charisms in his 1943 encyclical *Mystici Corporis*, but only in a limited sense.[182] Charisms, Congar emphasized, should be treated not simply as gifts for personal spiritual enrichment or ornamental additions to a self-sufficient ecclesial institution but rather as a contribution to the church's very constitution. Even subsequent to the Second Vatican Council, he noted with concern, "we are still a long way from opening the life of the Church, its parishes and its organizations to the free contribution of the charisms."[183]

As Gotthold Hasenhüttl explained, the charisms are the *Ordnungsprinzip* of the church—the principle of ecclesial order and construction—a position Congar accepted with the qualification that Hasenhüttl's theology must be placed in the proper context of the sacrament of orders and given christological balance.[184] The ordained ministries must not be reduced to one charism among others, for they have a foundational role in the life of the church. One of Congar's criticisms of Hans Küng's *The Church* was its presumption that the forms of church life of the Pauline era could serve as a comprehensive basis for contemporary ecclesiology; Küng's book had its value and merits (among which, Congar noted, was the reintroduction of spiritual anthropology into ecclesiology)[185]; yet it was a kind of *Scriptura sola* approach to theology that neglected the importance of the development of ecclesial tradition.[186] Despite this qualification of Hassenhüttl and critique of Küng, Congar affirmed that charisms do contribute to the very constitution of the church, and consequently they do not, as is often presumed, stand in opposition to the ecclesial institution. Inevitably, there will be some tension between ecclesial charisms and institution.[187] Yet many charisms can be rightfully designated as actual ministries, and the institutionalized or ordained ministries, in turn, have a charismatic dimension. "Although not everyone possessing the gifts of the Spirit is instituted as a minister, those who are instituted do in fact possess such gifts."[188]

The charisms manifest themselves not only in their contribution to a plurality of ministries but also in the diversity of local and particular churches. The local church is the church in a certain place (e.g., Paris, Santiago, Philadelphia), and the particular church is a church in which the members share a common characteristic, such as language or ethnicity.[189] The distinctive features of local and particular churches are charisms insofar as they are orientated to the mission of the church universal, and the church universal must call these charisms forth. "[T]he Church is only Catholic," Congar maintained, "when, by the communion of the local or particular churches she applies to herself the gifts distributed to all. No man can say to another, 'I do not need you' (cf. 1 Cor 12:21; Rv 3:17)."[190]

The Holy Spirit Is the Principle of Ecclesial Communion

The Holy Spirit not only inspires a rich diversity of charisms but also brings all persons and all local and particular churches into communion with one another. A pneumatological ecclesiology that embraces manifold gifts and ministries does not result in anarchy or fragmentation, for the same Spirit who enlivens a diversity of charisms is also (by appropriation) the principle of ecclesial communion. Congar had been devoted to the service of ecclesial unity ever since he championed the cause of ecumenism very early in his career; yet Famerée observes that in the later stages of Congar's life, his call for "unity" became a vision of diversity within ecclesial *communion*.[191] The church is graced with the *koinōnia tou hagiou pneumatos* (2 Cor 13:13). This Pauline passage uses the objective genitive rather than the genitive of author, for ecclesial communion is not simply something produced by the Spirit but a participation *in* the Holy Spirit of God.[192] One and the same Holy Spirit dwells within all the members of the church as their principle of unity, "for by one Spirit we were all baptized into one body" (1 Cor 12:13).[193] Although faith, the sacraments, and common life and action are also principles of ecclesial unity, the Spirit is the personal and living principle of the communion of the church.[194] "That which makes us one is that each of us has a personal relation with the unique, living God, thanks to the Holy Spirit who is given to us."[195]

In the Spirit of God, persons of every time, place, race, and culture are incorporated into the body of Christ. Communion of such profound extent is possible only through the One who is "unique and present everywhere, transcendent and inside all things, subtle and sovereign, able to respect freedom and to inspire it."[196] From Abel to the last of the chosen people, from earth to heaven, from the church's head to every member, the same Holy Spirit is in all.[197] No human person, Congar emphasized, could ever unify people in the boundless manner of the Spirit of God.[198] No human institution or human law could secure this unlimited communion.[199] No human being could make of many persons one body without annihilating their unique individuality and personhood.[200] Ecclesial communion is a mysterious act of grace that comes from above—from God through Jesus Christ in the Holy Spirit.

Human persons contribute to this communion through their cooperation with grace. Congar believed that the church is built up by the graced initiatives of all who are members of the church universal, for the church does not exist as an unchanging institutional form that absorbs new members who are homogenized to a common mold. Rather, the church is a living communion that grows dynamically as each person and each local community contribute its gifts to the service of others. Inspired by the great evangelical commitment of so many Catholics in postwar France and in the post–Vatican II church, Congar wrote:

> Henceforth, we may confidently speak of an ecclesiology of communion: communion between persons who are seen as so many individual subjects of gifts which they communicate to others, in accordance with the apostolic exhortation of 1 Pet 4:10, which Vatican II repeats, applying it equally to the particular communities or local Churches. A communion, in fact, of Churches that each have their [sic] own gifts and cannot be reduced to the condition of merely quantitative parts of one integrally homogeneous whole, which has all too often been a dominant tendency in Latin Catholicism over the past ten centuries. This supposes that we take account, both in general and in the *de Ecclesia* theology, of the interiorization of the fullness of Christ in individual subjects, which is the specific work of the Holy Spirit.[201]

Congar emphasized the centrality of initiative and renewal in a church in which the Spirit and the human person act together in liberty.[202] He stressed the importance of conciliar life and collegiality, and he described the reception of church teaching as an active process of church members who are not passive objects but persons in communion through the Holy Spirit of God.[203]

As a communion of unique persons, the church is richly diverse. The Spirit takes living roots in every person in a strictly original and personal way, bringing persons to communion "by respecting and even stimulating their diversity."[204] The church is consequently not a homogeneous uniformity but rather a uniplurality of unique persons. The unique personhood of everyone who receives the Spirit of God is one reason for this diversity; the second and more foundational reason is the transcendence of the infinite, incomprehensible, and inexhaustible God. There will never be one hymn that exhausts God's glory, one prayer that captures God's mystery, or one theology that explains God's economy.²⁰⁵ "Communion is precisely unity without uniformity, the harmony or symphony of diverse voices. There is nothing more sublime, nothing more concrete."²⁰⁶ Famerée, following Jean-Pierre Jossua, observes that Congar's accentuation of the importance of ecclesial diversity represents a qualitative shift in his thought. In *Divided Christendom* (1937), Congar stressed unity and treated diversity as a provisional and secondary reality. In contrast, *Diversity and Communion* (1982) treated diversity as a necessary and positive correlative of communion.²⁰⁷ Ultimately, Congar realized, diversity and communion are not opposed, because both have their source in the Spirit of God who is "guarantee both of that communion and of the diversity of the gifts."²⁰⁸ This diversity must never degenerate into division, and Congar regarded it as the responsibility of the pastoral ministry to guard against this possibility.²⁰⁹ Yet he cautioned that the Spirit "does not bring about unity by using pressure or by reducing the whole of the Church's life to a uniform pattern. He does it by the more delicate way of communion."²¹⁰ Congar expressed concern that "excessive emphasis has been given in the Catholic Church to the role of authority and there has been a juridical tendency to reduce order to an observance of imposed rules, and unity to uniformity."²¹¹ External ecclesial authority exists only to serve the spiritual finality of personal union with God and should always be subordinate to this end.²¹²

The Spirit Is the Principle of the Church's Holiness

Our *koinōnia* in the Spirit is a communion with the God who is absolutely holy, as the seraphs extolled in awe when God appeared to Isaiah in the Temple (Is 6:1–3). Jesus Christ—the Word of God and the anointed of the Spirit—was holy and sinless and established the church as a holy nation, a holy priesthood, and a holy temple (1 Pt 2:5, 9 and Eph 2:21). In the Spirit, Jesus Christ instituted the *ecclesia congregans* (the gathering church)—the apostolic institution with its magisterial and sacramental functions—which, by virtue of God's promise to Peter (Mt 16:18–19), enjoys what Congar termed a perpetual and objective holiness.²¹³ All the acts of the apostolic institution are not de facto holy, but holiness is assured of all the "decisive structures and operations of the ecclesial institution."²¹⁴ This holiness does not result from any human virtue but is grounded in the institution of the *ecclesia congregans* by the Incarnate Word and sustained by God's fidelity to God's own promises.²¹⁵ "Only God is holy," Congar insisted, "and only he can make us holy, in and through his incarnate Son and in and through his Spirit."²¹⁶ The Spirit of God is (by appropriation) the principle of this promised holiness.

In the Spirit, holiness is extended from the *ecclesia congregans* to the *ecclesia congregata* (the assembled church). Human persons are washed clean of their sins in the waters of baptism and begin new lives of total orientation to God. Our conversion from sin is an ongoing process; all members of the church are in continual need of purification and struggle forward as the "holy Church of sinners."[217] Nonetheless, holiness is the true vocation of the baptized. The entire church is to be an icon of holiness, a sign of communion with God that reveals the "reality and the presence of another world."[218] Something is holy, Congar explained, insofar as it is oriented to God, comes from God, belongs to God, and is totally referred to God.[219] Holiness is evident in worship, beauty, and acts of charity; the grandeur of Chartres Cathedral; the harmonious dulcidity of Gregorian chant; and the lives of men and women such as Seraphim of Sarov, Charles de Foucauld, and Mother Teresa, who have given themselves totally and unconditionally to God.[220] "It is the Holy Spirit," Congar wrote, "who causes this radiation of holiness."[221] Holiness is not an individual but an ecclesial reality. There is an intercommunication of spiritual energy that is the basis of the prayers for the departed, the baptism of infants, and the communion of saints.[222]

The Holy Spirit Is the Principle of the Church's Catholicity

The church's many expressions of holiness are one dimension of its catholicity. Catholicity is an embrace of the universal truth that is manifest in the uniqueness of every creature. The term "catholic," Congar noted, made its first known appearance in ancient Greek philosophical texts; in Aristotle's works, *kath'olou* meant "according to the whole, in general," while for Philo *katholokis* connoted the general in opposition to the particular.[223] When Christian theology adopted this term, its meaning was transposed, for the God of Jesus Christ is not "general" but unique. "It is because God is unique, because he is the unique sovereign reason behind all that is, that his Plan is universal. . . . If God makes something according to his image, he makes it at the same time one and universal."[224] Catholicity has its ultimate source in God who is simultaneously unique and universal and who creates a cosmos in which every creature is both unique and destined to universal communion. Creation's destiny to communion is fulfilled in Jesus Christ, who is the "concrete universal"; in the mystery of the hypostatic union, the concrete and particular human nature of Jesus of Nazareth is united fully to God and through God to all that is.[225] Paul, Congar noted, described Christ's mission as the reconciliation of all beings (*ta panta*) with God (Col 1:19–20); in and through the cosmic Christ of the *plērōma*, the Spirit of Christ unites what Congar called the sources of catholicity from below (human nature and the cosmos) with the source from above (God).[226] All creatures in their own uniqueness are incorporated into the universal body of

Christ, for the Spirit fosters "that mutual interiority of the whole in each which constitutes the catholic sense: *kath'holou*, being of a piece with the whole."[227] A truly catholic ecclesiology "requires a pneumatology."[228]

The catholicity of the church is evident in its universal geographic extension. The Spirit of Christ carried the church throughout the Mediterranean and then across the globe, and Congar spoke of this geographic breadth as quantitative catholicity.[229] As the church incorporated the unique peoples of East and West, Asia and Africa, and North and South America, it developed a diversity of rites, prayers, languages, and theologies that Congar described as qualitative catholicity. Quantitative and qualitative catholicity, he emphasized, are indissociable.[230] As Congar grew in appreciation for ecclesial diversity, his theology of catholicity became more rich and expansive; catholicity is not just the inclusion of persons in the church universal but the celebration of the unique contributions that diverse persons and cultures bring to the ecclesial body.[231] Congar lauded the emphasis of the Second Vatican Council on local and particular churches.[232] He regarded missionary work as an effort driven by the Spirit to bring all into the *plērōma* of Jesus Christ and noted that Christianity needed to learn to encounter, recognize, and welcome different religions and cultures in a new way.[233] Catholicity requires attentiveness to the presence of the Spirit beyond the borders of the institutional churches, openness to the signs of the times, receptivity to the new, and vigilance for the future.[234]

The Holy Spirit Keeps the Church Apostolic

Catholicity is a dimension of the church's apostolic fidelity. This apostolicity, Congar explained, is based above all in the faithfulness of God.[235] God's steadfast love for creation is manifest in the Incarnation of the Word, the ongoing presence of the glorified Christ, and the continuation of Christ's mission by the apostles and those who unfailingly take up the apostolic task in each successive generation. God's faithfulness requires in response our own fidelity, and this is enabled by the Spirit who "is given to the Church as its transcendent principle of faithfulness."[236] The indwelling Spirit generates an ecclesial apostolicity manifest in the service, witness, suffering, and struggle of all the faithful.[237] We profess, Congar emphasized, that the Holy Spirit makes the *church* apostolic.[238] "[A]postolicity does not consist in a pure external structure, that is in the identity of forms of doctrine and of institutions, but rather the interior principle of apostolicity in the unity of the church is the Holy Spirit."[239]

Only within this communion of the whole church can apostolic succession in the strict sense of the term—that is, the succession of the bishops—take place.[240] Jesus Christ commissioned Peter, James, Andrew, and the other apostles to govern the church, and this mission and its requisite charism of truth is passed from the apostles to the bishops. This succession, however, is not simply a vertical bestowal of charism from Christ to the episcopacy but a gift of fidelity that permeates the entire church through the power of the Spirit.[241] New bishops are thus consecrated by several bishops in the midst of the people who bear witness to the faith of the bishop elect.[242] Consecrated bishops exercise the apostolicity made manifest in them through general pastoral governance, the convocation of ecumenical councils, and the exercise of the magisterium.[243] The special teaching authority of the magisterium that has been designated "infallible" would be better described as "indefectible," for the Spirit's promise to us in our finitude and limitation is that error will not ultimately prevail (Mt 16:18).[244] Congar noted that the Spirit's inspiration of the episcopacy has been described in an automatic and juridical fashion in the Counter-Reformation period, but he stressed that "in principle, no automatic, juridical formalism" is involved, "since the 'hierarchical' function exists within the communion of the *ecclesia*."[245]

Apostolicity is often described as conformity to the church's first-century origins, but Congar emphasized that apostolicity has a forward-looking sense and thrust.[246] The apostolicity of the church is not simply an act of historical memory but also a dynamic affirmation of the ongoing presence and power of God. Apostolicity is conformity to Christ who is Alpha and eschatological Omega. The Spirit brings the mystical body to its fullness amidst the novelty of history and the variety of cultures through which will come the "Christ that is to be."[247] Precisely as the Spirit of Christ, Congar wrote, the Spirit is God-before-us.[248] For "what Christ has *given* has still to come to pass; in a manner not yet realized. History is the realization of what has not yet taken place."[249]

The Holy Spirit Kindles the Eschatological Mission of the Church

The eschatological activity of the Spirit extends beyond the visible community of the baptized, for the Spirit acts secretly in places where the institutional church does not reach.[250] Congar believed that the principle *extra ecclesiam, nulla salus* does not limit the activity of the Spirit to the institutional church but is rather an affirmation of the indispensable role of the church in the execution of God's plan. This is the fundamental meaning of the *extra ecclesiam, nulla salus* tradition, although Congar thought this required so much explanation that the formula was in practice not very useable.[251] The activity of the Spirit extends beyond the church—as Ambrosiaster wrote, "All truth, no matter where it comes from, is from the Holy Spirit."[252] Yet the manifestations of the Spirit beyond the walls of chapels and cathedrals are not foreign to the church's life. One mission of the church is to gather together all truths scattered and dispersed and to offer all to God in a hymn of cosmic praise, voicing the doxology of those persons who do not have explicit knowledge of God and the praise of all speechless creatures. We offer all, Congar wrote, in "that sheaf that has been bound together invisibly by the Holy Spirit."[253]

The church acts to realize God's plan of communion in both its historical and suprahistorical dimensions. Its mission is to struggle for justice, to participate in the transformation of the world, and to gather all people into one through Christ and the Spirit. The church, Congar reflected, in 1975, is "totally and entirely praise for God and totally and entirely mission, in the service of humanity."[254] God's plan will ultimately be fulfilled when all human persons created in the divine image live in harmony and peace and when all are regenerated through Christ in the Holy Spirit so as to behold together the glory of God.[255]

The Integration of Pneumatological Anthropology and Pneumatological Ecclesiology

For purposes of clarity, Congar's pneumatological anthropology and his pneumatological ecclesiology have been treated separately in the first two sections of this chapter; yet, in fact, these two dimensions of Congar's thought cannot be disjoined. A separation of Congar's anthropology and ecclesiology would misrepresent the genesis of Congar's thought and betray the character and content of his theology. According to Hervé Legrand, a Dominican confrère of Congar who is himself now a prominent French ecclesiologist, it would be wrong to imagine that Congar first developed an anthropology and then set forth an ecclesiology and then finally attempted to synthesize these components of his theology.[256] Rather, theological anthropology and ecclesiology coincided in Congar's thought and evolved concomitantly as his theology developed. Moreover, it should be evident from the exposition earlier in this chapter that Congar's *anthropologie pneumatologique* and *ecclésiologie pneumatologique* are not two discrete theological realms but two inseparable dimensions of the one gift of the Holy Spirit, two ways of approaching the one mystery of deification and communion. Many of the themes discussed under the rubric of Congar's anthropology arose again in the exposition of his ecclesiology: conversion, communion, incorporation in Christ, holiness, human/divine synergy, eschatology, and the praise and glorification of God.

A number of theological principles contribute to this integration of spiritual anthropology and ecclesiology in Congar's theology of the Holy Spirit. The first is the strong theocentric emphasis of his theology. Neither the human person nor the church—nor even the gift of the Holy Spirit—is an end in itself. The Spirit of Christ comes from God and calls us to return to God—to convert from sin and selfishness and to live in holiness, justice, charity, and communion. In our great need we call upon the Spirit in the prayer of epiclesis, and in response to the gift of God's love we return to God our praise and thanksgiving through the power of the Spirit who is the fire of this divine charity. The indwelling of the Spirit in the human person and the mission of the church are united in their common orientation toward the transcendent God; Christian spirituality and ecclesial life are both rooted in doxology.

A second principle that contributes to Congar's integration of pneumatological anthropology and ecclesiology is his theology of nature and grace. Congar joined de Lubac, Blondel, and Rahner in challenging the extrinsicism of neoscholastic theologies of grace. He affirmed that we have an inefficacious desire for the grace of God and that from the moment of our creation in the divine image God has destined us for divine communion. The grace of the Holy Spirit, moreover, does not eclipse our natural human constitution even as grace transcends the gift of our creation in the *imago Dei*. Grace offers a supranatural and eschatological principle of deification and new life, and yet the order of redemption is not incongruous with who we are as human creatures. Congar's affirmation of the continuity of creation and redemption, it should be noted, not only drew upon the work of de Lubac, Blondel, and Rahner but also contributed an important pneumatological and ecclesiological dimension to the discussion they initiated. Whereas de Lubac gave limited explicit attention to pneumatology, Congar emphasized that grace *is* the Holy Spirit of God.[257] And, whereas Rahner's primary emphasis was theological anthropology, Congar reminds us that Christian anthropology cannot be divorced from an ecclesiological framework and context.[258]

Congar's communitarian anthropology was another key to his synthesis of anthropology and ecclesiology. Congar emphasized that human persons manifest the *imago Dei* through knowledge and love—we are created to live in relation with God and other persons in a perpetual being-toward (*être-à*) one another. The deification of the human person by the indwelling of the Holy Spirit is a perfection of our relation with God and with others—a necessarily ecclesial mystery, celebrated in the *koinōnia* of the church that is the one body of Christ. The communitarian life of the church is thus not a negation of our humanity nor a threat to human authenticity but rather the place in which all the dimensions of our human personhood can at last be fully realized. In our fallen world, Congar remarked, human institutions typically abrogate either our communion with others or our personal uniqueness and freedom. But "Christianity brings together two things that are often in opposition to one another: 'inwardness' or personal life, and the communal principle or unity."[259]

Congar's emphasis on the active initiative of human subjects and human cooperation with grace is another important principle integrating his ecclesiology and anthropology. Congar stressed that our creation in the *imago Dei* means that we are free and active human subjects, called to cooperate with grace. The life of the church is entirely dependent on the action of the Spirit, but the Spirit does not destroy human freedom, volition, and natural gifts and talents. The human capabilities described in Congar's anthropology are thus not abrogated by Congar's ecclesiology but rather perfected and elevated by the Spirit in the service of God. We are created not as passive objects but as active human subjects, and it is as active subjects that we are redeemed. The church is not a uniformity but a uniplurality of unique persons who bring their gifts to the service of God. Indeed, Congar believed, our personal uniqueness and capacity for free action finds ultimate fulfillment only in the catholicity of the church where our unique gifts are enriched with those of others and all are offered up to God. "Christian existence of which the Holy Spirit is in us the principle, realizes in a radical fashion our quest to be fully [human]."[260]

Another key principle in Congar's integration of anthropology and ecclesiology was his pneumatological Christology. In the 1970s and 1980s, Congar emphasized that Jesus Christ is constituted to be Messiah for us through the action of the Spirit in the events of his life, death, and resurrection. It is through the Holy Spirit that the humanity hypostatically united to the eternal Word passes from the *forma servi* to the *forma Dei*, and it is in the Spirit that Jesus Christ serves as the foundation of the church and sustains it throughout the centuries. This Christology was fundamental to Congar's affirmation that the Spirit is the co-institutor and life principle of the church. "A pneumatological ecclesiology presupposes a pneumatological Christology."[261] A pneumatological anthropology requires the same presupposition, for, just as the Spirit transforms the humanity of Christ from the *forma servi* to the *forma Dei*, so, too, the Spirit deifies the human person.[262] The Spirit's transformative activity in the life of Jesus Christ is the foundation and context for the Spirit's deification of humanity within the mystery of the church.

Finally, Congar's emphasis on the Spirit's power of communion was critical to his synthesis of pneumatology, ecclesiology, and anthropology. The importance of this dimension of Congar's pneumatology is particularly pronounced when Congar's work is compared with the late-nineteenth- and early twentieth-century approaches to pneumatology discussed in the Introduction. Neoscholastic *De Ecclesia* treatises and popular authors such as Cardinal Henry Edward Manning discussed the activity of the Spirit in the church in terms of infallibility, perpetuity, and unity. Infallibility and perpetuity are strictly ecclesiological terms, whereas communion is simultaneously an anthropological and ecclesiological mystery. Communion is also, as Famerée highlights, a more pneumatological term than unity.[263] The rich biblical, liturgical, and theological connotations of the term *koinōnia* simultaneously span pneumatology, ecclesiology, and theological anthropology. The triune God of communion has created and redeemed us as persons in communion, a holy mystery that is fulfilled through the ecclesial body in the *koinōnia* of the Holy Spirit.

4

The Indivisibility of Pneumatological Anthropology and Pneumatological Ecclesiology

One way to approach Congar's integration of a pneumatological anthropology and a pneumatological ecclesiology is to consider the theological principles that unite these two dimensions of his theology,
as I have done in chapter 3. Another way to approach this question
is to examine some of the biblical images that are foundational to
Congar's thought. Congar believed that the church is a supernatural
mystery that cannot be defined but only described with a plurality of
complementary theological images. Three such images with strong
biblical roots that Congar employed extensively throughout the
course of his career are the mystical body of Christ, the people of
God, and the temple of the Holy Spirit.[1] Each of these biblical paradigms has an anthropological, an ecclesiological, and a pneumatological dimension and can therefore serve as a lens through which
to view the integration of these components of Congar's theology.
Discussion proceeds in the order of each paradigm's chronological
importance in Congar's theology. According to van Vliet, the theology of the mystical body was dominant in Congar's work between
1931 and 1944; the theology of the people of God, between 1959 and
1968; and the theology of the temple of the Holy Spirit, between
1969 and 1991.[2] Of course, all three themes permeate Congar's entire corpus of writings, and van Vliet did not intend his schematiza-
tion to be taken in an absolute sense. Nonetheless, it is useful to
proceed within a chronological framework, at least in a broad sense.
Congar first spoke explicitly of a pneumatological anthropology and
a pneumatological ecclesiology only in the 1970s and 1980s, and

this must be borne in mind when considering publications from earlier periods.

The Mystical Body of Christ

In the post-Reformation period, the ancient theological tradition of the mystical body of Christ was eclipsed in Roman Catholicism by the *societas perfecta* ecclesiology. When Clement Schrader attempted to reincorporate the theology of the mystical body into the ecclesiological deliberations of the First Vatican Council (1869–1870), his efforts found favor with some bishops but were ultimately rejected by the conciliar gathering. Msgr. Ramadié insisted that the mystical body tradition was a matter of spirituality rather than dogmatic theology, while others argued that it suggested a Protestant or Jansenist ecclesiology and was thus inappropriate to the current needs of the Catholic Church.[3] Between 1920 and 1925, however, interest in the theology of the mystical body burgeoned in Catholic circles. In this five-year period, there appeared as many articles on the mystical body of Christ as had been published in the twenty years preceding. Between 1930 and 1935, the number of publications quintupled.[4] During this time, Congar noted, one could always draw a large audience if the mystical body was the topic of discussion.[5] There was much enthusiasm for the theology of the mystical body among participants in Catholic Action, and the liturgical movement also fueled interest in this theological tradition.[6]

Among the most important publications of this theological renewal are the two monumental works of the Belgian Jesuit Emile Mersch: *Le Corps mystique du Christ: Études de théologie historique* (1933) and *La Théologie du corps mystique* (1944). Mersch, according to Hervé Legrand, was an important influence on Congar's own thinking on the mystical body tradition.[7] Congar also referenced the Swiss theologian Charles Journet's three-volume *L'Église du Verbe incarné* (1941, 1951, 1969).[8] Another theological landmark was Pius XII's *Mystici Corporis* (1943), the first publication of the church's teaching office devoted expressly to the topic of the mystical body.[9] One year later, Henri de Lubac's *Corpus mysticum: L'Eucharistie et l'Église au Moyen Age* stimulated further discussion on the theology of the mystical body.[10] New Testament scholars also contributed to the renewal of this tradition, although Congar noted that exegetes and theologians often seemed to talk past each other on this issue, and he regretted the lack of a more fruitful working relationship between biblical and theological specialists.[11]

Congar had his own contribution to make to the renewal of the theology of the mystical body. According to van Vliet, the mystical body of Christ was the predominant ecclesiological paradigm in the writings of the first period of Congar's career (1931–1944).[12] In 1937, indeed, Congar described the mystical body of Christ as the true definition of the church.[13] Congar's appropriation of this biblical and theological paradigm enhanced his responsiveness to the laity, contributed to his ecumenical efforts, and supported his position that the church is a *theo*logical and not simply a juridical reality.[14] The theology of the mystical body also fostered the integration of pneumatological anthropology and pneumatological ecclesiology in Congar's theology. As Congar reflected on the mystery of the *Corpus mysticum*, he moved seamlessly from discussion of each human person's filiation in Christ to reflection on the structure and sacraments of the church.

The Anthropology of the Mystical Body Theology

Congar's discussion of the mystical body tradition presumed an *imago Dei* anthropology and the theology of divine filiation. God not only created humankind in the divine image with the capacities for knowledge, love, and freedom but also destined humanity to communion in the divine life. We were created to become sons and daughters of God, a divine plan that is fulfilled through the Incarnation of the Word and the gift of the Spirit. In Christ and the Spirit, humanity is incorporated into the mystical body of the one who is *the* Image of God. This deification elevates humanity to a new level of participation in the life of God; yet it does not eclipse our human faculties or subsume our human personhood.

The incorporation of human persons into the mystical body of Christ is fundamentally different from the hypostatic union of the divine Word with the human nature of Jesus Christ. The hypostatic union was a union of being (*dans l'être, par esse, secundum esse*) of the Word of God and the one human nature assumed, whereas humanity is united to Christ in a mystical communion.[15] "Christian mysticism," Congar emphasized, "is a mysticism of communion, not a mysticism of union (in the sense of a fusion or a complete unity)."[16] The mystical body is not ontologically *the* body of Christ but precisely the *mystical* body of Christ.[17] In philosophical terms, we should speak of the mystical body not with the language of being but rather with the category of relation.[18] In theological terms, however, it is more precise to use the language of espousement or covenant.[19] This language emphasizes that the life of the mystical body is a life of communion among free persons. "[T]he Body of Christ," Congar wrote, with reference to Pascal, "is not a reality in the sense of a physical substance, but a body 'full of thinking members.' "[20] These thinking members are human subjects, each having conscience, freedom, and a self-subsistent existence (*existence pour soi* or *être à soi*).[21] Human members of the mystical body do not share Christ's *esse*, and "the life of the mystical Body is not simply a repetition of that of Christ; it is the content of the life of Christ received, no longer properly by him . . . but by free persons."[22]

This is not to suggest that the mystical body is simply an aggregate of human persons. St. Paul testified that Christians are truly one in Jesus Christ

(Gal 3:28),[23]Augustine described the church as the *totus Christi*, and Aquinas spoke of Christ and his members as *una mystica persona*.[24] In Christ, human persons both retain their own proper existence *and* become truly incorporated into one body in a very real sense. This incorporation and communion is the work of the Holy Spirit. "What brings it about," Congar wrote, "that there is a single body in Christ is that animating this body is a single spirit, the Spirit of Christ."[25] The Holy Spirit is *idem numero*—identically the same—in both Christ (the head) and in the members of the mystical body.[26] Human persons truly live in Christ, for they have received Christ's Spirit (Rom 8:14; Gal 4:6).[27] As Paul exhorted repeatedly, Christ is in us, and we are in Christ. Such expressions, Congar noted, occur in the Pauline literature not fewer than 144 times.[28] We rejoice in Christ (Phil 3:3), hope in Christ (1 Cor 15:19), speak the truth in Christ (Rom 9:1), and triumph in Christ (2 Cor 2:14). Indeed, the Christian does all of his or her daily work in Christ, for the Spirit of Christ is gradually communicated "to all that is material, to the whole range of human actions . . . professional, social, cultural."[29] This theology should be understood with absolute realism: "It is not simply a question of moral consecration of our life to Christ and of a greater or lesser fidelity to his inspiration, but our acts are to be considered as his own and they must be so in fact."[30]

In Christ, our human acts of knowledge and love participate in the knowledge and love of God. We know as God knows, we see as Christ sees, we gaze with the gaze of God, "which is also my gaze, since it is really engrafted and adapted in my own life."[31] In the Spirit of Christ, we will as God wills and love as God loves, for "the love of God is shed abroad in our hearts by His Spirit which He hath given us (Rom 5:5)."[32] God loves without limits, and so, therefore, must we. Congar believed that Jesus Christ's injunction to love even our enemies and our persecutors (Mt 5:43–48) must be taken absolutely literally.[33] Such love is not an innate capacity of any created being, and in this sense Christ *is* the profound personality of the mystical body. Our life in Christ is a life in the "pneumatological order, in which the faithful exist only in Christ, to realize Christ in his plentitude, through a participation in a life that is his own."[34]

Nonetheless, human members of the mystical body do retain their existence as proper subjects of existence and action. Congar's theological anthropology presumed, following Aquinas, that every act of God's love for the creature causes some good to exist within the creaturely being. The love with which God created the cosmos bestowed on each creature a nature proper to its created end—powers and principles of operation fitted to its particular purpose in the created order. The special love (*dilectio specialis*) whereby God then draws rational creatures to participation in a divine life that is beyond the condition of created nature likewise bestows powers and operative principles proper to this love.[35] Members of the mystical body not only participate in the love and knowledge of God, but in consequence of this love God infuses into the human

soul a habitual gift whereby rational creatures are enabled to receive and respond to God's eternal goodness.[36] Through the exercise of this gift of created
grace, members of Christ's mystical body "are not instruments but true subjects of action existing and acting according to the quasi-nature that is the grace
diffused in them in the Holy Spirit."[37] Within the mystical body of Christ, acts
of faith, hope, and charity are both works of God and properly human activities,
exercises of the theological virtues that proceed from the principle of grace
infused in our soul. "If we go on to inquire what part we are called to contribute
to the building up of the mystical Body," Congar commented, "we shall have
to speak, along with St. Paul, of faith and charity, and, from that, of the whole
moral life considered as a *vita in Christo*."[38]

The Ecclesiology of the Mystical Body Theology

The *vita in Christo* is the life of the church, a life of charity that is nourished,
maintained, and expressed in ecclesial communion.[39] "Union with Christ,"
Congar reflected, "which is the interior life of the individual soul, is lived and
acquired socially, in the Church."[40] The mystery of the mystical body is not
only an ineffable participation of human persons in the knowledge and love
of God but also the visible, concrete, and tangible life of the ecclesial communion. Congar considered the Protestant theology of the invisible church a
misconstrual of the mystical body tradition. In pre-Constantinian ecclesiology,
there is a "plainness and absence of distinctions with which the mystical Body
of Christ and the Church in its social being are identified as a single reality."[41]
Aquinas, too, affirmed this identification of the *Corpus mysticum* and the concrete *societas fidelium*.[42] The mystical body, Congar maintained, "is not some
spiritual entity unrelated to the world of human realities and activities but is
the visible Church itself."[43]

The inseparability of the mystical body from its visible and human dimensions is preeminently manifest in the church's sacramental life. Congar believed that sacramental activity and sacramental causality constitute the mystical body "at the deepest level of its being."[44] In an essay written in 1941, he
noted that the constitutional role of the sacraments in the church had been
ignored in the preceding forty years, and he credited Protestant theologians
such as Schweitzer and Goguel with bringing this point of incalculable importance to the fore.[45] It is through the sacraments—particularly the sacraments of baptism and Eucharist—that the church *is* the mystical body of
Christ.[46] The sacramental rites were established by Jesus Christ for the purpose
of our union with him, and they have a special efficacy to assimilate persons
into his body.[47] This efficacy operates in the unique mode of the symbolical/
real.[48] Sacramental acts are symbolic in the sense that they are not, strictly
speaking, new events; the Eucharist does not repeat Christ's sacrifice on the
cross. But sacraments are not simply nostalgic enactments of old memories,

for Christ *is* really present at the Eucharistic synaxis, and his power is truly operative in the waters of the baptismal font. Baptism is the sacrament of our incorporation into the mystical body, and the Eucharist is the sacrament of unity, a mystery that results in an increase of grace and a substantial unity of life with Jesus Christ.[49]

Through the sacraments of baptism and Eucharist, Congar believed, the unity that exists between Jesus Christ and his mystical body is real and profound. "The Church is, in the first place, the Body of Christ; it forms, with him, a single reality."[50] Congar did not mean to imply an absolute ontological identification of the church and Jesus Christ, for he maintained that Jesus Christ and the church are analogously related, not identical.[51] Whereas the human nature of Jesus Christ is hypostatically united to the divine Logos in being (*par esse, secundum esse*), the church is united to Jesus Christ only operationally (*per operationem, in operatione*).[52] Divinity and humanity are thus united in the church without confusion but not without division, and the christological communication of idioms does not apply to the church.[53]

Congar's caution concerning the ontological difference between Jesus Christ and the mystical body is one point where the intersection of his theological anthropology and ecclesiology is evident. The human persons who are members of the mystical body do not partake of the *esse* of Jesus Christ but retain their own proper *être à soi*, and accordingly the church is not, strictly speaking, divine. At the same time, however, Congar did believe that the church is a means of grace, and here one sees that his anthropology and ecclesiology diverge. The church, unlike the human person, plays a causal role in the communication of grace. Throughout the period in which the mystical body paradigm predominates in Congar's ecclesiology, he ascribed prophetic, sacramental, and governing powers to the hierarchical apostolic body, which he described in Aristotelian terms as the church's formal cause.[54] For Congar, Famerée comments, "the church thus has a *proper causality* of salvation and takes rank of cause *with* God or cooperates *directly* for the constitution of the Kingdom through her own *powers*."[55] This exercise of power stands in pronounced disjunction from the indwelling of the Spirit in the human person, disjoined from any consideration of pneumatological anthropology, for members of Christ's body can never cause grace. When the ministers of the church act in their sacramental capacities, they "do not operate as persons, i.e. as beings with an existence *pour soi* acting on their own responsibility (with an immanent principle of operation) but as causes of something outside of themselves."[56] Ordained ministers are purely the vehicle of the sacramental, governing, and prophetic powers bestowed upon the apostolic body by Christ. The ordained exercise these powers not through a created habitus that is their own proper principle of operation but rather as instruments of Christ's divine power.[57] On this point, there is a significant incongruity between the anthropology and the ecclesiology of the mystical body theology.

The Pneumatology of the Mystical Body Theology

With strong patristic and medieval precedent, Congar described the Holy Spirit as the soul of the mystical body of Christ.[58] The soul is the actualizing and unifying principle of any living being, and in the mystical body this role belongs (by appropriation) to the Holy Spirit.[59] This must be understood in a qualified sense, for the Holy Spirit is not the soul of the mystical body in precisely the same sense in which the human soul is the unifying principle of the human body; if this were the case, the church would be ontologically divine. The Spirit is the uncreated soul of the church but only as a soul indwelling—not composing—the mystical body. According to Congar's writings of this period, the indwelling and composing formal cause of the church is not the Holy Spirit but the hierarchical apostolic body.[60] Ultimately, it is the Holy Spirit (by appropriation) who unifies the mystical body, but penultimately this unity is wrought by the formal efficacy of the apostolic body, which serves as a unique instrument of Christ's governing, sacramental, and prophetic power, a divinely instituted means of grace.

Famerée is critical of this aspect of Congar's preconciliar mystical body theology, for it has the unfortunate consequence of undulying autonomizing (autonomiser) the church and "tends necessarily to hide the pure and permanent dependence of the Church with respect to the Spirit of the resurrected Christ."[61] The apostolic means of grace appear less as instruments of the Spirit than a sensible and collective means of salvation with their own proper efficacy, and they thus become a second autonomous cause of grace.[62] Famerée believes that Congar's discussion of the Spirit as the uncreated soul of the mystical body does not resolve this problem of autonomization but rather creates further theological difficulties. Whereas Congar's construal of the apostolic powers unduly autonomized the church, his description of the Spirit as the church's uncreated soul generates the opposite problem and binds the Spirit to the church in quasi-hylomorphic fashion.[63] The Spirit as uncreated and transcendent soul of the mystical body is substantially attached to the church in a manner that engenders an ecclesial monophysitism that eclipses the human and sociological dimension of ecclesial life. Furthermore, this theology reduces the freedom of the Spirit, who seems assigned to reside in a church that monopolizes the Spirit's presence.[64]

According to Famerée, the fundamental source of these pneumatological tensions in Congar's mystical body theology is the underlying christocentrisme and incarnationnisme of this approach.[65] If the church is truly Christ's body, it must have a certain salvific causality and cooperate directly in the constitution of God's Kingdom, just as the humanity of Christ was a free instrument of Christ's divinity.[66] Yet Congar explicitly denied an absolute parallel between Jesus Christ's humanity and the mystical body.[67] Furthermore, he always qualified his discussion of the Spirit as the mystical body's uncreated soul precisely to avoid the suggestion that the church is substantially divine. He explicitly critiqued ecclesial monophysitism and repeatedly stated that a truly incarnational ecclesiology must emphasize the human and social character of the church.[68] The autonomization of the church that Famerée perspicaciously identifies in Congar's mystical body theology comes not from *incarnationnisme* per se but rather from the incomplete convergence of the anthropological and ecclesiological dimensions of Congar's approach at this time. Congar portrayed the hierarchical apostolic body as a formal cause of the mystical body that exists above and apart from the human persons who are its members, exercising spiritual power over them. The apostolic body is identical neither with Jesus Christ nor with the Holy Spirit, for the church itself is not divine. Nor, however, is the apostolic hierarchy identifiable with the human members of the mystical body, for, unlike human persons, the hierarchy is a cause and means of grace. The church thus appears as an autonomous entity—it is not Jesus Christ, nor the Holy Spirit, nor, strictly speaking, the human persons who compose it. Ecclesiology then becomes a domain removed from both pneumatology and spiritual anthropology.

Congar's appropriation of the mystical body tradition did contribute in many respects to his construction of a pneumatological anthropology and pneumatological ecclesiology; the Holy Spirit incorporates human persons into Christ's mystical body in and through the communion of the church. Yet, in this theology, as formulated between 1931 and 1949, anthropology and ecclesiology are not fully integrated. In Famerée's terms, Congar has "autonomized" the church, portraying the ecclesial hierarchy as a cause of grace that exercises spiritual powers over the human persons who are members of Christ's body. This critique, however, should not eclipse the importance of Congar's contribution to a recovery of the mystical body tradition, nor should one conclude that an autonomization of the church is an inevitable component of a mystical body theology. In Congar's later works, as we shall see in chapter 5, he himself critiqued the autonomization of the ecclesial hierarchy characteristic of his earlier ecclesiology. Even as he disclaimed this dimension of his earlier work, he never abandoned the mystical body tradition that continued to ground his sacramental ecclesiology and his vital sense of Christian spirituality.

The People of God

On the heels of the renewal of the mystical body tradition came the rediscovery of the theology of the people of God, a biblical idea that spread in popularity in the Roman Catholic Church between 1937 and 1942.[69] Participants in Catholic Action and the liturgical movement were living witnesses that the church *is* the people who work for the rights of laborers, live together as Christian families, and worship with one another. Scholars reflected on the theology of the people of God, building on biblical research that had begun decades earlier.[70] For some, this theology was a refreshing change from ecclesiastical juridicism, while for others it was a viable alternative to the ecclesiology of the mystical body. In 1940, M. D. Koster critiqued the mystical body tradition as prescientific mysticism and offered as an alternative a theology of the people of God, which he believed would provide ecclesiology with a firm foundation and a true definition of the church.[71] In 1942, Lucien Cerfaux published a philological and exegetical study of Pauline theology that reinforced Koster's argument.[72] For Paul, Cerfaux explained, the fundamental and defining concept of the church is not the mystical body of Christ but rather the people of God; the language of the mystical body is only an explicative attribute of the more foundational people of God paradigm. The work of Koster and Cerfaux received both appreciation and critique.[73] Congar himself believed that the people of God paradigm was not the foundation of Pauline or patristic ecclesiology, although Augustine and others did occasionally define the church in these terms.[74]

Reflection on the church as the people of God continued in the 1950s and 1960s. Congar considered the work of German scholars such as M. Schmaus and I. Backes particularly important in the ecclesiological development of this paradigm.[75] The revitalization of this tradition culminated in the decision of the Coordinating Commission of the Second Vatican Council to add a chapter entitled *De Populo Dei in genere* to what would become *Lumen gentium*.[76] Council commentators repeatedly note the importance of this addition to the Pastoral Constitution on the Church and emphasize the significance of the placement of the chapter on the "People of God" between *Lumen gentium*'s first chapter on the mystery of the church and the third chapter on the ecclesial hierarchy.[77] One of the original reasons given for this arrangement of chapters was simply the methodological concern that the generic (the people of God) should precede the specific (the hierarchy).[78] Quickly, however, it was recognized that there was greater significance to the new order of the document—an implicit recognition, as Congar put it, of the "primacy of the ontology of grace" above organizational structures.[79] The structure of *Lumen gentium* as it now stands demonstrates the priority and primacy of Christian existence (*l'être chrétien*) above ecclesial organization.[80] This placement affirms that the church is foundationally composed of all the baptized prior to any distinction between members of the hierarchy and laity. Congar believed that the Council's addition of the chapter on the people of God to *Lumen gentium* was one of the most important decisions made at Vatican II, a decision that "has the greatest promise for the theological, pastoral and ecumenical future of ecclesiology."[81]

Indeed, subsequent to the Council, the people of God ecclesiology was enthusiastically received both in the Roman Catholic Church and in ecumenical discussion. Congar noted that this ecclesiology was particularly conducive to discussion with Protestants because it connotes election and call, implies an historical and eschatological framework, and offers an alternative to what Protestants perceived as the institutionalism, substantialism, and romanticism of other forms of Catholic ecclesiology.[82] An ongoing stream of publications on the theology of the people of God indicates that this continues to be an important ecclesiological paradigm in the postconciliar period. In Congar's own theology, according to the analysis of van Vliet, the people of God became a dominant theme between 1959 and 1968. Van Vliet observes that Congar appeared to scarcely notice the importance of the work of Koster, Cerfaux, and Vonier in his original reviews of their publications, but by 1959 the people of God had become an important theme in his own theology.[83] "The expression People of God," Congar wrote in 1964, "in itself has such depth of meaning and such dynamism that it is impossible to use it in reference to the reality that is the Church, without orienting our thoughts in certain perspectives."[84] This orientation of thought is simultaneously anthropological, ecclesiological, and pneumatological.

The Anthropology of the People of God Theology

In an essay written in 1964, Congar observed that one of the merits of the people of God paradigm is its anthropological value.[85] He lamented that ecclesiological writings and ecclesiastical publications often contrasted or opposed "the Church" to the people who composed it, as if the church were a self-standing entity that could exist apart from its members. He was confident that a people of God theology would challenge this opposition and renew the anthropological dimension of ecclesiology.[86] The very language of the *people* of God implies that the church is composed of the faithful men, women, and children who have dedicated their lives to God.

The people of God paradigm contributes a markedly corporate theological anthropology to ecclesiological discussion. This ecclesiological tradition is grounded in the Hebrew Scriptures and the life of the people of Israel, who had a strong sense of their communal identity. The British theologian H. Wheeler Robinson maintained that an anthropology of corporate personality is necessary to a proper interpretation of the Hebrew Scriptures, for the Hebrew people understood their common existence with a corporate realism that easily escapes modern persons who read the Scriptures with contemporary presumptions about individual existence.[87] In the biblical period, the *people* Israel was conceived as a real entity. Hebrew law presumed a communal responsibility for transgression, Hebrew families extended into the past and into the future so as to include in a very real sense both ancestors and the unborn, and Hebrew prophets moved with fluid reference from the one to the many and the many to the one as they communicated the messages entrusted to them. In the psalms, the "I" of the psalmist easily passed into the "I" of the community, and in the Servant songs of Deutero-Isaiah (Is 42:1–4; 49:1–6; 50: 4–9; 52:13–53:12), the Servant is Israel.[88] "The view we have presented," Robinson explained, "is neither allegory nor personification, but a primitive category of thought which is very different from our own antithesis of the collective and the individual."[89]

Robinson's interpretations of Hebrew anthropology have received both commendation and critique.[90] Congar himself believed that Robinson's work contributed to an appreciation of the mutual interdependence that characterizes the life of the people of God.[91] Among the Hebrew and Christian peoples, there is indeed a "sort of interpenetration of the personal and the collective."[92] In Daniel 7, Congar noted for example, the messianic Son of Man is inseparable from the people who will receive the kingdom:

> [H]ere we already have, in a highly significant way, one of the features which will be dominant, even decisive, in the Christian idea of the Kingdom and of the Church—the real identity of an individual and a collectivity, all being in a single one, all belonging to a single one, and yet all being realized in a collectivity, all belonging to a people. . . . The religious consciousness of Israel and the call of each person are bound up with the destiny of the group.[93]

Each member of the people of Israel and of the church is what the Scripture scholar Wilhelm Vischer described as a *pars pro toto*, or what Oscar Cullman referred to as "one for many"—one who is not simply a discrete or detachable part of a whole but one who carries in himself or herself the destiny of a whole people.[94] The people of God paradigm emphasizes the corporate character of human existence and our inseparability from one another.

The Ecclesiology of the People of God Theology

Congar's people of God ecclesiology reflected the corporate realism of Hebrew anthropology. Drawing on Vischer's discussion of the *pars pro toto* and on Cullman's theology of one for many, Congar maintained that the life of the church is advanced by a divine summons given to one person on behalf of an entire people.[95] The people of God was formed originally through the call of Abraham (Gn 12:1–2) and then through the person of Jesus Christ (Rom 8:29–30).[96] Abraham and Jesus Christ, through their fidelity, carried forward God's plan for the salvation of the whole people of Israel and for the entire human race. Each person, indeed, who responds to his or her vocation furthers God's plan and advances the destiny of all. Narratives of the lives of the faithful consequently are not simply inspiring spiritual stories but are properly ecclesiological testimonies. The church fathers, Congar noted, "so often described their vision of the Church in terms of typical biblical personages (Abraham, Rahab, Mary Magdalene, etc.), or of some Gospel parable. The Church indeed

is composed of men who open themselves to God's call."⁹⁷ Every member of
the church contributes to its common destiny. In like vein, the ecclesial body
as a whole is the *pars pro toto* of all humankind. Strictly speaking, Congar
believed, the people of God includes only Jews and baptized Christians—on
this point, he differed from Karl Rahner, who interpreted this tradition in a
more inclusive fashion.⁹⁸ Nonetheless, Congar affirmed, the church realizes
proleptically the communion with God that is the destiny of the entire human
race. The people of God paradigm is appropriately suggestive of the inextricable
connection between the church and the entire human family.⁹⁹

A people of God ecclesiology emphasizes not only the church's communitarian destiny but also the church's corporate identity and action. The church,
Congar noted, with reference to early Christian professions of faith, is the "we"
of Christians; we who preach the Gospel, we who heal the sick, we who teach
the unlettered, we who advocate for justice, we who reconcile the divided, and
we who gather for worship.¹⁰⁰ Indeed, the corporate identity of the church
implies that the entire liturgical assembly is a celebrant of the church's sacraments and even a consecrator of the Eucharistic gifts.¹⁰¹ This ecclesial "we"
does not jeopardize the uniqueness of every person and every local church. To
the contrary, an ecclesiology of the people of God enhances appreciation for
the particularity of each person and each local ecclesial gathering. In patristic
and liturgical texts, *populus* often denotes the local Eucharistic assembly, an
assembly to which each person brings his or her unique personal history.¹⁰²
The people of God are the athletes and the crippled, the poets and the parents,
the field laborers and the teachers and the assembly line workers—the people
who are "to be found in the midst of every population unit—my village, my
city, my apartment building, the train on which I am traveling, the hospital in
which I am sick."¹⁰³ A people of God ecclesiology contributes to a greater appreciation of catholicity precisely because it reaffirms the anthropological dimension of ecclesiology.¹⁰⁴ The church "is itself composed of diverse historical
peoples, each of which brings its own resources: *Volkerkirche.*"¹⁰⁵ This corporate
"we" of the *Volkerkirche* does not exist independent of institutional form. The
people of God is not a loose association but rather a structured people with its
assemblies, its hierarchy, its rites and customs, for "God is a God not of dis-
order but of peace" (1 Cor 14:33).¹⁰⁶

The people of God paradigm contributes to ecclesiology not only a strong
sense of collective identity but also an emphasis on the historical and eschatological mission of the church.¹⁰⁷ Congar observed that references to the *Populus Dei* in liturgical prayers typically recount the history of the people of God
from creation, the call of Abraham, the crossing of the Red Sea, and on through
history.¹⁰⁸ The term "people of God" connotes historical human relativities and
events at the same time as it suggests a movement and progression toward the
eschatological end of the Kingdom of God (Rom 8:19–25; 1 Cor 15:24–28).
This unites the human and historical with the eschatological so as to impel the

church to eschatological hope within the density of temporal life; it calls us to service and to mission.[109] The "idea of the People of God," Congar commented, "lends itself to an extremely realistic catechesis and it communicates an understanding of the Church that is both concrete and dynamic."[110]

Finally, a people of God ecclesiology contributes to our awareness of the church's sinfulness and failings. Insofar as the church is a divinely established institution, it is pure and sinless, but, insofar as the church is composed of people, it is marred by pride, egoism, and human weakness. Years before the people of God became a dominant theme in Congar's ecclesiology, he had already raised Catholic consciousness about the sinfulness of the church precisely by emphasizing that the church is composed of fallible human persons; the church is both the *ecclesia de Trinitate* and the *ecclesia ex hominibus*.[111] The former is indefectible and holy; the latter, marred by sin. The anthropological connotations of the people of God theology enabled Congar to reiterate this point. Indeed, he noted, the very terminology of the people of God resonates with the penitential prayers in which the community implores God's mercy for God's people (*Populus tuus*).[112] "As Dom Anscar Vonier saw so well, this [the people of God] is the *locus* in the Church where there are failures and sins, the struggle for a more perfect fidelity, the permanent need for reform and for the effort this involves."[113] To a greater degree than the ecclesiology of the mystical body of Christ, an ecclesiology of the people of God expresses the need for conversion and the importance of entreaty for help and mercy. The church is an "assembly of sinners."[114]

The Pneumatology of the People of God Theology

The theology of the people of God clearly contributed to the coincidence of anthropology and ecclesiology in Congar's thought. This biblical paradigm includes a corporate anthropology that readily becomes an ecclesiology, and an ecclesiology that emphasizes the church's anthropological dimension. But does the theology of the people of God include a *pneumatological* anthropology and a *pneumatological* ecclesiology? Congar believed that the Holy Spirit was responsible for the very development of a contemporary theology of the people of God, a beautiful notion with which "the Holy Spirit must secretly have inspired everyone . . . sometime between 1937 and 1943."[115] Yet, in the essays in which Congar discussed the church as the people of God, there is surprisingly scant reference to pneumatology. Congar's essay "The Church: The People of God," for example, does not mention the Holy Spirit at all in its first twenty pages. When he finally does speak of the Spirit in the final pages of this article, it is with reference not to the theology of the people of God itself but rather to the ecclesiology of the mystical body of Christ.[116] The essay "The People of God" mentions the Spirit five times, but in each instance the reference is not directly to Congar's own people of God theology but rather to a citation from the documents of the Second Vatican Council or a reference to Dom Anscar Vonier's *The Spirit and the Bride*.[117]

The relative infrequency with which Congar referenced the Holy Spirit in his essays on the people of God does not necessarily mean that there is no operative pneumatology underlying these reflections. The Spirit is the Spirit of God, and the people of God are thus the people of the Spirit of God, whether or not this is explicitly stated. Congar, in fact, underscored the theological (and hence pneumatological) character of the people of God paradigm, cautioning that the term "people" must be interpreted in a theological, rather than a general or ordinary, sense.[118] The church is the people of *God*.[119] Furthermore, Congar's theology of the people of God highlighted dimensions of ecclesial life that clearly have a pneumatological foundation: the corporate destiny and communion of the ecclesial body, the catholicity of the church, the church's eschatological mission, and the importance of ecclesial penitence and conversion; it is the Holy Spirit, Congar later wrote in *I Believe in the Holy Spirit*, who is the principle of the church's communion and catholicity, the bearer of the church's eschatological mission, and the kindler of conversion.[120] "People of God connotes Plan of God and therefore sacred history," and this sacred history is shaped by the two divine missions of the Word and the Spirit.[121]

There is, however, an obstacle to any argument for the existence of an implicit pneumatology in Congar's theology of the people of God. Congar believed that the people of God paradigm linked the church particularly to the phase of the economy recorded in the Hebrew Scriptures, and, as was described in chapter 2, Congar maintained that in this period the Spirit was present only in a limited manner. The Spirit intervened as necessary to ensure the realization of God's plan, but only as a transitory collective presence, rather than a permanent personal indwelling.[122] Further development of the pneumatological dimension of the people of God paradigm would require some reformulation of this position. Congar's position that there is only a collective rather than a personal presence of the Spirit among the Hebrew people was critiqued by his own fellow Dominicans, and it is not consistent with the anthropology of corporate personality that Congar himself appropriated from Robinson. If there is indeed no antithesis between the individual and the collective within a Hebrew worldview—as Robinson affirmed and Congar concurred—the collective presence of the Spirit among the Hebrew people must be also a personal presence.[123] In conjunction with an account of a corporate Hebraic anthropology, one should thus be able to construct a Hebrew spiritual anthropology of indwelling that would in turn enhance the pneumatological dimension of a people of God theology.

A reformulation of Congar's account of the activity of the Spirit among the people of Israel could build upon Congar's observation that the plan of God in the Old Testament period emphasized election and call, covenant, consecration to God, and the promise of eschatological fulfillment. Congar mentions all of these dimensions of Hebrew life in his essays on the church as the people of God, but he does not place these ideas in an explicitly pneumatological framework.[124] Clearly, however, the mysteries of election, covenant, consecration, and eschatological promise must ultimately have a pneumatological foundation. Congar did note, in his essays on the people of God, that election and call presuppose God's grace, and in *I Believe in the Holy Spirit* he stated that uncreated grace *is* the Holy Spirit.[125] Consecration to God requires a life of service, praise, and worship—all of which are gifts of the Spirit.[126] The eschatological character of the life of the people of God must likewise have a pneumatological ground, for the Spirit is the promised one and the bearer of the eschaton.[127]

The pneumatological dimension of a people of God theology could also be strengthened by emphasizing the pneumatological character of God's covenant with Israel and its continuity with the covenant enacted through Jesus Christ. If both covenants are an act of grace, both are in some sense a bond between God and God's people through the Holy Spirit.[128] Congar believed that an ecclesiology of the people of God has the merit of highlighting the kinship between Christians and the people of Israel,[129] and he advocated the inclusion of Vatican II's declaration on the Jews within *Lumen gentium*'s chapter on the people of God in order to accentuate this relationship.[130] Yet Congar's denial of a personal indwelling of the Spirit among the Hebrew people implies a decisive discontinuity between Israel and the church. Indeed, Congar believed that, insofar as the church is truly the church of Jesus Christ, it cannot be adequately described with the theology of the people of God (inherited from Israel), for this theology "cannot express a properly *Christian* ecclesiology."[131] Insofar as the church is the church of Jesus Christ, it transcends the designation "people of God" and receives a new title: the mystical body of Christ.[132] Congar's pronounced contrast between the people of God and the mystical body of Christ weakens his affirmation of the kinship between Israel and the church. Congar believed that Koster—whose work had been such a stimulus to the development of a contemporary theology of the people of God—had erred in opposing the people of God theology to the ecclesiology of the mystical body, which Koster disdained; yet, in a different manner, Congar himself has opposed these two paradigms.[133] Had he given more emphasis to the pneumatological dimension of the theology of the people of God, he could have expressed more emphatically the continuity and complementarity of the people of God and the mystical body theologies. Indeed, Congar believed that it is the Holy Spirit who is the bond between the ancient promise made to Abraham and its fulfilment in Jesus Christ, for the Spirit is called the "Promise."[134] The paradigm of the people of God that has become so important in the post–Vatican II era would have been enhanced if Congar had developed more fully and explicitly a pneumatology corresponding to the rich anthropological and ecclesiological dimensions of this theology.

The Temple of the Holy Spirit

The mystical body of Christ was not the only ecclesiological model that Congar thought could transcend the people of God paradigm and express the newness and fullness of the Christian dispensation; the theology of the temple of the Holy Spirit could serve the same purpose. The biblical theme of the temple of the Holy Spirit has not been the subject of intense theological and exegetical attention in contemporary Roman Catholic theology to the same degree as the theology of the mystical body or that of the people of God.[135] But this Pauline theme (1 Cor 3:16–17; 1 Cor 6:19; 2 Cor 6:16; Rom 8:9; Eph 2:19–22) did play an increasingly important role in Congar's own work. As Congar was writing *Lay People in the Church* (French edition, 1953), he reflected, "[I] continually came upon the idea that the essential point of God's plan and the place of the faithful within it could be well formulated in terms of a temple built of living stones."[136] While in exile in Jerusalem in 1954, Congar devoted himself to writing *The Mystery of the Temple*, a biblical and theological survey of the significance of the temple throughout the economy of salvation. Between 1969 and 1991, as he focused increasingly on pneumatology, the temple of the Holy Spirit continued to be a prominent theme in his theology.[137] This theme recurs throughout the second volume of *I Believe in the Holy Spirit* (1979–1980),[138] and the "Temple of the Holy Spirit" is the subtitle of the first major subdivision of the chapter entitled "A Pneumatological Ecclesiology" in Congar's article "Pneumatologie dogmatique" (1982).[139] In the 1969–1991 period that van Vliet characterizes as the fourth and final phase of Congar's scholarly life, Congar spoke explicitly of an *anthropologie pneumatologique* and an *ecclésiologie pneumatologique* for the first time, and the Pauline paradigm of the temple of the Holy Spirit contributed to Congar's ability to develop these dimensions of his theology in a synthetic way. In Paul's letters, Congar observed, "we find simultaneously a twofold application of the idea of the temple, to the body of the individual Christian and to the Church considered as a whole."[140] This multivalent resonance is found in Congar's own use of the temple of the Holy Spirit tradition.

The Anthropology of the Temple of the Holy Spirit Theology

"Do you not understand," exhorted Paul, "that you are God's temple [*naos*], and that God's Spirit has his dwelling in you?" (1 Cor 3:16). God no longer dwells only in the Ark of the covenant or in the Temple in the Holy City of Jerusalem, but God has taken flesh in Jesus Christ and dwells henceforth in all those who are members of Christ's body. The human *person* has become the sanctuary of the Lord. Paul's talk of God's dwelling (from the Greek verb *oikein*) connotes a stable presence and the idea of habitation and ownership.[141] This divine inhabitation is the basis of human sanctification and holiness.

The Spirit, Congar explained, abides in our soul or heart, which forms a substantial unity with our bodies.[142] The anthropology implicit in the temple of the Holy Spirit theology gives striking importance to human corporeality. Although Congar cautioned that Paul's language of the indwelling of the Spirit should not be understood in a spatial sense, the communion with God that Paul's language connotes is a communion that includes our human corporeality.[143] "The place of this indwelling [of the Spirit]," Congar wrote, "with all the consequences it involves, is *our body*."[144] Paul's theology does not denigrate the body in the manner of Greek philosophy or spiritualize the soul in the manner of the Jewish philosopher Philo.[145] Rather, Paul operated from the Hebrew presumption that the body is the whole living person, the outward manifestation of personal activity.[146] Paul was also influenced by the event of Easter, from which he drew the firm conviction that our bodies—together with that of Jesus Christ—will rise again: "And if the Spirit of him who raised up Jesus from the dead dwells in you, he who raised up Jesus Christ from the dead will give life to your perishable bodies too, for the sake of his Spirit who dwells in you" (Rom 8:11).[147] Congar urged his readers to "take very seriously those statements which claim that our bodies can be transfigured and are able, in their own way, to reflect God's glory and the peace and joy of the Holy Spirit."[148] He recounted the ancient story of Leonidas, who came one evening to bid goodnight to his young son Origen and tenderly kissed his chest, convinced that his small body was truly a temple of the Holy Spirit.[149] Congar also highlighted the accounts of bodily transfiguration found in the mystical tradition—the testimonies of people like St. Gertrude, St. Teresa of Avila, or Seraphim of Sarov, whose face became radiant as he spoke about the Holy Spirit with his friend Motovilov in a field on a wintry Russian day.[150]

Because the Holy Spirit truly indwells our persons, we must lead lives of purity and holiness. "God," Paul exhorts, "has not called us for uncleanness, but in holiness . . . God, who gives his Holy Spirit to you" (1 Thes 4:7–8).[151] The same purity required of those who entered the Temple gates is now required of us in every moment of our daily lives, and Congar emphasized the importance of constant prayer, a prayer that is simultaneously our own entreaty and the work of the Spirit who cries "Abba!" in our hearts (Gal 4:6; Rom 8: 15).[152] Congar also exhorted his readers to offer themselves in union with Jesus Christ as a spiritual sacrifice to God each day—indeed, every instant of their lives.[153] In the mystery that the very Spirit of God has tabernacled in our soul and body, Congar found the foundation for a rich spirituality, an exigent Christian ethics, and the ontological dignity of the Christian.[154]

The Ecclesiology of the Temple of the Holy Spirit Theology

The indwelling of the Holy Spirit in the human person is inseparable from the activity of the Spirit in the church. As the church Fathers had written, " 'Each soul is the Church.' "[155] Congar cautioned that this patristic maxim does not mean that the indwelling of the Spirit in the human soul is causally prior to the action of the Spirit in the church.[156] Nor, however, is the activity of the Spirit in the church causally prior to the Spirit's indwelling of the human person. "We might be tempted to conclude," Congar acknowledged, "that . . . the question of the Church comes first and, like a principle in relation to its consequences, is the determining factor in the idea of the individual believer as the temple of the Holy Spirit."[157] In fact, however, as St. Paul affirmed, "there is no opposition, no systematic and exclusive priority as between the Church and the individual believer. Each needs the other and in them both the Holy Spirit is the principle of life."[158]

The Holy Spirit is the principle of the church's life, and the church is the Spirit's temple. Like the Temple of Solomon, the church is a temple in the very concrete sense of a building consecrated to God. Congar did not discount this simple meaning of the theological tradition of the temple of the Holy Spirit. He believed that the church building itself has a sacramental character; it fosters the union of Christians in one body and is a sign of God's love even when its pews are unpeopled.[159] Congar reveled in the beauty of church architecture and artistry, confident that the glory of Chartres and of Le Thoronet was surely the work of the Spirit of God.[160]

The foundation stone of the church, however, is ultimately not a hewn piece of marble but Jesus the Christ (Eph 2:20).[161] Upon this foundation, the church is built with the living stones who are the church's members (1 Pt 2: 5).[162] Just as each stone laid upon a temple wall contributes to its construction and its beauty, so every member of the church contributes his or her own unique gifts and charisms to the temple of the Spirit. Congar believed that the importance of charisms as ecclesial realities had been undervalued, and he reintroduced a theology of charisms into Catholic ecclesiology. Charisms are "talents of which the Holy Spirit makes us *pros to sumpheron,* 'for the common good,' so that the community of the Church will be built up."[163] Charisms of preaching, teaching, healing, advocacy for justice, reconciling, and so forth contribute to the very construction of the church—they are not peripheral or threatening to the ecclesial institution. Congar wrote:

> Theologically, if the false opposition is accepted and a sharp division is made between charism and institution, the unity of the Church as the Body of Christ is destroyed. . . . The essential element of pneumatology would also be eliminated from ecclesiology, and it is pre-

cisely this element that I am attempting at least to suggest in this work.[164]

Full appreciation of the charisms requires a proper understanding of the inseparability of Jesus Christ and the Holy Spirit. The entire life of Jesus Christ was guided by the Spirit, and hence the institutions established by Christ necessarily have a charismatic dimension. Ordination to an ecclesial office, for example, is accompanied by the gift of the charisms required to carry out this instituted ministry.[165] At the same time, the Spirit who inspires new forms of ministry is the Spirit of the glorified Christ, and hence new charisms are not opposed to the ancient dominical institutions.[166] In 1984, the French church was in a state of crisis as the number of priests dropped precipitously and the diocesan organization failed to provide a vital structural framework for ecclesial life. Yet, Congar reflected,

> although we are living in what might be described as a comfortable desert, a Church is being constantly refashioned as the Gospel makes fresh springs rise again in the lives of men and women. . . . The Gospel and the Spirit are constantly rising again in hundreds, even thousands of springs from an underground source of water below the contemporary desert of France. These springs are giving new life, stimulating fresh initiatives and reshaping the attitudes of many members of the People of God and the Church. They are an expression of the charisms or the talents which the Spirit is giving to so many people for the building up of the Body of Christ and which can be seen as the "principle of order" of a Church that is being reborn from its foundations.[167]

Through the ongoing gift of charisms, the temple of the Holy Spirit is a cathedral ever under construction.[168]

The temple of the Holy Spirit ecclesiology is not only charismatic and dynamic but also cosmic. The people of Israel, as well as adherents of other ancient religions, conceived their temples as places where heaven and earth were mysteriously united; the temple was the sacred center of the universe, the place from which the waters of life poured forth.[169] Congar believed that the Christian church must also have a cosmic character, for the redemption wrought by Jesus Christ is cosmic in scope.[170] Jesus Christ is the temple of the new creation, the foundation stone from which the springs of life-giving water flow to those who are thirsty (Jn 7:37–8; cf. 4:14).[171] The life, death, and resurrection of Christ is the source of the restoration of the fallen created order, and the human persons who are living stones of the temple are a microcosm of the restored cosmos, for they are made of both spirit and matter, and the holiness of the saints is proleptic of the redemption of the entire universe.[172]

Indeed, the church building itself is a sign of the incipient transformation of the fallen cosmic order, for it is constituted of both material elements and the labor of human persons in response to the grace of God.[173]

Finally, the paradigm of the temple of the Holy Spirit implies an ecclesiology of effusive praise and worship. Just as the human person becomes a temple of the Spirit through constant prayer, so, too, the church is a temple whose walls echo with the sound of voices united in praise of God. The Spirit animates the celebration of the Christian mysteries and the church's liturgical worship, a ceaseless chorus that follows the rising sun as it steadily circles the earth:

> The Church is the holy temple in which, through the strength of the living water that is the Holy Spirit, faith is celebrated in baptism and love or *agapē* is celebrated in the Eucharist. How beautiful the Church's liturgy is, filling time and space with praise of God the creator and savior—to the Father, through the Son, in the Spirit. When our praise ceases here, it begins a little further to the west, as the sun rises. It goes around the world without interruption, "uniting all things in him, the Christ."[174]

This praise spills over into the streets as those gathered for liturgy are commissioned to go forth and serve the Lord.

The Pneumatology of the Theology of the Temple of the Holy Spirit

The temple of the Holy Spirit paradigm fully incorporates both a pneumatological anthropology and a pneumatological ecclesiology. This pneumatology affirms that God is truly given and truly present, that God is truly in communion with us to such a degree that our very bodies are a temple of the Lord. Although the Spirit does not yet abide with eschatological fullness, the Spirit is substantially present within us to such an extent that the distance between God and creature is overcome.[175] In the Spirit, God has given the gift of God's own love, and the principle of our movement toward salvation is now of its very substance heavenly and divine.[176] Congar believed that this indwelling of God within us is appropriated to the Spirit, rather than being personally proper to the Spirit in a technical trinitarian sense. But he did affirm that the divine indwelling—like all of God's actions—originates with God the Father and takes place through the Son in the Holy Spirit. In this trinitarian *taxis*, the hypostatic property of the Spirit is manifest to us.[177]

The trinitarian *taxis* is also a reminder that the temple of the Holy Spirit theology must be understood in its properly christological context. Jesus Christ himself is the temple of the Spirit; in the course of his life, death, and resurrection it becomes clear that "the true dwelling-place of God among men is none other than the person of Jesus himself."[178] Through Jesus Christ, members of his body also become the dwelling-place of God:

> During his life on earth, Jesus was the temple of the Holy Spirit, containing all men with the intention and the power to accept them as children of God. After the Lord's glorification, the Holy Spirit has that temple in us and in the Church and he is active in the same way in us, enabling us to be born *anōthen* (from above and anew: see Jn 3:3) and to live as a member of the Body of Christ.[179]

The theology of the temple of the Holy Spirit is thus closely related to the theology of the mystical body of Christ. There are nonetheless some important nuances that distinguish the two approaches. Within the temple of the Holy Spirit paradigm, Congar achieved a closer integration of theological anthropology and ecclesiology than was the case in his theology of the mystical body of the 1930s and 1940s. As discussed earlier, Congar's theology of the mystical body made qualitative distinctions between Jesus Christ (who is divine), the church (which is not itself divine but which is an instrumental cause of grace and possesses spiritual powers), and the human persons who are members of the mystical body (who neither cause grace nor possess spiritual powers). This resulted in a certain disjuncture of anthropology and ecclesiology and what Famerée described as an "autonomization" of the church—a theology in which the church exercises a causality in the communication of grace in a manner that is abstracted from both Christ and the Spirit and from the human persons who compose the ecclesial body. In Congar's theology of the temple of the Holy Spirit, in contrast, there is no autonomization of the church. Through Jesus Christ, both the church and the human person are truly a dwelling-place of the Spirit, and everything that can be said about the church as temple of the Spirit can also be said of the human person: the Spirit indwells, transfigures the corporeal, bestows charisms, fosters holiness, and evokes praise in the human persons who are the living stones of the church. Within the paradigm of the temple of the Holy Spirit, pneumatological anthropology and pneumatological ecclesiology are more thoroughly integrated than was the case in Congar's mystical body theology of the 1940s or his theology of the people of God of the 1960s. In its own way, however, each of these biblical themes has in fact made an important contribution to Congar's ecclesiology, anthropology, and pneumatology.

5

The Significance of Congar's Legacy

Yves Congar's distinctive contribution to a contemporary Roman Catholic theology of the Holy Spirit is his insight into the pressing need to reunite spiritual anthropology and ecclesiology. He himself advanced this reunion through his elaboration of both a pneumatological anthropology and a pneumatological ecclesiology. The many demands on Congar's time and talents precluded a comprehensive systematization of these dimensions of his theology of the Holy Spirit, but it is a theology rich with potential to contribute to a variety of ongoing discussions in areas such as spirituality, liturgical and sacramental theology, ethics, ecumenism, and ecclesiology. While there are many topics that could be examined in light of Congar's work, this chapter focuses on the significance of Congar's theology for three issues in contemporary systematic theology: the discussion as to whether the Catholic Church is a hierarchy or a democracy, the use of "persons in communion" as a framework for theological anthropology and ecclesiology, and the *proprium* of the Holy Spirit and the theology of appropriations.

The Catholic Church—A Hierarchy or a Democracy?

In 1947, Congar lamented that much of Roman Catholic ecclesiology from the seventeenth century on was little more than "hierarchology."[1] Catholic theology emphasized precisely what Protestant Reformers, Enlightenment thinkers, Gallicanism, Conciliarism, and Modernism had challenged: the divinely established authority of a pyramidal structure of clergy to govern and sanctify the lives of their immediate subordinates and the body of the faithful as a whole. Catholicism's emphasis on hierarchical authority and power grew in response to the critique to which the hierarchy was subjected, and the laity increasingly appeared to be a dispensable append-age to a self-sufficient ecclesiastical institution.[2] As Möhler noted, in his critical review of Theodor Katerkamp's study of church history, it appeared that "God has created the hierarchy and so has shown more than enough care for the church until the end of the world."[3] From the post-Reformation period on, the dominant ecclesiological model in Roman Catholicism was that of the church as a *societas perfecta* or *societas hierarchica*.[4] Even into the twentieth century, many Catholics assumed that the word "church" meant simply the hierarchy.[5]

In the decades prior to the Second Vatican Council, Congar and others developed alternative theologies of the church, and the promulgation of the Council's Pastoral Constitution on the Church (*Lumen gentium*) was a funda-mental turning point in Roman Catholic ecclesiology. According to *Lumen gen-tium*—a document that the Council bishops approved with near unanimity—the church is first and foremost a mysterious sacrament of God's love (*LG* 1) and exists as the entire people of God (*LG* 2). Only after having established this does *Lumen gentium* then proceed to discuss in detail the church's hier-archical structure (*LG* 3). Congar repeatedly noted the importance of the Coun-cil's deliberate decision to place *Lumen gentium*'s chapter on the people of God before the chapter on the hierarchy, a reversal of the original order of the document and a sign of the Council's intention to emphasize that the church is first and foremost the *populus Dei*.[6]

Congar was one of the key architects of the Council documents, and he believed that Vatican II was not an end in itself but only the beginning of the church to come. Both theologically and pastorally, there remained much to do for a full *aggiornamento*. Yet, forty years after the Vatican Council, there is no consensus in the Catholic Church as to the meaning of the Council and its significance for the future of the church. One of the most fundamental ongoing debates concerns church structure and governance. Joseph Cardinal Ratzinger believes that some persons have taken *Lumen gentium*'s theology of the people of God too far; he is critical of programs of reform that "in place of all hier-archical tutelage will at long last introduce democratic self-determination into the Church."[7] Hans Urs von Balthasar also critiques the idea that the church is a democracy, and Walter Kasper stresses that if the church is to be a trini-tarian *communio*, it must be hierarchically structured.[8] Other theologians, in contrast, hold that a full *aggiornamento* of the church requires the implemen-tation of decidedly nonhierarchical forms of governance. Leonard Swidler ad-vocates the establishment of democratic forms of government in the Catholic Church and the formulation of a Catholic Constitution.[9] Elisabeth Schüssler Fiorenza is very critical of ecclesial hierarchy and advocates instead a church structured as a discipleship of equals.[10] Edward Schillebeeckx, for his part, observes that throughout history the church has adapted to the structures of the society in which it finds itself; the organization of the church by gradations of power is one example of the cultural influence of the Roman Empire, feudalism, and Neoplatonic cosmologies on Catholicism, and such cultural influences and societal structures are not normative for the church whose ultimate criterion is the life of Jesus Christ. According to the Gospels, there should be no structure of lordship among the disciples (Mt 20:25–26; Mk 10:42–43; Lk 22:25). Although there is necessarily authority and leadership in the church, it is a historical misunderstanding to maintain that the church has a divinely willed hierarchy. Schillebeeckx is not opposed to the use of the term "hierarchy" as a designation for those persons who exercise ecclesial authority and leadership, but he emphasizes that church authority properly understood "in no way excludes *a priori* a democratic church government."[11] A call for ecclesial democracy comes not only from theologians but also from Catholic organizations. In April 1994, for example, the Plenary Assembly of the *Bund der Deutschen Katholischen Jugend* (BDKJ, Association of German Catholic Youth), an official ecclesial organization with more than a half-million members, approved a program titled "Plan to Promote Democracy in the Catholic Church."[12]

In the context of this ongoing discussion as to whether the church is a hierarchy or a democracy, there is a need to determine precisely what is meant when someone uses these terms and a need to consider how the apparent conflict of views might be reconciled. Both the language of ecclesial democracy and that of ecclesial hierarchy have limitations and can be subject to misinterpretation. Congar's theology of the Holy Spirit can contribute to a clarification of this terminology, bringing a pneumatological perspective to bear on the discussion. From this perspective, a common ground can be constructed that incorporates some of the concerns of both those who advocate ecclesial hierarchy and those who call for democracy.

In order to discuss Congar's contribution to this conversation, it is necessary to bear in mind not only the synopsis of Congar's pneumatological anthropology and pneumatological ecclesiology, presented in preceding chapters, but also Congar's explicit reflections on ecclesial hierarchy. Congar's theology of the ecclesial hierarchy cannot be comprehensively summarized here, but it is important at least to make note of some of the main features of Congar's thought in this regard and to do so with awareness of the changes and development his own ecclesiology underwent in the 1970s and 1980s as he elaborated his theology of the Holy Spirit.

Congar's Reflections on Ecclesial Hierarchy

From at least as early as 1947, Congar was sharply critical of what he termed the "hierarchology" of the dominant neoscholastic *De Ecclesia* treatises. He faulted Catholic ecclesiology for attending solely to the church's hierarchical principle and neglecting what he termed the church's "principle of collective life."[13] But Congar's critique of hierarchology was not a criticism of the hierarchy per se. To the contrary, from 1931 through roughly 1968, Congar described the ecclesial hierarchy—the deaconate, presbyterate, and episcopacy—as a divinely instituted means of grace that has both ontological and temporal precedence to the faithful and mediates the authority and salvific power of Jesus Christ.[14] Using the Aristotelian terminology that was in widespread use in Roman Catholic theology of this period, Congar described the hierarchy as the formal cause of the church and identified the members as the material cause.[15] This precedence of the hierarchy over the baptized ensures that the church is not simply a congregation of human beings but rather a divine institution from above (de en haut). The church, Congar emphasized, finds its source, foundation, authority, and salvific power not in the decision of like-minded human beings to gather, congregate, and organize a structure of common life; rather, the church's origin and foundation is the Incarnate Word and the offices Jesus Christ himself established to continue the mediation of the mystery of Incarnation in the aftermath of his death and resurrection. The relationship between hierarchy and laity is, accordingly, a relationship of superior to subordinate, for the hierarchy mediates not a human mandate to govern but the divine authority of the Incarnate Word. "Hierarchical persons," as Congar termed the holders of ecclesial office, are equal to the laity insofar as the clergy themselves are also baptized members of the one body of Christ, but insofar as clergy exercise hierarchical powers they are superior to those who do not. In 1951, Congar stated, in his introduction to *Lay People in the Church* (a book that affirmed the importance of the laity), that "lay people will always be a subordinate order in the Church."[16] Congar insisted that hierarchical superiority must be exercised in a mode of service, undertaken in the spirit of Jesus Christ's humble foot washing of the apostles (Jn 13:1–17) and his silencing of James and John who desired to sit at his right and left hands (Mk 10:42–45; Mt 20:25–28). We must not, Congar warned, let the church be "ruined by the spirit of domination" or mired by the weight of glory, power, and prestige; a hierarchy that dominates rather than serves is not exercising its office in fidelity to the intention, teaching, and example of Jesus Christ.[17] The hierarchy's mission to serve the church, nonetheless, exists within the context of the fundamental religious relation of superior to subordinate.

In the 1970s and 1980s, Congar's appreciation for the remarkable growth of lay initiatives in the postconciliar church and his growing emphasis on the theology of the Holy Spirit bore fruit in an ecclesiology that differed in some important respects from that of his earlier works.[18] Congar's advocacy of a pneumatological ecclesiology as well as developments in his theology of the relationship between Christ and the Spirit served as theological grounds for ecclesiological reformulations. In 1971, when Congar was sixty-seven years old, he professed, "I now see many things differently and, I hope, better in comparison with forty years ago. . . . I have gradually corrected my vision, which at first was principally and spontaneously clerical."[19]

The origins of the church, Congar emphasized in his publications from the period 1969–1991, cannot be adequately explained with reference only to the acts of the historical Jesus. Rather, in light of a pneumatological Christology, we must recognize the Holy Spirit as the church's co-institutor.[20] The Holy Spirit guided Jesus' earthly acts, raised him from the dead, and fostered the growth of the church after Pentecost through the inspiration and assistance given to the apostles. Throughout the centuries, the Spirit continues to build up the church in a process that is ultimately eschatological in scope.[21] "The Church," Congar wrote in 1973, "is not ready-made. . . . She is not prefabricated and placed in a frame which has already been prepared."[22] The Spirit of the glorified Christ indwells each of the faithful and fosters the church's ongoing organic growth. God, Jesus said, will give *you* the Spirit, will send the Spirit to *you;* the Spirit will teach *you*, lead *you*, reveal to *you* . . . (Jn 14 and 16). In Congar's interpretation of these Johannine passages, he noted that the "you" refers both to each particular believer and to the ecclesial body as a whole.[23] "All have received the Spirit or can receive him . . . ," he wrote. "The total Church only enjoys the fullness of the Spirit's gifts by welcoming and integrating the contributions brought from all sides. . . ."[24] The very same Spirit who is in Christ is given to all the church's members—*unus numero in Christo et in omnibus.*[25]

Congar's evolving pneumatology and his attendant rejection of a pyramidal ecclesiological schema led to a reformulation of his theology of ordained ministry. In a 1971 article entitled "My Path-Findings in the Theology of Laity and Ministries," Congar explicitly critiqued his earlier reflections on the hierarchy's ontological and temporal precedence above the body of the faithful as a whole. "The risk I ran," he explained, "was to define the ministerial priesthood purely in itself, along a line of thought which extended the Scholasticism of the twelfth and thirteenth centuries (where character is identified with the conferring of a power)."[26] This, he continued,

> translates into a linear scheme of this type: Christ makes the hierarchy and the hierarchy makes the Church as community of faithful. Such a scheme, even if it contains a part of the truth, presents inconveniences. At least in temporal priority it places the ministerial priest before and outside the community. Put into actuality, it would in fact reduce the building of the community to the action of the hierarchical ministry. Pastoral reality as well as the New Testament presses on us a much richer view. It is God, it is Christ who by his Holy Spirit does not cease building up his Church.[27]

Congar now emphasized that the hierarchical ministries exist not apart from or before or above the members of the Church but *within* the ecclesial communion. He schematized his earlier ecclesiology as follows:

Jesus Christ
↓
Hierarchy
↓
Church as Community of Faithful

In contrast, he offered two alternative ecclesiological models that were developed in ecumenical consultations (see figure 1).[28]

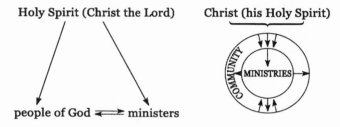

FIGURE I

Notably, these latter diagrams include the Holy Spirit, whereas the Spirit was not even mentioned in Congar's earlier ecclesiological model. In these new models, it is rather the term "hierarchy" that does not appear at all. "As to terminology," Congar himself said of the new approach, "it is worth noticing that the decisive coupling is not 'priesthood/laity,' as I used it in *Jalons*, but rather 'ministries/modes of community service.' "[29] He emphasized that the term "ministries" takes the plural form, for the church is built up by a multitude of ministries, some ordained and some lay.[30] "There is not a purely vertical descent," Congar commented elsewhere, "as would be the case within a purely christological logic of the 'valid' succession of the apostles: there is rather the operation of the entire body in which the Spirit dwells and acts."[31]

In Congar's publications between 1969 and 1991, he continued to affirm—as he had done in his earlier writings—that the ordained ministries of the church are a means of grace with an essential soteriological function. Clearly, however, there are some important differences in his explication of the manner in which the ordained exercise this role. First, Congar emphasized that the capacity of the ordained ministers to mediate grace is dependent not only on the institution of their ecclesial office by Jesus Christ but also on the continuing activity of the Holy Spirit. "Every action performed by the ministry," he wrote, "calls for an epiclesis. Orthodox Christians are right when they say that the life of the Church is entirely epicletic."[32] Second, Congar emphasized that the activity of the Spirit in response to the prayer of epiclesis is an activity mediated not by the ordained minister alone but rather by the ordained minister *in relation to the ecclesial body as a whole* in whom the Spirit dwells and through whom the Spirit works. The priest who acts *in persona Christi* can do so only because the minister stands also *in persona Ecclesiae:*

> If, on the other hand, the pneumatological aspect is emphasized, as the Eastern tradition loves to do, the *in persona Christi* is more easily seen as situated within the *in persona Ecclesiae*. There is no denial here of the fact that the priest has received, through his ordination, the "power" to celebrate the Eucharist and therefore to consecrate the bread and wine. . . . but this does not mean that he can do it alone, that is, when he remains alone. He does not, in other words, consecrate the elements by virtue of a power that is inherent in him and which he has, in this sense, within his control. It is rather by virtue of the grace for which he asks God and which is operative, and even ensured, through him *in the Church*.[33]

As is evident in this passage and in his ecclesiological diagrams (figure 1), Congar's publications from this later period of his career emphasize not the ontological and temporal precedence of ordained minsters over the baptized but rather the mutuality and communion of all members of the church within which ministers have a unique role. An ordained minister cannot be a priestly mediator of the grace of Christ apart from the communion of the baptized on whose behalf the priest stands *in persona Ecclesiae*. Nor can the ministerial office be efficacious without the activity of the Holy Spirit who acts not only through this office but also through the ecclesial body as a whole. This reformulation of Congar's ecclesiology led him to question his earlier portrayal of the relationship of hierarchy and laity as a relation of superiority and subordination. "I now wonder," he pondered, in 1971, "whether this is a happy mode of procedure."[34] He never entirely abandoned the language of hierarchy as a term of reference to ordained ministry, but, in keeping with his expressed preference for the coupling "ministries/modes of community service" as opposed to the distinction of "hierarchy/laity," Congar's references to ecclesial hierarchy decrease sharply in frequency in his later works. In the first sixty-four pages of his *Lay People in the Church* (1957), the word "hierarchy" appears thirty-five times.[35] In contrast, the most explicitly ecclesiological portion of *I Believe in the Holy Spirit*—a sixty-four-page section of volume 2 entitled "The Spirit Animates the Church"—employs the term "hierarchy" only once and the adjective "hierarchical" only twice. In *I Believe*, moreover, Congar placed these terms in quotation marks and discontinued his former practice of capitalizing the nominative form.[36]

Is the Church a Hierarchy or a Democracy?

What, then, of the current discussion as to whether the church should be a hierarchy or a democracy? In what follows I draw from both Congar's theology of the Holy Spirit and the preceding synopsis of the development of his thinking on ecclesial ministry to respond to this question. In speaking to this issue, it is important to clarify what is signified by the terms "hierarchy" and "democracy." Congar presumed that the word "hierarchy" necessarily connotes a relation of superiority and subordination. This, in fact, is a common usage of the term. In both secular and theological literature, "hierarchy" typically connotes gradations of rank and value and/or the dominance of some persons over others.[37] "Hierarchy" and "inequality" were nearly synonymous terms in the dominant preconciliar theology that described the church as a *societas inaequalis, hierarchica.*[38] The term "democracy," in contrast, is commonly understood to mean precisely the opposite: a relation of governance among people who are all of equal stature and have equal voice. This term also implies that "people are the origin of all just power" (David Hume) or that "power is inherent in the people" (Thomas Jefferson).[39]

From the perspective of Congar's theology of the Holy Spirit, the church is neither a hierarchy nor a democracy in the most common understanding of these terms. The church is not a hierarchy if this means a social body structured by relationships of superiority and subordination. Even in their capacity as mediators of grace, those who hold ministerial office in the church are not superior to those who do not. Rather, they stand with the baptized in a relation of mutuality and communion. The ordained minister cannot exercise priestly office apart from the community as a whole, nor can the ordained act as a mediator of grace apart from the activity of the Holy Spirit whose empowerment of priestly ministry is distinct from but nonetheless inseparable from the indwelling of the Holy Spirit in the entire ecclesial communion. The ordained minister has a unique role in the mediation of grace but acts in communion with the other members of the church, not in superiority over them. Reflecting on the Holy Spirit as the principal agent in the sacrament of ordination, Hervé-Marie Legrand writes that "one can see how all Christians are equal within the variety established by the Spirit, and why a hierarchical understanding of the ordained ministry is inadequate."[40]

This does not mean, however, that the church is a democracy in the sense of an organization of equals in which power is inherent in the people. The power of the church is not inherent in the people but rather comes from the Spirit of Christ, the Spirit of God. The church, as Congar said, is completely dependent on its co-institution by Jesus Christ and the Holy Spirit and exists only by virtue of the ongoing activity of the Spirit of the glorified Christ in the ecclesial body—the Spirit who is implored in the prayer of epiclesis. The church differs in some important respects from civil democratic societies; as

Catherine Mowry LaCugna wrote, "The church makes a claim that civil governments do not: that it is the people of God, Body of Christ, and Temple of the Holy Spirit. The life of the church is to be animated by the life of God; the church is to embody in the world the presence of the risen Christ, showing by its preaching and by its own form of life that sin and death have been overcome by Jesus Christ."[41] The terminology we use to describe the church should reflect the church's unique character and mission and emphasize its absolute dependence on the Spirit of God. The conciliarity by which the church governs and organizes its life does bear some resemblance to the processes of democratic societies, and Congar, as we have seen, stressed the importance of conciliarity, reception, and other participatory forms of ecclesial governance and decision making. Nonetheless, it is more precise to speak of the church as a communion in the Spirit of Christ rather than as a democracy.[42] The language of communion better expresses the theocentric character of the church, whose life and power come ultimately not from the people (in a Jeffersonian sense) but from the Spirit of God.

Having just questioned the use of both "hierarchy" and "democracy" as appropriate ecclesiological terms, however, one must also affirm the truth that underlies the positions of the proponents of both of these two forms of ecclesiology. Congar's emphasis on the hierarchical character of the church in his publications between 1937 and 1968 stemmed from an important conviction that continues to shape his ecclesiology even in his later works: the church does not come *de en bas* (from below) but rather *de en haut* (from on high). The church, Congar wrote, in 1953, is not just an association of people in the manner of a pagan *collegium* but rather an institution with a divine origin— "she was and is an institution formed from on high, hierarchically built."[43] In Congar's ecclesiology of this period, the term "hierarchy" expresses that the church comes from on high by emphasizing the ontological and temporal precedence of the ecclesial hierarchy over the members of the church to whom the ordained relate as superiors to subordinates, or as formal to material cause. Even when one prescinds from the language of hierarchy, as Congar himself was inclined to do in his later years, one must still preserve his underlying conviction that the church comes *de en haut*—from the grace of God. Indeed, one could argue that *it is precisely this mystery of the church's divine origin*, rather than the institution of relations of superiority and subordination that is ultimately at the heart and core of the term "hierarchy." This term comes from the Greek prefix *hier*, which means "sacred," and from the Greek noun *archē*, meaning origin, principle, or rule.[44] In this etymological sense, the church is most certainly a *hier-archē*, for sacred origin and sacred rule are ecclesiological sine qua non. Hierarchical language, however, has so overwhelmingly connoted social subordination for so long that it is very difficult to purge the terminology of this connotation.[45] The development of alternative forms of expression of the church's sacred origin and divine rule is thus imperative to

the formulation of a contemporary ecclesiology that can forthrightly communicate what *hier-archē* truly means. It is notable, indeed, that the pneumatological ecclesiology that Congar developed in the 1970s and 1980s expresses the
sacred origin and divine rule of the church not primarily with the language of
hierarchy but rather with an accentuation on Christology, sacramental theology,
and the epiclesis of the Holy Spirit. In 1979, in *I Believe in the Holy Spirit*,
Congar continued to hold, as he had in 1953, that the church comes *de en haut*,
but he has found a new way to express this mystery: "The life of the Church,"
he emphasized, "is one long epiclesis."[46] The church finds its divine rule and
sacred origin in the Spirit of Christ whom the church implores in prayer and
worship.

From the perspective of Congar's theology of the Holy Spirit, then, there
is an important truth that underlies the position of those who advocate ecclesial
hierarchy insofar as these persons use this term, as Congar himself had done,
to express the church's divine origin. From the perspective of Congar's pneumatology, however, there is also an important truth that underlies the position
of those who advocate ecclesial democracy. Proponents of this form of ecclesiology surely do not intend to reduce the church to a human political organization; rather, they seek to express a truth that is rooted in the mystery of
baptism and the church's Eucharistic and communitarian life. As Congar's
theology of the Holy Spirit expresses so well, the Spirit of Christ actively indwells all of the faithful. Even when the ordained ministers mediate grace, they
do so not apart from the faithful but in a relation of mutuality and communion
with other ministers and all the baptized. The minister who acts *in persona
Christi*, Congar emphasized, stands also *in persona Ecclesiae*. If we are to take
seriously Congar's pneumatological ecclesiology and pneumatological anthropology, we cannot conceive of the activity of the Spirit in the church apart from
the personal indwelling of the Spirit in all the baptized, for the mediation of
the Spirit by the ordained ministers of the church is distinct from but nonetheless inseparable from the indwelling of the Spirit in all of the faithful. Those
who advocate ecclesial democracy call our attention to the presence of the Holy
Spirit in each and every person and ask that we take seriously the consequences
of this presence for the life and mission of the church. We may—as Congar
himself did—criticize the ecclesiological use of the language of democracy
insofar as this term does not of itself express the divine origin and divine rule
of the church.[47] From the perspective of Congar's theology, however, we must
also recognize the truth that underlies the position of the proponents of ecclesial democracy, even as we give this truth a more pneumatological expression:
the Holy Spirit indwells all of the faithful, and this personal indwelling has
important implications for the life, structure, and mission of the church.

"Persons in Communion" as a Framework for Contemporary Theological Anthropology and Ecclesiology

Congar's theology of the Holy Spirit can contribute not only to current discussions about the structure of the church but also to the construction of a broad theological framework in which reflection on theological anthropology and ecclesiology can proceed. As we have seen, Congar used pneumatology to bridge these two domains—domains that had been separated by neoscholastic treatises that divorced *De Ecclesia* schemas from reflection on the personal indwelling of the Holy Spirit found in treatises on grace. Today, pneumatology, ecclesiology, and theological anthropology are no longer completely disjoined. Numerous books, articles, and ecumenical conferences have developed the pneumatological dimension of ecclesiology, and reflection on the human person and the church proceeds under such rubrics as "the individual and the community,"[48] "the individual in the church,"[49] or "persons in communion."[50] In light of Congar's theology of the Holy Spirit, "persons in communion" emerges from among these alternatives as a preferable paradigm for contemporary theological reflection. This paradigm serves the pneumatological dimension of theological anthropology and ecclesiology more adequately than the framework of "individuals and community."

The difference between the person and the individual and the distinction between communion and community are discussed in the section that follows. An argument is then made for the serviceablity of persons in communion as a paradigm for contemporary theology. Congar's pneumatology is the theological vision that serves as the overarching context for this discussion. The reflection, however, draws from the writings not only of Congar but also from other theologians whose work contributes to the question at hand.

The Difference between the Person and the Individual

In contemporary discourse, it is often presumed that "person" and "individual" are synonymous or interchangeable terms. The philosopher Catherine McCall, for example, describes the concept of person as one of three different modes of understanding the individual (the other two being self and human).[51] Edward Henderson uses the terms "person" and "individual" interchangeably in his article "Knowing Persons and Knowing God."[52] And the English translators of Congar's writings often used the term "individual" in places where Congar himself had written simply *personne*.[53]

The roots of the presumption that "person" means individual reach back at least as far as Boethius's sixth-century treatise *Contra Eutyches and Nestorius*, which provided the Western tradition with a formal definition of the term *persona*. "Person," Boethius determined, after considering how this word was

employed in common speech, is an "individual substance of a rational nature."[54] This definition proved to be enormously influential in the Western
theological tradition.[55] It was adopted with some modifications by Thomas
Aquinas and thereby exerted particular influence in Roman Catholic theology.
In recent years, nonetheless, Boethius's approach has been widely criticized.
Bernd Hilberath identifies a number of German scholars who consider Boethius's definition of the person to be overly determined by philosophy, insufficiently theological, inappropriate for use in trinitarian theology, and even inadequate to the very christological problem it was originally intended to resolve.
Hilberath himself is sympathetic to this critique.[56] Meanwhile, contemporary
philosophers and theologians have sought other ways to elucidate the meaning
of personhood. In this process, some have systematically distinguished the
meaning of the term "person" from that of "individual." This distinction can
be found in varying forms in personalist schools of thought, some contemporary appropriations of Aquinas's theology, the spiritual writings of Thomas
Merton, and the work of the Greek Orthodox theologian John Zizioulas. This
is not an exhaustive inventory of those who distinguish person and individual,
nor can the approaches here presented be explicated in their entirety, but the
manner in which these schools of thought or particular authors distinguish
the person from the individual is briefly described.

PERSONALIST SCHOOLS OF THOUGHT. The term "personalism" was first used
in 1903 by Charles Renouvier to describe his approach to philosophy.[57] Over
the course of the twentieth century, personalism developed as a school of
thought that emphasized the human person's irreducible uniqueness, freedom, responsibility, and relationality in the face of determinism, materialism,
mass society, and individualism. Writers associated with personalism include
Max Scheler, Nicholas Berdyaev, Ferdinand Ebner, Franz Rosenzweig, Paul
Landsberg, Paul Ricoeur, Maurice Nédoncelle, Jean Lacroix, Martin Buber, John
Macmurray, Gabriel Marcel, and Karl Jaspers, some of whom wrote from a
strictly philosophical perspective and some of whom took a theological approach. Among Christian personalists, Emmanuel Mounier is one of the most
significant figures. He is the founder of the personalist journal *Esprit* (1930)
and the author of numerous personalist articles and monographs, and his work
can serve as a good example of personalist thought.[58]

    Mounier declined to define the meaning of the term "person" as a matter
of principle. He believed that we can define only observable objects, and, although human persons do have observable characteristics (e.g., a body) and
can be classified in terms of their social functions and roles (e.g., a Frenchman,
a bourgeois, a Catholic, a socialist), none of these identifications captures the
uniqueness of a given personal existence. We may describe Bernard Chartier
as *a* Frenchman and *a* bourgeois and *a* Catholic, but Bernard is nonetheless
"not *a* Bernard Chartier, he is Bernard Chartier."[59] The essence of the person

is indefinable, and the meaning of personal existence can be expressed only by an actual encounter with someone who realizes a fully personal life and thereby awakens others to their own personal potential, or by a philosophical description of the person that proceeds from reflection on the objective universe but that in so doing hints obliquely at a reality that is not primarily objective and can be only imperfectly conveyed.[60] Mounier attempted the latter approach, and in so doing he deliberately distinguished the person from the individual. He affirmed that individual self-reflection is a component of human development; yet he insisted that the first condition of personalism is a decentering of the individual. The person, he explained,

> is only growing in so far as he is continually *purifying himself from the individual* within him. He cannot do this by force of self-attention, but on the contrary by making himself *available* (Gabriel Marcel) and thereby more transparent both to himself and to others. Things then happen as though the person, no longer "occupied with himself" or "full of himself," were becoming able—then and thus only—to be someone else and to enter into grace.[61]

In Mounier's thought, to be a person is to live wholly within a communion of love. "I love," he writes, "therefore I am."[62]

CONTEMPORARY APPROPRIATIONS OF THE THEOLOGY OF THOMAS AQUINAS. Personalist philosophy and theology influenced the work of a number of twentieth-century Catholic theologians who were trained in the theology of Thomas Aquinas. Aquinas's theology was shaped by his encounter with Aristotle, a biologist turned philosopher whose philosophical concepts and categories were equally well suited to speculation on plants, animals, artifacts and human persons like Socrates. As personalist thinkers highlighted the difference between the human person and the purely material world, a number of Catholic theologians called for a Thomism that would take this difference into account. Congar himself commented, "there is a danger in Thomism, although I do not think that Thomas himself succumbed to it, . . . a danger of homogeneity almost at any price, to the degree that the human beings are themselves conceived of in the manner of natural things."[63] Congar feared that this homogenization had become widespread in Catholic metaphysical reflection, and he warned that "there is an ontology of the person which cannot be reduced to a pure ontology of nature."[64] In like vein, the Dominican Edward Schillebeeckx critiqued Roman Catholic sacramental theology for its use of categories taken predominantly from the physical realm, categories that resulted in an impersonal and mechanical theology.[65] Schillebeeckx himself elaborated an alternative sacramental theology based on categories of personal encounter and communion. The neo-Thomist Norris Clarke, meanwhile, developed a theological anthropology that emphasized the interpersonal and intersubjective di-

mensions of the person, aspects that he thought had not been clearly or explicitly developed by Aquinas or his ancient predecessors.[66]

The twentieth-century Thomist most associated with personalism is
Jacques Maritain, with whom Congar himself had some contact in his youth
through his connection to Father Daniel Lallement. Maritain's anthropology
made a clear distinction between the person and the individual. It is "extremely
important to distinguish the person from the individual," Maritain affirmed,
"and it is also extremely important to grasp the exact significance of this distinction."[67] Human beings, he explained, are both individuals and persons. We
are individuals insofar as we are made of matter, which is the metaphysical
principle of the individuation of all created material beings. But we are also
persons, for we are not simply individuated material beings but also spiritual
beings endowed with a soul that gives us the capacity for freedom, knowledge,
and love. "I am wholly an individual by reason of what I receive from matter,
and I am wholly a person, by reason of what I receive from spirit."[68] Maritain
believed that this basic truth generates a perennial tension in human life—the
individual pole of our existence pulls us toward fleshly passions and threatens
to disperse us in an amorphous sea of *materia prima*. All too often, the person
is eclipsed by the individual and bourgeois individualism, communist anti-
individualism, and dictatorial totalitarianism result—forms of social existence
that ignore the human person and consider only the material individual
alone.[69] Discipline, asceticism, and education are necessary so that the person
can elevate the individual through freedom, knowledge, and love. The aim is
not to extinguish the individual—this would be metaphysically impossible—
but rather to achieve a balance between what Maritain termed individuality
and personality.[70]

THE SPIRITUALITY OF THOMAS MERTON. Maritain's formulation of the distinction between person and individual influenced Thomas Merton, one of the
most popular spiritual writers of the twentieth century. Merton studied Maritain in graduate school, and years later he appropriated Maritain's differentiation of the individual and the person as a metaphysical analogue for his own
distinction between the false self and the true self. The individual or false self,
Merton explained, is the egoistic, illusory, and sinful self, as contrasted to the
true self, our true identity in Christ.[71] Merton decried the confusion and ab-
surdity of the false, worldly self and exhorted that "the person must be rescued
from the individual."[72] He called his readers to transcend divisive self-
exaltation, for "the man who lives in division is not a person but only an
'individual.'"[73] This death to the self-exaltation of the individual is a birth to
eternal life:

> There just aren't individuals after death. There are persons, but not
> individuals. I think this is a very important point because we as

Christians do not believe in the afterlife of the individual. We believe in the afterlife of the person, who is free, who is in God already, who is one with God from the beginning. The person returns to God and finds the self in God on a much deeper level than an individual ever could, because an individual has to know the self as an isolated little entity from which everything else is shut off. As long as we're individuals, we can never be with one another.[74]

Notably, Merton's usage of the term "individual" has a more negative cast than Maritain's. In Maritain's Thomism, our existence as individuals is metaphysically necessary and only becomes problematic insofar as the individual eclipses the person; in Merton's New Seeds, in contrast, the individual is the false self, which is not something to be balanced with the true self but something to be entirely overcome. Merton was not entirely consistent in his use of this terminology; after stating that we cannot—insofar as we are individuals—truly be with one another, he added, "but, of course, it's as individuals that we work the thing out."[75] His reflections on the individual as the false self nonetheless do contribute to the discussion at hand and have been influential in contemporary spirituality.

THE WORK OF THE ORTHODOX THEOLOGIAN JOHN ZIZIOULAS. Whereas Merton drew from Maritain, the Greek Orthodox theologian John Zizioulas approaches theology from a starting point that is intentionally different from Thomism and Scholasticism.[76] Zizioulas—described by Congar as "one of the most original and profound theologians of our epoch"[77]—grounds his work in Greek patristic theology, particularly that of the Cappadocians, whom Zizioulas credits with a new approach to ontology that is radically different from both Platonic and Aristotelian thought. Zizioulas believes that within both Platonic ontology and the Aristotelian alternative, the question "Who am I?" can never receive an authentic answer. Classic Greek philosophy can give no definitive foundation to the true uniqueness of the "I," for it derives the particular human being from a general human ousia—the Platonic ousia hyperkeimene or the Aristotelian ousia hypokeimene—of which the human being is simply an instantiation.[78] In the biblical view, in contrast, humanity is derivative not from an ideal man (as in Plato) or a generic human nature (as in Aristotle) but rather from Adam, a particular human being.[79] This biblical ontology has its source in the divine being, for God ultimately exists not because of a generic divine substance but because of the person of God the Father. The Cappadocians developed this insight and gave ontological ultimacy to particularity for the first time in the history of philosophy. They emphasized, furthermore, that the particular person of God the Father exists in eternal relationship with the Son and the Spirit; relationality is therefore ontologically ultimate. Zizioulas explains, "in trying to identify a particular thing we have to make it part of a relationship and not isolate it as an individual, as the *tode ti* of Aristotle."[80] He critiques Augustine, Boethius, and the subsequent Western tradition for equating person and individual.[81] Greek patristic thought affirms that "there is no true being without communion. Nothing exists as an 'individual,' conceivable in itself. Communion is an ontological category."[82]

For Zizioulas, indeed, God is in no sense an individual. The human being, on the other hand, *is* an individual in consequence of the conditions of our created existence. Creation had a beginning, exists in a spatio-temporal realm, and lives in a being-unto-death (Heidegger); the result is a separation (*chorismos*) of creatures from one another and hence a fallen state in which humans do in fact have an individual existence.[83] "[T]he conditions that we have set out for [an] ontology of personhood," Zizioulas acknowledges, "exist only in God."[84] The human being generated by sexual procreation in exile from Eden is not a true person but only a biological hypostasis, a body that "tends towards the person but leads finally to the individual."[85] Zizioulas does believe, however, that this tragic human condition can be overcome through the grace of God. The Holy Spirit de-individualizes the baptized through incorporation into the hypostasis of Jesus Christ—an hypostasis that is eternal, unlimited by space and time, and unconstricted by being-unto-death. Through participation in the hypostasis of Jesus Christ, the human being too may finally become a person rather than an individual.[86] In Christ, our biological hypostasis becomes what Zizioulas terms an ecclesial hypostasis, a true person.[87] "The individual dies as such and rises as the person."[88]

The preceding summary has not done full justice to the thought of Mounier, Maritain, Merton, or Zizioulas. It should at least be evident, however, that there is reason to question the presumption that "person" and "individual" are synonymous or interchangeable terms. The work of the philosophers and theologians I have discussed demonstrates that there is a basis for carefully distinguishing the person and the individual, a distinction that can take different forms in different contexts. Maritain, working out of a Thomist perspective, affirms that we are both individuals and persons, whereas Zizioulas constructs an ontology of communion in which we are called to transcend our existence as fallen human individuals in order to finally become true persons. Whatever one's approach, some form of distinction of the person and the individual is well suited to the pneumatological anthropology advocated by Congar. All of the theologians mentioned use the word "person" with connotations of freedom, grace, uniqueness, mystery, relationality, and communion—qualities that are foundational to pneumatological anthropology and pneumatological ecclesiology. Indeed, William Hill believed that the Holy Spirit's transformation of the person is something real within believers, "but it is real within them not as individuals but as persons."[89] The suitability of the term "person" for use within pneumatology is further discussed later in this chapter, after a consideration of the distinction between community and communion.

The Distinction between "Community" and "Communion"

In contemporary parlance, discourse about the individual or the person seldom stands alone. Typically, it is only one side of a couplet in which its partner is discourse about community or society. One readily finds books with titles such as Kegley's *Genuine Individuals and Genuine Communities* or McLean and Meynell's *Person and Society*.[90] Computer databases catalog countless articles with similar titles—González-Faus's "Anthropology: The Person and the Community," for example, or Frances Moore Lappé's and J. Baird Callicott's "Individual and Community in Society and Nature."[91] In like vein, theological discussions often counterpose the individual and the community or the individual and the church. As Ann O'Hara Graff writes, "in the study of the church today, no term is more important than community. We are not merely individuals before God, but a people."[92] Yet Congar's pneumatological ecclesiology centered around the idea of communion, a concept by which he believed one could enter into the theology of the church.[93] The terms "communion" and "community" have different nuances of meaning. Justice cannot be done here to all the literature on the significance of these terms, but a comparison of Congar's ecclesiology with the ideas expressed by James Gustafson in *Treasure in Earthen Vessels: The Church as a Human Community* can at least indicate some of the issues involved.

"COMMUNITY" IN JAMES GUSTAFSON'S *TREASURE IN EARTHEN VESSELS.* Gustafson's book *Treasure in Earthen Vessels* has been selected for exposition because it offers a representative and systematic account of the meaning of the term "community" in contemporary discourse. Gustafson is a Protestant theologian who is well versed in sociology, and his book *Treasure in Earthen Vessels: The Church as a Human Community* was hailed by H. Richard Niebuhr as "the first real sociology of the church."[94] Gustafson acknowledges that the church transcends sociological analysis, and he does not consider his book a comprehensive ecclesiology. He is concerned, however, that theologians all too often slight the church's human dimension, eclipsing the human character of the church with doctrinal claims or ambiguous mystical statements.[95] Gustafson's intention in *Treasure in Earthen Vessels* is to demonstrate the manifold ways in which the church manifests the same sociological processes as all other human communities. "Community" is the central term of his analysis, and he uses this term in a loose sense to refer "to a body of persons who share some measure of common life, and a common loyalty."[96] Such bodies include not only the church but also families, business corporations, trade and labor unions, clubs and voluntary associations, political parties, and entire nations.

Gustafson explains that the church differs from other forms of community in that it has a distinctive center of common loyalty. The loyalty of the church is centered on Jesus Christ, whereas a trade union is loyal to the principles of the labor movement and a state to the principles of its constitution and national history.[97] Different communities have different fidelities, but Gustafson insists that there is a singular *process* by which all communities are formed, despite variance in the purpose or intention of community organization.[98] In *Treasure in Earthen Vessels*, Gustafson explicates the various aspects of this process of community formation as evident in the life of the church. The church is organized in such a way that it serves natural human needs—physical, psychological, and emotional.[99] This process of organization is inherently political, for the church perdures through the institutionalization of patterns of relationship, authority, and power.[100] The church also maintains itself through time as a continuous community by virtue of a common language (Scripture and creed) that is internalized by the church's members and that establishes boundaries between those who belong to the church and those who stand outside the community lines.[101] This common language is passed on from generation to generation in a process of interpretation that both preserves the community's past and also adapts the past to present circumstances, such that the church is a community of both memory and understanding.[102] Finally, the church is a community of belief and action, a moral community that professes a faith that it puts into practice.[103]

Gustafson emphasizes throughout *Treasure in Earthen Vessels* that everything he has said about the church can also be said about other human communities. All communities serve natural human needs, have some form of political organization, share a common language, and preserve continuity over time through processes of memory and interpretation. Many communities other than the church are also moral communities of belief, action, and even faith.[104] A theologian, Gustafson notes, would argue that the church is nonetheless distinctive because its own community-formation process proceeds through the divine action of Jesus Christ and the Holy Spirit. But "perhaps," Gustafson reflects, "God acts through the very processes of Church life that can be interpreted from the point of view of social theory."[105]

"COMMUNION" IN CONGAR'S PNEUMATOLOGICAL ECCLESIOLOGY. Congar would certainly not deny that God works through human social processes or that ecclesiologists can fruitfully employ the sociological discipline. In fact, he believed that contemporary sociology can enrich Roman Catholic ecclesiology, which for so long defined the church as *societas* within a purely philosophical delineation of this term.[106] Congar did not believe, however, that sociology can be the sole or primary entrée into ecclesiology. Rather, the ecclesiologist must take a theological approach to the mystery of the church—and in this context there can also be a place for sociological analysis. "In the end," wrote Congar, "the Church is certainly a society, but that is not what one should begin with. The first thing is the spiritual communion, a communion on the basis of the

Word of God received in faith and grace, of which the sacraments are one of the principle vehicles."[107]

Neoscholastic treatises on the church typically defined *societas* as a "moral and stable unity of many people to a certain end, from which common action should follow," and Congar considered this a useful definition.[108] This particular usage of the term "society" is very similar to Gustafson's definition of the word "community"—"a body of persons who share some measure of common life, and a common loyalty."[109] Despite F. Tönnies's influential distinction of *Gemeinschaft* (community) and *Gesellschaft* (society), there can be considerable continuity in the usage of these two terms.[110] Ecclesiologically speaking, indeed, more important than the differentiation of community from society is the distinction of both community and society from communion. These concepts should not be starkly contrasted or opposed, for the church is surely a form of communal and social existence. The differentiation of communion from both society and community is nonetheless necessary in order to preserve the distinctively theocentric and trinitarian character of ecclesial life. As Congar explained, the church cannot be understood by simply determining the general characteristics of all human societies and then applying this definition of society to the church with the modification "Christian" appended, for the church is not simply a human society but a participation in the mystery of God.[111] The church is different from other human communities, not simply because it has its own particular center of community loyalty (as Gustafson held) but because it is not only a community but also a communion in the life of God.

Dictionary definitions cannot capture the rich range of meaning and signification that the term "communion" has carried throughout the biblical, liturgical, and theological tradition of the church.[112] This English term is a translation of the Greek word *koinōnia*, which occurs nineteen times in the New Testament, primarily in the Pauline epistles. It is used there with reference to the sharing of goods with those in need (2 Cor 9:13; Rom 15:26); the fellowship of Christians with one another (Gal 2:9–10); the sharing of the Eucharistic assembly in the body and blood of Jesus Christ (1 Cor 10:16); the sharing of Christians in the suffering of Christ (Phil 3:10); and the gift of the Holy Spirit (Phil 2:1; 2 Cor 13:13). In the second epistle of Peter, the word *koinōnia* is also used with reference to humanity's participation (*koinōnoi*) in the divine nature through Jesus Christ (2 Pt 1:4). These important theological connotations of the word "communion" have been preserved in the handing on of the Christian tradition, and "communion" thus bears christological and pneumatological resonances that the term "community" does not necessarily convey. Communion, Congar explained, means participation (*metochē*) in the goods that come from God or in God's very life.[113] In standard sociological usage, "community" refers to the relationships of human persons with one another, whereas the theological language of communion places these human relationships in the context of our relationship to God through Jesus Christ in the Holy Spirit. "When we consider the New Testament use of the word," Hamer insists, "we must beware of reducing *koinōnia* to mere friendly relationships between man and man. The vertical dimension is the primary one: *koinōnia* is founded wholly on Christ and on the Spirit."[114] The relationship to God connoted by the term *koinōnia* is by no means exclusive of human relationships, but within a theocentric context human relationships take on a different cast.

Indeed, Gustafson's discussion of the church as a community differs from Congar's portrayal of the church as a communion in some important respects.[115] For Gustafson, the church is a community because it serves basic human physical, psychological, and emotional needs, whereas for Congar the church is oriented not simply to human need but also to the elevation of the human person to participation in the supranatural life of God. For Gustafson, the church is a community because it has institutionalized forms of political organization, but for Congar these political forms are properly understood only if placed in the context of Christology and pneumatology, for the foundational institutions of the church are sacramental rather than political in the strictly secular sense of this term. Gustafson explains that the church's common language (Scripture and creed) differentiates those who belong to the church from those who stand outside ecclesial boundaries, whereas Congar affirmed that communion with the Christian church can extend to people of goodwill who may never have heard the name of Jesus Christ and even to creatures of the earth that speak no human language at all.[116] Gustafson held that the church perdures in time as a continuous community through its use of ongoing textual interpretation, whereas Congar believed that the church's transgenerational unity comes primarily from the Spirit of God, who transcends the limits of space and time such that the church is not simply in continuity with Christians of ages past, but also in an actual ongoing relationship with the entire communion of saints. Finally, Gustafson held that the church is a community because it engages in purposive action, whereas for Congar the church must not simply undertake common action but rather specific *kinds* of communal actions: acts of sharing, fellowship, love, and the continuous praise and adoration of God. The sacramental theologian Michael Lawler explains his own preference for the term "communion" over the word "community" as follows: "History demonstrates the many human and ecclesial groups arrogating to themselves the name community, while giving absolutely no sign of any genuine human communication, communing, or communion."[117] The concept of community as used by Gustafson can apply with equal validity not only to the Christian church but also to the Nazi party, the Klu Klux Klan, or other such organizations whose orientation is fundamentally antithetical to the Gospel. The Nazi Party and the KKK are political organizations with a common language that undertake common actions—they meet Gustafson's definition of "community." They do not, however, meet the criteria of communion.

This is not to deny that the church has all the various features that Gustafson identified: the church does serve human needs, perdure through institutionalized patterns of relationship, share a common language, maintain continuity through textual interpretation, and undertake common action. But the church does all of these things with a theological intention that fundamentally reorients and reconfigures these activities in a manner that is best described with the language of communion. In the last chapter of *Treasure in Earthen Vessels*, Gustafson himself warns against sociological reductionism and reminds his readers that his book was not intended as a comprehensive ecclesiology. In this chapter, he, too, speaks of *koinōnia*:

> The common inner life of the Church is not only the effect of processes of internalization of objectified meanings. It is not only the subjective counterpart to the objective signs and marks of life given in institutional forms. It is *koinōnia*, a fellowship given by Jesus Christ and sustained by the activity of the Holy Spirit of God. It is a gift, and not just a natural outcome of a social process. God himself is present among men, and makes himself and his actions known in the common life of the Church.[118]

Gustafson translates *koinōnia* as "fellowship." He notes that the word "communion" is preferable, but he declines to use it to avoid confusion with the sacrament of the Eucharist.[119] From Congar's perspective, however, a concern for confusion is unfounded, for the sacramental connotations of the word "communion" enhance rather than detract from its ecclesiological usage. Precisely because of the liturgical connotations of this term, it is uniquely suited to express the mystery of God's presence, the gift of the Holy Spirit. This is not to suggest that ecclesiology and theological anthropology should use the language of communion to the exclusion of the language of community or society. Clearly, the church is both a communion and a community—or, as Congar said, "a communion in the form of a society."[120]

Indeed, Congar readily used the language not only of communion but also of community (*communauté*), and in the context of his constructive theology this term takes on many of the theological connotations of the New Testament *koinōnia*.[121] "Community" need not have the strictly sociological connotations Gustafson identifies with this term. In Congar's ecclesiology, this term assumes a deeper meaning precisely because Congar contextualizes this terminology within a trinitarian theology of communion. In turn, Congar's position that the church is both a communion and a society (or community) preserves his theology of the church from the weaknesses that Avery Dulles observes in ecclesiologies based strictly on the model of the church as a mystical communion. These ecclesiologies do not make clear the importance of the visible church and may fail to give Christians a clear sense of mission; they also tend to exalt and unduly divinize the church and can generate a tension between the church as a fellowship of interpersonal relations and the church as a mystical communion of grace.[122] Congar avoided these weaknesses and demonstrated that a theology of communion, grounded in strong trinitarian foundations and accompanied by an account of the church as a human society or community, can provide a strong foundation for a pneumatological ecclesiology. The church, he wrote, is a "communion of persons."[123]

Persons in Communion as an Appropriate Framework for Pneumatological Anthropology and Ecclesiology

The work of Congar, as well as that of the other theologians discussed, suggests that the most adequate theological framework for the integration of theological anthropology and ecclesiology is the paradigm of persons in communion. This paradigm is theologically more suitable than that of either "individuals and society" or "individuals and community." As Mounier, Maritain, Merton, and Zizioulas have demonstrated, the terms "person" and "individual" have different connotations, and the discussion of Gustafson and Congar has highlighted some of the different nuances that distinguish the discourse of community and communion. These differences are particularly important if contemporary theology is to follow Congar in the elaboration of a thoroughly pneumatological anthropology and ecclesiology. "Persons in communion" is a pneumatologically suitable paradigm, given the trinitarian foundations of Christian theology, the analogical nature of theological language, the apophatic character of theological speech, and the perichoretic quality of the persons in communion paradigm.

THE TRINITARIAN FOUNDATIONS OF CHRISTIAN THEOLOGY. Trinitarian theology is the formative context for theological anthropology and ecclesiology, and the trinitarian tradition typically speaks of Father, Son, and Spirit not as individuals but rather as persons. In fact, some theologians trace the very origin of the term "person" as used in Western culture to patristic theological discussions and the consequent elaboration of trinitarian and christological doctrine.[124] Tertullian, Athanasius, the Cappadocians, and others adopted the terms *persona, prosopon,* and *hypostasis* from Greco-Roman courtrooms and theaters, where these words had meant simply role or mask, and they gave these terms a new theological import and meaning. The Cappadocian formulation that God exists in the *hypostases* of Father, Son, and Spirit proved to be particularly influential. According to the historian R. P. C. Hanson, the Cappadocians used the term *hypostasis* to communicate that Father, Son, and Spirit all have their own irreducible realities.[125] In the context of later christological debates, Boethius did define *persona* as an individual substance of a rational nature, but he himself rarely used this concept with respect to God.[126] Richard of St. Victor sought an alternative theology of person that prescinded from use of the term "individual," and Thomas Aquinas noted that "individual" can be predicated of God only insofar as it means indivisible.[127] Aquinas himself described the persons of Father, Son, and Spirit as subsistent relations.[128]

The trinitarian tradition has emphasized not only the language of person but also the language of divine communion. Basil of Caesarea, for example, spoke of the communion (*koinōnia*) of the Spirit with the Father and the Son.[129] Contemporary theologians such as Jürgen Moltmann and other advocates of what has been called a social trinitarianism do use the language of society and community even when speaking of God.[130] Others caution, however, that this approach can be subject to a tritheistic misinterpretation. Catherine Mowry LaCugna maintained, moreover, that trinitarian theology reflects "a much deeper kind of communion than the word 'community' can possibly convey."[131] The profound communion of which LaCugna speaks is the work of the Spirit of God, and this mystery of communion is the proper context not only for trinitarian theology but also for pneumatological anthropology and ecclesiology.

THE ANALOGICAL NATURE OF THEOLOGICAL LANGUAGE. "Person" and "communion" are used in trinitarian theology in a manner analogical to the use of these terms in the realms of theological anthropology and ecclesiology. Within the Roman Catholic tradition, Aquinas's work has been particularly influential in clarifying the character of analogical discourse. Aquinas held that we cannot univocally predicate qualities such as goodness of both God and creature given the profound difference between God and the created order. Nor, however, are the affirmations "God is good" and "Mary is good" entirely equivocal, for the created order does participate in the goodness of God in a limited and creaturely manner. Qualities such as goodness that pertain to the divine essence can be predicated of both God and creature, but only in a manner proportionate to each—that is, analogically.[132] These qualities apply primarily and preeminently to God and secondarily to creatures.[133] Or, more precisely, the perfections that these terms signify (*res significata*) belong properly to God and less properly to creatures, whereas the limited human words used to comprehend and express these perfections (*modus significandi*) belong properly to creatures and do not strictly apply to God at all.[134]

Aquinas reflected on analogical method in *ST* I[a], q. 13 "On the Divine Names." Later, in *ST* I[a], q. 29 "On the Divine Persons," Aquinas considered the question "Whether the word 'person' should be said of God?" and he determined:

> "Person" signifies what is most perfect in all nature—that is, a subsistent individual of a rational nature. Hence, since everything that is perfect must be attributed to God, forasmuch as His essence con-

tains every perfection, this name *person* is fittingly applied to God; not, however, as it is applied to creatures, but in a more excellent way; as other names also, which, while giving them to creatures, we attribute to God; as we showed above when treating of the names of God (Q. 13, A.2).[135]

The perfection signified by the word "person" belongs properly to God, and human beings participate in this perfection in a limited manner that is proportionate to their creaturely status. In the preceding passage, Aquinas defined "person" in Boethius's sense as an individual of a rational nature, but it is interesting to note that Aquinas focused on "person" rather than "individual" as the term of his analogy between God and creature ("this name *person* is fittingly applied to God"). "Person" has served as an analogical bridge between trinitarian theology and theological anthropology in a way that the term "individual" has not.[136] The Reformed theologian Alan Torrance comments that "the concept of person is possibly the only concept that can be predicated properly and without the risk of anthropomorphism of both the divine and human realms."[137] The contemporary Thomist Norris Clarke considers "person" the primary analogate between God and the human creature, even as he attributes to the person an interpersonal and intersubjective character that he does not find explicit in Aquinas.[138]

THE APOPHATIC CHARACTER OF THEOLOGICAL SPEECH. Analogical speech has a strong apophatic dimension. Even as Aquinas affirmed that God and creature are both good, he denied that the human intellect can conceive of perfect goodness as it exists in God. Aquinas also negated the idea that the word "good" (the *modus significandi*) properly applies to God, even as he maintained that the perfection of goodness itself (the *res significata*) is properly divine. "The *via eminentiae*," David Tracy reflects, "is possible only on condition of its constant fidelity to the *via negationis*."[139] The *via negationis* has a long history in Christian theology and is currently the focus of renewed interest. Tracy notes "the contemporary rediscovery of the importance of radical apophaticism for all naming of God."[140]

Catherine Mowry LaCugna believed that an apophatic approach is particularly crucial to pneumatology, and she highlighted the suitability of the terms "person" and "communion" to the *via negativa*.[141] The *via negativa* is a path of knowing through *unknowing*, a movement away from our own fantasies, projections, and images and toward the true living God.[142] Words like "relation," "communion," and "person" are particularly suited to this apophatic way, since they point us away from ourselves and toward God and contribute to the ascetic discipline of the *via negativa*. In this movement of unknowing, the words "relation," "communion," and "person" must themselves be negated; yet, at the same time, they orient us toward God such that the way of unknowing is simultaneously a way of knowing—a way to enter into the divine presence. When we use the term "person" of God, LaCugna explained, we are not defining God but using a term that points beyond itself to the divine ineffability, and when we stand in awe of God's ineffability we are approaching true theological knowledge.[143]

LaCugna is not alone in noting the apophatic character of the terms "person" and "communion." Hanson suggests that the term *hypostasis* as used by the Cappadocians cannot be strictly defined other than to say that it means "*not* substance."[144] Studer and Hilberath, in like vein, have highlighted the apophatic character of Augustine's use of the word *persona* in his *De Trinitate*, where the term is used not to express difference but rather to deny singularity.[145] And Christos Yannaras believes the entire Orthodox tradition practices what he terms an "apophasis of the person."[146] Zizioulas reflects accordingly:

> [E]xactly as the Greek Fathers spoke of the divine persons, we cannot give a *positive qualitative content* to a hypostasis or person, for this would result in the loss of his absolute uniqueness and turn a person into a classifiable entity. . . . [A] true ontology of personhood requires that the uniqueness of a person escape and transcend any qualitative *kataphasis*.[147]

Zizioulas believes that the attempt to conceive of the human being as an *individuum* forces us toward definition, whereas the human person must be "approached as an indefinable being."[148] As we have seen, personalists like Mounier also stressed the indefinability of the person.

THE PERICHORETIC QUALITY OF THE PERSONS IN COMMUNION PARADIGM. The paradigm of persons in communion is theologically serviceable, not only because it is eminently apophatic but also because of its perichoretic quality. Contemporary theologians emphasize that to be a person—divine or human— is to exist in relationship and communion; communion, in turn, fosters the realization of each person's unique mystery.[149] To be a person *is* to exist in communion with others, and to exist in communion *is* to be a person. The paradigms of the "individual and community" or "individual and society," in contrast, tend to oppose the individual and the social body. Individuals and society often stand in an antagonistic relationship, such that emphasis on the individual detracts from the needs of the social body and emphasis on the society threatens individual fulfillment. According to Schillebeeckx, Cartesian dualism leads Westerners to perceive the individual and society as two independent entities, separated by a mysterious wall that cannot be precisely identified.[150] The enduring influence of seventeenth-century contract theories also shapes our use of the individual and society paradigm. Charles Taylor believes that social contract philosophy is so deeply entrenched in our thinking that we are habitual atomists, convinced that we exist first as individuals and only subsequently (if we so choose) as social bodies.[151] This is implicit in the discourse of "the individual *and* society." Trinitarian theology, in contrast, speaks of "persons *in* communion." The shift from "and" to "in" is telling. We do not first exist as persons and then only subsequently enter into communion, but, rather, person and communion are correlative terms.

In sum, Congar's theology of the Holy Spirit is better served by the paradigm of persons in communion than by the discourse of "individuals and community" or "individuals and society." The work of personalist thinkers such as Mounier, twentieth-century Thomists such as Maritain, spiritual writers such as Merton, and Orthodox theology as represented by Zizioulas suggests that there is an important distinction to be made between the "person" and the "individual." The ecclesiology of Congar as contrasted with Gustafson's sociology has likewise demonstrated that the terms "communion" and "community" may have different connotations. In a theological context, "person" connotes love, relationality, freedom, uniqueness, and ineffability, while "communion" connotes the grace of participation in the life of God through Christ and the Spirit. "Persons in communion" as a paradigm for pneumatological anthropology and ecclesiology expresses these realities and also serves theology's trinitarian, analogical, apophatic, and perichoretic character. "The line of words," Annie Dillard wrote, "is a miner's pick, a wood-carver's gouge, a surgeon's probe. You wield it, and it digs a path you follow. Soon you find yourself deep in new territory. Is it a dead end, or have you located the real subject?"[152] The words "person" and "communion," just like all our human language, are limited probes, but they are probes that may be able to lead into the mysterious territory of the Spirit.

The Person of the Holy Spirit and the Theology of Appropriations

This chapter concludes with a consideration of the contribution of Congar's theology of the Holy Spirit to contemporary discussions about the personhood of the Holy Spirit and the theology of appropriations. The Spirit is, in the words of von Balthasar, the "unknown one beyond the Word," and theologians have always struggled to describe who the Spirit is and in what sense the Spirit is a "person."[153] Moltmann is not alone in his view that the discernment of the Holy Spirit's personhood is the most difficult problem in trinitarian theology.[154] Congar's contributions to contemporary discussions about the personhood of the Holy Spirit and the theology of appropriations are twofold. First, Congar's theology of the Holy Spirit transforms the framework in which reflection on the *proprium* of the Holy Spirit and the theology of appropriations proceeded within Roman Catholic theology in the first half of the twentieth century. During this period, theologians debated whether the indwelling of the Spirit in the just soul is proper to the Spirit or simply appropriated. As this discussion proceeded, there was little explicit attention to the ecclesial context of this indwelling; Congar's pneumatology here offers an important corrective. Second, Congar's unshaken commitment to the use of a theology of appropriations can be instructive to those theologians of the second half of the twentieth century who criticized the appropriations methodology and sought other means to speak about the Holy Spirit's personhood. Congar used the appropriations tradition to highlight the absolute inseparability of the Holy Spirit from God (Father) and the Son, and this communion is an important truth that must be preserved even if contemporary theology no longer employs the method of appropriations.

Twentieth-Century Discussions of the Theology of Appropriations and the Indwelling of the Holy Spirit

Appropriation is the practice by which divine attributes, divine names, or divine activities that are absolutely common to the divine persons (and thus to the divine essence) are predicated of God (Father), Son, or Holy Spirit. The attribute of goodness and the activity of sanctification, for example, are typically appropriated to the Holy Spirit, although in fact the quality of goodness and the act of sanctification are not unique to the Spirit but rather are shared by the Father and the Son. In contrast, the relations that distinguish the divine persons from one another—paternity/filiation and spiration/procession—result in what are called "personal notions" that are uniquely proper (*proprium*) to each: paternity is proper to God, filiation to the Son, and procession to the Holy Spirit. These personal notions are constitutive of the persons of Father, Son, and Spirit in a way that merely appropriated qualities are not. Ideally, there is to be a fittingness between the attributes or activities that are attributed to Father, Son, and Spirit and a divine person's true *proprium*. According to Aquinas, for example, goodness is common to all the divine persons but fittingly appropriated to the Spirit, for the spiration of the Spirit is an act of love, and goodness is love's nature and object.[155] Strictly speaking, however, an appropriated quality, name, or activity does not express the uniqueness of the Spirit's person or tell us who the Spirit is.

The history of the theology of appropriations is recounted differently by different theologians. Scholars disagree, for example, on the status of the theology of appropriations in Patristic literature. De Régnon does not find a theory of appropriations in the Greek theology of the third and fourth centuries, while Paul Galtier affirms that there is an implicit theology of appropriations in Basil of Caesarea, Gregory of Nyssa, Didymus the Blind, John Chrysostom, and Cyril of Alexandria, although he acknowledges that the term "appropriation" does not appear in early Greek patristic texts.[156] Some reviewers of Galtier's work believe that his reading of Greek theology is overly influenced by his own theological commitments.[157] Within the Latin tradition, both contemporary theologians and medieval authorities such as Aquinas trace the theology of appropriations to Hilary of Poitiers and Augustine, although in fact Hilary and Augustine do not expressly use the term "appropriation."[158] Richard of St. Victor (d. c. 1173) offers one of the earliest explicit attestations of this terminology in his treatise De tribus appropriatis, and, a century later, Aquinas defined appropriation as a "manifestation of the divine persons by the use of the essential attributes."[159] The Council of Florence (1438–1445) made another important contribution to the theology of appropriations with their promulgation of the axiom In Deo omnia sunt unum, ubi non obviat relationis oppositio. This axiom was intended to counter the tritheism of the Jacobites, but it also bolstered the theology of appropriations, for it suggested that the uniqueness of the divine persons consists only in the relationis oppositio (paternity/filiation, spiration/ procession); by implication, all other divine activities, names, and attributes cannot be predicated properly of Father, Son, or Spirit but must be strictly appropriated.[160] This Florentine axiom and a modified version of Aquinas's theology of appropriations were incorporated into the neoscholastic theological manuals that were the basis for Roman Catholic seminary education from the late nineteenth century until Vatican II.

In the decades prior to Vatican II, the theology of appropriations was an ongoing topic of conversation. Theologians debated whether the divine indwelling of God in the souls of the justified entailed a divine presence proper (proprium) to the person of the Holy Spirit or whether we can speak of the indwelling of the Spirit only in an appropriated sense.[161] Most theologians writing on this issue took the position that the divine indwelling was technically an indwelling of God and therefore only appropriated to the Holy Spirit.[162] A leading argument on their behalf was the aforementioned Florentine axiom— In Deo omnia sunt unum, ubi non obviat relationis oppositio—from which it was deduced that the divine activity ad extra was absolutely and indistinguishably common to God (Father), Son, and Spirit.[163] Some theologians, however, did take the position that sanctifying grace entails a nonappropriated indwelling of the Spirit.[164] Johannes Beumer supported this position with references to the Pauline texts that speak of the soul as the temple of the Spirit, not the temple of the Father or the temple of the Son,[165] while Malachi Donnelly argued that the Florentine axiom applied only to God's actions by means of efficient causality in the order of creation, not to God's quasi-formal causality proper to the supernatural order of grace.[166] Still others tried to develop a middle position between the appopriation and the proprium theologies.[167]

Notably, even those theologians who endorsed some form of a nonappropriated indwelling of the Spirit could affirm an indwelling proper to the Spirit only in a limited sense. Scheeben, for example, argued for a nonappropriated relation of the just soul to the Holy Spirit but denied that the Holy Spirit has a nonappropriated activity in the economy of salvation.[168] De Letter took a similar position; he affirmed three "special or distinct relations" of the just soul to the three divine Persons but at the same time held that the activity of sanctification is absolutely common to Father, Son, and Spirit and can only be appropriated to the Holy Spirit. The result is such a limited sense of the indwelling Spirit's *proprium* that de Letter himself wondered whether this theology of appropriated activity and distinct relations was in fact simply a continuation of a pure appropriations theology in a different guise:

> But it may, and must, be asked: Does this manner of conceiving our special relations to each of the three divine Persons say or mean anything more than the appropriation theory? Since the three "do" exactly the same thing, as far as doing means producing a reality, the whole idea of a special relation to each of the three or of a special role (which is only a relation of mere reason in them) of each of the three seems, to put it bluntly, to boil down to a question of mere words. Is there a difference of realities?[169]

There were many dimensions to this theological discussion: the meaning of the *ad intra* and *ad extra* distinction employed in trinitarian theology, the character of divine causality, the meaning of created grace, and so forth.[170] Much of this is beyond the scope of this chapter. Here, I would simply like to illustrate one way in which Congar's advocacy of a pneumatological anthropology and a pneumatological ecclesiology could have enhanced this debate on the theology of appropriations.

When one peruses the literature generated by this discussion in light of Congar's theology of the Holy Spirit, it is striking that all parties concerned—both those who abided by a strictly appropriated account of the Spirit's indwelling and those who advocated some form of a proper indwelling—limited their reflection to consideration of the divine indwelling in the just soul abstracted from interpersonal or ecclesial relationships. De Letter's article "Sanctifying Grace and Our Union with the Holy Trinity" illustrates this common practice. De Letter argued that there is a special (that is, nonappropriated) relation between the graced human person and each of the three divine persons—Father, Son, and Holy Spirit. In the course of his article, he spoke exclusively of the relation between the human soul and God—the "union of the essence of the soul with the essence of God," the "supernatural relation . . . from the soul to God," the "supernatural presence of God in the just soul," and so forth.[171] All told, de Letter made thirty references to the union of God and the soul and no explicit references to the union of Christians with one another in the life of the church.[172] In the conclusion of the article, de Letter did address the "practical import of special [i.e., nonappropriated] relations [i.e., of the soul to each of the divine persons]," but here again he said nothing about ecclesiology. He observed only that the trinitarian pattern of supernatural relations that he has set forth can provide a theological foundation for the devotional life of Christians who spontaneously take different attitudes to Father, Son, and Spirit.[173]

Malachi Donnelly shared de Letter's commitment to a theology of non-appropriated indwelling, but he responded to de Letter's article with a critique of what he perceived as an insufficient emphasis on created grace and an extrinsic, rather than intimate, account of the soul's communion with God.[174] Yet Donnelly, too, presumed that the relation between God and the soul was an adequate framework for the discussion of sanctifying grace. He spoke of the "inhabitation of the Holy Spirit in the just soul" and of "Uncreated Grace, the loving guest of every just soul." Like de Letter, Donnelly made no explicit reference to interpersonal relationships or ecclesial life. This is also largely true of Donnelly's other articles, which are not constrained by his intention of responding to de Letter's position, although, in the conclusion to an article on M. J. Scheeben's theology of indwelling, Donnelly does state:

> As brought out in [Scheeben's] *Mysterien*, the holiness of the soul is
> like the twofold holiness of a church. First hallowed by the bishop's
> seal and consecration, the church receives an additional holiness
> with the entrance of the Blessed Sacrament. Similarly, to the essen-
> tial and *in se* perfect holiness which the soul has through created
> grace the advent of uncreated grace adds a super-fullness of sanctity
> which can be had only through substantial cohesion with God.[175]

Even in this reference to the church as an analogue to the just soul, however, Donnelly speaks of the church as a cathedral or building and does not develop the idea of the church as the *communio sanctorum* or the *populus Dei*.

De Letter, Donnelly, and other writers of this period surely presumed an ecclesial context, even though there is very little or no explicit reference to ecclesial communion in their reflections on divine indwelling. Congar's pneumatology, in contrast, makes this ecclesial context explicit, and therefore he can offer a more relational and sacramental account of the sanctifying grace of the Spirit. In light of Congar's work, a theology of indwelling that focuses strictly on God and the soul appears anthropologically and ecclesiologically incomplete. Congar's theology of the Holy Spirit provides a new framework in which to consider the appropriation debate and suggests new possibilities for describing the *proprium* of the Spirit. The activity of the Spirit in the economy of sanctification is an eminently ecclesial activity, a mission to gather all creatures into communion with God and with one another. Paul's conversion, for example, impelled him to found churches in Corinth, Ephesus, and Rome; the indwelling of the Spirit in the soul of Paul did not take place in abstraction or isolation from others but in communion with Peter, Cornelius, Chloe, Crispus, Gaius, and Stephanas. Indeed, William Hill suggests that an affirmation of the Spirit's *proprium* requires "an awareness of the activity of the Holy Spirit as having its locus not in the individual but within the communal sphere of the ecclesial community."[176] It is notable that Heribert Mühlen, the contemporary theologian who has made the most detailed and extensive argument for a non-appropriated activity of the Holy Spirit, has accomplished this precisely by combining pneumatology with ecclesiology and a phenomenology of interpersonal relations.[177] Mühlen believes that the Spirit's distinct *proprium* is to be "one person in many persons"—one person in the *perichōresis* of the Father and Son and one person in Christ and in Christians.

Contemporary Discussion of the Viability of the Theology of Appropriations

In 1953, de Letter spoke of a current dissatisfaction with the appropriations theory "apparently inspired by the thirst for realism and the aversion to nominalism which are characteristic of our time."[178] As contemporary theologians develop alternatives to the neoscholastic methodologies that predominated until Vatican II, they have expressed further dissatisfactions with the appropriations approach. Indeed, the fundamental issue of discussion is no longer whether divine indwelling is proper to the Holy Spirit or strictly appropriated but whether the theology of appropriations is itself viable as a theological methodology. Heribert Mühlen believed that the method of ascribing the divine activities *ad extra* to Father, Son, or Spirit only by appropriation is antithetical to Scripture.[179] Karl Rahner argued that an exclusive use of the doctrine of appropriations to speak of the divine persons *ad extra* violates the principle that revelation is the self-communication of God; if God exists as Father, Son, and Spirit, then God thereby communicates God's self in the economy in the persons of Father, Son, and Spirit in a sense proper to each.[180] Catherine Mowry LaCugna believed that the axiom of the Council of Florence has been especially problematic in pneumatology; in conjunction with the *Filioque*, she maintained that the Florentine axiom has obscured the *proprium* of the Holy Spirit in the economy of salvation.[181] Other theologians who have no explicit critique of the theology of appropriations have simply dropped this method and terminology from their works.

Clearly there is a need not only to reevaluate the theology of appropriations but also to determine what contribution this approach has made to trinitarian theology so that this contribution can be preserved even if the method and language of appropriations are no longer employed. It is in this latter respect that Congar's pneumatology is particularly helpful. Congar himself consistently defended the theology of appropriations even as he acknowledged its shortcomings, for he believed this theology was consonant with the perennial affirmation of both East and West that Father, Son, and Spirit are one. His qualified defense of the theology of appropriations reminds contemporary theologians that the Holy Spirit is utterly inseparable from the Father and the Son and exists in consummate communion. If contemporary theology dispenses with the theology of appropriations because of its limitations, it must find some other manner to preserve this truth. Without the theology of appropriations, there is a danger that trinitarian theology may portray Father, Son, and Spirit as a numerical threesome, or a community of individuals. LaCugna advised against a tendency in contemporary theology to overhypostasize the Spirit and cautioned: "[W]e must remember that the Spirit never stands alone. In the enthusiasm to remedy our 'forgetfulness' of the Spirit, we might find ourselves 'singling out' the Spirit in an artificial way, as if the Spirit of God, Spirit of Christ exists by itself."[182] Congar's adherence to the theology of appropriations is an important reminder that the Spirit cannot be singled out, for the Spirit is the Spirit of God and the Spirit of Jesus Christ. Contemporary reflections on the personhood of the Spirit must bear this in mind. In this light, Mühlen's discussion of the Holy Spirit as "one person in many persons" (in God, in Jesus Christ, and in us) appears particularly valuable, for Mühlen describes the uniqueness of the Spirit's person not by hypostasizing the Spirit apart from God, Jesus Christ, or human persons but rather by speaking of the Spirit's activity precisely in terms of the communion of persons with one another. Kilian McDonnell's formulation that Jesus Christ is the "what" of the Gospel and the Holy Spirit the "how" also offers a way to affirm the centrality of the mission of the Spirit without separating the activity of the Spirit from that of Jesus Christ.[183] Congar's theology of the Holy Spirit reminds us that we must speak of the person of the Spirit in such a manner that the communion of the Spirit with God and Jesus Christ is never eclipsed. Any theological formulation that explicitly or implicitly separates the Spirit from God and Christ is ultimately not an affirmation of the Spirit's distinct personhood but a negation of the Spirit's person and activity of communion.

Conclusion

The theology of the Holy Spirit of the French Dominican Yves Congar is a milestone in Roman Catholic theology. Congar recognized the importance of the reunification of spiritual anthropology and ecclesiology, and he himself contributed to this reunion through his *anthropologie pneumatologique* and *ecclésiologie pneumatologique*. From the Reformation through the twentieth century, much of Catholic theology divorced these two domains of theological reflection. Theologians and spiritual writers reflected on the indwelling of the Holy Spirit in the human soul and the consequent bestowal of spiritual gifts and fruits but assumed that this indwelling had no significant consequences for the life, mission, and structure of the church. In the era of Congar's youth, as we have seen, the neoscholastic manuals used in seminary curricula set forth a treatise, *De Gratia*, that described at some length the indwelling of the Spirit in the human soul. This treatise stood in juxtaposition to the treatise *De Ecclesia*, which typically referred to the Spirit simply as the guarantor of the authority of the magisterium and the authenticity of tradition; in some cases, Congar observed, *De Ecclesia* treatises made no mention of the Holy Spirit at all. The result was a juridical ecclesiology inconsistent with biblical theology and the best of the patristic and medieval traditions. The spiritual disciplines of prayer, ethical practice, and ascesis and the spiritual gifts of faith, hope, and love seemed strangely extraneous to the structure of the church, which seemed to hover above the faithful as an autonomous reality defined by its own system of authority.

Congar's entire theological career was tirelessly and passionately devoted to the renewal of the Catholic Church and the reunion of a Christian family fragmented into denominational divisions. In the 1970s and 1980s, Congar's scholarly attention turned increasingly to the theology of the Holy Spirit, and his vision for ecclesial renewal took an expressly pneumatological form. Drawing from his biblical study, patristic and medieval *ressourcement*, the inspiration of Möhler, ecumenical encounters, and the event of the Second Vatican Council, Congar called for an *ecclésiologie pneumatologique* united to an *anthropologie pneumatologique*.

This theological vision, as we have seen, was dependent on a broad trinitarian framework, a pneumatological Christology, and a theology of grace, such as those of de Lubac and Rahner, in which grace is not extrinsic to the human being created in the *imago Dei*, even as grace transcends and surpasses our creaturely condition and existence. In this framework, Congar articulated a communitarian anthropology in which to-be is to-be-in-relation to God and one another (*être-à, être-pour*). He understood our fall into sin as a fracture of the relationality that was our intended destiny, and he described grace as the healing of these broken relationships and the elevation of human existence to a new level of participation in the life of God. For Congar, the Incarnation of the Word of God and the gift of the Holy Spirit are events of a communion between God and creature so profound that we scarcely have the words to speak of these mysteries. Incorporated into Christ through the power of the Spirit, we become sons and daughters of God in a very real sense. "We are truly deified!" Congar exclaimed.[1] His pneumatological anthropology presents a vision of human persons transformed by grace like iron glowing in fire. Through the indwelling of the Holy Spirit, human persons know and love with the very knowledge and love of God. We are called to live in communion and holiness through cooperation with the grace of the Spirit of Christ, a vocation that has radical implications for our daily life, our ecclesial life, and the responsibilities of Christians in a world fractured by injustice, hatred, and division.

We begin to realize this eschatological destiny in the church. The Spirit of God is given to us not as individuals but as persons in communion with one another, persons united through the common praise and worship of God, whose grace we implore with our prayer of epiclesis. A pneumatological anthropology requires a pneumatological ecclesiology—an account of the indwelling of the Holy Spirit in the sacramental, communitarian, and missionary life of the *ecclesia*. Fundamental to Congar's pneumatological ecclesiology as it developed in the last decades of his life is his conviction that there is no reified church apart from the persons of the baptized themselves. Ordained ministers have a unique role in the church as mediators of God's grace, but they exercise this role not removed from or above the body of the faithful but rather in communion with all the baptized, apart from whom they can stand neither *in persona Ecclesiae* nor *in persona Christi*. Congar's pneumatological ecclesiology is neither a congregationalism in which individuals touched privately by the

Spirit join together in common cause nor a hierarchology in which some persons have the autonomous power to dispense God's grace to others. Rather, it is a complex theology of the church that takes the communitarian character of both nature and grace with utmost seriousness. The Spirit of Christ acts through relationships of mutuality and communion.

This is a theocentric vision that emphasizes our dependence on God, our orientation toward God, and our destiny to share the very life of God through Christ and the Spirit. It is a vision that respects our character as active subjects and requires our commitment to conversion and our disciplined participation in the new life of the Spirit. It is a profoundly sacramental vision in which baptism and Eucharist remake us as the body of Christ and the temple of the Holy Spirit. It is a vision of the church as a dynamic communion of persons rooted in the event of Incarnation and bearing an eschatological orientation. Ceaselessly co-instituted throughout history by Christ and the Spirit, the church is open to new interpretations of revelation and new developments as it lives from the Spirit of the glorified Christ. This is an ecclesial vision in which all the baptized are indispensable members of the church, each bringing gifts and talents that become part of the *plērōma* of Christ, a vision in which charisms are not simply a matter of personal spiritual enrichment but gifts that contribute to the very constitution of the church. It is a vision that celebrates and welcomes diversity, striving toward a catholicity that is inclusive of all God's creatures, each of which bears its own particularity and uniqueness. Indeed, it is an ecclesiology with cosmic scope that incorporates not only human persons but all God's creatures. It is a vision of a church governed through conciliarity and reception as it seeks to discern the counsel of the Spirit of Christ, who is active in all its members. Moreover, it is a theology in which the church is not self-oriented or self-concerned but turned in mission toward a world of suffering humanity and turned in praise and worship toward God.

The theological and ecclesial landscape at the dawn of this new twenty-first century differs from that of the dawn of the twentieth. The neoscholastic ecclesiology that dominated Roman Catholicism in 1904, when Congar was born, is no longer standard seminary fare. The Second Vatican Council was a remarkable *aggiornamento* of the Roman Catholic Church that bore fruit in liturgical reform, a dramatic increase in the active participation of all the faithful in the life of the church, the development of new forms of ministry and new possibilities for ecumenism and interreligious dialogue, and a commitment of the church to embrace the joys and sorrows of all humanity and to work for God's kingdom of justice and peace. Congar's legacy can be seen in all of these developments.

Nonetheless, forty years after the Council, there is no consensus in the Catholic Church about the meaning of this council and no common ecclesial vision for the future. Disagreement persists about church structure, ministry, the relation of the local and universal church, issues of gender and sexuality, liturgy, and matters of ecumenism and interreligious dialogue. There is evidence, moreover, that the reunion of spiritual anthropology and ecclesiology that Congar envisioned has yet to be realized in the actual lived experience of many Catholics.

The most public manifestation of this failure is the scandal perpetrated by a number of sexually abusive clergy and those bishops who knowingly moved abusive priests from one position to another with an apparent lack of concern for their victims—men and women whose lives have been broken by this violation of their personal integrity and holiness. Another symptom of the continuing disjunction of spiritual anthropology and ecclesiology is the refrain one often hears (especially among young Catholics) that "I am spiritual but not religious" or that "I am spiritual but not interested in institutional religion." This common attitude may reflect the individualism of our culture, but it also suggests that many people sincerely have not found spiritual nourishment in churches. It is an indication of the importance of ecclesial reform rooted in the principle of the reintegration of spirituality and ecclesiology that Congar advocated. Meanwhile, the world again faces the very scourge of war that propelled Congar as a young man in France to seek a sacerdotal vocation such that he might preach conversion to humanity. Our world threatened by injustice, violence, and ecological degradation is in dire need of the moral leadership and hope that the Christian church should be able to offer. The exalted vision of Christian life that Congar sets forth—a vision of deification, of participation in the very life and love of God through the Spirit of Christ—sets the failings of Christianity in stark relief. Congar's theology of the Holy Spirit reveals to us how far we have fallen from our vocation and reminds us that life in the Spirit begins with repentance and conversion.

In our current context, Congar's theology of the Holy Spirit can serve theology and the church at many different levels. His work, of course, has its limitations. He did not have intellectual training or personal experience in many of the important issues demanding the attention of theologians today— postmodernism, interreligious dialogue, feminism, conversations between theology and science, and so forth. Nonetheless, his vision of the reunification of spiritual anthropology and ecclesiology—a vision solidly rooted in the biblical, patristic, and medieval traditions—is an important contribution that together with other voices can guide and inspire work to build the church of the twenty-first century. As indicated in chapter 5, Congar's legacy can help build common ground between those in the church who advocate ecclesial democracy and those who call for hierarchical structure; it also supports the articulation of "persons in communion" as a broad framework for theological reflection and contributes to a heightened consciousness of the profoundly communitarian character of the person and activity of the Holy Spirit. Congar's vision of the reintegration of spirituality and ecclesiology also has the potential to bear fruit in areas not explored in these pages—sacramental theology, ecumenism,

Christian ethics, and a wide variety of specific topics within the discipline of ecclesiology.

Congar compared his theological labor to the stretching and tuning of the strings of a harp; such labor was the austere task of research. The Spirit, he hoped, would make of this human labor a true song of prayer and life, blowing over his taut chords to create music, beauty, and harmony. In the preceding pages, I have tried to stretch once again the strings that Congar tuned so finely, attempting to summarize, analyze, and synthesize the primary components of his theology of the Holy Spirit. The result is simply words on paper. The reality of which Congar spoke—the Gift of God of whom he testified—cannot be circumscribed in words but can be implored in prayer. "*Veni Sancte Spiritus* . . . Come, Holy Spirit, and send out a ray of your heavenly light."

Notes

AER	American Ecclesiastical Review
Ang	Angelicum
AugustinStud	Augustinian Studies
CBQ	Catholic Biblical Quarterly
Comm	Commonweal
Conc	Concilium
CT	Ciencia Tomista
CTSAP	Catholic Theological Society of America Proceedings
DCom	Doctor Communis
DTC	Dictionnaire de théologie catholique (1910–1950) Paris
EphThL	Ephemerides Theologicae Lovanienses
Fran	Franciscanum
Heythrop	Heythrop Journal
IPQ	International Philosophical Quarterly
Iren	Irénikon
ITQ	Irish Theological Quarterly
JEcSt	Journal of Ecumenical Studies
JRel	Journal of Religion
JTS	Journal of Theological Studies
LG	Lumen gentium
Lumen	Lumen vitae
M-D	La Maison-Dieu
MThZ	Münchener theologische Zeitschrift
NatCathRep	National Catholic Reporter
NewBlckfrs	New Blackfriars
NRT	Nouvelle revue théologique
PG	Migne, Patrologia Graeca

PL	Migne, *Patrologia Latina*
POC	*Proche orient chrétien*
RSR	*Recherches de science religieuse*
RAM	*Revue d'ascétique et de mystique*
REtAug	*Revue des études Augustiniennes*
RevTh	*Revue thomiste*
RHPR	*Revue d'histoire et de philosophie religieuses*
RRel	*Review for Religious*
RSPhTh	*Revue des sciences philosophiques et théologiques*
SCG	Aquinas, *Summa Contra Gentiles*
SChr	*Sources chrétiennes*
ScotJTh	*Scottish Journal of Theology*
ST	Aquinas, *Summa Theologiae*
SVS	*Supplément de la vie spirituelle*
SVTQ	*St. Vladimir's Theological Quarterly*
TheoDgst	*Theology Digest*
Thom	*The Thomist*
ThPh	*Theologie und Philosophie*
ThQ	*Theologische Quartalschrift*
ThToday	*Theology Today*
TI	Rahner, *Theological Investigations*
TS	*Theological Studies*
VieI	*Vie intellectuelle*
VS	*Vie spirituelle*
ZNW	*Zeitschrift für Neutestamentliche Wissenschaft*

INTRODUCTION

1. Yves Congar, *I Believe in the Holy Spirit*, 3 vols., trans. David Smith (New York: Seabury Press, 1983), 2:17.

2. Congar, *I Believe*, 2:92.

3. Congar, *The Word and the Spirit*, trans. David Smith (San Francisco: Harper and Row, 1986), 5.

4. Congar, *Word and Spirit*, 82.

5. For bibliography see Petro F. Chirico, *The Divine Indwelling and Distinct Relations to the Indwelling Persons in Modern Theological Discussion* (Rome: Pontificiae Universitatis Gregoriana, 1960).

6. Congar, "The Council as an Assembly and the Church as Essentially Conciliar," in *One, Holy, Catholic and Apostolic. Studies on the Nature and Role of the Church in the Modern World*, ed. Herbert Vorgrimler (London: Sheed and Ward, 1968), 45. Congar also offered anecdotal evidence of the eclipse of the Holy Spirit from ecclesiology. He recalled that a theologian of repute said to one of the *periti* at the Second Vatican Council, "You speak of the Holy Spirit, but that is for the Protestants. We have the teaching authority." Congar, "Pneumatology Today," *AER* 167 (1973): 436.

7. The emphasis on the Spirit as the guarantor of the church's inerrancy has been dominant in Roman Catholic theology since the Reformation. See Congar, *I Believe*, 1:151–52.

8. Congar, "Pneumatology Today," 439.

9. Congar, *I Believe*, 1:154.

10. Adolphe Tanquerey, *Brevior synopsis theologiae dogmaticae*, 9th ed. (Paris: Des-clée, 1952), 516–17 and 510. The original edition of the *synopsis* was published in 1931.

11. Tanquerey, *Brevior synopsis*, 103–4, 115, and 123. In "The Constitution of the Catholic Church," the immediately subsequent treatise, the Spirit is mentioned only twice, described as the vivifying soul of the mystical body of Christ. Tanquerey, 498–506.

12. Cardinal Henry Edward Manning, *The Internal Mission of the Holy Ghost* (London: Burns and Oates, 1895), 2–3.

13. Manning, *Internal Mission*, 2.

14. Cardinal Henry Edward Manning, *The Temporal Mission of the Holy Ghost* (London: Burns and Oates, 1909), 3.

15. Congar, *I Believe*, 1:156.

16. Congar, *I Believe*, 1:155–57. See also Congar, "Actualité de la pneumatologie," in *Credo in Spiritum Sanctum*, ed. P. José Saraiva Martins (Vatican City: Libreria Editrice Vaticana, 1983), 15. On the influence of Manning in North America, see Joseph P. Chinnici, O.F.M., *Devotion to the Holy Spirit in American Catholicism* (New York: Paulist, 1985), 16–34.

17. Barthélemy Froget, *De l'inhabitation du S. Esprit dans les âmes justes* (Paris: Leithielleux, 1890). Bede Jarret published a summary of Froget's work as *The Abiding Presence of the Holy Ghost in the Soul* (New York: Cathedral Library Association, 1918; Westminster, MD: Newman, 1957). Sydney Raemers later published the complete translation: *The Indwelling of the Holy Spirit in the Souls of the Just* (Baltimore, MD: Carroll, 1950).

18. Francis Blunt, *Life with the Holy Ghost: Thoughts on the Gifts of the Holy Ghost* (Milwaukee: Bruce, 1943); James Carroll, *God the Holy Ghost* (New York: P. J. Kenedy and Sons, 1940); G. F. Holden, *The Holy Ghost the Comforter* (London: Longmans, Green and Co., 1907); Edward Leen, *The Holy Ghost and His Work in Souls* (New York: Sheed and Ward, 1937); Luis M. Martínez, *El Espiritu Santo* (Mexico City: n.p., 1939), trans. M. Aquinas, *The Sanctifier* (Paterson, NJ: St. Anthony Guild, 1957).

19. Congar, *Tradition and Traditions: An Historical and a Theological Essay*, trans. Michael Naseby and Thomas Rainborough (London: Burns and Oates, 1966), 397.

20. Congar, *The Mystery of the Temple*, trans. Reginald F. Trevett (London: Burns and Oates, 1962), 153.

21. Congar, "The Council as Assembly and the Church as Essentially Conciliar," 59. On this point see also Congar's *Power and Poverty in the Church*, trans. Jennifer Nicholson (Baltimore: Helicon, 1964), 97.

22. Congar, "The Idea of the Church in St. Thomas Aquinas," *Thom* 1 (1939): 359. See also 339, 348, and 358.

23. Congar, "Le Saint-Esprit dans la théologie thomiste de l'agir moral," in *L'Agire morale. Atti del Congresso internazionale: Tommaso d'Aquino nel suo Settimo Centenario* (Naples: Edizioni Domenicane Italiane, 1974), 5:16.

24. Congar, *I Believe*, 2:66.

25. See Congar, "The Church: The People of God," *Conc* 1 (1964): 22 n. 13; "Preface" to Ignace de la Potterie and S. Lyonnet, *La Vie selon l'Esprit* (Paris: Cerf, 1965), 11; "Pneumatology Today," 435.

26. Congar, "The Council as Assembly and the Church as Essentially Conciliar," 59.

27. Congar, *I Believe*, 2:92.

28. Conversation with Hervé Legrand, O.P., upon the occasion of his visit to the University of Notre Dame, Fall 1997.

29. Peter Steinfels, *New York Times* (12 August 1995): 9.

30. Congar, *I Believe*, 1:x.

CHAPTER I

1. In Jean-Pierre Jossua, *Yves Congar: Theology in Service of God's People* (Chicago: Priory Press, 1968), 44.

2. Congar, *Blessed Is the Peace of My Church*, trans. Salvator Attanasio (Denville, NJ: Dimension Books, 1973), 99.

3. Robert Gildea, *The Past in French History* (New Haven: Yale University Press, 1994), 219.

4. Congar, *Blessed Is the Peace of My Church*, 99.

5. Congar, *Blessed Is the Peace of My Church*, 99. See also 9.

6. Congar, "Les Trois âges de la vie spirituelle," *VS* 92 (1955): 119.

7. Puyo, *Une vie pour la vérité. Jean Puyo interroge le Père Congar* (Paris: Centurion, 1975), 14. See also "Ardennes," in Henri Dubief and Jacques Poujol, *La France Protestante* (Montpellier: M. Chaleil, 1992), 233–38.

8. Puyo, *Une vie pour la vérité*, 73.

9. Congar, *Journal de la guerre 1914–1918* (Paris: Cerf, 1997), 30.

10. Congar, *Journal de la guerre*, 293.

11. Puyo, *Une vie pour la vérité*, 7.

12. Puyo, *Une vie pour la vérité*, 15.

13. Puyo, *Une vie pour la vérité*, 15.

14. Puyo, *Une vie pour la vérité*, 16.

15. Puyo, *Une vie pour la vérité*, 16.

16. Puyo, *Une vie pour la vérité*, 21.

17. Eugene Masure, *Le Sacrifice du Chef* (Paris: Beauchesne, 1932).

18. Congar, *Fifty Years of Catholic Theology: Conversations with Yves Congar*, ed. Bernard Lauret, trans. John Bowden (Philadelphia: Fortress, 1988), 20. I have not been able to locate a Tennyson poem that actually contains this verse. The verse does not appear in Arthur Baker's *A Concordance to the Poetical and Dramatic Works of Alfred, Lord Tennyson* (London: K. Paul Trench, Trübner and Co., 1914).

19. Congar, Preface to *Dialogue between Christians*, trans. Philip Loretz (Westminster, MD: Newman Press, 1966), 3.

20. Congar, "Letter from Father Yves Congar, O.P.," *TheoDgst* 32 (1985): 213. "Since then," Congar wrote elsewhere, "God knows how many times I have read it and even prayed it." *Fifty Years*, 79.

21. "The Unity of the Church" was the title of Congar's lectorate thesis, a Dominican requirement. This 1931 thesis was never published. In a note written to Cornelis van Vliet through the mediation of Hervé Legrand, Congar dismissed the thesis as one of the universe's many scholastic treatises on Thomas Aquinas. Cornelis van

Vliet, *Communio sacramentalis: Das Kirchenverständnis von Yves Congar—genetisch und systematisch betrachtet* (Mainz: Matthias-Grünewald, 1995), 61 n. 132.

22. Puyo, *Une vie pour la vérité*, 75.

23. Congar, Preface to *Dialogue between Christians*, 5–7 n. 5.

24. Congar, "The Reasons for the Unbelief of Our Time," *Integration* (August–September 1938 and December 1938–January 1939): 13–21 and 10–26. This is a translation of an essay Congar had been asked to write as a conclusion to *Vie intellectuelle*'s three-year series "Causes of Unbelief." See Yves Congar, "Une conclusion théologique à l'enquête sur les raisons actuelles de l'incroyance," *Viel* 37 (1935): 214–49.

25. Thomas F. O'Meara, O.P., "Ecumenist of Our Times: Yves Congar," *Mid-Stream* 28 (1988): 67. O'Meara described Congar thus after meeting him at Vatican II.

26. Puyo, *Une vie pour la vérité*, 45–47.

27. On *ressourcement* see Congar, "Chronique," in Congar, *Sainte Église. Études et approches ecclésiologiques*, Unam Sanctam, no. 41 (Paris: Cerf, 1963), 553–54.

28. Étienne Fouilloux, "Frère Yves, Cardinal Congar, dominicain. Itinéraire d'un théologien," *RSPhTh* 79 (1995): 381.

29. *Unam Sanctam*'s first volume included a flyer that introduced the series and described its goal. This announcement was not signed by Congar, but, as van Vliet observes, it certainly bears his stamp and expresses his theological vision. Copies of this prospectus are very difficult to find, so van Vliet has reproduced the French text in full in the appendix of *Communio sacramentalis*. Here is a translation of an excerpt:

> UNAM SANCTAM. These words of the creed are the title of a collection of studies on the Church, published by Editions du Cerf. The idea for this collection was born from a double concern. On the one hand, when one reflects on the great problems of Catholic life and expansion, on modern unbelief and indifference, and finally on the reunion of separated Christians, one is led to think that the amelioration of the present state of affairs, in so far as it depends on us, requires that a large, rich, vibrant, fully biblical and traditional idea of the Church penetrate Christianity: first the clergy, then the elite Christians, then the entire body. On the other hand, an incontestable renewal of the idea of the Church is manifest on all sides where, as it is normal, the impulse of interior and apostolic life precedes theology. Naturally the desire is born to respond to the need that one has perceived, to serve a movement that is manifestly sustained by the Holy Spirit. These two aspects at root call forth the same response: an intellectual effort directed to a truly broad, living and serious theology of the Church. This is the work that, for its part, without belittling the merit of other similar publications, *Unam Sanctam* wishes to pursue.
>
> This intention shapes the character and breadth of the effort. *Unam Sanctam* does not conduct pure history, nor apologetics, nor current analysis, nor missiology, nor liturgy, nor practical ecumenism; although all this obviously concerns the Church and can not, for this very fact, be entirely foreign to her. *Unam Sanctam* rather intends to make known the nature or if you will the mystery of the Church; historical works can here have their place, and even liturgical and missiological considerations, and also studies

concerning separated Christians and the problem of their reunion, *in so far* as such research serves a richer and more profound knowledge of the Church in her intimate nature and in the mystery of her life. In particular as theology, according to its own law, lives only through an intimate and organic contact with its spiritual origin *(donné)*, one applies oneself to make a serious study of the sources from which one derives an authentic knowledge of the one, holy, catholic and apostolic Church: the Holy Scripture, the Fathers, the liturgy, the life of ecclesiastical institutions, etc. (Introduction to *Unam Sanctam* [1937], reprinted in van Vliet, *Communio sacramentalis*, 285–87)

30. Jossua, *Yves Congar*, 65; Fouilloux, "Frère Yves," 386. *Unam Sanctam* published its seventy-seventh and last volume in 1967, as if to suggest, writes van Vliet, that, with Vatican II, the project, initiated in 1937, "had reached the first fulfillment of its program." *Communio sacramentalis*, 163.

31. Congar, Preface to *Dialogue between Christians*, 22; Puyo, *Une vie pour la vérité*, 100.

32. Timothy Radcliffe, "Church of God, My Mother," *Priests and People* 9 (1995): 340. For Congar's tribute to his fellow prisoners see Yves Congar, *Leur résistance. Mémorial des officiers évadés—anciens de Colditz et de Lübeck morts pour la France. Témoignage d'Yves Congar* (Paris: A. Renault, 1948). See also Congar, Preface to A. Maloire, *Colditz. Le grand refus* (Vincennes: Le Condor, 1982), 10–14. Congar received the following honors for his years of military service: Chevalier de la Légion d'Honeur, Croix de Guerre, and Médaille des Évadés.

33. Congar, 1955 journal manuscript, quoted in Fouilloux, "Frère Yves," 389. Translation by Christian Dupont, "Friar Yves, Cardinal Congar, Dominican: Itinerary of a Theologian," *U.S. Catholic Historian* 17 (1999): 73.

34. The book in question is Marie-Dominique Chenu, *Une école de théologie: Le Saulchoir* (Kain-lez-Tournai, Belgium: Le Saulchoir, 1937). Chenu's text is reprinted together with essays by Giuseppe Albergio, Étienne Fouilloux, Jean Ladrière, and Jean-Pierre Jossua in Chenu, *Une école de théologie: Le Saulchoir* (Paris: Cerf, 1985).

35. For an overview of the biblical and historical "return to the sources" that was a component of the *nouvelle théologie*, see Roger Aubert, *La Théologie catholique au milieu du XXᵉ siècle* (Paris: Casterman, 1954). Leaders of this effort included not only the Saulchoir Dominicans but also the Jesuits of Lyon-Fourvière, such as Henri de Lubac, Henri Bouillard, and Jean Daniélou. Monuments of their labors included the series *Sources chrétiennes*, founded in 1942. For a history of the liturgical movement, including a discussion of the Centre de Pastorale Liturgique, established in Paris in 1943, see Bernard Botte, *Le Mouvement liturgique: Témoignage et souvenirs* (Paris: Desclée, 1973).

36. See Oscar L. Arnal, *Priests in Working-Class Blue: The History of the Worker-Priests (1943–1954)* (Mahwah, NJ: Paulist Press, 1986).

37. Congar, Preface to *Dialogue between Christians*, 32.

38. Congar, "Letter from Father Yves Congar," 214.

39. Jacques Duquesne, *Un théologien en liberté. Jacques Duquesne interroge le Père Chenu* (Paris: Centurion, 1975), 140.

40. Jean-Marie Le Guillou, "Yves Congar," in *Bilan de la théologie du XX*ᵉ *siècle*, ed. Robert Vander Gucht and Herbert Vorgrimler (Paris: Casterman, 1970), 2:797.

41. Le Guillou, "Yves Congar," 2:797.

42. Fouilloux, "Frère Yves," 390.

43. Jossua, *Yves Congar*, 51.

44. Le Guillou, "Yves Congar," 2:795.

45. This is the assessment of Étienne Fouilloux and of Jean-Pierre Jossua. See Fouilloux, "Frère Yves," 391; Jossua, *Yves Congar*, 28.

46. Congar, Preface to the second revised edition of *Vraie et fausse réforme dans l'Église*, Unam Sanctam, no. 72 (Paris: Cerf, 1968), 8 n. 2.

47. Le Guillou thinks *Vraie et fausse réforme* thus lost its transparency; pastoral concern led Congar to redraft a work "more useful for the Church but apparently less satisfying." Le Guillou, "Yves Congar," 2:793.

48. Congar, Preface to *Dialogue between Christians*, 40.

49. Congar, Preface to *Dialogue between Christians*, 34.

50. Congar, Letter to Gagnebet, cited in Fouilloux, "Frère Yves," 393.

51. Puyo, *Une vie pour la vérité*, 99. On Congar's difficulties with Rome see Fouilloux, "Recherche théologique et magistère romain en 1952. Une 'affaire' parmi d'autres," *RSR* 71 (1983): 269–86.

52. Thomas F. O'Meara, O.P., " 'Raid on the Dominicans': The Repression of 1954," *America* 170 (4 February 1994): 8–16.

53. Congar, "L'Avenir des prêtres-ouvriers," *Témoignage chrétien*, 25 September 1953.

54. See François Leprieur, *Quand Rome condamne. Dominicains et prêtres-ouvrieres* (Paris: Cerf, 1989).

55. Fouilloux, "Frère Yves," 394. Congar's recently published personal journals discuss at length his conflict with Rome, his conviction that he must continue to persevere in pursuit of truth, and his struggle with the meaning of obedience. See Congar, *Journal d'un théologien (1946–1956)*, edited and annotated by Étienne Fouilloux (Paris: Cerf, 2001).

56. Congar, Preface to *Dialogue between Christians*, 44–45. Congar also reflected on patience in "La Patience; le respect des délais," *Vraie et fausse réforme*, 2d ed., 277–300. This great patience, however, did not take away the pain of exile and ostracism. The pages of Congar's recently published personal journals expresses his anguish during this period. Fouilloux notes in his commentary that "It is necessary to read and reread these pages in order to comprehend how a member of a religious order who consecrated his life to the church was made to suffer by the church." Fouilloux, in Congar, *Journal d'un théologien*, 400.

57. On this point see Fouilloux, "Frère Yves," 398.

58. In a personal letter to Richard Beauchesne dated October 17, 1971, Congar wrote, "At the Council . . . I worked in Chapter II of *Lumen gentium* (numbers 9, 13, 16, and 17 are mine, and also parts of number 28 and of Chapter I); in *Presbyterorum ordinis* of which I am one of the principal redactors with Father Lécuyer; in *Ad gentes* (Chapter I is completely my work), and on the various texts of the Sectretariat for Unity." Richard Beauchesne, "Heeding the Early Congar Today, and Two Recent Roman Catholic Issues: Seeking Hope on the Road Back," *JEcSt* 27 (1990), 536 n. 3.

Congar also discussed his work on these documents in *Fifty Years*, 10 and 14. For Congar's chronicle of the Council sessions see Congar, *Vatican II: Le Concile au jour le jour*, 4 vols. (Paris: Cerf, 1963–1966), and *Mon journal du Concile*, 2 vols. (Paris: Cerf, 2002). For an account of Congar's work with the Council see Étienne Fouilloux, "Comment devient-on expert à Vatican II? Le cas du Père Yves Congar," in *Le Deuxième Concile du Vatican II (1959–1965)* (Rome: Ecole française de Rome, 1989), 307–31.

59. Fouilloux, "Frère Yves," 398 and 400; trans. Dupont, "Friar Yves," 81 and 83. In a similar vein, Richard McBrien writes, "No modern theologian's spirit was accorded fuller play in the documents of Vatican II than Congar's. Vatican II was a council of the church, and Congar has been a theologian of the church *par excellence*." Richard McBrien, "Church and Ministry: The Achievement of Yves Congar," *TheoDgst* 32 (1985): 203. See also Joseph Komonchak, "A Hero of Vatican II: Yves Congar," *Comm* 15 (December 1, 1995): 15–17. Congar himself remarked, "If there is a theology of Congar, that [Vatican II] is where it is to be found." "Letter from Father Yves Congar," 215.

60. Congar, "Reflections on Being a Theologian," *NewBlckfrs* 62 (1981): 405.

61. Puyo, *Une vie pour la vérité*, 149.

62. Congar, *Mon journal du concile*, 1:354–55.

63. Congar, *Mon journal du concile*, 1:177.

64. Puyo, *Une vie pour la vérité*, 131–32.

65. Jossua, "Yves Congar," 9. See also Congar, "Reflections on Being a Theologian," 408.

66. Puyo, *Une vie pour la vérité*, 131–32.

67. He found the journal too *germano-hollandaise* and was concerned that the articles were often insufficiently theological. He nonetheless agreed to serve as editor because of the importance of the journal's postconciliar mission and its international breadth. See Puyo, *Une vie pour la vérité*, 158.

68. Congar, "My Path-Findings in the Theology of Laity and Ministries," *The Jurist* 32 (1972): 169–88.

69. Congar, "My Path-Findings," 169–70.

70. Fouilloux, "Frère Yves," 403–4.

71. Fouilloux, "Frère Yves," 402. On Congar's eventual appointment to the College of Cardinals, see Richard McBrien, "The Long-Overdue Elevation of an Extraordinary Theologian," *NatCathRep* 31 (9 December 1994): 2.

72. Dominique Congar, Preface to Congar, *Journal de la guerre*, 12.

73. O'Meara, "Ecumenist of Our Times," 67.

74. O'Meara, "Ecumenist of Our Times," 67.

75. Congar, "Pour un bon usage de la maladie," *VS* 117 (1967): 528.

76. Congar, *Fifty Years*, 86.

77. Van Vliet, *Communio sacramentalis*, 237.

78. The homily, given by Timothy Radcliffe, Master General of the Dominican Order, is published as "Church of God, My Mother," *Priests and People* 9 (1995): 340–42. Commemorative reflections include Avery Dulles, "Yves Congar: In Appreciation," *America* 173 (15 July 1995): 6–7; Keith Egan, "Yves Congar: 1904–1995," *Christian Spirituality Bulletin* 3 (1995): 22–24; William Henn, "Yves Congar, O.P. (1904–95)," *America* (12 August 1995): 23–25; Fergus Kerr, "Cardinal Yves Congar O.P.," *NewBlckfrs* 76 (July–August 1995): 314–16; Thomas O'Meara, "Reflections on Yves Congar

and Theology in the United States," *U.S. Catholic Historian*, 17 (1999): 91–105; Paul Philibert, "Yves Congar: Theologian, Ecumenist, and Visionary," *U.S. Catholic Historian*, 17 (1999): 116–20; Cardinal Johannes Willebrands, "Cher frère Yves Congar," *CT* 123 (1996): 5–6.

79. Congar, "Nunc et in hora mortis nostrae," *VS* 45 (1935): 119.

80. Congar, *Fifty Years*, 71.

81. Puyo, *Une vie pour la vérité*, 38–39. See also André Duval, "Yves Congar: A Life for the Truth," *Thom* 48 (1984): 505–11. The expression "I have loved the truth as one loves a person" is a profession Congar took from Madame Swetchine.

82. Puyo, *Une vie pour la vérité*, 47. See also Congar, *La Foi et la théologie* (Tournai: Desclée, 1962), 125–36. For further study of Congar's theological method see Congar's *A History of Theology*, trans. Hunter Guthrie (Garden City, NY: Doubleday, 1968); *Tradition and Traditions: An Historical and a Theological Essay* (London: Burns and Oates, 1966); *Tradition and the Life of the Church*, trans. A. N. Woodrow (London: Burns and Oates, 1964); and *Situation et tâches présentes de la théologie* (Paris: Cerf, 1967). Congar remarked in a letter to Thomas Lehning that *Tradition and Traditions* is more representative of his thought than *La Foi et la théologie*. The latter work was intended as a manual for use in seminaries, and this constricted its composition. See "A Letter from Yves Congar," in the appendix of Lehning, "The Foundations, Functions and Authority of the Magisterium in the Theology of Yves Congar, O.P." (Ph.D. diss., Catholic University of America, 1985), 409–11. Congar's letter referred specifically to his discussion of the magisterium in *Tradition and Traditions* and *La Foi et la théologie*, but presumably his preference for *Tradition and Traditions* prevails generally.

83. Puyo, *Une vie pour la vérité*, 47. See also 34.

84. Chenu's methodological works include "Les Yeux de la foi," *Rev. Dominicaine* 38 (1932): 653–60; "Position de la théologie," *RSPhTh* 24 (1935): 232–57; *Une école de théologie; La théologie est-elle une science?* (Paris: A. Fayard, 1957); *Saint Thomas d'Aquin et la théologie* (Paris: Éditions du Seuil, 1959).

85. Congar, "Le Père M.-D. Chenu," in Vander Gucht and Vorgrimler, *Bilan de la théologie du XXᵉ siècle*, 2:773.

86. Jean-Pierre Torrell, "Yves Congar et l'ecclésiologie de Saint Thomas d'Aquin," *RSPhTh* 82 (1998): 205.

87. Congar, *Foi et théologie*, 139–40. See also "Situation et tâches," in Yves Congar, *Situation et tâches*, 77.

88. Congar, *Foi et théologie*, 169–79.

89. Congar, *L'Ecclésiologie du haut Moyen Âge. De Saint Grégoire le Grand à la désunion entre Byzance et Rome* (Paris: Cerf, 1968), 10.

90. Congar distinguished positive theology from historical theology, which is materially but not formally theological. See his "Théologie historique," in *Initiation à la pratique de la théologie*, ed. Bernard Lauret and François Refoulé (Paris: Cerf, 1982), 1:237.

91. Congar, *Martin Luther. Sa foi, sa réforme. Études de théologie historique*, Cogitatio Fidei, no.119 (Paris: Cerf, 1983), 10.

92. Congar, *Foi et théologie*, 144–68; *Tradition and Traditions*, 425–26.

93. See for example Congar's *Tradition and Traditions*, 310; *I Believe*, 2:29–30.

94. Congar, "La Recherche théologique entre 1945–1965," in Congar, *Situation et tâches*, 36; *I Believe*, 1:x.

95. Congar, *I Believe*, 1:vii.

96. For Congar's reflections on the significance of Scripture and the use of Scripture in theology, see "Que pouvons-nous trouver dans les Écritures?" *VS* 81 (1949): 227–31; "Holy Writ and Holy Church," *NewBlckfrs* 41 (1960): 11–19; "Inspiration des Écritures canoniques et apostolicté de l'Église," *RSPhTh* 45 (1961): 32–42; *The Revelation of God*, trans. A. Manson and L. C. Sheppard (New York: Herder and Herder, 1968); "Scripture and Tradition in Relation to Revelation and to the Church," *Tradition and Traditions*, 376–424; "The Debate on the Question of the Relationship between Scripture and Tradition from the Viewpoint of Their Material Content," in *A Theology Reader*, ed. R. W. Gleason (New York: Macmillan, 1966), 115–29.

97. Congar, "The Psalms in My Life," in Congar, *Called to Life*, trans. William Burridge (New York: Crossroad, 1987), 19.

98. Congar, "A God Who Has Spoken," in Congar, *Called to Life*, 38.

99. Congar, "A God Who Has Spoken," 33.

100. Congar, "A God Who Has Spoken," 38; *I Believe*, 1:ix.

101. Congar, "La Recherche théologique entre 1945 et 1965," 36.

102. Congar, "A God Who Has Spoken," 39.

103. Congar, "A God Who Has Spoken," 40.

104. Congar's *Foi et théologie* implied a subordination of theologians to the magisterium. In other writings, Congar maintained that the title of teaching church belongs properly to the magisterium, but he discussed the relationship between theologians and the magisterium in more complementary terms. He noted, for example, that men working on the periphery of the church had prepared the way for the Council. Congar, "Theology in the Council," *AER* 155 (1966): 220–21. He also described the tasks of bishops and theologians as complementary. "Situation et tâches," 58.

105. Congar, *Foi et théologie*, 157–68.

106. Congar, *Tradition and Traditions*, 434–35, with reference to Dom Prosper Guéranger, *Institutions liturgiques*, 2d ed. (Paris: Société Générale de Librairie Catholique, 1878).

107. Puyo, *Une vie pour la vérité*, 30. For further reflections on the liturgy see Congar, *Foi et théologie*, 146–48; *Tradition and Traditions*, 427–35; "Liturgical Celebration and Witness," in Congar, *Called to Life*, 130–38.

108. Congar, *I Believe*, 1:x.

109. Congar, "Les Saints Pères, organes privilégiés de la tradition," *Iren* 35 (1962): 489.

110. Congar, *Foi et théologie*, 148–53; *Tradition and Traditions*, 435–50. See also his "L'Esprit des Pères d'après Möhler," *SVS* 55 (1938): 1–25.

111. Congar, *Foi et théologie*, 153–54; *Tradition and Traditions*, 450–51. Congar's own reflections on the presence of God in ordinary existence and in the lives of the saints include the essays in his *Faith and Spiritual Life*, trans. A. Manson and L. C. Sheppard (New York: Herder and Herder, 1968).

112. Joseph Famerée, *L'Ecclésiologie d'Yves Congar avant Vatican II: Histoire et Église. Analyse et reprise critique* (Leuven: Leuven University Press, 1992), 79. "A subsequent stage," he adds, "will discern in the events of the world themselves the signs of the times, the signs of God." Famerée's comments come in the context of a discussion of Congar's collection of essays *Esquisses du Mystère de l'Église*, Unam Sanctam, no. 8 (Paris: Cerf, 1941), particularly the essay "Vie de l'Église et conscience de la

catholicité," originally published in *Bulletin des missions* 18 (1938): 153–60. An English translation appeared as "The Life of the Church and Awareness of Its Catholicity," in *The Mystery of the Church* (Baltimore: Helicon Press, 1960), 138–46.

113. Puyo, *Une vie pour la vérité*, 52–53.

114. Congar, "Theology in the Council," 224.

115. Congar, *I Believe*, 1:172.

116. See Puyo, *Une vie pour la vérité*, 41; Congar, "Reflections on Being a Theologian," 407.

117. Congar, *Foi et théologie*, 178–79. See also "La Théologie depuis 1939," in Yves Congar, *Situation et tâches* (Paris: Cerf, 1967), 17–18. Here, Congar reiterated the rich possibilities of phenomenology and existentialism but warned against exclusive attention to the experience of existence to the neglect of foundational ontology.

118. Congar, "Chenu," 777.

119. Van Vliet, *Communio sacramentalis*, 50.

120. Puyo, *Une vie pour la vérité*, 20.

121. Congar, "La Théologie depuis 1939," 16–17. See also "La Recherche théologique entre 1945–1965," 31–33.

122. Congar, "Situation et tâches," 72. It should be noted that although such an approach may have been new to many in the post-Vatican II era, it was not new to Congar himself. His recently published personal journals express his commitment to a theology and a church that is open to the questions and needs of the world, and his frustration with preconciliar Rome, which seems to be an "unreal, artificial world, characterized by a triumphant immutability and a false air of glory." *Journal d'un théologien*, 119. Congar perceived a wide breach between those theologians who attempted to respond in a viable way to the true questions of humanity, and the ecclesiastical authorities whose pronouncements so often did not speak to the human situation. There was a need, he was convinced, for an open Christianity and a Christian theology that dealt in human realities, not just repeated formulas. *Journal d'un théologien*, 95, 106, 185, 219, 225, 294–95. See also *Mon journal du Concile*, 1:31, 1:107, and 1:115.

123. Congar, "La Recherche théologique entre 1945–1965," 27. For Congar's critique of horizontalism see "Situation et tâches," 63–66. Congar offered Rudolph Bultmann and some forms of popular prayer as examples of horizontalism. He also saw Harvey Cox and Thomas Altizer moving in this direction.

124. A Parisian Dominican colleague of Congar shared this anecdote with van Vliet. Van Vliet, *Communio sacramentalis*, 15 n. 17.

125. Pietro Quattrocchi, "General Bibliography of Yves Congar," in Jossua, *Yves Congar*, 189–241; Aidan Nichols, "An Yves Congar Bibliography 1967–1987," *Ang* 66 (1989): 422–66. These bibliographies enumerate not only the French originals but also the translations of Congar's writings into Italian, German, English, Spanish, Dutch, and Portuguese.

126. For Congar's discussion of the distinction between theological scholarship and preaching, as well as his reflections on kerygmatic theology, see his *Foi et théologie*, 185–88.

127. Thomas O'Meara, "Beyond 'Hierarchology': Johann Adam Möhler and Yves Congar," in *The Legacy of the Tübingen School: The Relevance of Nineteenth-Century Theology for the Twenty-First Century*, ed. Donald J. Dietrich and Michael J. Himes (New York: Crossroad, 1997), 173. Richard McBrien writes, in like vein, "By any reasonable

account, Yves Congar is the most distinguished ecclesiologist of this century and perhaps of the entire post-Tridentine era." "Church and Ministry: The Achievement of Yves Congar," 203.

128. Congar, "Reflections on Being a Theologian," 405.

129. Congar, *Lay People in the Church*, trans. Donald Attwater (Westminster, MD: Newman Press, 1965), xxi.

130. Congar, *I Believe*, 1:viii.

131. Le Guillou, "Yves Congar," 2:804–5.

132. Van Vliet, *Communio sacramentalis*, 98–99 and 219.

133. Aidan Nichols, *Yves Congar* (Wilton, CT: Morehouse-Barlow, 1989); Timothy I. MacDonald, *The Ecclesiology of Yves Congar: Foundational Themes* (Lanham, MD: University Press of America, 1984). Macdonald identified the dialectic of "structure" and "life" as the foundational principle of Congar's lifelong ecclesiological work. Van Vliet argues, however, that this dialectic was simply used by Congar to demonstrate both the necessity and limits of church reform; he denies that it is the foundation of Congar's thought and notes that MacDonald himself acknowledges that this dialectic does not encompass Congar's discussion of the church as a communion. Van Vliet, *Communio sacramentalis*, 22.

134. Ramiro Pellitero, "Congar's Developing Understanding of the Laity and Their Mission," *Thom* 65 (2001): 327–59.

135. Famerée, *L'Ecclésiologie d'Yves Congar;* van Vliet, *Communio sacramentalis.*

136. Van Vliet, *Communio sacramentalis*, 33–80.

137. Famerée, *L'Ecclésiologie d'Yves Congar*, 83.

138. Famerée, *L'Ecclésiologie d'Yves Congar*, 417–18.

139. Van Vliet, *Communio sacramentalis*, 91–153. Famerée also observes that a duality in some form (e.g. "structure and life," or "hierarchy and communion") characterized Congar's work in the period 1937–1959.

140. Van Vliet, *Communio sacramentalis*, 144.

141. Van Vliet, *Communio sacramentalis*, 155–228.

142. Van Vliet, *Communio sacramentalis*, 229–83.

143. Famerée, *L'Ecclésiologie d'Yves Congar*, 451–52.

144. See Gerald A. McCool, *Catholic Theology in the Nineteenth Century: The Quest for a Unitary Method* (New York: Seabury, 1977); Thomas F. O'Meara, *Romantic Idealism and Roman Catholicism: Schelling and the Theologians* (Notre Dame: University of Notre Dame Press, 1982); O'Meara, *Church and Culture: German Catholic Theology, 1860–1914* (Notre Dame: University of Notre Dame Press, 1991).

145. On the different schools and traditions of Thomism, see Thomas F. O'Meara, O.P., *Thomas Aquinas: Theologian* (Notre Dame: University of Notre Dame Press, 1997), 167–95.

146. Congar, *Fifty Years*, 70.

147. Puyo, *Une vie pour la vérité*, 38.

148. Torrell, "Yves Congar et l'ecclésiologie de Saint Thomas d'Aquin," 204 and 202.

149. Congar, "Vision de l'Église chez Thomas d'Aquin," *RSPhTh* 62 (1978): 523.

150. Congar, "Saint Thomas serviteur de la vérité," *VS* 50 (1937): 259–79.

151. Congar, *Fifty Years*, 72.

152. For a comprehensive, international bibliography of work on Aquinas's pneu-

matology from 1870 to 1993, see Arnaldo Pedrini, *Bibliografia Tomistica sulla Pneumatologie* (Vatican City: Libreria Editrice Vaticana, 1994).

153. Congar discussed the structure of the *Summa* in "Vision de l'Église chez Thomas d'Aquin," 524–25. Elsewhere, he observed with puzzlement that it is "a little astonishing and even deceiving" that Aquinas did not explicitly exploit the centrality of the divine missions described in q. 43 in the remainder of the *Summa*. Congar, "Chronique de pneumatologie," *RSPhTh* 64 (1980): 447.

154. Congar, "Vision de l'Église chez Thomas d'Aquin," 525. See also 529–36.

155. Congar, "Vision de l'Église chez Thomas d'Aquin," 535.

156. Aquinas wrote: "Et ideo quidquid fit per Spiritum Sanctum, etiam fit per Christum." *In Ephes. 2.18, lect. 5*, no. 121.

157. Congar, "Le Moment 'économique' et le moment 'ontologique' dans la sacra doctrina (révélation, théologie, *Somme théologique*)," in *Mélanges offerts à M.-D. Chenu*, Bibliothèque Thomiste, no. 37, ed. André Duval (Paris: Librairie Philosophique, 1967), 174.

158. Congar, "The Idea of the Church in St. Thomas Aquinas," 337.

159. Congar, "Vision de l'Église chez Thomas d'Aquin," 533. See also *I Believe*, 3: 118–121, where Congar referenced *ST* I^a q. 36, a. 2 and observed that there Aquinas treated the *Filioque* in a "dialectic and highly rationalized way." For a more scriptural account drawing on the fathers, Congar directed the reader to *Contra Gent.* IV, 24 and *De Pot.* q. 10, a. 4.

160. Congar, *I Believe*, 3:117. See also *I Believe*, 1:88–90, and Congar, "Bulletin de théologie," *RSPhTh* 56 (1972): 307.

161. Congar, "Vision de l'Église chez Thomas d'Aquin," 532. Congar made reference here to Aquinas's *Compend. theol.* I c. 147; *Contra Gent.* IV, 20; *ST* I^a q. 45, a. 6, ad 2; *In Galat.* c. 5, lect. 4.

162. Congar, "Le Saint Esprit dans la théologie thomiste de l'agir moral," 10. Congar referred here to *Contra Gent.* IV, 21 and 22; *Compend. theol.* I, 147.

163. Congar, "Vision de l'Église chez Thomas d'Aquin," 534–35.

164. Congar, "Le Saint Esprit dans la théologie thomiste de l'agir moral," 11. See also *I Believe*, 3:117, where Congar referred the reader to *ST* I^a q. 37 and 38.

165. Congar, "The Idea of the Church in St. Thomas Aquinas," 346. Other interpreters of Aquinas differed from Congar on this point. William Hill, for example, held that Aquinas "makes clear that the presence of the Spirit is not a mere appropriation." Hill, *The Three-Personed God: The Trinity as Mystery of Salvation* (Washington, DC: Catholic University of America Press, 1982), 305.

166. Congar, "Vision de l'Église chez Thomas d'Aquin," 533; "Le Saint-Esprit dans la théologie thomiste de l'agir moral," 13–14; *I Believe*, 1:128.

167. Aquinas, *ST* II^a–II^{ae} q. 106, a. 1, c. with reference to Rom 8:2 and to Augustine's *De Spiritu et littera*, xxiv and xxi. See also Aquinas, *ST* II^a–II^{ae} q. 106, a. 3, c.

168. Congar, "Le Sens de l''économie' salutaire dans la 'théologie' de saint Thomas d'Aquin (*Somme théologique*)," in *Glaube und Geschichte, Festgabe J. Lortz*, ed. E. Iserloh and P. Mann (Baden-Baden: Bruno Grimm, 1957), 2:86, 2:118.

169. Congar, "Le Saint-Esprit dans la théologie thomiste de l'agir moral," 13–14. See also "The Idea of the Church in St. Thomas Aquinas," 336.

170. Aquinas, *ST* II^a q. 106, a. 1, c.

171. Congar, "Le Sens de l''économie' salutaire dans la 'théologie' de saint Tho-

mas d'Aquin," 90. See also "Le Saint–Esprit dans la théologie thomiste de l'agir moral," 15.

172. Congar, "Le Saint-Esprit dans la théologie thomiste de l'agir moral," 16.

173. Congar, "The Idea of the Church in St. Thomas Aquinas," 340.

174. Congar, "The Idea of the Church in St. Thomas Aquinas," 358.

175. Congar, "The Idea of the Church in St. Thomas Aquinas," 339.

176. Congar, *Word and Spirit*, 6. Congar commented to Bernard Lauret that "beyond question I developed, and in a way even parted company with Thomism." Congar, *Fifty Years*, 71.

177. Congar, *Word and Spirit*, 6.

178. Congar, Introduction to *Martin Luther*, 9. On Congar's recognition of the limits of scholasticism see also Fouilloux, "Frère Yves," 382–83.

179. Congar, "Vision de l'Église chez Thomas d'Aquin," 536–38.

180. Torrell, "Yves Congar et l'ecclésiologie de Saint Thomas d'Aquin," 217.

181. Congar, *Fifty Years*, 70.

182. For a comprehensive exposition of Möhler's thought, see Michael J. Himes, *Ongoing Incarnation: Johann Adam Möhler and the Beginnings of Modern Ecclesiology* (New York: Crossroad, 1997). On Möhler's pneumatology see Bradford Hinze, "The Holy Spirit and the Catholic Tradition: The Legacy of Johann Adam Möhler," in *The Legacy of the Tübingen School*, 75–94.

183. Johann Adam Möhler, *Unity in the Church or the Principle of Catholicism Presented in the Spirit of the Church Fathers of the First Three Centuries*, trans. Peter C. Erb (Washington, DC: Catholic University of America Press, 1996). Originally published as *Die Einheit in der Kirche Oder das Prinzip des Katholizismus dargestellt im Geiste der Kirchenväter der ersten drei Jahrhunderte* (Tübingen: Heinrich Laupp, 1825).

184. Möhler, in *Johann Adam Möhler. Bd. 1: Gesammelte Aktenstücke und Briefe*, ed. Stephan Lösch (Munich: Josef Kösel and Friedrich Pustet, 1928), 511; trans. Peter Erb, in "Introduction" to *Unity in the Church*, 2.

185. Johann Adam Möhler, *Symbolism or Exposition of the Doctrinal Differences between Catholics and Protestants as Evidenced by Their Symbolical Writings*, trans. James Burton Robertson (London: Gibbings and Company, 1894). Originally published as *Symbolik oder Darstellung der dogmatischen Gegensätze der Katholiken und Protestanten nach ihren öffentlichen Bekenntnisschriften* (Mainz: Kupferberg, 1832). This work underwent several editions in Möhler's lifetime. For the critical German edition see Josef Rupert Geiselmann, *Symbolik* (Cologne and Olten: Hegner, 1958).

186. On Congar's importance as a conveyer of Möhler's theology see Thomas O'Meara, "Beyond 'Hierarchology': Johann Adam Möhler and Yves Congar," 173–91.

187. Puyo, *Une vie pour la vérité*, 48.

188. Puyo, *Une vie pour la vérité*, 48.

189. Congar, Preface to *Dialogue between Christians*, 24.

190. Congar, "L'Esprit des Pères d'après Möhler," *SVS* 55 (1938): 1–25; "Sur l'évolution et l'interprétation de la pensée de Möhler," *RSPhTh* 27 (1938): 205–12; "La Signification oecuménique de l'oeuvre de Möhler," *Iren* 15 (1938): 113–30. Other essays on Möhler by Congar include "L'Hérésie, déchirement de l'unité," in *L'Église est une. Hommage à Möhler*, ed. Pierre Chaillet (Paris: Bloud and Gay, 1939), 255–69; "La Pensée de Möhler et l'ecclésiologie orthodoxe," *Iren* 12 (1935): 321–29.

191. Pablo Sicouly, "Yves Congar und Johann Adam Möhler: Ein theologisches Gespräch zwischen den Zeiten," *Catholica* 45 (1991): 38.

192. Puyo, *Une vie pour la vérité*, 48. A reflection on Möhler from the later part of Congar's career is "Johann Adam Möhler: 1796–1838," *ThQ* 150 (1970): 47–51.

193. Congar, Preface to *Dialogue between Christians*, 24.

194. Möhler, *Unity in the Church*, §2, 84.

195. Möhler, *Unity in the Church*, §3, 85. "Community" is Erb's translation of *Gemeinheit*.

196. Möhler, *Unity in the Church*, §52, 217–18.

197. Möhler, *Symbolism*, §10, 85.

198. Möhler, *Symbolism*, §10, 86.

199. On the merits of Protestant views see Möhler, *Symbolism*, §17–§18. Möhler critiqued Protestantism in *Symbolism*, §2, 32.

200. One of many indications of this change of emphasis is Möhler's exegesis of John 17, a passage, as we have seen, that is of much significance to Congar. In *Unity in the Church*, Möhler cites Origen, who interpreted John 17:21 pneumatologically: " 'That they may all be one; even as you, Father, are in me, and I in you, that they also may be in us' (Jn 17:21), namely, through the fullness of love that is given through the Holy Spirit." *Unity in the Church*, §1, 83. In *Symbolism*, in contrast, the interpretation of this passage is christological. "The Lord putteth up a prayer for the gift of unity," he writes, "and the union of all who shall believe; and for a unity too, which finds its model only in the relation existing between the Father and the Son of Man. *'In us* shall they be one.' " *Symbolism*, §36, 273.

201. Möhler, *Symbolism*, §38, 281, and §36, 260.

202. Congar, "Sur l'évolution et l'interprétation de la pensée de Möhler," 211.

203. Congar, "La Pensée de Möhler et l'ecclésiologie orthodoxe," 324 and 328.

204. Congar, "Johann Adam Möhler," 47. See also Congar, " 'Lumen Gentium,' No. 7," in Congar, *Le Concile de Vatican II. Son Église, peuple de Dieu et corps du Christ*, Théologie historique, no. 71 (Paris: Beauchesne, 1984), 148f.

205. Congar, " 'Lumen Gentium,' No. 7," 149.

206. Möhler, *Die Einheit*, §3. Cited by Congar in *Tradition and Traditions*, 194.

207. Congar, *Tradition and Traditions*, 324. For further discussion of Congar, Möhler, and tradition, see Thomas O'Meara, "Beyond 'Hierarchology': Johann Adam Möhler and Yves Congar," 179–80.

208. Congar, "Johann Adam Möhler," 50.

209. Congar, "Bulletin de théologie," *RSPhTh* 27 (1938): 656–57. See also Congar's "Sur l'évolution et l'interprétation de la pensée de Möhler."

210. See for example Congar, *Word and Spirit*, 115.

211. Congar, "Johann Adam Möhler," 50.

212. Congar, "Johann Adam Möhler," 50–51.

213. For a general history of ecumenism during this period in France see Étienne Fouilloux, *Les Catholiques et l'unité chrétienne du XIXe au XXe siècle. Itinéraires européens d'expression française* (Paris: Centurion, 1982); *Au coeur du XXee siècle religieux* (Paris: Cerf, 1993).

214. Puyo, *Une vie pour la vérité*, 76.

215. Jossua, *Yves Congar*, 58.

216. Congar, *Divided Christendom: A Catholic Study of the Problem of Reunion*, trans. M. A. Bousfield (London: Centenary Press, 1939).

217. Joseph Famerée, "*Chrétiens désunis* du P. Congar: 50 ans après," *NRT* 110 (1988): 666–86.

218. Jossua, *Yves Congar*, 51.

219. Jossua, *Yves Congar*, 46 and 85.

220. Congar, Preface to *Dialogue between Christians*, 15.

221. Congar, "Renewed Actuality of the Holy Spirit," *Lumen* 28 (1973): 23.

222. Congar, "The Call to Ecumenism and the Work of the Holy Spirit," in Congar, *Dialogue between Christians*, 101.

223. Congar, Preface to *Dialogue between Christians*, 4. Congar told Puyo that he was absolutely convinced that this act of Calvinist generosity was the beginning of his ecumenical vocation. Puyo, *Une vie pour la vérité*, 14.

224. Congar, Preface to *Dialogue between Christians*, 5–6.

225. For Congar's thoughts on Kierkegaard see his "Actualité de Kierkegaard," *VieI* 32 (1934): 9–36.

226. Congar, Preface to *Dialogue between Christians*, 11.

227. In retrospect, Congar realized "that my project may have been somewhat irritating to Protestants. I would have liked Protestants themselves to explain their position more frequently." Preface to *Dialogue between Christians*, 13.

228. Fouilloux, *Les Catholiques et l'unité chrétienne*, 226.

229. Puyo, *Une vie pour la vérité*, 59–60. Congar was reproached in Rome for designating Luther a religious genius. The church fathers, Congar was told, would never have used the word "genius" of a heretic. *Journal d'un théologien*, 316.

230. Puyo, *Une vie pour la vérité*, 59. See also Congar's Introduction to his own *Martin Luther*, 8.

231. Congar noted this difficulty in his *Martin Luther*, 9; "Luther réformateur. Retour sur une étude ancienne," in *Martin Luther*, 42; "Nouveaux regards sur la christologie de Luther," in *Martin Luther*, 129–30.

232. Congar, *Vraie et fausse*, 2d ed., 13. See also Introduction to *Martin Luther*, 15.

233. Congar, "Considerations and Reflections on the Christology of Luther," in Congar, *Dialogue between Christians*, 372–406. This essay was originally written in 1950 and published as "Regards et réflexions sur la christologie de Luther," in *Das Konzil von Chalkedon. Geschichte und Gegenwart*, ed. G. Grillmeier and H. Bacht (Würzburg: Echter, 1954), 3:457–86. It stands in contrast with Congar's "Nouveaux regards sur la christologie de Luther," 105–34.

234. Congar, "Luther réformateur," 34.

235. Puyo, *Une vie pour la vérité*, 49.

236. Congar noted Luther's theological emphasis in "Luther réformateur," 22, 41, and 44.

237. On Luther see Congar's *Vraie et fausse*, 2d ed., 362. For Congar's critique of Luther's theology of nature and grace see *Vraie et fausse*, 2d ed., 347, 354–55, 363; "Luther réformateur," 75. Congar found a similar problem in Barth and questioned his tendency to "consider exclusively the sovereign causality of God in God himself without realizing that this causality injects something real *into us* and ultimately confers on us the capacity for con-causality with God!" Preface to *Dialogue between Christians*, 12.

238. Congar noted Luther's emphasis on the *pro me* in *Vraie et fausse*, 2d ed., 357; "Luther réformateur," 26, 29, 71; "Théologie de l'eucharistie," in Congar, *Martin Luther*, 93, 102. He critiqued Luther's lack of attention to the properly ecclesial in *Vraie et fausse réforme*, 2d ed., 367, 373, and 377; "Théologie de l'eucharistie," 102. Congar also critiqued Luther's dissociation of the interior act of the Spirit from the exterior means of grace. In *Vraie et fausse réforme*, for example, Congar wrote that Luther shows no recognition of the proper reality of the ecclesial means of grace and writes only of the entirely transcendent action of the Holy Spirit. *Vraie et fausse*, 2d ed., 379, with reference to Luther's *Great Catechism*. See also "Luther reformateur," 62. Congar had a similar assessment of Barth. See *Vraie et fausse*, 2d ed., 381.

239. See for example Congar's *Vraie et fausse*, 2d ed., 373–74.

240. Congar, *Divided Christendom*, 91.

241. Congar, *I Believe*, 1:138–40.

242. Congar, *I Believe*, 1:148 n. 8.

243. Puyo, *Une vie pour la vérité*, 51. See also Congar, "J'aime l'Orthodoxie," in *2000 ans de christianisme* (Paris: Aufadi, 1975), 2:97–99.

244. Congar, "Chronique: Années 1939–1946," in Congar, *Sainte Église*, 564. Some have postulated that the affinity of Khomiakov's work and that of Möhler can be accounted for through the common influence of Greek patristic theology.

245. Albert Gratieux, *A. S. Khomiakov et le mouvement slavophile*, Unam Sanctam, nos. 5 and 6 (Paris: Cerf, 1939); Georges Samarine, *Préface aux oeuvres théologiques de A. S. Khomiakov*, Unam Sanctam, no. 7 (Paris: Cerf, 1939).

246. Joseph Famerée, "Orthodox Influence on the Roman Catholic Theologian Yves Congar, O.P.: A Sketch," *SVTQ* 39 (1995): 409.

247. Famerée, "Orthodox Influence," 410, 412, 414.

248. Famerée, "Orthodox Influence," 412–13, 415–16.

249. Congar, "Letter from Father Yves Congar," 215.

250. Congar, "La Pneumatologie dans la théologie catholique," *RSPhTh* 51 (1967): 251; "Pneumatologie ou 'christomonisme' dans la tradition latine?" in *Ecclesia a Spiritu Sancto edocta. Mélanges théologiques. Hommage à Mgr. Gérard Philips* (Gembloux: Duculot, 1970), 41–63; "Renewed Actuality of the Holy Spirit," 20. In apparent contradiction, Congar also wrote that "to return to the question of the decisive and universal impact of the *Filioque*, I would agree that the criticism of 'Christomonism' in Western Catholicism is to some extent right, but I have, I think, shown that this is being corrected." *Word and Spirit*, 117. Perhaps here he did not strictly distinguish "christomonism" and "christocentrism."

251. In Congar, *I Believe*, 2:66.

252. Congar, *Word and Spirit*, 122; *La Parole et le Souffle* (Paris: Desclée, 1984), 191.

253. Avery Dulles, "Yves Congar: In Appreciation," 6. On Congar's tremendous influence at the Council see also Joseph Komonchak, "Yves Congar: A Hero of Vatican II," 15; Fouilloux, "Frère Yves," 398.

254. Congar, "Theology in the Council," 224.

255. Famerée, *L'Ecclésiologie d'Yves Congar*, 437–57.

256. Congar noted the importance of the addition to the sacramentary of Eucharistic prayers that include an explicit epiclesis in "Renewed Actuality of the Holy Spirit," 29.

257. Congar, "Pneumatology Today," 440.

258. Congar, *Vraie et fausse*, 2d ed., 7–12.

259. Congar, Letter to Thomas O'Meara, cited in O'Meara, "Beyond 'Hierarchology,'" 182.

260. Van Vliet identifies *I Believe in the Holy Spirit* as Congar's best-known postconciliar work in *Communio sacramentalis*, 235.

CHAPTER 2

1. Congar, "Renewed Actuality of the Holy Spirit," 21. See also *Word and Spirit*, xi.

2. Congar, *I Believe*, 3:160; "Le Troisième article du symbole. L'Impact de la pneumatologie dans la vie de l'Église," in *Dieu, Église, Société*, ed. J. Doré (Paris: Cerf, 1985), 292.

3. Congar, "La Tri-unité de Dieu et l'Église," *VS* 128 (1974): 687.

4. Congar, *Word and Spirit*, 2.

5. Congar, *I Believe*, 3:xv.

6. Congar, "Pneumatologie et théologie de l'histoire," in *La Théologie de l'histoire. Herméneutique et eschatologie*, ed. Enrico Castelli (Paris: Aubier, 1971), 68.

7. Congar, "Le Christ dans l'économie salutaire et dans nos traités dogmatiques," in Congar, *Situation et tâches*, 94.

8. Congar spoke of "le temps *constitutif* du peuple de Dieu" in "Pneumatologie dogmatique," in *Initiation à la pratique de la théologie*, ed. Bernard Lauret and François Refoulé (Paris: Cerf, 1982), 2:485.

9. Congar, *Fifty Years*, 62. Presumably he is using the term "revelation" here in the technical sense of special, rather than general, revelation. Even so, it is difficult to reconcile this position with Congar's conviction that the Spirit works in history to bring about the "'Christ that is to be.'" *Word and Spirit*, 71, with reference to Tennyson. "What Christ has *given*," Congar explained, "has still to come to pass; in a manner not yet realized. History is the realization of what has not yet taken place." "Pneumatology Today," 446–47.

10. Congar, "Pneumatologie dogmatique," 485.

11. Congar, *Mystery of the Temple*, ix; *I Believe*, 1:ix.

12. Congar, *Mystery of the Temple*, 51–52.

13. Congar, *Tradition and Traditions*, 238.

14. Congar, "Pneumatologie et théologie de l'histoire," 61–62.

15. Notes from a sermon preached at St. Séverin in Paris on Dec. 7, 1952, published as Yves Congar, "The Christian Idea of History," in Congar, *Priest and Layman* (London: Darton, Longman and Todd, 1967), 280.

16. Congar, *Mystery of the Temple*, ix.

17. Congar, *Mystery of the Temple*, 53.

18. Congar, "*Dum Visibiliter Deum Cognoscimus*: A Theological Meditation," in Congar, *The Revelation of God*, 89–90. This is a reflection Congar wrote on the feast of Christmas.

19. Congar, "The Church and Pentecost," in Congar, *The Mystery of the Church*, trans. A. V. Littledale (Baltimore: Helicon, 1960), 12.

20. Congar, "La Pneumatologie dans la théologie catholique," 256. See also *I Believe*, 3:149.

21. Congar, *The Wide World, My Parish*, trans. Donald Attwater (Baltimore: Helicon, 1961), 58. See also *I Believe*, 2:83.

22. See for example Congar, *Word and Spirit*, 95; *I Believe* 3:149; *I Believe* 3:171.

23. "What is necessary and what is free in God should, it is true, not be confused, but, on the other hand, both are identified in him." Congar, *I Believe*, 2:68.

24. Congar, *I Believe*, 3:171. In the French original, *réellement* is italicized. *Je crois en l'Esprit Saint* (Paris: Cerf, 1980), 3:228. Pondering the meaning of the identity of liberty and essence in God, Congar continued, "We affirm that identity in our own inability to represent it and to understand it. We can only revere that mystery and make it the object of our praise." *I Believe*, 3:171.

25. On St. Paul, see *I Believe*, 2:68. As to the eternity of the incarnation, Congar echoed Bouyer who maintained that the divine Word assumed a human nature at a definite moment of time but qualified that "as far as He is concerned, He assumes it eternally. Then the Father eternally generates his Son, not only as before His incarnation but also as the Word made flesh." *Word and Spirit*, 97. Reference is to Louis Bouyer, *The Eternal Son* (Huntington, IN: Our Sunday Visitor, 1978), 401.

26. Congar, *Word and Spirit*, 11.

27. Congar, *Fifty Years*, 30.

28. See for example Congar, *Mystery of the Temple*, 262–99; *I Believe*, 1:7 and 2: 76.

29. Congar discussed the meaning of *rûach* in the Old Testament—where the term occurs 378 times with a variety of connotations—in *I Believe*, 1:3–14.

30. See for example Congar, *I Believe*, 1:4 and 1:5.

31. Congar, *Mystery of the Temple*, 4. He elaborated: "It remains true that in the Old Testament and in Judaism, at least before certain rather late developments in Jewish piety, the Holy Spirit (literally: the spirit of holiness), (i) is not considered a divine person; (ii) is above all the power through which God provides for the carrying out of the Covenant." *Mystery of the Temple*, 271.

32. Congar, *I Believe*, 2:75 and 2:78 n. 6.

33. Congar, *I Believe*, 2:73–77.

34. See for example Congar, *Mystery of the Temple*, 262–99; *I Believe*, 2:76. Congar thought that theologians such as Mgr. Waffelaert and Gérard Philips were moving in this same direction.

35. See for example Congar, *Mystery of the Temple*, 16 and 271; *I Believe*, 1:4; *Word and Spirit*, 44.

36. Congar, *Mystery of the Temple*, 16 and 18.

37. Congar, *I Believe*, 1:9.

38. See for example Congar, *Mystery of the Temple*, 262.

39. Congar, *Mystery of the Temple*, 232.

40. Congar, *Mystery of the Temple*, 240.

41. Congar, *Mystery of the Temple*, 237.

42. Congar, *Mystery of the Temple*, xi.

43. Congar, *Word and Spirit*, 85–87. See also *I Believe*, 3:166. Congar believed that Aquinas should have given more emphasis to the humanity of Jesus Christ and to the growth in knowledge and love that occurred throughout his life, and he found Aquinas's presentation of Jesus' life in *ST* III^a qq. 1–60 historically unsatisfactory. He also commented that "The question in the *Summa* devoted to Jesus' baptism goes

back to a theology that is both analytical and typological, not to say metaphorical, and certainly disappointing." *I Believe,* 1:22. At the same time, Congar had great respect for Aquinas's theology of hypostatic union as set forth in *ST* III ª qq. 7–8. See for example *Word and Spirit,* 85.

44. Congar, *Word and Spirit,* 92. See also *I Believe,* 1:16, 3:169–71. This point is expressed more tentatively in *I Believe,* 1:106.

45. Congar credited Heribert Mühlen with raising awareness that "Christ" is not simply a proper name as the scholastic theologians presupposed; biblically, the term means the anointed one or, in Hebrew, the Messiah. *I Believe,* 1:23.

46. On the constitutive importance of Jesus' baptism see Congar, *I Believe,* 1:16, 1:18, 3:166, 3:169. On the designation of Jesus as Servant and the relation of his baptism to his sacrifice and death, see *I Believe,* 1:19.

47. Congar commented on these events in *I Believe,* 1:18.

48. Congar discussed Jesus' growth in knowledge and pondered the question of his consciousness of his identity in *I Believe,* 1:17–18; 3:166–68.

49. On this point see Congar, *Fifty Years,* 20–21.

50. The Holy Spirit, Congar stated, "raised Jesus from the dead (Rom 1:4; 8:11)." *I Believe,* 1:105. See also *I Believe,* 3:144. Elsewhere Congar spoke of the Spirit as the agent of resurrection. *I Believe,* 1:95.

51. See Congar, *I Believe,* 3:169, 1:104. On the need for evil to be overcome before the kingdom of God can be achieved see *Fifty Years,* 20–21.

52. Congar, *I Believe,* 3:169.

53. Congar, *I Believe,* 1:53.

54. Congar, *I Believe,* 2:44–47. The church fathers, Congar noted, understood Pentecost as a reversal of Babel, and Luke himself likely made this connection. See also "Pneumatologie dogmatique," 499 and 499 n. 36.

55. Congar, *I Believe,* 1:44. Elsewhere, Congar drew a parallel between the baptism of Jesus and the significance of Pentecost for the church. *I Believe,* 1:19.

56. Congar, *I Believe,* 1:57.

57. Congar, *I Believe,* 1:55–56.

58. Congar read the books of Acts as a testimony of the communication rather than replacement of Jesus Christ in *I Believe,* 1:45. He spoke of the Spirit of Christ as the power of new birth from above in *Word and Spirit,* 92 and 103.

59. Congar, *Word and Spirit,* 102.

60. Congar distinguished the constitutive period of the church from subsequent centuries in "Pneumatologie dogmatique," 485. He also spoke of a "classical" period in church history, which he identified as the time between Nicaea (325) and the death of St. Gregory the Great (604) and St. Isidore (636). *I Believe,* 1:104.

61. See for example "Pneumatologie dogmatique," 485.

62. On the activity of the Spirit in church councils and elections and the provision of church teachers see Congar, *I Believe,* 1:151. On tradition and the magisterium see *I Believe,* 1:168. On the Spirit in the lives of the saints see for example *Tradition and Traditions,* 263.

63. Congar, *I Believe,* 1:115. On the Holy Spirit and the emergence of new religious orders see also *I Believe,* 1:129. On the ecumenical movement as a work of the Spirit see "The Church and Pentecost," 28. Congar also described the many revivals

that have punctuated the life of the Protestant church as an activity of the Spirit in *I Believe*, 1:146.

64. See for example the reflection "The Spirit secretly guides God's work in the world," in *I Believe*, 2:220–21.

65. Congar, "Pneumatologie et théologie de l'histoire," 70. On the other hand, Congar readily affirmed—as we have seen—that the Spirit guided the church's councils, preserved the church in holiness, and inspired renewal movements throughout ecclesial history. He also explicitly identified some apparently secular historical events as components of God's plan. He was convinced, for example, by B. Duhm's argument that the growth of great empires in the ninth century BCE challenged tribal and nationalistic theologies and provided the framework for the Hebrew prophet's proclamation of God's universal sovereignty. *Mystery of the Temple*, 62. Reference is to B. Duhm, *Israels Propheten* (Tübingen: Mohr Siebeck, 1916), 1–3. Congar also described the destruction of both the Temple and the throne in 587 as a condition for a higher stage of development in the Hebrew people's relationship with God. *Mystery of the Temple*, 44. And he believed that the diaspora contributed to Israel's movement to a higher form of spirituality. *Mystery of the Temple*, 89.

66. Congar, *Word and Spirit*, 125. Reference is to Rom 8:22–23.

67. Congar, *Word and Spirit*, 125.

68. Congar, *Mystery of the Temple*, 149.

69. Congar, *Mystery of the Temple*, 174. Reference is to Heb 11:13–16.

70. See for example Congar, *Word and Spirit*, 19.

71. Congar, *Fifty Years*, 18–19. See also *I Believe*, 3:144; "The Holy Spirit in the Cosmos," in *Word and Spirit*, 122–29.

72. On the Spirit as the one who completes all things see Congar, *I Believe*, 3:144.

73. Congar, *Fifty Years*, 61–62.

74. On the end of the economy as deification, see for example Congar, *I Believe*, 1:95.

75. Congar contrasted his own position on this matter with Luther's in "Luther réformateur," 22. "Il y a un en soi de Dieu," Congar here insisted, "on dirait, si l'on osait, une ontologie de Dieu: cela, c'est pour lui."

76. Congar, "Christ dans l'économie," 87 n. 1.

77. Congar, "Christ dans l'économie," 87. This position is admittedly somewhat at odds with Congar's statement that there is no *Ens a se*, mentioned earlier in the discussion of his theology of creation. The two approaches could conceivably be reconciled in what Congar calls "an ontology of charity," although this is not something he develops in a systematic fashion.

For Congar's further discussion of the differences among "ontology," "ontological," "ontic," "economy," "economic," and "functional," see "Le Moment 'économique' et le moment 'ontologique' dans la sacra doctrina," 135–36.

78. Congar, "Christ dans l'économie," 87.

79. Congar, *Word and Spirit*, 43. Reference is to B. D. Dupuy, *Vatican II. La Révélation divine*, Unam Sanctam, no. 70b (Paris: Cerf, 1968), 563–66; M.-D. Chenu, "Vérité évangélique et métaphysique wolffienne à Vatican II," *RSPhTh* 57 (1975): 632–40.

80. Congar, *Word and Spirit*, 42.

81. Congar, "Christ dans l'économie," 99.

82. Congar, "Christ dans l'économie," 105.

83. Congar, "Christ dans l'économie," 100–101.

84. Congar, "Christ dans l'économie," 102.

85. Congar, *Word and Spirit*, 95.

86. Theodore de Régnon, *Études de théologie positive sur la Sainte Trinité*, 3 vols. (Paris: Retaux, 1892–1898).

87. G. L. Prestige, *God in Patristic Thought* (London: SPCK, 1952), 233.

88. Congar, *I Believe*, 3:xvi.

89. Congar, *I Believe*, 3:xvii.

90. Congar, *I Believe*, 3:34.

91. Congar, *I Believe*, 3:73.

92. Lossky, *In the Image and Likeness of God* (London: Mowbrays, 1975), 79; cited in Congar, *I Believe*, 3:74.

93. Congar, *I Believe*, 3:72.

94. Congar, *I Believe*, 3:200;*Word and Spirit*, 105.

95. Congar, *I Believe*, 3:xvi and 3:72.

96. Congar, *Fifty Years*, 60. See also *I Believe*, 1:78, 3:105.

97. Congar, *I Believe*, 3:116.

98. Congar, *I Believe*, 3:133.

99. Congar, *Word and Spirit*, 10. Congar consistently used "Father" and masculine pronouns in reference to God in accordance with common practice. Anne Harnett explains that Congar's work must be supplemented by feminist theology. See Harnett, "The Role of the Holy Spirit in Revelation and Its Transmission. The Interpretation of Yves Congar," Ph.D. diss., Catholic University of America, 1989. For Congar's discussion of "The Motherhood in God and the Femininity of the Holy Spirit," see *I Believe*, 3:155–64.

100. Congar, *Word and Spirit*, 18.

101. See "The Father, the Absolute Source of Divinity," in Congar, *I Believe*, 3:133–43. He identifies his sources as follows: Origen, *Comm. in Ioan.* II, II, 20 (*SChr* 120, 121): Pseudo-Dionysius, *De div. nom.* II, 7 (*PG* 3, 645B); Gregory Nazianzen, *Orat.* 2, 38 (*PG* 35, 445) and 20, 6 (*PG* 35, 1072C); Greogry Nazianzen, *Orat.* 25, *In laudem Heronis Philos.* 15 (*PG* 35, 1220); Basil, *Ep.* 125, 3 (*PG* 32, 549); Bonaventure, *In I Sent.* d. 29, dub. 1 (Quaracchi ed., I, p. 517); Bonaventure, *Breviloquium*, p. 1, c. 3 (Quaracchi ed., V, p. 212); Alan of Lille, *Reg. theol.* 3 (*PL* 210, 625) and 53–54 (*PL* 210, 647) and Thomas Aquinas, *In I Sent.* d. 29, q. 1, a. 1 sol. end; Albert the Great, *In I Sent.* d. 12, a. 5 (ed. A Borgnet, XXV, 359); Bonaventure, *In I Sent.* d. 27, p. 1, q. 2, ad. 3 (Quaracchi ed., 470–71); Philippe de Gamaches, *Summa theologica* (Paris, 1634), I, 270.

102. Congar, *I Believe*, 3:88, 3:120, and 3:202.

103. Congar, *I Believe*, 3:120 and 3:202.

104. Congar, *I Believe*, 3:121.

105. On Anselm see Congar, *I Believe*, 3:99.

106. Congar, "Renewed Actuality of the Holy Spirit," 22.

107. Congar, *I Believe*, 2:90 and 3:140; *Word and Spirit*, 15. Reference is to Rahner's "*Theos* in the New Testament," *TI* (Baltimore: Helicon, 1961), 1:79–148.

108. Congar, *Mystery of the Temple*, 287.

109. Congar, *I Believe*, 2:89. In this passage Congar is summarizing the position of Greek patristic theology but in an affirmative manner that suggests his accord. Elsewhere he himself reiterated that God is not first a divine essence that is subsequently differentiated into divine persons. See *Fifty Years*, 59.

110. Congar, *Fifty Years*, 60.

111. Congar, *I Believe*, 3:140.

112. Congar, "Dum Visibiliter Deum Cognoscimus," 90.

113. Congar, "Dum Visibiliter Deum Cognoscimus," 90. Elsewhere, Congar spoke of two levels of existence: the biological and the level of *vere esse*. *Word and Spirit*, 46.

114. Congar, *Esprit de l'homme, Esprit de Dieu*. Foi Vivante, no. 206 (Paris: Cerf, 1983), 86.

115. Congar, "La Tri-unité de Dieu," 692.

116. Karl Rahner, *The Trinity*, trans. Joseph Donceel (New York: Herder and Herder, 1970; New York: Crossroad, 1997), 103–15; Barth, *Church Dogmatics* I/1, 2d ed. (Edinburgh: T & T Clark, 1975), 355.

117. See Aquinas, *ST* I^a q. 29, a. 4. In a review of Bouyer's *Le Consolateur* that critiqued Aquinas on this point, Congar maintained that the expression "subsistent relation" has a precise and profound meaning. "Chronique de pneumatologie," *RSPhTh* 64 (1980): 446.

Congar rendered *relationis oppositio* in French as *opposition de relation*, which David Smith translated into English as "opposition of relationship." See for example *Je crois*, 3:140, as compared to *I Believe*, 3:98. Smith's translation is not precise, since in fact the technical trinitarian term is "relation" rather than "relationship." Furthermore, the English word "opposition" is misleading, since it has connotations of contrariness. Throughout this chapter I thus use the Latin expression, since it is less prone to misunderstanding. It is also less prone to inversion. Congar noted that some Orthodox theologians believe that the West postulates "relationships of opposition," but Congar insisted that "to speak of 'a relationship of opposition' instead of an 'opposition of relationship' (as in the case of Father—Son or Son—Father) could mean that, for the Latins, the persons are pure relations in essence, but this would point to a lack of understanding, both of the idea of subsistent relationships and of the way in which the Latins think of the diversity of the persons in the unity and simplicity of the divine Absolute." *I Believe*, 3:78 n. 11.

118. Congar, "La Tri-unité de Dieu," 693. See also: "All is common to the Three Divine Persons except that by which the first Person is the Father, the second is the Son, and the third is the Holy Spirit, and hence all the order in which the Three divine Persons exist, since this order derives from the relations which make them what they are as Persons." *Mystery of the Temple*, 286.

119. This axiom is not found verbatim in Anselm, Congar explained, but is implicit in Anselm's argument in *De proc. spir. sanct.* 1 (Schmitt, II, p.180, 1.27; 181, 1. 2–4; 183, 1.3). *I Believe*, 3:98 and 3:102 n. 9; *Word and Spirit*, 119 n. 20.

120. Congar, *I Believe*, 3:98. See also *Word and Spirit*, 108.

121. Paul Evdokimov, *L'Esprit Saint dans la tradition orthodoxe* (Paris: Cerf, 1969), 41.

122. Congar, *I Believe*, 3:78 n. 11.

123. Congar, "La Tri-unité de Dieu," 693.

124. Congar believed that was also the teaching of the Greek Fathers. *I Believe*, 3: 37.

125. See for example Congar, *I Believe*, 3:114.

126. Congar, *I Believe*, 2:89.

127. On the identity of *esse* and *essentia* in God see for example Aquinas, *ST* Iᵃ q. 3, a. 3 and a. 4.

128. Congar, *I Believe*, 1:89. Indeed, in Western theology at large, Congar stated elsewhere, "There is no activity of the nature or essence of the divinity that exists prior to or independent of the Persons." *I Believe*, 2:85.

129. Congar described the divine substance as love in *Esprit de l'homme*, 86. Elsewhere he wrote of God the Father: "*Agapē*—love flowing like a source, love initiating being and life—is attributed to God as a hypostatic mark, that is, as a personal characteristic (see 2 Cor 13:13; 1 Cor 13:11). The Father is the subject of this *agapē* (see 1 Jn 2:15; Jn 3:14; Eph 2:4)." *I Believe*, 3:140. See also *I Believe* 2:86, where this point is discussed in light of the work of A. Nygren. Elsewhere Congar wrote that the Word and the Spirit do "whatever the Father, who is Love" wishes to do. *Word and Spirit*, 25.

130. Congar, *Mystery of the Temple*, 240. In the Incarnation God is united to humanity "personally and in his own being." *Mystery of the Temple*, 240. The old dispensation in contrast was limited because God did not yet communicate himself *personnellement*. *Mystery of the Temple*, 18; French edition, 34.

131. Congar, *Mystery of the Temple*, 239. This should not, Congar emphasized, be understood as if grace were a "substance" in the sense of a "thing." See *I Believe*, 2: 83.

132. Congar, *Mystery of the Temple*, 264. Elsewhere Congar wrote that grace is the "substantial indwelling of the divine persons and divinization." *I Believe*, 2:75.

133. *Mystery of the Temple*, 112. It is also notable that Congar distinguished two kinds of substantial and personal presence: "God, who is already present through his activity as creator and is therefore also substantially present—since his action is himself—but only as the cause of being and working, gives himself and becomes substantially present as the object of our love and knowledge, as the end of our return to him as our Father. His presence is also personal. He is not only in us, but also with us, and we are with him." *I Believe*, 2:83–84. Evidently Congar here has distinguished two kinds of divine presence: (a) causal presence and (b) presence as the object of knowledge and love. These two kinds of presence are proper to the realms of creation and grace, respectively.

134. See for example Congar, *Fifty Years*, 60.

135. Congar, *Word and Spirit*, 5. Reference is to *In III Sent.* d. 25, q. 1, a.1, qᵃ 1, obj. 4 and *ST* IIᵃ IIᵃᵉ, q. 1, a. 6. Congar noted that Albert the Great and Bonaventure also described articles of faith in this manner.

136. Congar, *Word and Spirit*, 5.

137. Congar, *Word and Spirit*, 6. He is citing here Claude Geffré, in *Initiation à la pratique de la théologie*, ed. Bernard Lauret and François Refoulé (Paris: Cerf, 1982), 1:124. On this point see also Congar's "The Spirit and Truth: The Spirit Is Truth," chapter 4 of *Word and Spirit*, 42–47.

138. Congar, *Word and Spirit*, 5.

139. Congar, "Dum Visibiliter Deum Cognoscimus," 90.

140. Congar, *Word and Spirit*, 11 and 97.

141. Congar, "Christ dans l'économie," 106.

142. Congar, "Christ dans l'économie," 106.

143. Congar, *Word and Spirit*, 4. This stands in contrast with an earlier statement: "The revelation of the mystery of the Trinity has been made as much through the economy itself as through theoretical statements." *Mystery of the Temple*, 286.

144. Congar, "Christ dans l'économie," 107. See also 89.

145. Congar, "Le Troisième article du symbole," 290.

146. Congar, "L'Influence de la société et de l'histoire sur le développement de l'homme chrétien," *NRT* 96 (1974): 686. Elsewhere he wrote: "[W]hen he [God] is not content to speak from afar off, as it were through a representative, but when he comes *himself* to be seen and heard in person—'Philip, he who has seen me has seen the Father' (John 14:9)—God speaks more than ever in human terms and lives more than ever a human history, since HE BECOMES MAN." *Tradition and Traditions*, 238.

147. Congar spoke of the Incarnate Word as suprahistorical in *Tradition and Traditions*, 260 n. 1.

148. Rahner, *The Trinity*, 22.

149. Congar, *Word and Spirit*, 104.

150. Congar, *I Believe*, 3:13–14.

151. Congar, *I Believe*, 3:15. See also *Word and Spirit*, 105.

152. Congar, *I Believe*, 3:15–16.

153. Congar, *Word and Spirit*, 105.

154. Congar, *Esprit de l'homme*, 29.

155. See for example Congar, *I Believe*, 2:68. This passage may help clarify Congar's position: "We may therefore conclude that it is possible to speak of the Word *without* Jesus' assumption of humanity, although it is not possible to speak of the existence of that Word *before* the incarnation. This is the condition by which justice is done to the difference between the necessary mystery of the Tri-unity of God and the free mystery of his election of grace." *Word and Spirit*, 95.

156. Congar, *Tradition and Traditions*, 265 n. 1 and 342 n. 1.

157. Congar's "The Holy Spirit and the Apostolic Body: Continuators of the Work of Christ" and "The Church and Pentecost" appeared in English in Congar, *The Mystery of the Church*, trans. A. V. Littledale (Baltimore: Helicon, 1960), 147–86 and 1–57.

158. Congar, "Church and Pentecost," 7.

159. Congar, "Church and Pentecost," 7.

160. Congar, "Church and Pentecost," 33.

161. Congar, "Church and Pentecost," 19.

162. My emphasis.

163. Congar, "The Holy Spirit and the Apostolic Body," 149–50.

164. Congar, "The Holy Spirit and the Apostolic Body," 158.

165. Congar, "The Holy Spirit and the Apostolic Body," 154. Emphasis original.

166. Congar, "The Holy Spirit and the Apostolic Body," 151.

167. Congar, "The Holy Spirit and the Apostolic Body," 161. See also 150 and 158–59.

168. Congar, "Church and Pentecost," 14.

169. Congar, "The Holy Spirit and the Apostolic Body," 150.

170. Congar, "Church and Pentecost," 14.

171. Congar, "Church and Pentecost," 15.

172. Congar, "Church and Pentecost," 15. Emphasis original. See also "The Holy Spirit and the Apostolic Body," 170.

173. Congar noted that this distinction between Christ's objective work and the Spirit's subjective activity was not original to him. He commented that theologians speak in these terms, although he did not reference any particular authors. "Church and Pentecost," 15.

174. Congar, "Church and Pentecost," 15. Emphasis original.

175. Congar, "Church and Pentecost," 24. See also "The Holy Spirit and the Apostolic Body," 151 and 165.

176. Congar, "The Holy Spirit and the Apostolic Body," 148.

177. Congar believed that Joachim betrayed the principle that the Spirit simply completes the work of Christ. See for example "The Holy Spirit and the Apostolic Body," 152.

178. Congar, "The Holy Spirit and the Apostolic Body," 178.

179. On the duality in the Spirit's work of both "Institution" and "Event" see for example "Holy Spirit and the Apostolic Body," 177.

180. Congar, "Holy Spirit and the Apostolic Body," 180. Congar thought his position was comparable to that of Walter Kasper as presented in his *Dogma unter dem Wort Gottes* (Mainz: Matthias-Grünewald, 1965); French trans. *Dogme et évangile* (Tournai: Casterman, 1967). Kasper believed the Spirit was active in the church first as the "Spirit of Christ" but also "in the freedom which is peculiar to him." See Kasper, *Dogme et évangile*, 88–90, and Congar, *I Believe*, 2:14 n. 32. Congar's discussion of the free sector of the Spirit was critiqued by P. Bonnard, "L'Esprit et l'Église selon le Nouveau Testament," *RHPR* 37 (1957): 81–90; M.-A. Chevallier, *Esprit de Dieu et paroles d'homme* (Neuchâtel: Delachaux et Niestlé, 1966), 212 n. 3; F. Malmberg, *Ein Leib—Ein Geist. Vom Mysterium der Kirche* (Freiburg: Herder, 1960), 192ff.

181. Congar, *I Believe*, 2:23 n. 16. Congar referred here particularly to *Tradition and Traditions*, 257–70.

182. Famerée, *L'Ecclésiologie d'Yves Congar*, 429, 408, and 418. Isaac Kizhakkeparampil is of the opinion that christocentrism remains dominant in Congar's thought even in this later period, and he argues that Congar's work would have been enhanced if he had more thoroughly integrated Spirit Christology into his approach. Kizhakkeparampil, *The Invocation of the Holy Spirit as Constitutive of the Sacraments According to Cardinal Yves Congar* (Rome: Gregorian University Press, 1995), 147.

183. Congar, *Word and Spirit*, 21. Emphasis is Famerée's. The French is "La Parole et l'Esprit opèrent conjointement l'oeuvre de Dieu." *La Parole et le Souffle*, 43. One could also note that the first paragraph of Congar's 1982 essay "Pneumatologie dogmatique" includes the statement *L'Esprit inspire la poursuite de l'oeuvre de Dieu.* "Pneumatologie dogmatique," 485. Congar italicized this line.

184. Famerée, *L'Ecclésiologie d'Yves Congar*, 450.

185. Congar, *I Believe*, 2:104.

186. Statements that the Spirit completes and continues the work of Christ can be found in Congar, *I Believe*, 2:12, 3:162; "Pneumatologie dogmatique," 508, 509. Jesus Christ is presented as actualizing his own mission in the Spirit in *I Believe*, 3:165–73.

187. See Congar, *I Believe*, 1:37–38 and 1:55–56; "Pneumatologie dogmatique," 506–7.

188. Congar, "Le Troisième article du symbole," 291.

189. See "Towards a Pneumatological Christology," in Congar, *I Believe*, 3:165–73; "The Place of the Holy Spirit in Christology," in *Word and Spirit*, 85–100.

190. Congar, "Pneumatologie dogmatique," 495–96.

191. Congar, *I Believe*, 2:5–14. See additionally Famerée, *L'Ecclésiologie d'Yves Congar*, 451.

192. Congar, "Pneumatologie dogmatique," 496.

193. Congar, *Word and Spirit*, 57. The English actually reads "co-existent here and now with the church of the incarnate Word" but the French is "*co–instituant* actuel de l'Église du Verbe incarné." *La Parole et le Souffle*, 99. See also an Appendix to *Word and Spirit* entitled "The Spirit as co-instituting the Church" (78–84) and "L'Esprit est co-instituant de l'Église," in "Le Troisième article du symbole," 292–94.

194. Congar, *I Believe*, 2:11.

195. Congar, *Word and Spirit*, 61.

196. "He sees them as in the same sphere of existence and function or of action." Congar, *Word and Spirit*, 25.

197. Congar, *Word and Spirit*, 71. Although "an irreducible personal factor enters into the instituted framework [of the church] . . . this does not mean that it is not Christological. It could be called an element of Christological pneumatology or pneumatological Christology." *Word and Spirit*, 53.

198. Congar, *I Believe*, 2:12.

199. Congar, *Word and Spirit*, 1. See also *Word and Spirit*, 62; "Chronique de pneumatologie," 448. Just as Congar opposed a Christology divorced from pneumatology, so, too, he cautioned against a pneumatology removed from Christology. "The soundness of any pneumatology is its reference to Christ." *I Believe*, 2:35. Elsewhere Congar warned against *pneumatocentrisme*. "Pneumatologie dogmatique," 502 and 510.

200. Congar, *I Believe*, 1:157.

201. Congar, *I Believe*, 2:12. See also *Word and Spirit*, 53.

202. According to Congar, rudiments of a *Filioque* theology can be found in someform in Tertullian, Hilary of Potiers, Marius Victorinus, and Ambrose of Milan. It was Augustine, however, who was the major influence in the development of the *Filioque* theology in the West. "He did not initiate the idea," but he "continued to be the major source in the question of the *Filioque*." *I Believe*, 3:134. Augustine's point of departure was the scriptural witness that the Spirit is of both the Father (Mt 10:28) and the Son (Gal 4:6; Jn 14:26; Lk 6:19; Rom 8:15). *I Believe*, 3:86. Reference is to *De Trin* I 4, 7; 5, 8; 8, 18. Augustine himself, of course, lived during a period when the *Filioque* as such was not a contested issue, but other theologians had recourse to his writings when the *Filioque* debate began.

203. This is the phrase of Photius, *On the Mystagogy of the Holy Spirit* (PG 102, 280).

204. Congar believed that political and sociological divisions also contributed to the breach of East and West. See *Divided Christendom*, trans. M. A. Bousfield (London: Centenary Press, 1939), 3–14.

205. Vladimir Lossky, *The Mystical Theology of the Eastern Church* (Crestwood, NY: St. Vladimir's Seminary Press, 1976), 56f.

206. Congar noted that Lossky did become "less obstinate on this point as he got older," although in the meantime he had won over a large number of followers to his position. *I Believe*, 3:xv. In discussion with Lossky, Congar pointed out that Reformation theologians vociferously contested Roman Catholic ecclesiology and yet defended the *Filioque*. Congar also called attention to the work of Sergei Bulgakov, an Orthodox theologian who was "particularly allergic to juridicism" but who believed that the *Filioque* theology had no ecclesiological repercussions. *I Believe*, 3:210–11.

207. Congar, *Diversity and Communion*, trans. John Bowden (London: SCM Press, 1984), 98.

208. Congar, "Le Troisième article du symbole," 301. Congar also believed, however, that "the quarrel about the ecclesiological consequences of the *Filioque* is of doubtful value." *I Believe*, 3:211.

209. Congar, *I Believe*, 3:208. The Aquinas reference is *Contra Err. Graec.* II, 32 (Leonine ed., 87).

210. Epiphanius, *Anc.* 6 (*PG* 43, 25C), 7 (*PG* 43, 28A), 11 (*PG* 43, 36C), 67 (*PG* 43, 137B), 73 (*PG* 43, 153A), 120 (*PG* 43, 236B); *Panarion, Haer.* LXII (*PG* 41, 1056). Cited in *I Believe*, 3:27 and 3:28 n. 14. Epiphanius, Congar explained, based this position on John 16:14, 15: "he will take (receive) from me."

211. Cyril of Alexandria, *Comm. in Ioel.* XXXV (*PG* 71, 377D); *De recta fide ad Theod.* XXXVII (*PG* 76, 1189A); *De SS. Trin. Dial.* VII (*PG* 75, 1093A); *Comm. in Ioan.* II (*PG* 71, 212B); *Adv. Nest.* IV, 1 (*PG* 76, 173A–B); *De recta fide ad Reg. Or. alt* LI (*PG* 76, 1408B); *De ador.* I (*PG* 68, 148A); *Adv. Nest.* IV, 3 (*PG* 76, 184D). Cited in Congar, *I Believe*, 3:35 and 3:46 nn. 48, 50, 51, and 52.

212. Congar, "Church and Pentecost," 19.

213. Congar, *I Believe*, 3:187.

214. Aquinas, *ST* I^a, q. 36, r. 2.

215. Congar, *I Believe*, 3:120.

216. Congar, *I Believe*, 3:87.

217. Congar noted that the idea of "complementarity" was introduced by the physicist Niels Bohr in 1927 to express wave/particle duality. Bohr himself generalized this phenomenon into an epistemological principle, although Congar expressed concern about the concept's vagueness. *Diversity and Communion*, 75.

218. Congar, *I Believe*, 3:188, 3:206.

219. Congar, *Diversity and Communion*, 76. See also "Pneumatologie ou 'christomonisme,' " 62; "Chronique de pneumatologie," 446.

220. Congar, "Chronique de pneumatologie," 448.

221. Congar, *I Believe*, 3:8.

222. Congar noted his change of position on this issue in *I Believe*, 3:204.

223. Congar, *I Believe*, 3:54.

224. Congar, *I Believe*, 3:130.

225. Congar, *I Believe*, 3:49.

226. Congar, *I Believe*, 3:206.

227. On Augustine see *I Believe*, 1:79. Reference is to Augustine's *De Trin.* XV, 17, 29 and 26, 45–47. On Aquinas see *Word and Spirit*, 107. Reference is to Aquinas's *Contra Gent.* IV, 24.

228. Congar, *I Believe*, 3:51.

229. Congar, *I Believe*, 3:32 and 3:39. He thought Photius ignored such texts in his determination to starkly oppose Eastern and Western theologies. *I Believe*, 3:58.

230. Congar, *I Believe*, 3:76.

231. Congar, *Word and Spirit*, 107.

232. Paul Evdokimov, *L'Esprit Saint*, 46.

233. "If it were simply a question of the birth of the Word made flesh in time, there would be no problem, but we have a discussion of eternal being. The formula [Evdokimov's *ex Patre Spirituque*] can therefore be disputed, because it does not respect the order of the Persons in their eternal being and the fact that, as Basil the Great pointed out, the Spirit is numbered together with the others, but third. Athanasius can also be quoted in this context. Nonetheless, we should welcome this idea of the in-existence of the hypostases one within the other, the idea, in other words, of exchange and reciprocity." Congar, *I Believe*, 3:75.

234. Congar, *Word and Spirit*, 93.

235. Congar, *I Believe*, 1:vii.

236. Congar, *I Believe*, 1:vii.

237. This, Congar commented, is "one of the most profound reflections made on the Holy Spirit." "Pneumatology Today," 448. The expression comes from von Balthasar's "Der Unbekannte jenseits des Wortes," in Helmut Kuhn, ed., *Interpretation der Welt; Festschrift R. Guardini* (Würzburg: Echter, 1965), 638–45.

238. Congar, *I Believe*, 1:vii–viii. Congar also wrote of the kenosis of the Spirit in "Le Troisième article du symbole," 289.

239. Congar, *I Believe*, 1:xvii.

240. Congar, *I Believe*, 3:149.

241. Congar, "Pneumatologie dogmatique," 508.

242. Congar, *Esprit de l'homme*, 80.

243. Aquinas, *ST* I^a, q. 37, c.

244. Congar, *I Believe*, 3:146. Reference is to Augustine, *De Trin.* VI, 10, 11.

245. See "The Theme of the Holy Spirit as the Mutual Love of the Father and the Son," in Congar, *I Believe*, 1:85–92, and "Speculative Triadology Constructed in Faith and under the Sign of Love," in *I Believe*, 3:103–15.

246. Congar, *I Believe*, 3:148.

247. H. F. Dondaine, *S. Thomas d'Aquin, Somme Théologique. La Trinité* (Paris: Desclée, 1946), 2:397–401. Cited in Congar, *I Believe*, 1:90.

248. Congar, *I Believe*, 1:92 n. 5. Reference is to Yves Raguin, *La Profondeur de Dieu* (Paris: Desclée, 1973) and *L'Esprit sur le monde* (Paris: Desclée, 1975). Congar reiterated the problem of anthropomorphism created by the mutual love theology in *I Believe*, 3:122.

249. See Congar, *I Believe*, 3:117 and 1:88–90; "Bulletin de théologie," *RSPhTh* 56 (1972): 307.

250. Congar, *I Believe*, 1:85.

251. Congar, *I Believe*, 3:147.

252. Congar, *I Believe*, 3:147–48.

253. Aquinas, *ST* I^a q. 32, a. 3, c.

254. Aquinas, *ST* I^a, q. 39, aa. 7–8.

255. Congar, *I Believe*, 2:85. Indeed, "the fact that attributes are constantly chang-

ing their position points to the non-exclusive nature of appropriations." *I Believe*, 2:
86.

256. Congar, *I Believe*, 2:85.

257. Heribert Mühlen, "Person und Appropriation," *MThZ* 16 (1965): 37–57;
Karl Rahner, "Some Implications of the Scholastic Concept of Uncreated Grace," *TI*
(Baltimore: Helicon, 1961), 1:345–46.

258. Rahner, *The Trinity*, 24–27.

259. Congar, "Pneumatologie ou 'christomonisme,' " 61.

260. Congar, "Pneumatology Today," 444. Appropriation is suggestive and fosters prayer but "is not entirely satisfactory in the rational sense." *I Believe*, 2:85. See
also 2:86–87.

261. Congar, "La pneumatologie dans la théologie catholique," 251.

262. In the same article cited earlier in which Congar stated that "our theology
does not see enough that the mission of the Spirit is proper and original," Congar
wrote that in the Latin tradition the "indwelling of God in the souls of the just (John
14:24) is appropriated to the Holy Spirit" and that the Spirit is by appropriation "the
principle of generosity through which God extends his family to his creatures." "La
pneumatologie dans la théologie catholique," 253 and 255. Congar also remarked that
Louis Bouyer's critique of appropriation in his *Le Consolateur* (Paris: Cerf, 1980) had
not done justice to the theology of appropriation's positive character. "Chronique du
pneumatologie," 446.

263. Congar, *I Believe*, 2:85–6. He believed, for example, that St. Paul had appropriated *koinōnia* (2 Cor 13:13) to the Holy Spirit and *agapē* to the Father. *Mystery of the
Temple*, 287. It should be noted, however, that the published form of *Mystery of the
Temple* does not give full expression to Congar's views on this subject. Congar's personal journal reveals that in his attempt to obtain a *nihil obstat* for *Mystery of the Temple*, he is told that the book has several problems—it is (among other things) too severe in its discussion of the Holy Spirit and the Western theology of appropriations.
Fouilloux notes that the published version of the text avoids asperity on this topic.
Journal d'un théologien, 388 and 388 n. 95.

264. On the person of the Word as the principle of a proper causality see Congar, "Pneumatologie ou 'christomonisme,' " 59. See also *I Believe*, 2:85.

265. Congar, "Pneumatologie ou 'christomonisme,' " 42.

266. Congar, "Pneumatologie ou 'christomonisme,' " 59; *Mystery of the Temple*,
289. See also *Mystery of the Temple*, 288 and 292.

267. Congar, *I Believe*, 2:20.

268. Congar, *I Believe*, 2:89–90.

269. Congar, "Renewed Actuality of the Holy Spirit," 21. See also "Pneumatologie dogmatique," 508.

270. For additional references see Congar, *I Believe*, 3:4–5.

271. Congar, *I Believe*, 3:144.

272. Hilary of Poitiers, *De Trinitate*, II, 1 (*PL* 10, 50); cf. II, 29 (*PL* 10, 70A).
Cited by Congar in *I Believe*, 3:146.

273. Augustine, *De vera religione*. Cited by Congar in *I Believe*, 3:146–47. See also
1:79–80.

274. Peter Lombard, *I Sent.*, d. 18; Aquinas, *ST* I^a, q. 37 and q. 38. Cited by Congar in *I Believe*, 3:147.

275. Congar, *I Believe*, 3:146.

276. Congar, *I Believe*, 3:145 and 147.

277. Congar, *I Believe*, 1:80.

278. Congar, *I Believe*, 3:149.

279. Congar, *I Believe*, 3:144.

280. For additional scriptural references to the Spirit as gift see Congar, *I Believe*, 3:144–45.

281. 2 Cor 1:22. See also Acts 5:32; Acts 8:18; Acts 15:8; Lk 11:13; Rom 5:5; 2 Cor 5:5; Eph 1:17; 1 Thes 4:8; 2 Tim 1:7; Jn 3:34; Jn 4:14; Rv: 21:16; Rv 14:16; 1 Jn 3:24; 1 Jn 4:13. For references to the Spirit using *lambanō* constructions see Acts 1:8; Acts 2:33; Acts 2:38; Acts 8:15; Acts 8:18; Acts 8:19; Acts 10:47; Acts 19:2; 1 Cor 2:12; 2 Cor 11:4; Gal 3:2; Gal 3:14; Jn 7:39; Jn 14:17; Jn 20:22. Cited by Congar in *I Believe*, 3:152 n. 6.

282. Congar, *I Believe*, 3:144. See also 2:69.

283. Congar, *I Believe*, 3:149.

CHAPTER 3

1. Simeon the New Theologian, *Hymns 1–15*, SChr no. 156 (Paris: Cerf, 1969), 151. Cited in Congar, *I Believe*, 2:112.

2. See Congar, "Renewed Actuality of the Holy Spirit," 20; *I Believe*, 1:156; "Le Troisième article du symbole," 292.

3. The phrase "pneumatological anthropology" appears in *Word and Spirit*, 122. The French is *"une anthropologie pneumatologique." La Parole et le Souffle*, 191. The expression "pneumatological ecclesiology" appears in "Actualité d'une pneumatologie," *POC* 2 (1973):124. The French is *une ecclésiologie pneumatologique*. Congar also used the expression *une pneumatologie ecclésiologique*. See "Pneumatologie dogmatique," 493.

4. See Congar, "The Council as an Assembly and the Church as Essentially Conciliar," 45.

5. Congar, "Poverty as an Act of Faith," *Conc* 194 (1977): 100. See also *Wide World, My Parish*, 37; "Religious Belief and the Life of the World," in Congar, *Faith and Spiritual Life*, 169. Congar's discussion of the inseparability of God and humanity frequently referenced Abraham Heschel's *God in Search of Man* (New York: Harper and Row, 1955). Congar expressed his great esteem for Heschel in *Fifty Years*, 37.

6. Interview with Yves Congar in *The Crucial Questions on Problems Facing the Church Today*, ed. Frank Fehmers (New York: Newman Press, 1969), 9.

7. Congar, *Wide World, My Parish*, 38.

8. "Interview with Yves Congar," *America* 155 (6 May 1967): 677. See also Congar's "Perspectives chrétiennes sur la vie personnelle et la vie collective," in *Socialisation et personne humaine*, Semaine sociale de Grenoble 1960 (Lyons: Chronique sociale de France, 1960), 195–96.

9. Interview with Yves Congar in *The Crucial Questions*, 9.

10. See Augustine's *De Trinitate*, VII, 10, 14; IX, 2, 2; IX, 3, 3; X, 11, 7; XI, 2, 2; XI, 3, 6–9; XII, 15, 25; XIII, 20, 26; XIV, 12, 15. For an important critique of the long-standing assumption that Augustine's *De Trinitate* intended to set forth a series of psychological analogies for the Trinity see John Cavadini, "The Structure and Intention of Augustine's *De Trinitate*," *AugustinStud* 23 (1992): 103–23.

11. William Hasker, "Tri-Unity," *JRel* 50 (1970): 1–32; Jürgen Moltmann, *The Trinity and the Kingdom* (San Francisco: Harper and Row, 1981), 199.

12. Congar, "La Tri-unité de Dieu," 693.

13. Congar, "La Tri-unité de Dieu," 688–90. Reference is to Augustine, *De Trinitate*, XII; Aquinas, *ST* I^a, q. 36, a. 3, ad 1; q. 93, a.6, 002.

14. Congar, "La Tri-unité de Dieu," 688.

15. Aquinas, *ST* I^a, q. 93, a. 6 and a. 7. Congar concurred: our nature "carries a reflection of the nature of God in its properties of intelligence and will." "Perspectives chrétiennes sur la vie personnelle," 205.

16. Congar, "La Tri-unité de Dieu," 689.

17. See Congar, "L'Homme est capable d'être appelé," *VS* 120 (1969): 377–84. Aquinas, in like vein, had written that the *imago Dei* is manifest in humanity's "natural aptitude for understanding and loving God; and this aptitude consists in the very nature of the mind, which is common to all men." *ST* I^a, q. 93, a. 4, c.

18. Congar, "La Tri-unité de Dieu," 693.

19. Congar, "La Tri-unité de Dieu," 693. Emphasis original.

20. Congar, *Lay People in the Church*, 444. When someone loves another, Congar wrote elsewhere, "He fulfills a need of human nature, deep below the superficial calls of selfishness, the need for fellowship with other people, and even with all living creatures. . . . Our true personality . . . is the one that loves and gives." *Wide World, My Parish*, 56.

21. Congar, *Blessed Is the Peace of My Church*, 64. This anthropology is given poignant expression in Congar's journal entries from his time in exile from his Dominican community and family in France. Standing outside under a tree in Cambridge in 1956 waiting for the rain to clear, he weeps bitterly: "Shall I always be a poor man all alone, shall I travel without end to suitcases, shall I always be alone and with nothing, like an orphan? *Dominus autem assumpsit me*: these tears, will God not hear them?" Congar acknowledged that there are transcendent things that no person can ever take away from us, "but this is not sufficient. We are beings of flesh, with a heart of flesh. . . . With the exile, and perhaps also with age, and especially here at Cambridge, I have seen arise in me an ontological need—like thirst after a long road or an exhausting physical labor—to love and be loved." *Journal d'un théologien*, 419, 420, and 428.

22. Congar, *Wide World, My Parish*, 6.

23. Congar, *Blessed Is the Peace of My Church*, 62; interview with Yves Congar in *The Crucial Questions*, 10.

24. Congar, "L'Homme est capable d'être appelé," 391.

25. Congar, *Wide World, My Parish*, 140–41.

26. God "is pure act and is also the first cause of being for all things. . . . Therefore, if He has communicated His likeness, as far as actual being is concerned, to other things, by virtue of the fact that He has brought things into being, it follows that He has communicated to them his likeness, as far as acting is concerned, so that created things may also have their own actions." *SCG*, III.69.14. "The dignity of causality is imparted even to creatures." *ST* I^a, q. 22, a. 3, c. This is true in a special way of humankind.

27. Aquinas, *ST* II^a–II^{ae}, Prologue. Aquinas here referenced the work of John Damascene.

28. Congar, *Esprit de l'homme*, 55. See also: The person is "a spiritual subject having as such, at its own level, an absolute value." "L'Influence de la société et de l'histoire," 691. In social life "what is done should be the activity of a person, that a person, with his own personal conviction, should be really the subject of that activity." *Word and Spirit*, 55. Such references could be multiplied.

In Congar's personal journals, this issue surfaces repeatedly as a point of contention between Congar and ecclesiastical authorities in Rome. The ecclesiology of the Curia, Congar laments, is based in an anthropology that has no confidence in human persons and treats them in an infantile fashion. *Journal d'un théologien*, 295. See also 303. He differed with Lallement on this point as well. *Journal d'un théologien*, 43.

29. Congar, *Vraie et fausse réforme*, 2d ed., 48.

30. Congar, *Esprit de l'homme*, 38. "Today people no longer want to be objects but subjects." *Fifty Years*, 67. Despite these affirmations, occasionally one does find passages where Congar speaks of persons as both subjects and objects. For example: "Lay people are not only *objects* in the Church, objects though they are of her goodness and care; they are also religious *subjects*, and therefore active persons." Yves Congar, "Holy Spirit and Spirit of Freedom," address presented during the Fourth Franco-German Week at Freiburg im Breisgau, in 1958, reprinted in Congar, *Laity, Church, World*, trans. Donald Attwater (Baltimore: Helicon, 1960), 22.

31. Congar, "L'Influence de la société et de l'histoire," 680. See also Congar's "Perspectives chrétiennes sur la vie personnelle et la vie collective," 195–221.

32. Thus there is a "dialectic of structures and of the person." "L'Influence de la société et de l'histoire," 680. See also "Perspectives chrétiennes sur la vie personnelle et la vie collective," 195–221.

33. On the importance of human choice and judgment see for example Congar's statement: "For freedom is the mode of action that befits a spiritual being and a person who exists in his own being, with choice and judgement of his own activity." *Lay People in the Church*, 425.

34. Congar, *Wide World, My Parish*, 100. See also 84–92.

35. Congar, *Wide World, My Parish*, 73.

36. Congar, *Wide World, My Parish*, 85.

37. Congar, "Holy Spirit and Spirit of Freedom," 14.

38. Congar, "L'Homme est capable d'être appelé," 377.

39. Congar, "L'Influence de la société et de l'histoire," 673.

40. Congar, "L'Influence de la société et de l'histoire," 688 and 678. See also "L'Historicité de l'homme selon Thomas d'Aquin," *DCom* 22 (1969): 297–304.

41. Congar, *The Catholic Church and the Race Question* (Paris: Unesco, 1961), 14–15; "L'Influence de la société et de l'histoire," 686.

42. Congar, *Catholic Church and the Race Question*, 15. Reference is to Tennyson's poem "The Making of Man." Congar again cites this poem in "L'Influence de la société et de l'histoire," 686.

43. "This is simply to recognize the reality of the human condition which is not purely constituting and situating but radically constituted and situated." Congar, "L'Homme est capable d'être appelé," 382.

44. Congar, "L'Influence de la société et de l'histoire," 675 and 680.

45. Congar, "L'Homme est capable d'être appelé," 381.

46. Congar, "L'Influence de la société et de l'histoire," 687.

47. Gregory of Nyssa, *De hominis opificio*, 16.16–18. This tradition was popularized in the twentieth century by Henri de Lubac's *Catholicism: A Study of Dogma in Relation to the Corporate Destiny of Mankind*, trans. Lancelot Sheppard (New York: Sheed and Ward, 1950).

48. Congar, "The Church, Seed of Unity and Hope for the Human Race," *Chicago Studies* 5 (1966): 29. See also *Catholic Church and the Race Question*, 13–15.

49. Cited by Congar in *Wide World, My Parish*, 17. No reference is given.

50. "Holy Spirit and Spirit of Freedom," 22. Congar's emphasis on personal uniqueness was influenced in part by personalist philosophy. See *Wide World, My Parish*, 17.

51. Congar, "La Tri-unité de Dieu," 690. Like the incommunicable divine persons, the human person is "something unique, a thing in itself and for itself." *Wide World, My Parish*, 40.

52. Congar, "Religious Belief and the Life of the World," 185–86.

53. Congar, "Perspectives chrétiennes sur la vie personnelle," 205–6.

54. Congar, "Perspectives chrétiennes sur la vie personnelle," 205.

55. Congar, "La Tri-unité de Dieu," 691.

56. Congar, "La Tri-unité de Dieu," 691.

57. Congar, "Holy Spirit and Spirit of Freedom," 8.

58. Congar, "L'Influence de la société et de l'histoire," 690.

59. Congar, *Wide World, My Parish*, 41.

60. Congar, *Word and Spirit*, 122.

61. Congar, *Wide World, My Parish*, 42. In like vein, Congar described hell as existence outside of God, leading life only for oneself. *Wide World, My Parish*, 76.

62. Congar identified human nature as the vehicle of transmission of original sin in *Divided Christendom*, 68; *Blessed Is the Peace of My Church*, 62.

63. Congar, *Wide World, My Parish*, 46–48, in reference to Sartre's "L'Enfer—c'est les autres."

64. Congar, *Wide World, My Parish*, 134. See also "Are St. Paul's 'Powers' Mythological?" in *Wide World, My Parish*, 128–130; *Esprit de l'homme*, 50–51; "Perspectives chrétiennes sur la vie personnelle et la vie collective," 215.

65. Congar, *Wide World, My Parish*, 48.

66. Congar, *Wide World, My Parish*, 91.

67. Congar, *Fifty Years*, 20. Here, Congar referenced also Mt 26:28; Mk 14:24; and 1 Cor 6:20.

68. This is implied by Congar's position that the Word was eternally begotten *incarnandus*—to become incarnate. *Word and Spirit*, 93. It is also suggested by Congar's position that humanity was created in the image of God for the purpose of incorporation into the Word who is *the* Image of God. In a reflection on A. Feuillet's *Le Christ Sagesse de Dieu*, Congar commented that "the plan of God with respect to creatures has two stages [creation and redemption] but one intention: from the beginning, it is a question of leading us to the condition of the 'glorious liberty of the children of God,' for we are predestined to reproduce the image of his Son, and the cosmos accompanies us in this destiny." Preface to A. Feuillet, *Le Christ Sagesse de Dieu: D'après les épîtres pauliniennes* (Paris: Librairie Lecoffre, 1966), 9.

69. Congar, *Fifty Years*, 20.

70. Congar, *Fifty Years*, 21.

71. Congar, "The Christian Idea of History," 283.

72. See Congar, *I Believe*, 3:150.

73. Congar, "The Church: Seed of Unity and Hope for the Human Race," *Chicago Studies* 5 (1966): 30. See also 31.

74. Congar, "Le Rôle de l'Église dans le monde de ce temps," in *L'Église dans le monde de ce temps*, Unam Sanctam, no. 65b, ed. Yves Congar and M. Peuchmaurd (Paris: Cerf, 1967), 2:315. For Congar's critique of extrinsicism and his affirmation that nature is dynamically oriented toward the supernatural, see Congar's Preface to A. Feuillet, *Le Christ Sagesse de Dieu*, 11–12. On de Lubac and Rahner, see Henri de Lubac, *Surnaturel: Études Historiques* (Paris: Aubier, 1946), and Karl Rahner, "Concerning the Relationship between Nature and Grace," *TI* (Baltimore: Helicon, 1961), 1: 297–317.

75. On the continuity of the orders of creation and redemption in Congar's theology see Congar's Preface to A. Feuillet, *Le Christ Sagesse de Dieu*, 7–15; Yves Congar, *Jesus Christ*, trans. Luke O'Neill (New York: Herder and Herder, 1966), 176 and 197; "Human Social Groups and the Laity of the Church," in *Priest and Layman*, 286; *Lay People in the Church*, 431.

76. "L'Homme est capable d'être appelé," 377–78. Congar referenced Maurice Blondel, *L'Action* (Paris: F. Alcan, 1936–37), and Karl Rahner, *Hearers of the Word* (New York: Herder and Herder, 1969).

77. Congar, *Esprit de l'homme*, 22 with reference to P. R. Régamey.

78. Congar, *Esprit de l'homme*, 11.

79. Congar, *I Believe*, 2:123.

80. Cited in Congar, *I Believe*, 1:54.

81. Congar, *I Believe*, 2:122–24.

82. Congar, "The Holy Spirit and the Apostolic Body," 166.

83. Other passages cited by Congar include: "You are not in the flesh but in the Spirit, if the Spirit of God really dwells in you (*oikei en humin*)" (Rom 8:9); "that Christ may dwell (*katoikēsai*) in your hearts through faith" (Eph 3:17); "And I will ask the Father and he will give you another Paraclete to be with you for ever, even the Spirit of truth . . . you know him, for he dwells with you and will be in you (*par' humin menei kai en humin estai*)" (Jn 14:16–17); "If we love one another, God abides in us (*en hēmin estin*) and his love is perfected in us. By this we know that we abide in him (*en autō menomen*) and he in us (*kai autos en hēmin*) because he has given us his Spirit" (1 Jn 4:12–13; see also 1 Jn 4:16). *I Believe*, 2:80.

84. Congar, *Mystery of the Temple*, 237.

85. Congar, *I Believe*, 2:100–1. "The causal rather than the local meaning of *en*," Congar commented, "and its relative equivalence to *dia* are so widely recognized that it would be pointless to provide references." *I Believe*, 2:109 n. 5.

86. Aquinas, *ST* I^a–II^ae, q. 2, a. 8; q. 3, a. 8.

87. Aquinas, *ST* II^a–II^ae, q. 6, a. 1, c. Möhler, another major influence on Congar, had also described the Spirit as a "new principle of life." *Einheit*, 10.

88. Aquinas, *ST* I^a–II^ae, q. 110, a. 1, c.

89. Aquinas, *ST* I^a, q. 93, a. 4, c.

90. Congar, *I Believe*, 2:116. This is a citation from J.-C. Sagne, "L'Esprit-Saint ou le désir de Dieu," *Conc* (French edition only) 99 (1974): 94. On this point, see also "Pneumatologie dogmatique," 494.

91. Congar, *I Believe*, 2:59. Reference is to "The Living Flame of Love" by John of the Cross. See also Yves Congar, "Aimer Dieu et les hommes par l'amour dont Dieu aime?" *REtAug* 28 (1982): 86–99.

92. Congar, "Pneumatologie dogmatique," 486 and 486 n. 2.

93. On the unity of love of God and neighbor see for example Congar's "God's Call," in *God's People on Man's Journey*, Proceedings of the Third World Congress for the Lay Apostolate (Rome: Permanent Committee for International Congresses of the Lay Apostolate, 1961), 1:118.

94. Congar, *Esprit de l'homme*, 20.

95. Congar, *Esprit de l'homme*, 21.

96. Congar, "Pneumatologie dogmatique," 498.

97. Congar, *I Believe*, 2:114.

98. Congar, "Aimer Dieu et les hommes par l'amour dont Dieu aime?" 86–99.

99. Congar, *I Believe*, 2:121.

100. *I Believe*, 2:70. See also Congar, "The Human Person and Human Liberty in Oriental Anthropology," in *Dialogue between Christians*, 232–45. The Protestant tradition, Congar maintained, differed from the Roman Catholic and from the Orthodox on this point. See his *Christ, Our Lady and the Church*, trans. Henry St. John (Westminster, MD: Newman Press, 1957), 16. For a comparison of Congar's reflections on divine-human synergy with the theology of Martin Luther, see Monika-Maria Wolff, *Gott und Mensch: Ein Beitrag Yves Congars zum ökumenischen Dialog* (Frankfurt: Josepf Knecht, 1990).

101. Congar, *I Believe*, 2:108. The definitive study of this issue in Aquinas is Joseph P. Wawrykow, *God's Grace and Human Action: 'Merit' in the Theology of Thomas Aquinas* (Notre Dame, IN: University of Notre Dame Press, 1995).

102. Congar, *I Believe*, 2:108.

103. Congar, *I Believe*, 2:57 with reference to Eph 4:30; *I Believe*, 2:70.

104. Congar, *I Believe* 2:69.

105. Congar, *Esprit de l'homme*, 5. Reference is to the Preface of Bonhoeffer's *Ethics* (London: SCM Press, 1955). On this point see also Congar's "Pneumatologie dogmatique," 491.

106. Congar, *Esprit de l'homme*, 18. See also "The Spirit and the Struggle against the Flesh, The Spirit and Freedom," in *I Believe*, 2:119–33.

107. Prayer, Congar reflected, actualizes "the profound dimension of our being." *Esprit de l'homme*, 40. On prayer see also "The Holy Spirit and Our Prayer," *I Believe*, 2:112–18; "The Psalms in My Life," in Congar, *Called to Life*, 11–17. On the need for elimination of distraction see *I Believe*, 2:115 and "L'Homme est capable d'être appelé," 383. In this later essay Congar alludes to Pascal's classic reflections on distraction.

108. Congar, "Life in the World and Life in the Lord," in Congar, *Faith and Spiritual Life*, 140–41. See also Congar, "St. Francis of Assisi: or the Gospel as an Absolute in Christendom," in Congar, *Faith and Spiritual Life*, 33–34; *Lay People in the Church*, 422–41.

109. Congar, "Life in the World and Life in the Lord," 135–42.

110. Simeon the New Theologian, *Orat.* XX, 12 (*PG* 35, 1080B). Cited in Congar, *I Believe*, 2:70. Elsewhere Congar quoted Marie de l'Incarnation: "ordinarily God gives

the Spirit after much toil in his service and fidelity to his grace." Cited in "Pneumatologie dogmatique," 491. No reference is given.

111. Reference is to Seraphim's dialogue with Motovilov as translated by Vladimir Lossky in *Essai sur la théologie mystique de l'Église d'Orient* (Paris: Aubier, 1944),
225ff. Cited in *I Believe,* 2:71.

112. Congar, *I Believe,* 2:71. Reference is again to the French translation of Seraphim's dialogue with Motovilov in Lossky, *Essai sur la théologie mystique de l'Église
d'Orient,* 225ff.

113. For Congar's account of deification in the Eastern tradition see "Deification
in the Spiritual Tradition of the East (In Light of a Recent Study)," in Congar, *Dialogue between Christians,* 217–31.

114. Congar, *I Believe,* 3:151.

115. Congar, *I Believe,* 2:125.

116. Congar, *I Believe,* 2:217. "Do we grasp the realism of such a statement?" he
asked. "We are really deified!" *I Believe,* 3:150.

117. *I Believe,* 2:100. Reference is to L. Cerfaux, *The Christian in the Theology of
St. Paul* (London: Geoffrey Chapman, 1967).

118. Congar, *I Believe,* 2:81.

119. Congar, *I Believe,* 2:84.

120. Congar, *I Believe,* 2:68–69. "It is regrettable," Congar commented elsewhere, "that our classic treatises on (created) grace did not make explicit the relationship between grace and the Trinity and the Spirit." "Pneumatologie dogmatique,"
494.

121. In the post-Reformation period, Congar noted, Roman Catholic ecclesiology
replaced the Spirit with a theology of created grace and the *gratia capitis.* "Pneumatologie dogmatique," 495–96.

122. Congar, *I Believe,* 2:89. Heribert Mühlen coined the term "personal causality" as an alternative way to talk about the action of the Spirit in our lives, but Congar
was dubious about this approach. *I Believe,* 2:95 n. 30. Reference is to Heribert
Mühlen, *Der Heilige Geist als Person. Beitrag zur Frage nach der dem Heiligen Geiste
eigentümlichen Funktion in der Trinität, bei der Inkarnation und im Gnadenbund* (Münster: Aschendorff, 1963).

123. Congar, *I Believe,* 2:96–97 nn. 40 and 41.

124. Congar, *I Believe,* 2:135. Reference is to *ST* I^a–II^{ae}, q. 68, a. 2 and to Aquinas's *Commentary on the Sentences.*

125. Congar, *I Believe,* 2:136.

126. See Eph 5:9 (goodness, righteousness, and truth); 1 Tim 6:11 (righteousness, godliness, faith, love, steadfastness, gentleness); Rom 14:17 and 15:13 (righteousness and peace and joy in the Holy Spirit); and 2 Cor 6:6–7 (purity, knowledge, forbearance, kindness, the Holy Spirit, genuine love, truthful speech, and the power of
God.) Cited in *I Believe,* 2:138.

127. Congar, *I Believe,* 2:138.

128. Congar, *Esprit de l'homme,* 39.

129. Congar, *I Believe,* 2:125.

130. Congar, "Pneumatologie dogmatique," 492.

131. Congar, *I Believe,* 2:129–30.

132. Congar, *Esprit de l'homme*, 38–39.

133. Congar, "Pneumatologie dogmatique," 498. Reference is to Eph 4:25.

134. Congar described communion in the Spirit as simultaneously sublime and concrete in *I Believe*, 2:22.

135. Congar, *I Believe*, 2:21–22.

136. Congar, *I Believe*, 2:115.

137. Congar, *I Believe*, 2:117. Emphasis original.

138. Congar, *I Believe*, 2:222–24.

139. Congar, *I Believe*, 2:121.

140. Congar, *I Believe*, 2:122. Emphasis original.

141. Congar, *I Believe*, 2:107.

142. Congar, *I Believe*, 2:76.

143. Congar, *I Believe*, 2:77.

144. For some of Congar's reflections on eschatology see *I Believe*, 2:106–7. Many of his essays on heaven, hell and purgatory have been translated and collected in *Wide World, My Parish*.

145. Congar, "Pneumatologie dogmatique," 496.

146. Congar, "Pneumatologie dogmatique," 496–97. Emphasis original.

147. Irenaeus, *Adv. haer.* III, 24, 1 (*PG* 7, 966; *SChr* 34, 399ff). Referenced by Congar in *I Believe*, 1:68.

148. On Augustine see *I Believe*, 2:5.

149. Congar observed that "[t]here is no real opposition or even break between the two: faith in the Holy Spirit who makes the Church one, holy, catholic and apostolic is in fact faith in the fulfillment of God's promise *in the Church*." *I Believe*, 2:6–7.

150. Congar, "Renewed Actuality of the Holy Spirit," 15.

151. Congar, "The Council as an Assembly and the Church as Essentially Conciliar," 45.

152. Congar, "Pneumatology Today," 439.

153. Congar, *I Believe*, 1:156.

154. Congar, "Pneumatologie dogmatique," 495–96.

155. Congar, "Pneumatologie dogmatique," 496.

156. Congar, *I Believe*, 2:9.

157. Congar, *I Believe*, 2:10.

158. "In speaking of Christ," Congar commented, "Saint Paul does not so much refer to him as founder (founder, in the past, of a completed society, *societas perfecta*), but as an ever-present foundation (cf. Cor 3:11 f.)." "Pneumatology Today," 442.

159. Thus he distinguished the original inspiration of the Spirit and the Spirit's ongoing assistance. See for example "Pneumatologie dogmatique," 496.

160. Congar, "Pneumatologie dogmatique," 496.

161. Congar, "Renewed Actuality of the Holy Spirit," 18.

162. Congar, "Pneumatology Today," 436.

163. Congar, "Renewed Actuality of the Holy Spirit," 18. Emphasis original. See also "Pneumatology Today," 441–42.

164. Congar, "Pneumatology Today," 443. Elsewhere he wrote: "The Church was not simply founded in the beginning—God continues without ceasing to build it up, which is, of course, the basic idea contained in 1 Cor 12." *Word and Spirit*, 80.

165. See for example Congar, *I Believe*, 3:271.

166. Congar, *I Believe*, 3:271. This is illustrated by an anecdote from Congar's personal journal. He recounts a conversation with Fr. Gilles Gourbillon who said provocatively, " 'Here is my Creed. I believe in the *holy* Church that burned Joan of Arc, that condemned Galileo, and that *emmerde* the world.' I answered him, 'Myself, I begin my Creed with the preceding article: I believe in the Holy Spirit.' " *Journal d'un théologien*, 219.

167. On baptism see Congar, *I Believe*, 2:189–201, 3:217–27.

168. On confirmation see Congar, *I Believe*, 3:217–27.

169. Congar, *I Believe*, 3:269. The formula of absolution declares, "God, the Father of mercies, through the death and resurrection of his Son, has reconciled the world to himself and sent the Holy Spirit among us for the forgiveness of sins."

170. Congar, *I Believe*, 3:268–69.

171. In the East, the crowning of the married couple is followed by a prayer that corresponds to the Eucharistic epiclesis. *I Believe*, 3:269.

172. Congar, *I Believe*, 3:229.

173. Congar considered it futile to try to isolate a specific moment of consecration of the Eucharistic elements since the entire Eucharistic anaphora is consecratory and must be considered as a whole. Within this prayer, however, the words of institution and the epiclesis are equally important. See *I Believe*, 3:228–49. Although the Roman Canon (now Eucharistic Prayer I) did not have an explicit epiclesis, Congar thought that the *Supplices te rogamus* served in this capacity. *I Believe*, 3:238 and 3:250. He also noted that the Latin West has always affirmed the consecratory activity of the Spirit, even in the absence of a more explicit epiclesis. See *I Believe*, 3:250–57. Reference is to S. Salaville's "Epiclèse eucharistique," *DTC*, V, cols. 194–300.

174. See "The Holy Spirit in Our Communion," in Congar, *I Believe*, 3:258–66.

175. Congar, *I Believe*, 2:224. Emphasis original.

176. Congar, *I Believe*, 2:224.

177. Congar, *I Believe*, 2:26.

178. Congar, *I Believe*, 2:162–63.

179. Congar, "Pneumatology Today," 443.

180. On the Second Vatican Council's treatment of charisms, see Congar, "Renewed Actuality of the Holy Spirit," 16.

181. Congar, "Pneumatology Today," 439.

182. On the charisms in *Mystici Corporis* see "Renewed Actuality of the Holy Spirit," 16; *Word and Spirit*, 79–80.

183. Congar, *I Believe*, 2:128.

184. Congar, "Renewed Actuality of the Holy Spirit," 19; "Pneumatology Today," 445; *Word and Spirit*, 78–84. On the need to balance the christological (institutional) and pneumatological (charismatic) dimensions of the church see *I Believe*, 2:11. The reference to Hasenhüttl is to his *Charisma, Ordnungsprinzip der Kirche* (Freiburg im Breisgau: Herder, 1970). His position is summarized in the French study "Les Charismes dans la vie de l'Église," in *Vatican II: L'Apostolat des laïcs*, Unam Sanctam, no. 75 (Paris: Cerf, 1970), 203–14.

185. Congar, "L'Église de Hans Küng," *RSPhTh* 4 (1969): 695. Review of Küng, *Die Kirche* (Freiburg: Herder, 1967).

186. Congar, "L'Église de Hans Küng," 697–700.

187. See for example Congar, *Word and Spirit*, 78–84.

188. Congar, *I Believe*, 2:10. See also "Pneumatology Today," 445.

189. Congar, *I Believe*, 2:26–27.

190. Congar, "Pneumatology Today," 444. See also "La Tri-unité de Dieu," 695.

191. Famerée, *L'Ecclésiologie d'Yves Congar*, 454.

192. Congar, "Pneumatologie dogmatique," 498. On the term *koinōnia* see *Mystery of the Temple*, 230 and 287; *L'Église, une, sainte, catholique et apostolique*, Mysterium Salutis, no. 15 (Paris: Cerf, 1970), 56–57; "Pneumatologie dogmatique," 497. On the church as a "communion," see *L'Église une*, 49–62; "Peut-on définir l'Église? Destin et valeur de quatre notions qui s'offrent à le faire," in Congar, *Saint Église*, 37–40; *I Believe*, 2:15–23; "Pneumatologie dogmatique," 495–502. Congar identified Ludvig Hertling, Möhler, and others as sources of a theology of communion in *L'Église une*, 49 n. 87.

193. In the Spirit, Congar noted, all members of the church have the same principle of supernatural operation. "La Tri-unité de Dieu," 691.

194. Congar, *L'Église une*, 60.

195. Congar, "Unité, diversités, et divisions," in *Saint Église*, 110. See also *I Believe*, 2:15.

196. Congar, *I Believe*, 2:17.

197. Congar, *I Believe*, 2:18–19.

198. Congar, "La Tri-unité de Dieu," 692.

199. Congar, *L'Église une*, 15.

200. Congar, "La Tri-unité de Dieu," 692.

201. Congar, "Renewed Actuality of the Holy Spirit," 19–20. See also "De la communion des Églises à une ecclésiologie de l'Église universelle," in *L'Episcopat et l'Église universelle*, Unam Sanctam, no. 39, ed. Yves Congar and B.-D. Dupuy (Paris: Cerf, 1962), 227–60. On the importance of Congar's experience of the active initiative of the Catholic faithful (particularly the laity) in the formation of his pneumatological ecclesiology see "Pneumatology Today," 439–40.

202. See for example "La Tri-unité de Dieu," 696–98. See also *Vraie et fausse réforme*, where Congar described the church as a result of the synergy between the grace of God and the free activity of humanity. *Vraie et fausse réforme*, 2d ed., 97.

203. On the pneumatological basis of conciliarity, collegiality, and reception, see "Pneumatologie dogmatique," 500–1; on reception as an active process see "La Tri-unité de Dieu," 698. See also "Reception as an Ecclesiological Reality," in *Election and Consensus in the Church*, ed. Giuseppe Alberigo and Anton Weiler (New York: Herder and Herder, 1972), 43–68.

204. Congar, *I Believe*, 2:17. See also "Unité, diversités, et divisions," 113.

205. Congar, *L'Église une*, 47; *Diversity and Communion*, 40.

206. Congar, *Esprit de l'homme*, 54.

207. Jossua, "L'Oeuvre oecuménique du Père Congar," *Études* 357 (1982): 552ff; Famerée, *L'Ecclésiologie d'Yves Congar*, 453–54; Famerée, "*Chrétiens désunis* du P. Congar: 50 ans après," *NRT* 110 (1988): 666–86.

208. Congar, *Word and Spirit*, 116. See also: "The Holy Spirit who was source of variety through the diversity of charisms is also the principle of communion and of unity." "Le Troisième article du symbole," 296.

209. See "Unité, diversités, et divisions," 111–12. Congar noted that the external

means of unity (the hierarchy) and the reality of communion should ideally be congruent. But spiritual unity can exist even where the external means of unity are absent, or one may partake of external means without being truly open to the Spirit. *L'Église une*, 118.

210. Congar, *I Believe*, 2:17.

211. Congar, *I Believe*, 2:16.

212. Congar, "Unité, diversités, et divisions," 112.

213. Congar differentiated the *ecclesia congregans* and the *ecclesia congregata*, a distinction he appropriated from Henri de Lubac's *Méditation sur l'Église* (Paris: Aubier, 1953), 78–85. See Congar, *L'Église une*, 130 n. 42. Congar also used this distinction in *I Believe*, 2:54. In an important aside in his review of Küng's *The Church*, Congar clarified that one should not conceive the *ecclesia congregans* as if it somehow existed above and apart from the *ecclesia congregata*. "In effect, there is no *substance* 'Church' that has a concrete existence outside of the members of this Church. Even when one distinguishes within the Church the aspect of *congregans* and the aspect *congregata*—or that of maternity on the one hand, and children and brothers on the other—the first of these aspects exists, just like the second, *in the faithful*." "L'Église de Hans Küng," 701–702.

214. Congar, *L'Église une*, 133–34.

215. In this respect, Congar referenced not only Mt 16:18–19 but also Mt 28:19–20 and Jn 14:16. See *I Believe*, 2:54–55. Congar believed that Protestants misunderstand this aspect of Catholic theology. See *L'Église une*, 129.

216. Congar, *I Believe*, 2:69.

217. Congar, *I Believe*, 2:57; *L'Église une*, 135. Congar also discussed the church's ongoing struggle to live out its vocation in *Vraie et fausse réforme*; "Comment l'Église sainte doit se renouveler sans cesse," *Iren* 34 (1961): 322–45; *Power and Poverty in the Church*; "L'Application à l'Église comme telle des exigences évangéliques concernant la pauvreté," in *Église et pauvreté*, Unam Sanctam, no. 57 (Paris: Cerf, 1965), 135–55; and "Péché et misères dans l'Église," in *L'Église une*, 136–44. In this reflection, Congar noted that the Virgin Mary is the one member of the church who did not sin and who fully realized in her person the holiness of the church.

218. Congar, *I Believe*, 2:58.

219. Congar, *L'Église une*, 125.

220. On worship, beauty, and charity as works of the Spirit see *I Believe*, 2:52–61.

221. Congar, *I Believe*, 2:58.

222. Congar, *I Believe*, 2:59–61. This passage contains both Congar's reflections and his interpretation of Aquinas's views on this issue. On the importance of the activity of the Holy Spirit in the baptism of infants, see also *I Believe*, 3:267–68.

223. Congar, *L'Église une*, 150.

224. Congar, *L'Église une*, 161.

225. For Congar's description of Christ as the "concrete universal," see *I Believe*, 2:34. Congar cautioned that the reality of Christ goes far beyond the philosophical connotations of this phrase.

226. Congar, *L'Église une*, 162–63, 165.

227. Congar, *I Believe*, 2:18.

228. Congar, *L'Église une*, 173.

229. As the church expanded, the church fathers explicitly identified this geographic extension as a sign of the church's catholicity. *L'Église une*, 154–55. Reference is to Optat of Mileve, Augustine, Cyril of Jerusalem, and others.

230. *L'Église une*, 171. He also acknowledged that cultural diversity has not always been respected. Rome has been paternalist, but this is not the authentic catholicity of the tradition. *L'Église une*, 172.

231. Famerée comments that "the 'catholicity' of Congar in 1982 has taken a different meaning than that of 1937." Famerée, *L'Ecclésiologie d'Yves Congar*, 453. Already in 1961, Congar had stressed that catholicity is not simply a quantitative expansion of an identical form of unity. He also acknowledged that to the extent that *Divided Christendom* (1937) suggested a purely quantitative catholicity, Vladimir Lossky had been right to criticize the book. "Unité, diversités, et divisions," 115.

232. *I Believe*, 2:26–27. Elsewhere, Congar cited Hervé Legrand: "Because the Church is catholic, it should be particular." "La Tri-unité de Dieu," 695.

233. Congar, *I Believe*, 2:24–27.

234. Congar, *I Believe*, 2:31–32. On the Spirit in the world see also *L'Église une*, 176.

235. Congar, *I Believe*, 2:39.

236. Congar, *I Believe*, 2:43.

237. Congar, *I Believe*, 2:45.

238. Congar, *I Believe*, 2:44. Emphasis original.

239. Congar, *L'Église une*, 187.

240. Congar, *I Believe*, 2:45.

241. Congar, "Pneumatologie dogmatique," 500–501.

242. Congar, *I Believe*, 2:45. Even the communion of saints in heaven is involved in this ordination.

243. *I Believe*, 2:44. On ecumenical councils see *Tradition and Traditions*, 346–47. On the magisterium, see *I Believe*, 2:46.

244. Congar considered infallible a "disturbingly heavy term." *I Believe*, 2:46. He acknowledged that the church's pastoral magisterium can fall short of its task and is limited by the historical nature of knowledge. He stressed that "the Holy Spirit helps the church *ne finaliter erret*—so that error will not ultimately prevail (see Mt 16:18)." He suggested indefectibility as the best concept to "express the whole of the Church's attempt throughout history to profess the saving truth." *I Believe*, 2:46. With respect to the Protestant position that the primary subject of indefectibility is the Holy Spirit rather than the Church itself, Congar commented that "we can gladly accept even this insistence, provided we can also say that grace is *given*." *I Believe*, 2:46. On the issue of infallibility see also Congar's "Infaillibilité et indéfectibilité," *RSPhTh* 54 (1970): 601–18; "Après *Infaillible?* de Hans Küng. Bilans et perspectives," *RSPhTh* 58 (1974): 243–52.

245. Congar, *I Believe*, 2:45. Thus, he continued, it is almost universally affirmed that a heretical Pope would cease to be Pope, since he would no longer be part of the communion of faith.

246. Congar, *I Believe*, 2:39.

247. Congar, *Word and Spirit*, 71. Congar is here citing Tennyson.

248. Congar, "Pneumatology Today," 448.

249. "Pneumatology Today," 447. Elsewhere Congar spoke of the pendulum

swing between the creativity of the Spirit and reference to Christ. See "Renewed Actuality of the Holy Spirit," 24. The latter formulation suggests more of a duality between Christ and the Spirit than the passage cited earlier and is not consistent with Congar's own emphasis on the indissociability of the activity of the Holy Spirit and the glorified Christ.

250. See for example *Word and Spirit*, 127.

251. Congar, *Divided Christendom*, 222, and *Wide World, My Parish*, 93–154.

252. Congar, *I Believe*, 2:219. Reference is to *PL* 17, 245.

253. Congar, *I Believe*, 2:223.

254. Puyo, *Une vie pour la vérité*, 218. See also Congar, *Un peuple messianique*, 179.

255. Congar, *I Believe*, 2:223. Reference is to *Ad gentes divinitus*, 7, 3.

256. Conversation with Professor Hervé Legrand, O.P., on the occasion of his visit to the University of Notre Dame, fall 1997.

257. Susan Wood notes de Lubac's weak pneumatology in "The Church as the Social Embodiment of Grace in the Ecclesiology of Henri De Lubac" (Ann Arbor: University Microfilms, 1986), 251.

258. The underdevelopment of Rahner's ecclesiology is mentioned in Michael E. Fahey, "On Being Christian—Together," in *A World of Grace: An Introduction to the Themes and Foundations of Karl Rahner's Theology*, ed. Leo J. O'Donovan (New York: Crossroad, 1987), 122.

259. Congar, "Holy Spirit and Spirit of Freedom," 19–20. "From its beginnings," Congar wrote elsewhere, "Christianity has succeeded in unifying collective and personal existence." *Mystery of the Temple*, 153. In the letters of Peter and Paul, "the personal and collective aspects are closely knit." *Mystery of the Temple*, 178. On this point see also *Wide World, My Parish*, 56–57; "The Christian Idea of History," 282–83; "L'Influence de la société et de l'histoire," 674; *I Believe*, 2:16.

260. Congar, *Esprit de l'homme*, 37–38.

261. Congar, "Pneumatologie dogmatique," 495.

262. Congar, *Word and Spirit*, 122.

263. Famerée, *L'Ecclésiologie d'Yves Congar*, 454.

CHAPTER 4

1. I speak loosely of these biblical formulations as theological themes or paradigms because Congar himself never explicitly reflected on the precise linguistic or theological status of this terminology. He referred to the "notion" or "theme" of the people of God and spoke of the mystical body of Christ as a "concept" or "idea." See his "Richesse et vérité d'une vision de l'Église comme 'peuple de Dieu'," in Congar, *Le Concile de Vatican II* (Paris: Beauchesne, 1984), 120; "D'une 'Ecclésiologie en gestation' à Lumen Gentium chap. I et II," in *Le Concile de Vatican II*, 127; "My Path-Findings," 170. Congar did not develop precise distinctions among ecclesial images, models, and paradigms in the manner of Avery Dulles's *Models of the Church*, rev. ed. (New York: Doubleday, 1987), 15–33.

2. See van Vliet, *Communio sacramentalis*, 83–87, 200–208, 244–46.

3. See Congar, " 'Lumen gentium' n° 7, 'L'Église, Corps mystique du Christ,' vu au terme de huit siècles d'histoire de la théologie du Corps mystique," in Congar, *Le Concile de Vatican II*, 150–51.

4. Congar, "My Path-Findings," 171. Reference is to J. Bluett, "The Mystical Body, A Bibliography, 1890–1940," *TS* 3 (1942): 260–89. From 1930 on, Congar regularly published reviews of the mushrooming publications on the theology of the mystical body. These are included in the collection of Congar's reviews in *Sainte Église*, 449–696.

5. Congar, "My Path-Findings," 171. See also *L'Église. De saint Augustin à l'époque moderne* (Paris: Cerf, 1970), 464.

6. On Catholic Action see Congar, *Lay People*, 55.

7. Conversation with Professor Hervé Legrand, O.P., on the occasion of his visit to the University of Notre Dame, fall, 1997.

8. Journet, *L'Église du Verbe incarné*, 3 vols. (Paris: Desclée de Brouwer, 1941, 1951, 1969). Congar generally referenced Journet favorably, although he disagreed with him on some issues, such as the role of the laity in the church. Congar described Journet as "profound" but "medieval" in *L'Église. De saint Augustin*, 464. For a comparison of Congar and Journet see Dennis M. Doyle, "Journet, Congar, and the Roots of Communion Ecclesiology," *TS* 58 (1997): 461–79.

9. *Mystici Corporis* was written under the influence of Sebastian Tromp, author of *Corpus Christi quod est Ecclesia*, 4 vols. (Rome: Pontificia Universitas Gregoriana, 1937–1960). Congar described Pius XII's encyclical as a "very ample and very well constructed synthesis" of the mystical body tradition. "Peut-on définer l'Église?" 30. He noted that the encyclical's theology was distinct from medieval approaches to the mystical body tradition and also differed from twentieth–century biblical exegesis. "Peut-on définer l'Église?" 27. Congar also commented on *Mystici Corporis* in "L'Eucharistie et l'Église de la Nouvelle Alliance," *VS* 82 (1950): 347–72; *Sainte Église*, 654; *Lay People*, 57.

10. Congar commented on de Lubac's contribution in *Fifty Years*, 42–43.

11. Congar, "Peut-on définer l'Église?" 29–30.

12. Van Vliet, *Communio sacramentalis*, 73–89.

13. Congar, *Divided Christendom*, 212. The French reads: "[L]a vrai définition de l'Église, c'est 'Le Corps mystique de Jésus-Christ.'" *Chrétiens désunis*, 266. Other early publications in which the theology of the mystical body is prominent include Congar's "Une fidélité dominicaine. La doctrine de l'Église, Corps mystique de Jésus-Christ," *ADom* 69 (1933): 239–45; "The Mystical Body of Christ," in Congar, *The Mystery of the Church*, 118–27; "The Church and Its Unity," in *The Mystery of the Church*, 58–96; "L'Église Corps mystique du Christ," *VS* 64 (1941): 242–54. Van Vliet considers the article "The Church and Its Unity," which Congar wrote in 1937 as the unofficial Catholic contribution to the Second World Conference for Practical Christianity, one of the most important of his early writings. Van Vliet, *Communio sacramentalis*, 76.

14. On these points, see van Vliet, *Communio sacramentalis*, 74–89.

15. Congar, "Dogme christologique et ecclésiologie: Vérité et limites d'un parallèle," in Congar, *Sainte Église*, 83.

16. Congar, "Dogme christologique," 87. Congar appropriated this distinction from A. Deissmann, *Paulus. Eine kultur-und religionsgeschichtliche Skizze*, 2d ed. (Tübingen: Mohr Siebeck, 1925), 118–22. Even within this same article "Dogme christologique," however, Congar himself did not entirely dispense with "union" language.

"[L]'union de l'Église à Dieu . . . ," he wrote for example, "est une union d'alliance."
"Dogme christologique," 93.

17. Congar, "Dogme christologique," 84, 92.

18. "L'unité entre l'Église et son hypostase divine ou sa quasi-hypostase divine
n'est pas une unité substantielle dans l'être, aboutissant à former une entité substantielle dans l'être, aboutissant à former une entité physique; c'est une union, une unité
relative qui, philosophiquement, se rangerait parmi les unités accidentelles, non pas
même par composition, mais selon l'ordre et la relation." Congar, "Dogme christologique," 92. English translations of other passages from Congar's writings occasionally
do use the language of being in reference to Congar's mystical body theology. See for
example: "If we form a single body and, as it were, a single *being* who loves in Christ,
that is so ultimately, because we are all interiorly animated by one and the same
soul." "The Mystical Body," 129. My emphasis. The French reads, however, "Si nous
formons un seul corps et comme un seul *Aimant* dans le Christ. . . ." "Le Corps mystique du Christ," 105.

19. Congar, "Dogme christologique," 93.

20. Congar, "Dogme christologique," 82. Reference is to Pascal, *Pensées,* ed.
Léon Brunschvicg (Paris: Cluny, 1934), #473, 171.

21. Congar, "Dogme christologique," 86. Within the mystical body, Congar reiterated, Christ's living reality comes to exist "in new and proper subjects of existence
and action, each having their *être à soi* and their freedom." "Dogme christologique,"
82.

22. Congar, "Dogme christologique," 82. "[L]'union des hommes à la divinité,
qui se réalise dans l'Église, n'est pas *per esse, secundum esse*: elle est seulement *per
operationem, in operatione,* et c'est pourquoi parfois on la dit 'mystique.' " "Dogme
christologique," 84.

23. Congar reads here a "single person in Christ." "The Church and Its Unity,"
68.

24. See Congar's "La personne 'Église,' " *RevTh* 71 (1971): 613–40. On Aquinas
see also "Dogme christologique," 89–91.

25. Congar, "The Church and Its Unity," 69.

26. Congar used the traditional *idem numero* formulation in *I Believe,* 2:19 and 2:
41. He noted that this idea is found classically in Aquinas, *In III Sent.* d. 13, q. 2, a. 1,
ad 2; q. 2, a. 2; *De ver.* q. 29, a. 4; *Comm. in ev. Ioan.* c. 1, lect. 9 and 10. It is also
used in *Mystici Corporis,* 54 and 77 ad sensum; *Lumen gentium* 7, 7. See *I Believe,* 2:23
n. 19.

27. Congar, *Divided Christendom,* 61.

28. Congar, "The Church and Its Unity," 69. The particular instance cited earlier
is Eph 2:13–18.

29. Congar, "The Church and Its Unity," 72.

30. Congar, "The Mystical Body," 120. "In this regard," he noted elsewhere, "the
idea of the mystical Body sets before us a highly realistic view. It makes us see how
Christ wills to continue his life in men, in a truly theandric way." "The Church and
Its Unity," 73.

31. Congar, "The Mystical Body," 124. See also *Divided Christendom,* 53–54.

32. Congar, *Divided Christendom,* 54–55 and 55 n. 1; "The Mystical Body," 126.

33. Congar, "The Mystical Body," 128.
34. Congar, "Dogme christologique," 92.
35. Aquinás, *ST* I^a–II^{ae}, q. 110, a. 1.
36. Aquinas, *ST* I^a–II^{ae}, q. 110, a. 2, c.
37. Congar, "Dogme christologique," 86.
38. Congar, "The Church and Its Unity," 70–71.
39. Congar, "The Church and Its Unity," 87.
40. Congar, "The Church and Its Unity," 87.
41. Congar, "The Church and Its Unity," 85. See also 73.
42. Congar, "The Idea of the Church in St. Thomas Aquinas," 348–58.
43. "It can no more be dissociated from this," he continued, "than, say, France considered in its spiritual reality can be dissociated in fact from the institutions and realities of the visible France, with its laws, constitution, government and so forth." Congar, "The Church and Its Unity," 85.
44. Congar, "The Church and Its Unity," 76. He continued on p. 78: "The Church is, of its essence, sacramental."
45. "The Church and Its Unity," 73 and 73 n. 1. In another essay, he wrote that the sacraments are "the point where the institutional or visible Church and the mystical Body meet and fuse in an organic unity." "The Mystical Body," 134.
46. On baptism and Eucharist see Congar's "The Church and Its Unity," 74–76; "The Mystical Body," 131–34.
47. Congar, "The Mystical Body," 129.
48. Congar used this terminology in "Unity of the Church," 74 and 76, and in "The Mystical Body," 130.
49. Congar, "The Mystical Body," 133.
50. Congar, "The Church and Its Unity," 68. This translation actually reads "a single entity," but the French is *une seule réalité.* "L'Église et son unité," 23.
51. Congar, "Dogme christologique," 78.
52. Congar, "Dogme christologique," 84.
53. Congar, "Dogme christologique," 78.
54. References to the investment of the apostolic body with spiritual powers can be found in "The Church and Its Unity," 79. For a discussion of Congar's use of this language of "powers" (*pouvoirs*) see Famerée, *L'Ecclésiologie d'Yves Congar,* 410–21. Famerée notes that this terminology is characteristic primarily of Congar's pre-Vatican II works. In 1978, Congar himself criticized the use of the term *spiritualis potestas* to describe the priestly office. See Congar, Preface to B.-D. Marliangeas, *Clés pour une théologie du ministère* (Paris: Beauchesne, 1978), 5–14.

For a discussion of the hierarchical apostolic body as the formal cause of the church, see "The Holy Spirit and the Apostolic Body," 180–82. Congar's use of this Aristotelian terminology was influenced by Charles Journet and by Ambroise Gardiel. Congar himself later critiqued the ecclesiological use of this Aristotelian framework. See "My Path-Findings," 175.

55. Famerée, *L'Ecclésiologie d'Yves Congar,* 414–15. Emphasis original. See also his statement: "Thus one can affirm that the Church as such has *proper* and decisive *causes* for the renewal of the Kingdom (royal, priestly and prophetic power of Christ and his Spirit) or that she *cooperates* in *direct* fashion in the constitution of the King-

dom of God through the exercise of powers that are properly hers." Famerée, *L'Ecclésiologie d'Yves Congar*, 413.

56. Congar, "Dogme christologique," 87.

57. On the governing, sacramental, and prophetic powers that the hierarchy carries out as Christ's vicar see for example "The Church and Its Unity," 88–90. Congar did make some distinctions between the manner in which the hierarchy exercised these various powers: "when St. Paul or the hierarchy celebrate the mysteries or announce the word of God, they act in a much closer dependence on Christ [than when they exercise jurisdictional powers]; they no longer act by a power that truly resides in them, and they are by no means free, at least as regards the essential, to do one thing or another as they please. Here, as the scholastics say, they are instrumental causes, acting under complete dependence on him who uses them." "The Church and Its Unity," 90. "So far from being an inducement for Christians to rely on and trust to human agency," Congar commented elsewhere, "[the sacraments] are but the affirmation and effective realization of the unique mediation of Christ." "The Mystical Body," 130.

58. This was also the position taken by Pius XII in *Mystici Corporis*. Mersch, in contrast, identified the soul of the mystical body as sanctifying grace.

59. Congar, *Divided Christendom*, 52. Elsewhere, however, Congar did describe the church as animated by *Christ* as by a soul: "For, as the body is animated by the soul, which it makes visible and expresses in all actions, so the Church is animated by Christ, makes him visible and expresses him in its various activities." "The Church and Its Unity," 70.

60. Congar, "The Holy Spirit and the Apostolic Body," 181.

61. Famerée, *L'Ecclésiologie d'Yves Congar*, 414–15.

62. Famerée, *L'Ecclésiologie d'Yves Congar*, 415–16.

63. Famerée, *L'Ecclésiologie d'Yves Congar*, 417.

64. Famerée, *L'Ecclésiologie d'Yves Congar*, 417–18.

65. Famerée, *L'Ecclésiologie d'Yves Congar*, 418.

66. Famerée, *L'Ecclésiologie d'Yves Congar*, 418.

67. Famerée himself notes that Congar never explicitly argued that the church as Christ's body must have a certain salvific causality, as did the humanity of Christ. He believes, however, that this is implied by a passage in *Le Christ, Marie, et l'Église*, 63. See Famerée, *L'Ecclésiologie d'Yves Congar*, 418 n. 1520.

68. For Congar's caution against ecclesial monophysitism see for example "Dogme christologique," 80. On the twofold character of the church as both divine and human see for example *Divided Christendom*, 75–89.

69. See Congar's "The Church: The People of God," 14–18.

70. Some of the works noted by Congar include Harold F. Hamilton, *The People of God*, 2 vols. (London: Oxford University Press, 1912). Exegetical contributions to this discussion included Nils A. Dahl, *Das Volk Gottes, Eine Untersuchung zum Kirchenbewusstsein des Urchristentums* (Oslo: I Kommisjon Hos Jacob Dybwod, 1941); Ernst Käsemann, *Das wandernde Gottesvolk. Eine Untersuchung zum Hebräerbrief* (Göttingen: Vandenhoeck and Ruprecht, 1938); H. Strathmann, "Laos," in *Theologische Wörterbuch zum N.T.* of Kittel, vol. IV, 29–57 (Fasc. appeared in 1938); A. Vonier, *The People of God* (London: Burns and Oates, 1937). Congar himself described the church

as the people of God as early as a 1937 essay. The idea of the people of God, he commented at that time, is "the simple fruit of the little effort made everywhere to relate the Church to its biblical bases and to the Plan of God begun with Abraham." See, "The Church: People of God," 14 n. 2.

71. M. D. Koster, *Ekklesiologie im Werden* (Paderborn: Bonifazius, 1940). Congar noted that World War II originally limited the circulation and discussion of Koster's writings to the German-speaking world. "D'une 'Ecclésiologie en gestation à Lumen Gentim chap. I et II,'" in *Le Concile de Vatican II*, 123.

72. Lucien Cerfaux, *La Théologie de l'Église suivant saint Paul*, Unam Sanctam, no. 10 (Paris: Cerf, 1942). Congar was in fact the inspiration for this book. He suggested to Cerfaux, a Louvain professor, that he pursue a philological study of Paul. A. Oepke reiterated Cerfaux's conclusions in *Das neue Gottesvolk in Schrifttum, Schauspiel, bildender Kunst and Weltgestaltung* (Gütersloh: Bertelsmann, 1950); "Leib Christi oder Volk Gott bei Paulus," *Theologische Literaturzeitung* 79 (1954): col. 363–8.

73. Karl Adam was one of the critics who expressed strong disagreement with Koster. See for example his *Volk Gottes im Wachsttum des Glaubens* (Heidelberg: Kerle, 1950). For bibliographic references to additional critical reviews see Congar, "D'une 'Ecclésiologie en gestation,'" 123 n. 2.

74. Congar, "Peut-on définir l'Église?" 23.

75. M. Schmaus, *Katholische Dogmatik* (Munich: Max Hueber, 1958), 3:204–39; I. Backes, "Die Kirche ist das Volk Gottes im Neuen Bund," parts I and 2, *Trierer Theologische Zeitschrift* 69 (1960): 111–17; 70 (1961): 80–93; "Das Volk Gottes im Neuen Bunde," in *Kirche, Volk Gottes*, ed. H. Asmussen (Stuttgart: Schwabenverlag, 1961), 97–129.

76. The history of the evolution of *Lumen gentium*, Congar noted in 1971, has not been written in its entirety. Nor can it be written in full detail because the documents that would be required for such a comprehensive study are inaccessible. "D'une 'Ecclésiologie en gestation,'" 128. In this article, Congar offered a partial reconstruction of the genesis of *Lumen gentium*, and in an addendum added in 1983 he noted the importance of Cardinal Suenen's work in the introduction of the chapter on the people of God. "D'une 'Ecclésiologie en gestation,'" 128–33 and 136.

77. Congar himself wrote in 1964 that "only time can tell what consequences will follow from the option made when the chapter *De Populo Dei* was placed in the sequence we have indicated. It is our conviction that these consequences will be considerable. A wholly new balance will be introduced in the treatise on the Church." "The Church: The People of God," 13.

78. See Congar, "The People of God," in *Vatican II: An Interfaith Appraisal*, ed. John Miller (Notre Dame, IN: University of Notre Dame Press, 1966), 198.

79. Congar, "The People of God," 198.

80. Congar, "Richesse et vérité," 105. Congar also observed that reference to the church as the people of God is not limited to *Lumen gentium*, where the phrase occurs thirty-nine times; it is also mentioned in ten of the other conciliar documents. "D'une 'Ecclésiologie en gestation,'" 134.

81. Congar, "The People of God," 197.

82. See Congar, "The Church: The People of God," 28–29; "Richesse et vérité," 121.

83. Van Vliet, *Communio sacramentalis*, 202 n. 253.

84. Congar, "The Church: The People of God," 12. See also "Richesse et vérité," 110; "The People of God," 202.

85. "The Church: The People of God," 21. Congar did not think, however, that *Lumen gentium* had developed the people of God idea "to the point of the formulation of a Christian anthropology, an image of the Christian man." "The Church: The People of God," 12. Elsewhere he noted that there were elements of a theological anthropology in other Council documents, particularly in *Gaudium et spes*. Here, "the Council studied the question more closely, without, however, taking up all the aspects of modern man or using all the resources of biblical tradition. Its vision remained too static." "The People of God," 198. He regretted that *Gaudium et spes* did not return more unreservedly to the categories "People of God" and "messianic people." "The People of God," 206.

86. "The Church: People of God," 22 and 22 n. 19. Congar offered the Austrian catechism of 1894 as an illustration of this common opposition of "the Church" and "men."

87. Robinson first presented these ideas at a professional conference in Germany in 1935. His paper was published in *Werden und Wesen des Alten Testaments: Vorträge gehalten auf der Internationalen Tagung Alttestamentlicher Forscher zu Göttingen vom 4.-10. September 1935*, ed. P. Volz, F. Stummer, and J. Hempel (Berlin: Töpelmann, 1936). Robinson's presentation was published in English in 1964 and then reprinted in 1980 as *Corporate Personality in Ancient Israel* (Philadelphia: Fortress). Prior to 1935, Robinson had broached his theory in *The Christian Doctrine of Man* (Edinburgh: T & T Clark, 2d ed. 1913), 8; "Hebrew Psychology," in *The People and the Book*, ed. A. S. Peake (Oxford: Clarendon, 1925), 376; *The Cross of the Servant* (London: SCM, 1926), 32–37. Further discussion of corporate personality in the biblical era can be found in Jean de Fraine, *Adam and the Family of Man* (New York: Alba House, 1965).

88. Robinson, *Corporate Personality*, 41.

89. Robinson, *Corporate Personality*, 38.

90. Appreciative commentary can be found in E. Best, *One Body in Christ* (London: Epworth, 1958), 3–41; R. P. Shedd, *Man in Community* 4, 10, 26, 37, 41, 87, 103; C. H. Dodd, *Epistle of Paul to the Romans* (London: Hodder and Stoughton, 1932); A. Nygren, *Commentary on Romans* (London: SCM, 1952), 213; H. Ridderbos, *Paul: An Outline of His Theology* (Grand Rapids: Eerdmans, 1975), 38, and 61–62 [although Ridderbos prefers the term "all-in-one" to the term "corporate personality"]; Th. C. Vriezen, *An Outline of Old Testament Theology*, 2d ed. (Oxford: Basil Blackwell, 1970), 327 n. 1 and 382–87. J. de Fraine's entire work *Adam et son lignage*, Museum Lessiánum. Sect. Bibl. (Bruges: Desclée, 1959), is devoted to the issue of corporate personality. Critics include G. E. Mendenhall, who refers to Robinson's ideas as cliché and mythological in "The Relation of the Individual to Political Society in Ancient Israel," in *Biblical Studies in Memory of C. C. Allemann*, ed. J. M. Myers et al. (Locust Valley, NY: Augustin, 1960), 91. J. R. Porter has been particularly critical of Robinson's use of the idea of corporate personality in his explications of Hebrew legal practice. "The Legal Aspects of the Concept of 'Corporate Personality' in the Old Testament," *Vetus Testamentum* 15 (1965): 361–80. J. W. Rogerson challenges Robinson's entire argument in "The Hebrew Conception of Corporate Personality: A Re-examination," *JTS* 21 (1970): 1–16, and *Anthropology and the Old Testament* (Oxford: Blackwell, 1978), 55–59. Wil-

liam Klein defends Robinson in *The Chosen People: A Corporate View of Election* (Grand Rapids, MI: Academie Books, 1990), 41–42.

91. Congar, "Perspectives chrétiennes sur la vie personnelle et la vie collective," 201.

92. Congar, "Perspectives chrétiennes sur la vie personnelle et la vie collective," 201.

93. Congar, "The Church and Its Unity," 60–61.

94. See Wilhelm Vischer, *The Witness of the Old Testament to Christ* (London: Lutterworth Press, 1949), 121, 122, 155, 188, 191. "The whole Bible," Congar concurred, "is permeated with the idea of *Pars pro toto*." "The Church: The People of God," 19. With respect to Cullman, Congar stated "I am a firm believer in the biblical idea of 'one for many,' an idea which Cullmann has developed in his numerous biblical studies." *Fifty Years*, 18.

95. Congar, "Perspectives chrétiennes sur la vie personnelle et la vie collective," 201.

96. Congar, "Richesse et vérité," 111.

97. Congar, "The Church: The People of God," 22.

98. "The People of God," 201. Unlike Rahner, Congar did not think one can extend the term "people of God" to include in some general sense all of the human community. Congar thought that "scriptural usage as well as liturgical and patristic tradition do not justify this way of speaking." "The People of God," 204–5. The Vatican Council itself, he noted, did not construe the term "people of God" in this sense. For Rahner's view, see "Membership of the Church According to the Teaching of Pius XII's Encyclical 'Mystic Corporis Christi,'" *TI* (Baltimore: Helicon, 1963), 2:82–83.

99. "[T]his People of God is *de iure* coextensive with humanity." Congar, "The People of God," 199. See also *LG*, 13.

100. Congar, *I Believe*, 2:52. Reference is to K. Delahaye, *Ecclesia Mater chez les Pères des trois premiers siècles*, Unam Sanctam, no. 46 (Paris: Cerf, 1964). "The Church is an institution," Congar reflected elsewhere, "but it is also and even primarily the 'we' of Christians." *I Believe*, 2:130. See also 2:66.

101. Congar, "Richesse et vérité," 113. This is not to suggest, Congar explained, that the entire congregation should recite the words of consecration, for this would be "an ecclesiological error and even a liturgical heresy." See also Congar's "L'Ecclesia' ou communauté chrétienne, sujet intégral de l'action liturgique," in *La Liturgie après Vatican II*, ed. J.-P. Jossua and Y. Congar, Unam Sanctam, no. 66 (Paris: Cerf, 1967), 241–82.

102. On the *populus* as the local assembly see "The Church: The People of God," 26.

103. Congar, "The Church: The People of God," 26–27.

104. Congar, "The People of God," 202.

105. Congar, "The People of God," 203.

106. Congar, "Richesse et vérité," 113.

107. Congar, "The People of God," 200–203.

108. Congar, "The Church: The People of God," 23.

109. Congar, "Richesse et vérité," 114–17.

110. Congar, "The Church: The People of God," 27.

111. See for example Congar's *Vraie et fausse réforme*, 2d ed., 102–8.

112. Congar, "The Church: The People of God," 23. Congar offered the example of the Lenten collects as collected by Michael Schmaus, *Ausdruckformer der lateinischen Liturgiesprache bis Elften Jahrhundert* (Mainz: Beuron, 1941), 205f and as found in the footnotes of A. Schaut, "Die Kirche als Volk Gottes. Selbstaussagen d. Kirche im röminischen Messbuch," in *Benediktinische Monatschrift* 25 (1949): 187–96.

113. Congar, "The Church: The People of God," 23–24. See also "The People of God," 202. Congar observed that after Vonier published *The Spirit and the Bride* (London: Burns and Oates, 1935)—a book that emphasized the holiness of the church—he felt a need to write *The People of God* (London: Burns and Oates, 1937), in which he emphasized the church's human and historical character. Elsewhere, however, Congar commented that Vonier overly contrasted the holy church and the human church: "it is the People of God who are the Church, and the Church is the People of God. In this dual unity, one can privilege one of the two aspects. The monastic and liturgical vision of Vonier is a little too glorious. We will see that, even from the point of view of cult, there is more to be said." "Richesse et vérité," 116.

114. Congar, "The People of God," 120.

115. Congar, Preface to Frank B. Norris, *God's Own People: An Introductory Study of the Church* (Baltimore: Helicon, 1962), v.

116. Congar, "The Church: The People of God," 31–35.

117. Congar, "The People of God," 199, 202, 203, 204.

118. Congar, "Richesse et vérité," 110.

119. See for example Congar's "The Church: The People of God," 27. Emphasis original.

120. On the Spirit as the principle of communion and catholicity, see Congar, *I Believe*, 2:15–38; on the Spirit and eschatology, see for example *I Believe*, 2:69–71, 2: 106–8, 3:144. On the Spirit and conversion and penitence, see *I Believe*, 2:122–24.

121. Congar, "People of God," 19. Indeed, he explained, the recovery of a people of God theology occurred through the efforts of Koster, Cerfaux, Vatican II, and others to place the Church in the perspective of salvation history. "The People of God," 14. Robinson, Congar believed, had unfortunately neglected this decisive element in his discussion of the Hebrew corporate personality; there is such a thing as corporate personality only because there is a plan of God, a plan that proceeds typologically such that the end of God's design is present in germ in those who serve as God's original representatives. "Perspectives chrétiennes sur la vie personnelle et la vie collective," 201.

122. See "The Church: The People of God," 31–33.

123. Congar himself stated that among the Jewish and Christian peoples there is a "sort of interpenetration of the personal and the collective." "Perspectives chrétiennes sur la vie personnelle et la vie collective," 201.

124. Congar, "The Church: The People of God," 19–20.

125. Congar noted that election and call presuppose grace in "The Church: The People of God," 19; "The People of God," 200. He emphasized that the Holy Spirit *is* uncreated grace in *I Believe*, 2:17–18; 2:68–69.

126. On the service, worship, and praise of God as gifts of the Spirit see for example Congar, *I Believe*, 112–18, and "Pneumatologie dogmatique," 494–95.

127. On the Spirit as the "Promised One" see Congar, *I Believe*, 2:69.

128. Heribert Mühlen discussed the pneumatological significance of God's Covenant with Israel in *Der Heilige Geist*, 245–49.

129. "The idea of the People of God, in the first place, enables us to express the continuity of the Church with Israel. . . . Placing the Church in the context of the history of salvation, the idea of the People of God makes it possible to examine the difficult but important question of Israel, that is, of the Jewish people according to the flesh who actually did stumble (Rom 11:11) but who continue to be the people chosen and loved by God." Congar, "The Church: The People of God," 19, 21.

130. Congar, "Richesse et vérité," 120; "D'une 'Ecclésiologie en gestation,'" 133.

131. Congar, "Richesse et vérité," 120.

132. "Under the new Dispensation, that of the promises realized through the Incarnation of the Son and the gift of the Spirit (the 'Promised One'), the People of God was given a status that can be expressed only in the categories and in the theology of the Body of Christ." "The Church: The People of God," 35. This, Congar noted, is not only his own view but also the position of exegetes such as N. A. Dahl and R. Schnackenburg, as well as of Catholic and Orthodox theologians such as M. Schmaus, I. Backes, J. Ratzinger, C. Algermissen, L. Bouyer, and G. Florovsky. For references see "The Church: The People of God," 35–36.

133. Congar, "The Church: The People of God," 36.

134. Congar, "Richesse et vérité," 121.

135. Works published on this topic that did influence Congar include E. C. Dewick, *The Indwelling God* (London: Oxford, 1938); A. Cole, *The New Temple* (London: Tyndale, 1950); Th. Hannay, "The Temple," *ScotJTh* 3 (1950): 278–87; J. Daniélou, *Le Signe du Temple ou de la Présence de Dieu*, Coll. catholique (Paris: Gallimard, 1942); H.-M. Féret, "Le Temple du Dieu vivant" in *Prêtre et Apôtre* (Paris: Bonne Press, 1947), 103–5, 135–37, 166–69, 181–84; M. Fraeyman, "La Spiritualisation de l'idée du temple dans les epîtres pauliniennes," *EphThL* 33 (1947): 378–412.

136. Congar, *The Mystery of the Temple*, ix. See also *Lay People*, 54, 57, 61, 96, 102–3, 113, 119–20, 121, 154 n. 78, 198, 405.

137. Van Vliet, *Communio sacramentalis*, 244–46. According to van Vliet, the other predominant ecclesiological theme of this period is a theology of the church as a "structured spiritual communion." See *Communio sacramentalis*, 240–44.

138. See especially Congar, *I Believe*, 2:53–55.

139. This chapter is his contribution to *Initiation à la pratique de la théologie*, ed. Bernard Lauret and François Refoulé (Paris: Cerf, 1982), 2:481–516. Congar's discussion of the church as "Temple of the Holy Spirit" is found on 493–95.

140. Congar, *Mystery of the Temple*, 153.

141. Congar, *Mystery of the Temple*, 155.

142. Congar, *I Believe*, 2:82.

143. Congar, *I Believe*, 2:100–101. See also 2:109 n. 5.

144. Congar, *Mystery of the Temple*, 155. Emphasis original.

145. Congar, *The Mystery of the Temple*, 155. Craig Koester, on the other hand, observes that Philo was the first in the Jewish tradition to identify God's tabernacle with the human soul, an interesting parallel with the Christian affirmation that the human person is the "Temple of the Holy Spirit." See Koester, *The Dwelling of God: The Tabernacle in the Old Testament, Intertestamental Jewish Literature, and the New Testament*,

CBQ Monograph Series, no. 22 (Washington, DC: Catholic Biblical Association of America, 1989), 65–66.

146. The Jerusalem Bible, Congar noted, thus appropriately translates "our bodies" in Rom 12:1 as "our persons." *Mystery of the Temple*, 156.

147. Referenced in Congar, *Mystery of the Temple*, 157.

148. Congar, *I Believe*, 2:82.

149. Congar, *I Believe*, 2:81.

150. Congar, *I Believe*, 2:70–71, 2:82, 2:82 n. 94.

151. Congar commented on this passage in *I Believe*, 2:107.

152. See Congar, *I Believe*, 2:114. See also "Pneumatologie dogmatique," 494.

153. Congar, "Richesse et vérité," 119–20.

154. Congar, *Mystery of the Temple*, 157.

155. Congar, *Mystery of the Temple*, 154. Congar noted that this phrase appears in the patristic literature again and again, although he does not give any specific citations. He himself repeated this formula in his essay "Pneumatologie dogmatique," 493; *I Believe*, 2:54.

156. Congar, *Mystery of the Temple*, 154. In other instances he simply cited the phrase without qualification.

157. Congar, *Mystery of the Temple*, 153.

158. Congar, *Mystery of the Temple*, 153.

159. Congar, *Mystery of the Temple*, 247; *I Believe*, 2:55. See also "Reflections on the Spiritual Aspect of Church Buildings" in *Priest and Layman*, 229–37.

160. Congar, *I Believe*, 2:58.

161. Congar discussed Jesus Christ as foundation stone of the church in *Mystery of the Temple*, 163–66.

162. On the "living stones" of the church see Congar, *Mystery of the Temple*, 166–72.

163. Congar, *I Believe*, 2:26.

164. Congar, *I Believe*, 2:11. See also *I Believe*, 2:152.

165. "Although not everyone possessing the gifts of the Spirit is instituted as a minister, those who are instituted do in fact possess such gifts." Congar, *I Believe*, 2:10.

166. See Congar, *I Believe*, 2:10–12 and *Word and Spirit*, 78–83.

167. Congar, *Word and Spirit*, 82.

168. Congar noted the dynamism of the Temple of the Holy Spirit ecclesiology in "Pneumatologie dogmatique," 493.

169. On the cosmic significance of the Temple of YHWH in the Old Testament and parallels with other ancient religions, see Congar, *Mystery of the Temple*, 94–100.

170. See Congar, *Mystery of the Temple*, 120, 199–201.

171. For further commentary see Congar, *Mystery of the Temple*, 198–99.

172. Congar, *Mystery of the Temple*, 244, 202, and 203.

173. Congar, *Mystery of the Temple*, 247 and 199.

174. Congar, *I Believe*, 2:54. Reference is to Eph 1:10, 13.

175. On substantial indwelling see Congar, *I Believe*, 2:24; *Mystery of the Temple*, 264. On Cyril of Alexandria's theology of substantial indwelling see *I Believe*, 2:84, and on Aquinas see *Mystery of the Temple*, 239–40, and *I Believe*, 2:54. On the abrogation of a certain distance between God and creature see *Mystery of the Temple*, 281.

176. Congar, *Mystery of the Temple*, 281.

177. Congar, "Pneumatologie dogmatique," 493–94.

178. Congar, *Mystery of the Temple*, 118.

179. Congar, *I Believe*, 2:67.

CHAPTER 5

1. Congar first used the term in "Bulletin d'ecclésiologie (1939–1946)," *RSPhTh* 31 (1947): 77–96. It recurs repeatedly throughout his work. See for example *Lay People*, 51; *Vraie et fausse*, 2d ed., 9; "My Path-Findings," 170; "Pneumatology Today," 43; "Moving towards a Pilgrim Church," in *Vatican II Revisited by Those Who Were There*, ed. Alberic Stacpoole (Minneapolis, MN: Winston Press, 1986), 133. Congar explained: "The *de Ecclesia* [treatise] was principally, sometimes almost exclusively, a defense and affirmation of the reality of the Church as a machinery of hierarchical mediation, of the powers and primacy of the Roman see, in a word, a 'hierarchology.'" *Lay People*, 45.

2. On the dispensability of the laity see for example Congar's *Lay People*, 51.

3. Möhler, Review of Theodor Katerkamp's *Des ersten Zeitalters der Kirchengeschichte erst Abtheilung: Die Zeit der Verfolgungen* (Münster, 1823), *ThQ* 5 (1823): 497. Congar cited this passage from Möhler repeatedly. See for example "My Path-Findings," 175 n. 14; "Rudolf Sohm nous interroge encore," *RSPhTh* 57 (1973): 275.

4. See, for example, Vellico, *De Ecclesia Christi: Tractatus apologetico-dogmaticus* (Rome: n.p., 1940), 104f; L. Billot, *Tractatus de Ecclesia Christi* (Rome: Polyglotta, 1898); C. Pesch, *Praelectiones dogmaticae De Ecclesia* (1894ff), M. d'Herbigny, *Theologica de Ecclesia* (Paris: Beauchesne, 1920–25); J. V. Bainvel, *De Ecclesia Christi* (Paris: Beauchesne, 1925). Cited in Congar, "Moving towards a Pilgrim Church," 131–32.

5. Congar made this observation in "The Church: The People of God," 22.

6. See for example Congar, "The Church: The People of God," 13; "The People of God," 97; "Richesse et vérité," 105.

7. Joseph Cardinal Ratzinger, *Called to Communion: Understanding the Church Today*, trans. Adrian Walker (San Francisco: Ignatius, 1996), 139.

8. Hans Urs von Balthasar, "Christology and Ecclesial Obedience," in *Explorations in Theology IV: Spirit and Institution*, trans. Edward Oakes (San Francisco: Ignatius, 1995), 162; Walter Kasper, "The Church as Sacrament of Unity," *Communio* 14 (1987): 10–11.

9. Leonard Swidler, *Toward a Catholic Constitution* (New York: Crossroad, 1996).

10. Elisabeth Schüssler Fiorenza, *Discipleship of Equals: A Critical Feminist Ekklesialogy of Liberation* (New York: Crossroad, 1994).

11. Edward Schillebeeckx, *Church: The Human Story of God* (New York: Crossroad, 1990), 188. He adds: "However, in all official documents of the Roman Catholic Church 'hierarchy' is used specifically as an argument for rejecting any democratic exercise of authority and thus democratic participation in the government of the church by the people of God on the basis of 'divine law'." *Church*, 217.

12. Swidler, *Toward a Catholic Constitution*, 100–101, with reference to *Macht teilen, Gleichheit anerkennen. Ein Demokratieförderplan für die katholische Kirche in Deutschland* (Düsseldorf: DKJ-Bundesstelle, 1994).

13. Congar, *Lay People in the Church*, 35. See also 38.

14. This time span reflects the periodizations of Congar's prolific writings provided by Joseph Famerée and Cornelis van Vliet. Both scholars note qualitative changes in Congar's theology of the Holy Spirit in the later stage of his life. See Famerée, *L'Ecclésiologie d'Yves Congar;* van Vliet, *Communio sacramentalis.*

15. Congar, *Lay People,* 52. See also 47 and *Vraie et fausse,* 2d ed., 95.

16. Congar, *Lay People,* xi.

17. Congar, *Power and Poverty,* 95; *Vraie et fausse,* 2d ed., 56. See also "Titles and Honours in the Church," in *Power and Poverty,* 101–31.

18. On the growth of myriad forms of new initiatives in the postconciliar church see Congar's "Pneumatology Today," 440; "Le Troisième article du symbole," 295.

19. Congar, "My Path-Findings," 169 and 181.

20. Congar, "Pneumatologie dogmatique," 496. See also *I Believe,* 2:5–14. In the former article Congar noted that he has come to understand the Spirit as "co-institutor" in an even broader sense than that expressed in *I Believe.*

21. See for example Congar, "Pneumatology Today," 447.

22. Congar, "Pneumatology Today," 443.

23. Congar, "Pneumatologie dogmatique," 496–97. Emphasis original. See also *I Believe,* 2:16.

24. Congar, "Renewed Actuality of the Holy Spirit," 17–18.

25. Congar, *I Believe,* 2:19, and "Pneumatologie dogmatique," 498 n. 31, with reference to Aquinas, *In III Sent.* d. 13, q. 2, a. 1, ad 2; q. 2, a. 2; *De ver.* q. 29 a. 4; *In Ioan.* 1 lect. 9 and 10; *ST* 1–2, q. 183, a. 3, ad 3; Pius XII, *Mystici Corporis,* 54 and 77; Vatican II, *Lumen gentium,* 7, 7.

26. Congar, "My Path-Findings," 174.

27. Congar, "My Path-Findings," 175.

28. Congar, "My Path-Findings," 178. See also "Ministères et structuration de l'Église," in *Ministères et communion ecclésiale* (Paris: Cerf, 1971), 38.

29. Congar, "My Path-Findings," 176. See also "The Liturgical Assembly" in Congar, *Called to Life,* 115.

30. Congar, "My Path-Findings," 176. On the importance of the plural ministries see also "The Liturgical Assembly," 116; "Pneumatologie dogmatique," 501.

31. Congar, "Pneumatologie dogmatique," 501. On this point see also "Pneumatology Today," 446.

32. Congar, *I Believe,* 2:46. On the importance of the epiclesis see also "Le Troisième article du symbole," 300; *I Believe,* 2:228–49 and 2:267–74.

33. Congar, *I Believe,* 3:235–36.

34. Congar, "My Path-Findings," 174. In Congar's subsequent writings, the terminology of superiority and subordination is absent in the section on "Pneumatological Ecclesiology" in the article "Pneumatology Today," 442–49, and in the section "Une pneumatologie ecclésiologique" in the article "Pneumatologie dogmatique," 493–502. It does appear in Congar's 1985 article "Le Troisième article du symbole," 298.

35. Congar, *Lay People,* 11, 15, 15, 25, 26, 26, 27, 27, 31, 34, 34, 35, 35, 35, 38, 38, 40, 42, 42, 42, 44, 45, 45, 45, 45, 45, 46, 46, 47, 47, 48, 51, 51, 52, 59. The six references to "hierarchy" that occur in pages 25–37 are part of a 1964 addition to the original edition.

36. The references are: "The Spirit supports the pastoral hierarchy of the Church and through it guides the Christian communities, but he does much more than this."

I Believe, 2:17. "There is therefore, in principle, no automatic, juridical formalism in this question, since the 'hierarchical' function exists within the communion of the *ecclesia*." *I Believe*, 2:45. "In concrete, this means that the Spirit must actively intervene in the case of any activity that is related to the sacramental or 'hierarchical' institution, whether it has to do with the Word, the pastoral government of the Church or the sacraments in the widest sense of the word." *I Believe*, 2:45.

37. For example, Gerald W. Creed and Barbara Ching note that anthropologists studying rural populations "have paid almost no attention to cultural hierarchies . . . they have generally failed to recognize the systematic *devaluation* of the rustic as a source of identity" (*Knowing Your Place: Rural Identity and Cultural Hierarchy*, ed. Ching and Creed [New York: Routledge, 1997], vii. Emphasis original.) The sociologist James Schubert contrasts the dynamics of small groups that demonstrate democratic qualities with those of groups that function as a "dominance hierarchy" (James N. Schubert, "Hierarchy, Democracy and Decision Making in Small Groups," in *Hierarchy and Democracy*, ed. Albert Somit and Rudolf Wildenmann [Carbondale, IL: Southern Illinois University Press, 1991], 79–101). Michael Richards notes that clergymen once hoped to climb to the top of a pyramid, for "[T]he Church . . . was a hierarchy. There were ranks and grades" (Richards, "Hierarchy and Priesthood," *Priests and People* 7 [1993]: 228).

38. Congar, "Rudolf Sohm nous interroge," 281; "Pneumatologie dogmatique," 495.

39. See Thomas Jefferson's letter to W. J. Cartwright in *Thomas Jefferson on Democracy*, ed. Paul K. Padover (New York: New American Library, 1939), 33. The Hume citation also comes from this letter of Jefferson.

40. Hervé-Marie Legrand, O.P., "Theology and the Election of Bishops in the Early Church," in *Election and Consensus in the Church*, ed. Giuseppe Alberigo and Anton Weiler (New York: Herder and Herder, 1972), 38.

41. Catherine Mowry LaCugna, *God for Us: The Trinity and Christian Life* (San Francisco: HarperCollins, 1991), 401.

42. On this point see again Hervé-Marie Legrand, "Theology and the Election of Bishops," 40–41.

43. Congar, *Lay People*, 34.

44. In early Christianity, the term *archē* became theologically important in part because of the LXX translation of Gen 1:1: "*en archē ho theos ton ouranon kai ten gen. . . .* " Origen had used an allegorical method to interpret *archē* in Gen 1:1 as a reference to the Logos in light of John 1 ("En archē én ho logos . . .") According to Basil of Caesarea's influential commentary on Genesis, *archē* in Gen 1:1 means "beginning" in the sense of a "beginning of movement"; beginning as "first foundation"; beginning as "principle" or "form"; and beginning in the sense of "goal." Basil, *In Hexaem*, I.6. See J.C.M. van Winden, "Frühchristliche Bibelexegese. 'Der Anfang,' " in *ARCHE: A Collection of Patristic Studies by J. C. M. van Winden*, ed. J. Den Boeft and D. T. Runia (Leiden: Brill, 1997), 3–36; idem, "In the Beginning: Early Christian Exegesis of the Term *archē* in Genesis 1:1," in *ARCHE*, 78–93. For a contemporary discussion of the significance of the term *archē* in trinitarian theology, see LaCugna, *God for Us*, 388–400.

45. For an example of an ecclesiology that redefines hierarchy, see Terence Nich-

NOTES 231

ols, *That All May Be One: Hierarchy and Participation in the Church* (Collegeville, MN: Liturgical, 1997).

46. This is the title of the last chapter of Congar's three-volume *I Believe in the Holy Spirit*. See "The Life of the Church as One Long Epiclesis," *I Believe*, 2:267–74.

47. Congar stated that the language of democracy works "so badly when applied to the Church or in the context of the Church. . . . [T]he Church has its own order of things, and its essential nature goes back more than seventeen centuries before the time of the French Revolution and nineteen centuries before the Russian Revolution." Congar, *Challenge to the Church: The Case of Archbishop Lefebvre*, trans. Paul Inwood (Huntington, IN: Our Sunday Visitor, 1976), 39.

48. See for example Brian Gaybba's *The Spirit of Love* (London: Geoffrey Chapman, 1987). Chapter 10 is entitled "The Spirit Creates the Community That Is the Church," and chapter 14 is entitled "The Spirit Enables Individuals to Share in What the Church Has."

49. See for example Michael Green, *I Believe in the Holy Spirit* (Great Britain: Hodder and Stoughton, 1975). Chapter 6 is entitled "The Spirit in the Individual," and chapter 7 "The Spirit in the Church."

50. Catherine Mowry LaCugna, *God for Us*; Alan Torrance, *Persons in Communion: An Essay on Trinitarian Description and Human Participation* (Edinburgh: T & T Clark, 1996); John Zizioulas, *Being as Communion: Studies in Personhood and the Church* (Crestwood, NY: St. Vladimir's Seminary Press, 1985).

51. Catherine McCall, *Concepts of Person* (Aldershot, England: Avebury, 1990), 178.

52. Edward Henderson, "Knowing Persons and Knowing God," *Thom* 46 (1982): 394–422. One example: he writes that "affirming God's existence should be judged by comparing it with affirming *the existence of persons* . . . we judge the believer's affirmation of God's existence by the best knowledge we have of *the existence of individuals*." "Knowing Persons," 396, my emphasis.

53. "The Holy Spirit," the English edition of *I Believe* reads, "is given to the community and individual persons." *I Believe*, 2:15. The French is: "Le Saint–Esprit est donné à la communauté et il est donné aux personnes." *Je crois*, 2:27. Here is another example: "Individual persons, however, want to be subjects of their actions." *I Believe*, 2:16. The French is: "Mais les personnes veulent être *les sujets* de leur acts." *Je crois*, 2: 27. Congar wrote of "quelque chose en faveur des personnes, des petits groups" (*Entretiens*, 25), and his remarks were translated as "some comments here in favor of individuals, of small groups" (*Fifty Years*, 17). His reflections on "l'action sur les personnes et l'action par les micro-réalisations" (*Entretiens*, 26) became "the effect of small-scale activity on the individual and the small group" (*Fifty Years*, 17). Congar's translators use "individual" not only as a translation for Congar's "personne" but also as a translation for "chacun." The "I" of the psalms, Congar wrote, is "représentatif du peuple de Dieu que chacun réalise d'une certaine façon." *Entretiens*, 80. In English this reads, "each individual represents the people of God in a particular way." *Fifty Years*, 61. And, whereas Congar spoke of charisms as "dons de chacun—institutionnels ou non—au bénéfice de tous" (*Entretiens*, 86), the translation reads, "individual gifts for the benefit of all" (*Fifty Years*, 66). There are however some occasions in which the English term "individual" does translate the French "individu." See for ex-

ample "si c'est une vote unanime chaque individu est impliqué" (*Entretiens*, 21) as compared with "each individual is involved" *(Fifty Years*, 13).

54. Boethius, *Liber de persona et duabus naturis* 3 (*PL* 64, 1343). This definition appears in the context of his attempt to defend the Council of Chalecedon's affirmation of the one person and two natures of Jesus Christ contra Eutyches and Nestorius.

55. Comblin writes that "in the West, classical theology adopted Boethius' definition, repeated it, and endlessly commented on it. It went no further." José Comblin, *Retrieving the Human: A Christian Anthropology* (Maryknoll, NY: Orbis, 1990), 50. This overstates the case, but even the editors of the Loeb library edition of Boethius's philosophical works made a point of footnoting Boethius's definition of person and remarking, "Boethius' definition of *persona* was adopted by St. Thomas, was regarded as classical by the Schoolmen, and has the approval of modern theologians." *Liber de persona et duabus naturis*, 84 n. a. This, too, is an oversimplification. On the difference between Aquinas's and Boethius's use of the term "person" see Bernd Hilberath, *Der Personbegriff der Trinitätstheologie in Rückfrage von Karl Rahner zu Tertullians "Adversus Praxean"* (Innsbruck: Tyrolia, 1986), 121–27.

56. Hilberath, *Der Personbegriff*, 104–15.

57. Emmanuel Mounier, *Personalism* (Notre Dame, IN: University of Notre Dame Press, 1952), xv. No reference to Renouvier is given.

58. Mounier, *Oeuvres de Mounier*, 4 vols. (Paris: Editions du Seuil, 1961–63). Works available in English translation include *Personalism* (Notre Dame, IN: University of Notre Press, 1952); *A Personalist Manifesto* (New York: Longmans, Green and Co., 1938); "Catholic Personalism Faces Our Times," in *Race: Nation: Person*, ed. Joseph T. Delos et al. (New York: Barnes and Noble, 1944).

59. Mounier, *Personalism*, xvi–xcvi.

60. Mounier, *Personalism*, xviii–xix.

61. Mounier, *Personalism*, 19. My emphasis.

62. Mounier, *Personalism*, 23.

63. Congar, *Fifty Years*, 71–72.

64. Congar, *Fifty Years*, 72.

65. Edward Schillebeeckx, *Christ the Sacrament of the Encounter with God* (New York: Sheed and Ward, 1963), 3.

66. W. Norris Clarke, "Fifty Years of Metaphysical Reflection: The Universe as Journey," in *The Universe as Journey: Conversations with W. Norris Clarke, S.J.*, ed. Gerald McCool (New York: Fordham University Press, 1988), 81.

67. Jacques Maritain, *Scholasticism and Politics* (Glasgow: University Press, 1940), 48. On Maritain's distinction of the person and the individual see especially chapter 3 of *Scholasticism and Politics*, entitled "The Human Person and Society," 45–70.

68. Maritain, *Scholasticism*, 52.

69. Maritain, *Scholasticism*, 63. On this point see also 47, 53, 62–70.

70. On individuality as distinct from personality see Maritain, *The Person and the Common Good* (Notre Dame, IN: University of Notre Dame Press, 1947), 31–46.

71. Merton himself does not reference Maritain in *New Seeds*, and the book has no footnotes, since it is not intended for academic reference. Carr is confident, however, that Maritain is the source of Merton's distinction of the individual and the per-

son. See Anne Carr, *A Search for Wisdom and Spirit: Thomas Merton's Theology of the Self* (Notre Dame, IN: University of Notre Dame Press, 1988), 27–30.

72. Merton, *New Seeds of Contemplation* (New York: New Directions, 1961), 38.

73. Merton, *New Seeds of Contemplation*, 48.

74. Merton, *The Springs of Contemplation* (Notre Dame, IN: Ave Maria Press, 1992), 93.

75. Merton, *The Springs of Contemplation*, 94.

76. Zizioulas is critical of Latin scholasticism for its heavy dependence on Greek philosophy. See for example "Human Capacity and Human Incapacity," *ScotJTh* 28 (1975): 403–4.

77. Congar, "Bulletin d'ecclésiologie," *RSPhTh* 66 (1982): 88.

78. Zizioulas, "On Being a Person. Towards an Ontology of Personhood," in *Persons, Divine and Human*, ed. Christoph Schwöbel and Colin Gunton (Edinburgh: T & T Clark, 1991), 34–38.

79. Zizioulas here draws on patristic exegesis, particularly that of the Cappadocians.

80. Zizioulas, "On Being a Person," 41.

81. Zizioulas, "The Doctrine of the Holy Trinity: The Significance of the Cappadocian Contribution," in *Trinitarian Theology Today: Essays on Divine Being and Act*, ed. Christoph Schwöbel (Edinburgh: T & T Clark, 1995), 58–59.

82. Zizioulas, *Being as Communion: Studies in Personhood and the Church* (London: Darton, Longman and Todd, 1985), 18.

83. Zizioulas, "Human Capacity and Human Incapacity," 416–18.

84. Zizioulas, "On Being a Person," 42.

85. Zizioulas, *Being as Communion*, 51.

86. On de-individualization in the Spirit see Zizioulas, "Human Capacity and Human Incapacity," 441. On the participation of the baptized in the hypostasis of Jesus Christ see 437–38.

87. On the ecclesial hypostasis see *Being as Communion*, 53–65.

88. Zizioulas, "Human Capacity and Human Incapacity," 442.

89. William Hill, *The Three-Personed God: The Trinity as a Mystery of Salvation* (Washington, DC: Catholic University of America Press, 1982), 306.

90. Jacquelyn Ann K. Kegley, *Genuine Individuals and Genuine Communities: A Roycean Public Philosophy* (Nashville: Vanderbilt University Press, 1997); George F. McLean and Hugo Meynell, eds., *Person and Society* (Lanham, MD: University Press of America, 1988). See also Robert Roth, ed., *Person and Community: A Philosophical Exploration* (New York: Fordham University Press, 1975); John H. Walgrave, *Person and Society: A Christian View* (Pittsburgh, PA: Duquesne University Press, 1965).

91. José Ignacio González Faus, "Anthropology: The Person and the Community," in *Mysterium Liberationis: Fundamental Concepts of Liberation Theology*, ed. Ignacio Elllacuría and Jon Sobrino (Maryknoll, NY: Orbis Books, 1993), 497–521; Frances Moore Lappé and J. Baird Callicott, "Individual and Community in Society and Nature," in *Religion and Economic Justice* (Philadelphia: Temple University Press, 1991), 245–52.

92. Ann O'Hara Graff, "The Struggle to Name Women's Experience," in *In the Embrace of God: Feminist Approaches to Theological Anthropology*, ed. Anne O'Hara

Graff (Maryknoll, NY: Orbis, 1995), 82. See also Lenn Goodman, "The Individual and the Community in the Normative Traditions of Judaism," in *Autonomy and Judaism*, ed. Daniel Frank (Albany: State University of New York Press, 1992), 69–119; Michael Novak, "Priority of Community, Priority of Person," in *Catholicism and Secularization in America*, ed. David L. Schindler (Huntington, IN: Our Sunday Visitor Publishing Division, 1990), 136–50; Bryan Schwartz, "Individuals and Community," *Journal of Law and Religion* 7 (1989): 131–72. These citations could be further multiplied.

93. Congar's contrast of the terms "communion" and "society" came in response to the long dominance of the *societas perfecta* ecclesiology in Roman Catholicism. "A concept other than that of 'society,' " he reflected, "is preferable in order to enter into the theology of the Church: that of 'communion.' " "Pneumatologie dogmatique," 496. The French is *communion*.

94. Comment on book jacket. No reference is given.

95. James Gustafson, *Treasure in Earthen Vessels: The Church as a Human Community* (Chicago: University of Chicago Press, 1961), 1–8.

96. Gustafson, *Treasure in Earthen Vessels*, 1 n. 1.

97. On Jesus Christ as the center of the church's loyalty see Gustafson, *Treasure in Earthen Vessels*, 45, 76, 89.

98. Gustafson, *Treasure in Earthen Vessels*, 8–9.

99. Gustafson, *Treasure in Earthen Vessels*, 14–28.

100. Gustafson, *Treasure in Earthen Vessels*, 29–42.

101. Gustafson, *Treasure in Earthen Vessels*, 42–56.

102. Gustafson, *Treasure in Earthen Vessels*, 56–85.

103. Gustafson, *Treasure in Earthen Vessels*, 86–99.

104. "Nations and ideological communities," he writes for example, "are also communities of faith." Gustafson, *Treasure in Earthen Vessels*, 90.

105. Gustafson, *Treasure in Earthen Vessels*, 13.

106. Congar, "Peut-on définir l'Église?" 34–35.

107. Congar, *Fifty Years*, 43.

108. The Latin is "Aunio moralis et stabilis plurium hominum ad aliquem finem, communi actione consequendum." Congar, "Peut-on définir l'Église?" 34.

109. James Gustafson, *Treasure in Earthen Vessels*, 1 n. 1.

110. F. Tönnies, *Gemeinschaft und Gesellschaft: Grundbegriffe der reinen Soziologie* (Berlin: K Curtis, 1887).

111. Congar, "Peut-on définir l'Église?" 42. The church, Congar explained, is not the species supernatural within the genre of societies. Because the church participates by grace in the mystery of God, it transcends definition.

112. Jerome Hamer comments on the limitations of definitions of communion as found in standard reference works in *The Church Is a Communion* (London: Geoffrey Chapman, 1964), 159.

113. Congar, "Pneumatologie dogmatique," 497. "It is because all the faithful participate in the gifts of God," Congar explained, ". . . that there is communion among them, that they are a communion." "Pneumatologie dogmatique," 498. See also Congar, "The Church as Communion of Faith," in Congar, *Called to Life*, 90–91.

114. Hamer, *The Church Is a Communion*, 162 and 175.

115. On Congar's communion ecclesiology see, for example, "Une Église qui est d'abord communion" in "Pneumatologie dogmatique," 495–500.

116. See for example Congar, *I Believe*, 2:222–23.

117. Michael Lawler, "*Perichoresis*: New Theological Wine in an Old Theological Wineskin," *Horizons* 22 (1995): 61.

118. Gustafson, *Treasure in Earthen Vessels*, 104.

119. Gustafson, *Treasure in Earthen Vessels*, 100.

120. Congar, "Une communion qui s'organise en société." See "Pneumatologie dogmatique," 500–502.

121. Communion and community are closely related in Congar's statement: "Le baptême (et la confirmation) créent la qualité de *personne* dans l'ordre chrétien de la nouvelle alliance. Il fonde les droits et devoirs d'une personne tant individuellement prise que prise dans ses rapports de communion dans la communauté des baptisés." "Rudolf Sohm nous interroge," 286.

122. See Dulles, *Models of the Church*, 59–62.

123. Congar, "Pneumatologie dogmatique," 502. The French is "communion de personnes."

124. See for example Joseph Cardinal Ratzinger, "Concerning the Notion of Person in Theology," *Communio* 17 (1990): 439; Zizioulas, *Being as Communion*, 27. The position that the Western conception of person originates with Christianity is questioned by J. C. Vogel, "The Concept of Personality in Greek and Christian Thought," *Studies in Philosophy and the History of Philosophy* 2 (1963): 20, 59–60. For further discussion see C. Anderson, "Zur Entstehung und Geschichte des trinitarischen Personbegriffs," *ZNW* 52 (1961): 1–39; G. Greshake, "Die theologische Herkunft des Personbegriffs," in *Personale Freiheit und pluraliste Gesellschaft*, ed. G. Pöltner (Wein: Herder, 1981), 75–86; B. Studer, "Der Personbegriff in der frühen kirchenamtlichen Trinitätslehre," *ThPh* 57 (1982): 161–77.

125. R. P. C. Hanson, *The Search for the Christian Doctrine of God* (Edinburgh: T & T Clark, 1988), 737.

126. Ghellinck observes that *persona* appears ninety times in Boethius's christological writings but only once in his treatise on the Trinity. "L'Entrée d'essentia, substantia, et autres mots apparentées, dans le Latin médiéval," *ALMA* 15/1 (1940): 77–112. The inapplicability of Boethius's definition of person to God has been noted by von Balthasar and Ratzinger. See Hans Urs von Balthasar, "On the Concept of Person," *Communio* 13 (1986): 22; Joseph Cardinal Ratzinger, "Concerning the Notion of Person in Theology," 448. Moltmann thinks that Boethius's definition can conceivably be used with reference to God the Father but not with respect to the Holy Spirit. Jürgen Moltmann, *The Spirit of Life: A Universal Affirmation* (Minneapolis: Fortress, 1992), 268 and 289.

127. Aquinas, *ST* I^a, q. 29, a. 3, ad. 4. Aquinas noted that there are some who believe that Boethius's definition of "person" does not apply to God. Richard of St. Victor, he continued, amends this definition "by adding that *Person* in God is *the incommunicable existence of the divine nature*." Father, Son, and Spirit are then not "individuals," although they are nonetheless distinct by virtue of their different relations of origin. *ST* I^a, q. 28, aa. 2 and 3. A divine person is a "relation as subsisting." *ST* I^a, q. 29, a. 4.

128. Aquinas, *ST* I^a, q. 29, a. 4, c.

129. Basil, *On the Holy Spirit* 16, 38 (*SChr* 17, p. 377).

130. A. Okechukwu Ogbonnaya, *On Communitarian Divinity: An African Interpre-*

tation of the Trinity (New York: Paragon House, 1994); Jürgen Moltmann, *The Trinity and the Kingdom* (San Francisco: Harper and Row, 1981).

131. LaCugna, Review of Moltmann's *The Spirit of Life*, *TS* 54 (1993): 757.

132. Aquinas, *ST* I[a], q. 13, a. 5.

133. Aquinas, *ST* I[a], q. 13, a. 6, c.

134. Aquinas, *ST* I[a], q. 13, a. 3, c.

135. Aquinas, *ST* I[a], q. 29, a. 3, c.

136. For approaches other than that of Aquinas see Peter Hoffmann, "Analogie und Person: Zur Trinitätsspekulation Richards von St.-Victor," *ThPh* 59 (1984): 191–234; Christof Theilemann, *Die Frage nach Analogie, natürlicher Theologie und Personenbegriff in der Trinitätslehre* (Berlin: Walter de Gruyter, 1995).

137. Torrance, *Persons in Communion*, 121. He adds that Barth's departure from the term "person" within trinitarian theology (in preference for *Seinsweise*) led to a gulf between his trinitarian theology and his theological anthropology. Torrance, *Persons in Communion*, 186–87.

138. Clarke, "What Is Most and Least Relevant in St. Thomas' Metaphyics Today?" *IPQ* 14 (1974): 425. See also Philip Rolnick, *Analogical Possibilities: How Words Refer to God* (Atlanta, GA: Scholars Press, 1993).

139. Tracy, *Analogical Imagination* (New York: Crossroad, 1981), 409.

140. Tracy, "Trinitarian Speculation and the Forms of Divine Disclosure," in *The Trinity: An Interdisciplinary Symposium on the Trinity*, ed. Stephen T. Davis, Daniel Kendall, S.J., and Gerald O'Collins, S.J. (New York: Oxford University Press, 1999), 292.

141. The *via negativa* was to have been central to the book on the Holy Spirit that LaCugna had hoped to write.

142. LaCugna, "1996 Sheedy Award Address," unpublished lecture delivered at the University of Notre Dame, 1.

143. LaCugna, *God for Us*, 305. On the apophatic character of the terms "person," "relation," and "communion" see also 302 and 332.

144. Hanson, *The Search for the Christian Doctrine of God*, 737.

145. "Quaesivit quid tria diceret et dixit substantias sive personas, quibus nominibus non diversitatem intelligi volui sed singularitatem noluit" (*De Trinitate*, 7, 4, 9, CCL 50, 259, 118–20, 131–33). Hilberath comments that the negative character of the term "person" in Augustine could not be expressed more pithily. Hilberath, *Der Personbegriff*, 100. Studer, in like vein, notes that in Augustine the negative character of the dogmatic use of the term "person" in early trinitarian theology is especially evident. Studer, "Der Personbegriff," 170–77.

146. Christos Yannaras, *Person und Eros: Eine Gegenüberstellung der Ontologie der griechischen Kirchenväter und der Existenzphilosophie des Westens* (Göttingen: Vandenhoeck and Ruprecht, 1982), 29–32.

147. Zizioulas, "On Being a Person," 46.

148. Zizioulas, "Human Capacity and Human Incapacity," 402. He continues: "There is something about the human phenomenon that seems to resist strongly any definition of man from the point of view of his 'substance' or qualities." "Human Capacity and Human Incapacity," 406.

149. On relationality see Elizabeth Johnson, *She Who Is* (New York: Crossroad, 1992), 191–245; Walter Kasper, *The God of Jesus Christ* (New York: Crossroad, 1984),

289–90; Catherine Mowry LaCugna, *God for Us*; Jörg Spell, *Leben als Mit-Sein: Vom trinitarisch Menschlichen* (Frankfurt: Josef Knecht, 1990); Carver Yu, *Being and Relation: A Theological Critique of Western Dualism and Individualism* (Edinburgh: Scottish Academic Press, 1987). On communion and personal uniqueness, see Congar's affirmation that the Holy Spirit brings persons to communion "by respecting and even stimulating their diversity." *I Believe*, 2:17. "Real love," said Mounier, "is creative of distinction." Mounier, *Personalism*, 23.

150. Schillebeeckx, *Church*, 46–47.

151. Charles Taylor, *Sources of the Self: The Making of Modern Identity* (Cambridge, MA: Harvard University Press, 1989), 106 and 196.

152. Annie Dillard, *The Writing Life* (New York: HarperPerennial, 1989), 3.

153. The von Balthasar expression comes from his "Der Unbekannte jenseits des Wortes," in *Interpretation der Welt: Festschrift R. Guardini*, ed. Helmut Kuhn (Würzburg: Echter, 1965), 638–45.

154. Moltmann, *The Spirit of Life*, 268.

155. Aquinas, *ST* I^a, q. 39, a. 8, c.

156. De Régnon, *Études de théologie positive sur la S. Trinité*, 3 vols. (Paris: Retaux, 1892–98), xvii and xxv; Paul Galtier, *Le Saint Esprit en nous d'après les Pères Grecs*, Analecta Gregoriana 35 (Rome: Gregorian University, 1946), 150–53, 188–91, 207–11, 200–203, 219, 244, 245, 265–71.

157. P. de Letter, "Sanctifying Grace and the Divine Indwelling," *TS* 14 (1953): 248. See also G. Philips, "Le Saint Esprit en nous, à propos d'un livre récent," *EphThL* 24 (1948): 127–35. Galtier's *Le Saint Esprit en nous* was written in response to Petau's theory of the special role of the Holy Spirit in the work of our sanctification, a theory that Galtier vigorously disputed.

158. Aquinas spoke of the "appropriation mentioned by Hilary" and stated that Augustine "appropriates *unity* to the Father, *equality* to the Son, *concord* or *union* to the Holy Ghost." *ST*, I^a, q. 39, a. 8, c. He referenced here Augustine's *De Doctrina Christiana* 1.5, where the term "appropriation" is not explicitly used. In our own day, George Sauvage affirms that the theory of appropriations is "established by the Latin Fathers of the fourth and fifth centuries, especially by St. Hilary (*De Trinitate*, II, n. 1; P. L., t. X, col. 50) and St. Augustine (*De Trinitate*, VI, x, P.L., t. XLII, col. 931)." The passages in Hilary and Augustine that Sauvage references, however, do not explicitly use the term "appropriation." One might argue that the theology of appropriations is operative even though the word "appropriation" does not appear, but one could also argue that it is anachronistic to read patristic theology through the lens of a terminology of another era.

159. Richard of St. Victor, *Opuscules théologiques*, ed. J. Ribaillier, Textes philosophiques du moyen âge 15 (Paris, 1967), 182–87. On the novelty of this terminology, see Jean Châtillon, "Unitas, aequalitas, concordia vel connexio: Recherches sur les origines de la théorie Thomiste des appropriations (*Sum. theol.*, I, q. 39, art. 7–8)," in *St. Thomas Aquinas, 1274–1974: Commemorative Studies*, ed. Étienne Gilson (Toronto: Pontifical Institute of Mediaeval Studies, 1974), 363 n. 117. On Aquinas see 337–79.

160. On the promulgation of this axiom by the Council of Florence and its influence on the theology of appropriations, see Heribert Mühlen, "Person und Appropriation. Um Verständnis des Axioms: In Deo omnia sunt unum, ubi non obviat relationis oppositio," *MThZ* 16 (1965): 38 and 43–44.

161. For summary of the debate and full bibliography see Petro F. Chirico, *The Divine Indwelling and Distinct Relations to the Indwelling Persons in Modern Theological Discussion* (Rome: Gregorian University, 1960).

162. See for example Galtier, *L'Habitation en nous des trois Personnes*, 2d rev. ed. (Rome: Gregorian University, 1950); B. Monsegû, "Unidad y trinidad, propriedad y appropriación en las manifestaciones trinitarias, según la doctrina de San Cirilo Alejandrino," *Revista española de teología* 8 (1948): 1–57, 275–328; William R. O'Connor, "A New Concept of Grace and the Supernatural," *AER* 98 (1938): 401–13; Victorino Rodriguez, "Inhabitación de la SS. Trinidad en el alma en gracia," *CT* 86 (1959): 101–2; T. Urdanoz, "Influjo causal de las divinas personas en la inhabitación en las ánimas justas," *Revista española de teología* 7 (1948): 141–202.

163. According to Malachi Donnelly, this principle of Florence and the arguments deduced from this axiom are "[t]he main reasons offered in support of appropriation." "The Inhabitation of the Holy Spirit: A Solution According to de la Taille," *TS* 8 (1947): 447.

164. In the nineteenth century, the most important advocates of this position included Petau, *De Trinitate*; de Régnon, *Études*; M. J. Scheeben, *Die Mysterien des Christentums* (1865). In post–World War II theology, proponents of a *proprium* theory in which each of the divine persons has a special relation to the just soul included F. Taymans d'Epyernon, *Le Mystère primordial: La Trinité dans sa vivante image* (Paris, 1941): 109–28; M. J. Donnelly, "The Indwelling of the Holy Spirit according to M. J. Scheeben," *TS* 7 (1946): 244–80; idem, "The Inhabitation of the Holy Spirit: A Solution According to de la Taille," *TS* 8 (1947): 445–70; idem, "The Inhabitation of the Holy Spirit according to St. Thomas and de la Taille," *CTSAP* (1949): 38–77; G. M. Dupont, *Foundations for a Devotion to the Blessed Trinity* (Calcutta, 1947); P. de Letter, "Sanctifying Grace and Our Union with the Holy Trinity," *TS* 13 (1952): 33–58.

165. Johannes Beumer, "Die Einwohnung der drei göttlichen Personen in der Seele des begnadeten Menschen: Versuch einer Erklärung auf Grund der Schrift," *Theologie und Glaube* 30 (1938): 510. See also Scheeben, *Mysteries*, 146.

166. Donnelly, "The Inhabitation of the Holy Spirit," 459 and 458.

167. S. I. Dockx proposed a middle way between pure appropriation and the *proprium* theory in *Fils de Dieu par grâce* (Paris: Desclée, 1948), 110–13. See also A. Bundervoet, "Wat behoort tot het Wezen van Gods heiligende Genade-Inwonin volgens St. Thomas I sent., dist. XIV–XVIII en XXXVII?" *Bijdragen der Nederlandsiche Jezuïeten* 9 (1948): 42–58. English summary in de Letter, "Sanctifying Grace and the Divine Indwelling," 256. Apperibay tries to combine appropriation and *proprium* theories in his study of mystical theology, "Influjo causal de las divinas personas en la experiencia mística," *Verdad y vida* 7 (1949): 74–97.

168. "This activity [of divine missions]," he wrote, "considered in itself is not a *proprium* of the sending or of the sent person, but is only an *appropriatum*." Scheeben, *The Mysteries of Christianity*, trans. Cyril Vollert (St. Louis: Herder, 1946), 176. "So far as the persons sent," he continued, "are really in us according to their personal characteristics, they have no individual activity. They are merely the prototype of the effect of the divine activity, as well as the object and motive of the creature's activity. If without appropriation we call the Holy Spirit alone the Comforter, the Paraclete, we can do so only so far as He affords us consolation not by any activity, but by His interior presence in us and His possession of us." *The Mysteries of Christianity*, 177.

169. P. de Letter, "Sanctifying Grace and Our Union," 51.

170. A survey of the issues at hand can be found in de Letter, "Sanctifying Grace and the Divine Indwelling," 242–72.

171. P. de Letter, "Sanctifying Grace and Our Union," 36, 37, 38.

172. The 30 references are found on pages 34, 36, 37, 38, 38, 38, 38, 38, 39, 39, 40, 41, 42, 43, 44, 44, 44, 45, 45, 45, 45, 46, 47, 47, 47, 48, 48, 48, 49, and 50. In several of these passages de Letter is citing other theologians.

173. de Letter, "Sanctifying Grace and Our Union," 57–58.

174. Donnelly, "Sanctifying Grace and Our Union," 190–91.

175. Donnelly, "The Indwelling of the Holy Spirit," 278. Reference is to Scheeben, Die Mysterien, 179.

176. William Hill, The Three-Personed God, 306. Hill is here summarizing what he thinks is a promising line of thought in Anthony Kelly's "The Gifts of the Spirit: Aquinas and the Modern Context," Thom 38 (1974): 193–231. Kelly did not explicitly discuss the theology of appropriations in this article, but Hill believes that Kelly rightly suggests that "the doctrine of the gifts [of the Spirit] can be more richly exploited in an ecclesial context. Here, the consciousness whose horizon is transformed by the Spirit is communal rather than individual. The Pneuma both transforms natures and unites the persons of such natures to himself. But the first achievement is only appropriated to the Third Person whereas the second is proper to him, an immediate effect of his mere presence." Hill, The Three-Personed God, 306.

177. See Heribert Mühlen, Der Heilige Geist als Person.

178. de Letter, "Sanctifying Grace," 244.

179. Mühlen, "Person und Appropriation," 41–43.

180. Rahner, The Trinity, 24–38.

181. LaCugna, God for Us, 298. On appropriation see also 212–13.

182. LaCugna, "Response to John R. Sachs," 43.

183. See Kilian McDonnell, "Pneumatology Overview," CTSAP 51 (1996): 191; "A Trinitarian Theology of the Holy Spirit?" TS 46 (1985): 215; "The Determinative Doctrine of the Holy Spirit," ThToday 39 (1982): 153.

CONCLUSION

1. Congar, I Believe, 3:150.

Selected Bibliography

WORKS BY YVES CONGAR

Works are cited chronologically in order of the date of the original French publication:

Monographs

Divided Christendom: A Catholic Study of the Problem of Reunion. Translated by M. A. Bousfield. London: Centenary Press, 1939. Originally published as *Chrétiens désunis. Principes d'un "oecuménisme" catholique,* Unam Sanctam, no. 1 (Paris: Cerf, 1937).

A History of Theology. Translated by Hunter Guthrie. Garden City: Doubleday, 1968. Originally published as "Théologie," in *Dictionnaire de théologie catholique,* edited by A. Vacant and E. Mangenot, vol. 15/1 (Paris: Letouzey et Ané, 1943): 341–502.

Vraie et fausse réforme dans l'Église. Unam Sanctam, no. 20. Paris: Cerf, 1950; 2d rev. ed., Unam Sanctam, no. 72, 1969.

Christ, Our Lady and the Church: A Study in Eirenic Theology. Translated by Henry St. John. Westminster, MD: Newman Press, 1957. Originally published as *Le Christ, Marie et l'Église* (Paris: Desclée, 1952).

The Catholic Church and the Race Question. Paris: Unesco, 1961. Originally published as *L'Église catholique devant la question raciale* (Paris: Unesco, 1953).

Lay People in the Church: A Study for a Theology of the Laity. Translated by Donald Attwater. Westminster, MD: Newman Press, 1965. Originally published as *Jalons pour une théologie du laïcat,* Unam Sanctam, no. 23 (Paris: Cerf, 1953; 2d ed., 1954; 3d rev. ed., 1964).

La Pentecôte—Chartres 1956. Paris: Cerf, 1956.

The Mystery of the Temple or the Manner of God's Presence to His Creatures from Genesis to the Apocalypse. Translated by Reginald F. Trevett. London: Burns and Oates, 1962. Originally published as *Le Mystère du Temple ou l'Économie de la Présence de Dieu à sa créature de la Genèse à l'Apocalypse*, Lectio divina, no. 22 (Paris: Cerf, 1958).

Tradition and Traditions: An Historical and a Theological Essay. Translated by Michael Naseby and Thomas Rainborough. London: Burns and Oates, 1966. Originally published as *La Tradition et les traditions. Essai historique* (Paris: Fayard, 1960); and *La Tradition et les traditions. Essai théologique* (Paris: Fayard, 1963).

Ecumenism and the Future of the Church. Chicago: Priory Press, 1967. Translated by John C. Guinness and Geraldine F. McIntosh. Chapters 1–6 originally published as *Aspects de l'oecuménisme* (Bruxelles: La Pensée Catholique, 1962). Chapter 7 originally published as "L'Avenir de l'Église," in *L'Avenir* (Paris: Fayard, 1963).

La Foi et la théologie. Tournai: Desclée, 1962.

Tradition and the Life of the Church. Translated by A. N. Woodrow. London: Burns and Oates, 1964. Originally published as *La Tradition et la vie de l'Église* (Paris: Fayard, 1963).

Vatican II. Le Concile au jour le jour. 4 vols. Paris: Cerf, 1963–1966.

Jesus Christ. Translated by Luke O'Neill. New York: Herder and Herder, 1966. Originally published as *Jésus-Christ, notre Médiateur et notre Seigneur.* Foi Vivante, no. 1 (Paris: Cerf, 1965).

Le Sacerdoce chrétien des laïcs et des prêtres. Bruxelles: La Pensée Catholique, 1967.

This Church That I Love. Translated by Lucien Delafuente. Denville, NY: Dimension Books, 1969. Originally published as *Cette Église que j'aime*, Foi Vivante, no. 70 (Paris: Cerf, 1968).

Blessed Is the Peace of My Church. Translated by Salvator Attanasio. Denville, NJ: Dimension Books, 1973. Originally published as *Au milieu des orages. L'Église affronte aujourd'hui son avenir* (Paris: Cerf, 1969).

L'Église. De saint Augustin à l'époque moderne. Paris: Cerf, 1970.

L'Église, une, sainte, catholique et apostolique. Mysterium Salutis, no. 15. Paris: Cerf, 1970.

Une passion: l'unité. Réflexions et souvenirs, 1929–1973. Foi Vivante, no. 156. Paris: Cerf, 1974.

Un peuple messianique. L'Église, sacrement du salut. Salut et libération. Cogitatio Fidei, no. 85. Paris: Cerf, 1975.

Challenge to the Church: The Case of Archbishop Lefebvre. Translated by Paul Inwood. Huntington, IN: Our Sunday Visitor, 1976. Originally published as *La Crise dans l'Église et Mgr. Lefebvre* (Paris: Cerf, 1976).

I Believe in the Holy Spirit. 3 vols. Translated by David Smith. New York: Seabury, 1983. Originally published as *Je crois en l'Esprit Saint*, 3 vols. (Paris: Cerf, 1979–1980).

Diversity and Communion. Translated by John Bowden. London: SCM Press, 1984. Originally published as *Diversités et communion. Dossier historique et conclusion théologique*, Cogitatio Fidei, no. 112 (Paris: Cerf, 1982).

Esprit de l'homme, Esprit de Dieu. Foi Vivante, no. 206. Paris: Cerf, 1983.

The Word and the Spirit. Translated by David Smith. San Francisco: Harper and Row, 1986. Originally published as *La Parole et le Souffle* (Paris: Desclée, 1984).

Fifty Years of Catholic Theology: Conversations with Yves Congar. Translated by John

Bowden. Edited by Bernard Lauret. Philadelphia: Fortress, 1988. Originally published as *Entretiens d'automne. Présentes par B. Lauret* (Paris: Cerf, 1987).

Journal de la guerre 1914–1918. Edited and annotated by Stéphane Audoin-Rouzeau and Dominique Congar. Paris: Cerf, 1997.

Journal d'un théologien (1946–1956). Edited and annotated by Étienne Fouilloux. Paris: Cerf, 2001.

Mon journal du Concile. 2 vols. Edited and annotated by Éric Mahieu. Paris: Cerf, 2002.

Collections of Articles and Essays

The Mystery of the Church. Translated by A. V. Littledale. Baltimore: Helicon, 1960. Originally published as *Esquisses du Mystère de l'Église,* Unam Sanctam, no. 8 (Paris: Cerf, 1941; 2d ed., 1953; 3d ed., 1963). A second English edition was published in 1965. Its pagination differs significantly from the 1960 edition that is the source of citations in my text.

Laity, Church, World. Translated by Donald Attwater. Baltimore: Helicon, 1960. Originally published as *Si vous êtes mes témoins. Trois conférences sur laïcat, Église et monde* (Paris: Cerf, 1959).

The Wide World, My Parish: Salvation and Its Problems. Translated by Donald Attwater. Baltimore: Helicon, 1961. Originally published as *Vaste monde, ma paroisse. Vérité et dimensions du salut* (Paris: Témoignage Chrétien, 1959).

Faith and Spiritual Life. Translated by A. Manson and L. C. Sheppard. New York: Herder and Herder, 1968. Originally published as Part II of *Les Voies du Dieu vivant: Théologie et vie spirituelle,* Cogitatio Fidei, no. 3 (Paris: Cerf, 1962).

Priest and Layman. London: Darton, Longman & Todd, 1967. Originally published as *Sacerdoce et laïcat devant leurs tâches d'évangélisation et de civilisation,* Cogitatio Fidei, no. 4 (Paris: Cerf, 1962).

The Revelation of God. Translated by A. Manson and L. C. Sheppard. New York: Herder and Herder, 1968. Originally published as Part I of *Les Voies du Dieu vivant: Théologie et vie spirituelle,* Cogitatio Fidei, no. 3 (Paris: Cerf, 1962).

Power and Poverty in the Church. Translated by Jennifer Nicholson. Baltimore: Helicon, 1964. Originally published as *Pour une Église servante et pauvre* (Paris: Cerf, 1963).

Sainte Église. Études et approches ecclésiologiques, Unam Sanctam, no. 41. Paris: Cerf, 1963.

Dialogue between Christians. Translated by Philip Loretz. Westminster, MD: Newman Press, 1966. Originally published as *Chrétiens en dialogue. Contributions catholiques à l'oecuménisme,* Unam Sanctam, no. 50 (Paris: Cerf, 1964).

Situation et tâches présentes de la théologie. Cogitatio Fidei, no. 27. Paris: Cerf, 1967.

L'Ecclésiologie du haut Moyen Âge. De Saint Grégoire le Grand à la désunion entre Byzance et Rome. Paris: Cerf, 1968.

Ministères et communion ecclésiale. Paris: Cerf, 1971.

Martin Luther. Sa foi, sa réforme. Études de théologie historique. Cogitatio Fidei, no. 119. Paris: Cerf, 1983.

Le Concile de Vatican II. Son Église, peuple de Dieu et corps du Christ. Théologie historique, no. 71. Paris: Beauchesne, 1984.

Thomas d'Aquin. Sa vision de théologie et de l'Église. London: Variorum Reprints, 1984.
Called to Life. Translated by William Burridge. Crossroad: New York, 1987. Originally
   published as *Appelés à la vie* (Paris: Cerf, 1985).

Articles and Essays

If an article has been published in more than one place or in more than one language, the version of the article that is referenced in the text of the dissertation is
cited first. Original or alternate publications are listed subsequently. As in the preceding sections, the bibliography is arranged in chronological order according to the date
of the original French publication.

"Actualité de Kierkegaard." *VieI* 32 (1934): 9–36.
"Pensée orthodoxe sur l'unité d l'Église." *VieI* 29 (1934): 394–414.
"Deification in the Spiritual Tradition of the East (in Light of a Recent Study)." In
   Congar, *Dialogue between Christians,* 217–31. Originally published as "La Déifica-
   tion dans la tradition spirituelle de l'Orient d'après une étude récente," *SVS* 43
   (May 1935): 91–107.
"Nunc et in hora mortis nostrae." *VS* 45 (1935): 113–25.
"La Pensée de Möhler et l'ecclésiologie orthodoxe." *Iren* 12 (1935): 321–29.
"The Reasons for the Unbelief of Our Time." *Integration* (August–September 1938
   and December 1938–January 1939): 13–21 and 10–26. Originally published as
   "Une conclusion théologique à l'enquête sur les raisons actuelles de
   l'incroyance," *VieI* 37 (1935): 214–49.
"The Mystical Body of Christ." In Congar, *The Mystery of the Church,* 118–27. Origi-
   nally published as "Le Corps mystique du Christ," *SVS* 50 (1937): 113–38.
"Saint Thomas serviteur de la vérité." *VS* 50 (1937): 259–79.
"L'Esprit des Pères d'après Möhler." *SVS* 55 (1938): 1–25.
"Sur l'évolution et l'interprétation de la pensée de Möhler." *RSPhTh* 27 (1938): 205–
   12.
"La Signification oecuménique de l'oeuvre de Möhler." *Iren* 15 (1938): 113–30.
"L'Hérésie, déchirement de l'unité." In *L'Église est une. Hommage à Möhler,* edited by
   Pierre Chaillet, 255–69. Paris: Bloud and Gay, 1939.
"The Idea of the Church in St. Thomas Aquinas." *Thom* 1 (1939): 331–59. Later pub-
   lished as "L'Idée de l'Église chez saint Thomas d'Aquin," *RSPhTh* 29 (1940): 3–
   58. Reprinted in English in Congar, *The Mystery of the Church,* 97–117.
"The Church and Its Unity." In Congar, *The Mystery of the Church,* 58–96. Originally
   published as "L'Église et son unité," in *Esquisses du Mystère de l'Église,* Unam
   Sanctam, no. 8 (Paris: Cerf, 1941), 11–57.
"L'Église Corps mystique du Christ." *VS* 64 (1941): 242–54.
"The Call to Ecumenism and the Work of the Holy Spirit." In Congar, *Dialogue between Christians,* 100–106. Originally published as "L'Appel oecuménique et
   l'oeuvre du Saint-Esprit," *VS* 82 (January 1950): 5–12.
"Dogme christologique et ecclésiologie: Vérité et limites d'un parallèle," in Congar,
   Sainte Église, 69–104. This is a slightly revised version of an article by the same
   title that appeared in *Das Konzil von Chalkedon. Geschichte und Gegenwart,* edited
   by A. Grillmeier and H. Bacht, 3:239–68 (Würzburg: Echter, 1954).

"The Holy Spirit and the Apostolic Body: Continuators of the Work of Christ." In Congar, *The Mystery of the Church*, 147–86. Originally published as "Le Saint-Esprit et le corps apostolique, réalisateurs de l'oeuvre du Christ," *RSPhTh* 36 (1952): 613–25 and 37 (1953): 24–48.

"The Human Person and Human Liberty in Oriental Anthropology." In Congar, *Dialogue between Christians*, 232–45. Originally published as "La Personne et la liberté humaine dans l'anthropologie orientale," *Recherches et débats* 1 (May 1952): 99–111.

"The Christian Idea of History." In Congar, *Priest and Layman*, 276–85. Originally a sermon preached at St. Séverin in Paris on Dec. 7, 1952, and published as "Conception chrétienne de l'histoire," *Bulletin de la Communauté Saint-Séverin* 21 (March 1953): 11–17.

"L'Esprit-Saint dans l'Église." *Lumière et vie* 10 (1953): 51–73.

"Human Social Groups and the Laity of the Church." In Congar, *Priest and Layman*, 286–99. Originally published as "Groupes sociaux humains et laïcat d'Église," *Masses ouvrières* 92 (December 1953): 25–40.

"Considerations and Reflections on the Christology of Luther." In Congar, *Dialogue between Christians*, 372–406. Originally written in 1950 and published as "Regards et réflexions sur la christologie de Luther," in *Das Konzil von Chalkedon. Geschichte und Gegenwart*, edited by. A. Grillmeier and H. Bacht (Würzburg: Echter, 1954), 3:457–86.

"Les Trois âges de la vie spirituelle." *VS* 92 (1955): 115–29.

"Life in the World and Life in the Lord." In Congar, *Faith and Spiritual Life*, 135–42. Originally published as "Vie dans le monde et vie dans le Seigneur," *VS* 96 (1957): 401–8.

"Le Sens de l'"économie" salutaire dans la 'théologie' de saint Thomas d'Aquin (*Somme théologique*)." In *Glaube und Geschichte: Festgabe J. Lortz*, edited by E. Iserloh and P. Mann, 2: 73–122. Baden-Baden: Bruno Grimm, 1957.

"Holy Spirit and Spirit of Freedom." In Congar, *Laity, Church, World*, 1–34. Originally an address presented during the Fourth Franco-German Week at Freiburg im Breisgau in 1958.

"Religious Belief and the Life of the World." In Congar, *Faith and Spiritual Life*, 164–93. Originally a lecture given at the meeting of the Responsables de la Fédération Française des Étudiants Catholiques, October 1958.

"The Church and Pentecost." In Congar, *The Mystery of the Church*, 1–57. Originally published as *La Pentecôte—Chartres* (Paris: Cerf, 1956).

"*Dum Visibiliter Deum Cognoscimus*: A Theological Meditation." In Congar, *The Revelation of God*, 67–96. First published as "*Dum Visibiliter Deum Cognoscimus*: Méditation théologique," *M-D* 59 (1959): 132–61.

"Perspectives chrétiennes sur la vie personnelle et la vie collective." In *Socialisation et personne humaine*, Semaine sociale de Grenoble 1960, 195–221. Lyon: Chronique sociale de France, 1960.

"Comment l'Église sainte doit se renouveler sans cesse." *Iren* 34 (1961): 322–45.

"Peut-on définir l'Église? Destin et valeur de quatre notions qui s'offrent à le faire." In Congar, *Sainte Église*, 21–44. Originally published in *Jacques LeClercq. L'Homme, l'oeuvre et ses amis*, edited by André Molitor et al. (Paris: Casterman, 1961), 233–54.

"Unité, diversités, et divisions." In Congar, *Sainte Église*, 105–30. Originally a presentation for the Semaine des Intellectuels Catholiques, November 8, 1961.

"De la communion des Églises à une ecclésiologie de l'Église universelle." In *L'Episcopat et l'Église universelle*, Unam Sanctam, no. 39, edited by Y. Congar and B.-D. Dupuy, 227–60. Paris: Cerf, 1962.

"The Hierarchy as Service." In Congar, *Power and Poverty in the Church*, 15–100. Originally published in two parts as "La Hiérarchie comme service, selon le Nouveau Testament et les documents de la Tradition," in *L'Episcopat et l'Église universelle*, Unam Sanctam, no. 39, eds. Y. Congar and B.-D. Dupuy (Paris: Cerf, 1962), 67–100, and "The Historical Development of Authority in the Church: Points for Reflection," in *Problems of Authority*, edited by John Todd (London and Baltimore: Darton, Longman & Todd, 1962), 119–56.

Preface to *God's Own People: An Introductory Study of the Church*, by Frank B. Norris. Baltimore: Helicon, 1962.

"Les Saints Pères, organes privilégiés de la tradition." *Iren* 35 (1962): 479–98.

"Title and Honours in the Church: A Short Historical Study." In Congar, *Power and Poverty in the Church* (1964; French edition, 1963), 101–31.

"The Church: The People of God." *Conc* 1 (1964): 11–37.

"L'Application à l'Église comme telle des exigences évangéliques concernant la pauvreté." In *Église et pauvreté*, edited by Georges Cottier et al., Unam Sanctam, no. 57, 135–55. Paris: Cerf, 1965.

Preface to *La Vie selon l'Esprit*, by Ignace de la Potterie and S. Lyonnet. Paris: Cerf, 1965.

"Theology in the Council." *AER* 155 (1966): 217–30. Originally published as *La Théologie au Concile. Le 'Théologiser' du Concile*, Vérité et Vie, series 71 (Strasbourg: Centre de pédagogie Chrétienne, 1965).

"Le Christ dans l'économie salutaire et dans nos traités dogmatiques." In Congar, *Situation et tâches*, 85–109. First published in *Conc* 11 (1966), 11–26.

"The Church: Seed of Unity and Hope for the Human Race." *Chicago Studies* 5 (1966): 25–40.

"The People of God." In *Vatican II: An Interfaith Appraisal*, edited by John Miller, 197–206. Notre Dame, IN: University of Notre Dame Press, 1966.

Preface to *Le Christ Sagesse de Dieu: D'après les épitres pauliniennes*, by A. Feuillet, 7–15. Paris: Librairie Lecoffre, 1966.

"La Recherche théologique entre 1945–1965." In Congar, *Situation et tâches*, 25–40. First published in *Recherches et débats* 54 (1966): 89–102.

"L'Ecclesia' ou communauté chrétienne, sujet intégral de l'action liturgique." In *La Liturgie après Vatican II*, Unam Sanctam, no. 66, edited by Jean-Pierre Jossua and Yves Congar, 241–82. Paris: Cerf, 1967.

"Interview with Yves Congar." *America* 155 (6 May 1967): 676–80.

"Le Moment 'économique' et le moment 'ontologique' dans la sacra doctrina (révélation, théologie, *Somme théologique*)." In *Mélanges offerts à M.-D. Chenu*, Bibliothéque Thomiste, no. 37, edited by André Duval, 135–87. Paris: Librairie Philosophique, 1967.

"La Pneumatologie dans la théologie catholique." *RSPhTh* 51 (1967): 250–58.

"Pour un bon usage de la maladie." *VS* 117 (1967): 519–30.

"Le Rôle de l'Église dans le monde de ce temps." In *L'Église dans le monde de ce temps*, Unam Sanctam, no. 65b, edited by Yves Congar and M. Peuchmaurd, 2:305–28. Paris: Cerf, 1967.

"Situation et tâches," in Congar, *Situation et tâches* (1967), 57–84.

"The Council as an Assembly and the Church as Essentially Conciliar." In *One, Holy, Catholic and Apostolic. Studies on the Nature and Role of the Church in the Modern World*, edited by Herbert Vorgrimler, 44–88. London: Sheed and Ward, 1968.

"La Théologie depuis 1939." In Congar, *Situation et tâches*, 11–23. Originally prepared as the Introduction to Congar's *A History of Theology* (Garden City: Doubleday, 1968), where it appeared in edited form.

"The Church as Communion of Faith." In Congar, *Called to Life*, 88–97.

"L'Historicité de l'homme selon Thomas d'Aquin." *DCom* 22 (1969): 297–304.

"L'Homme est capable d'être appelé." *VS* 120 (1969): 377–84.

"*L'Église* de Hans Küng." *RSPhTh* 4 (1969): 693–706.

Interview with Yves Congar. In *The Crucial Questions on Problems Facing the Church Today*, ed. Frank Fehmers, 7–14. New York: Newman Press, 1969.

" 'Lumen gentium' n° 7, 'L'Église, Corps mystique du Christ,' vu au terme de huit siècles d'histoire de la théologie du Corps mystique." In Congar, *Le Concile de Vatican II*, 137–62. Originally published in *Au service de la parole de Dieu. Mélanges offerts à Mgr. André-Marie Charue* (Gembloux, Belgium: Duculot, 1969), 179–202.

"Pneumatologie ou 'christomonisme' dans la tradition latine?" Reprinted in *Ecclesia a Spiritu Sancto edocta. Mélanges théologiques. Hommage à Mgr. Gérard Philips*, 41–63. Gembloux: Duculot, 1970. Originally published by the same title in *EphThL* 45 (1969): 394–416.

"Infaillibilité et indéfectibilité." *RSPhTh* 54 (1970): 601–18. Reprinted in Congar, *Ministères et communion ecclésiale*, 141–65.

"Johann Adam Möhler: 1796–1838." *ThQ* 150 (1970): 47–51.

"Ministères et structuration de l'Église." In Congar, *Ministères et communion ecclésiale*, 31–49. This is a revised version of an article by the same title that appeared in *M-D* 102 (1970): 7–20.

"Le Père M.-D. Chenu." In *Bilan de la théologie du XXᵉ siècle*, edited by Robert Vander Gucht and Herbert Vorgrimler, 2:772–90. Paris: Casterman, 1970.

"D'une 'Ecclésiologie en gestation' à Lumen Gentium chap. I et II." In Congar, *Le Concile de Vatican II*, 123–36. Originally published under the same title in *Freiburger Zeitschrift für Philosophie und Theologie* 18 (1971, Heft 1–2: Festch. M. D. Koster): 366–77.

"La Personne 'Église.' " *RevTh* 71 (1971): 613–40.

"Pneumatologie et théologie de l'histoire." In *La Théologie de l'histoire. Herméneutique et eschatologie*, edited by Enrico Castelli, 61–70. Paris: Aubier, 1971.

"My Path-Findings in the Theology of Laity and Ministries." *The Jurist* 32 (1972): 169–88.

"Reception as an Ecclesiological Reality." In *Election and Consensus in the Church*, Concilium, no. 77, edited by Giuseppe Alberigo and Anton Weiler, 43–68. New York: Herder and Herder, 1972. Originally published as "La 'Reception' comme réalité ecclésiologique," *RSPhTh* 56 (1972): 369–403.

"Renewed Actuality of the Holy Spirit." *Lumen* 28 (1973): 13–30. Originally published in the French version of *Lumen vitae* as "Actualité renouvelée du Saint-Esprit," *Lumen* 27 (1972): 543–60.

"The Liturgical Assembly." In Congar, *Called to Life*, 110–29. Originally published as "Réflexions et recherches actuelles sur l'assemblée liturgique," *M-D* 115 (1973): 7–29.

"Pneumatology Today." *AER* 167 (1973): 435–49. A popularized translation appeared as "The Spirit in Action," in Congar, *Called to Life*, 60–74. Originally published as "Actualité d'une pneumatologie," *POC* 2 (1973): 121–32.

"Rudolf Sohm nous interroge encore." *RSPhTh* 57 (1973): 263–94.

"Après *Infaillible?* de Hans Küng. Bilans et perspectives." *RSPhTh* 58 (1974): 243–52.

"L'Influence de la société et de l'histoire sur le développement de l'homme chrétien." *NRT* 96 (1974): 673–92.

"Le Saint-Esprit dans la théologie thomiste de l'agir moral." In *L'Agire morale. Atti del Congresso internazionale: Tommaso d'Aquino nel suo Settimo Centenario*, 5:9–19. Naples: Edizioni Domenicane Italiane, 1974.

"La Tri-unité de Dieu et l'Église." *VS* 128 (1974): 687–703.

"J'aime l'Orthodoxie." In *2000 ans de christianisme*, 2:97–99. Published by Société d'histoire chrétienne. Paris: Aufadi, 1975.

"The Psalms in My Life." In Congar, *Called to Life*, 11–17. First published as "Les Psaumes dans ma vie," *VS* 811 (1975): 876–87.

"Richesse et vérité d'une vision de l'Église comme 'peuple de Dieu.'" In Congar, *Le Concile de Vatican II*, 109–22. Originally published in *Les Quartre fleuves* 4 (1975): 46–54.

"Le Blasphème contre le Saint Esprit." In *L'Expérience de l'Esprit. Mélanges Schillebeeckx*, edited by Paul Brand et al., 17–29. Paris: Beauchesne, 1976.

"Liturgical Celebration and Witness." In Congar, *Called to Life*, 130–38. Originally published as "Témoignage et célébration liturgique," *Cahiers Saint Dominique* 164 (1976): 454–63.

"Bref historique des formes du 'magistère' et de ses relations avec les Docteurs." *RSPhTh* 60 (1976): 99–112. English summary in *TheoDgst* 25 (spring 1977): 15–20.

"What Belonging to the Church Has Come to Mean." *Communio* 4 (1977): 146–60.

"Bulletin de théologie. Aperçus de pneumatologie." *RSPhTh* 62 (1978): 421–42.

"A God Who Has Spoken." In Congar, *Called to Life*, 31–41. Originally published as "Un Dieu qui parle, un Dieu qui a parlé," *Cahiers Saint Dominique* 174 (1978): 5–17.

Preface to *Clés pour une théologie du ministère*, by B.-D. Marliangeas. Paris: Beauchesne, 1978.

"Saint Syméon le nouveau théologien. Une experience de l'Esprit." *VS* 132 (1978): 864–79. Reprinted as the fourth chapter of the second section of the first volume of Congar's *I Believe in the Holy Spirit*, 93–103.

"Vision de l'Église chez Thomas d'Aquin." *RSPhTh* 62 (1978): 523–42.

"Pour une christologie pneumatologique. Note bibliographique." *RSPhTh* 63 (1979): 435–42. This article was reprinted as chapter 4 of volume 3 of Congar's *I Believe in the Holy Spirit*.

"Chronique de pneumatologie." *RSPhTh* 64 (1980): 445–51.

"Le Monothéisme politique et la Dieu Trinité." *NRT* 103 (1981): 3–17.
"Reflections on Being a Theologian." *NewBlckfrs* 62 (1981): 405–8.
"Theology of the Holy Spirit and Charismatic Renewal." In Congar, *Called to Life*, 75–
87. Originally published as "Renouveau charismatique et théologie du Saint-
Esprit," *VS* 646 (1981): 735–49.
"Aimer Dieu et les hommes par l'amour dont Dieu aime?" *REtAug* 28 (1982): 86–99.
"Les Implications christologiques et pneumatologiques de l'ecclésiologie de Vatican
II." In Congar, *Le Concile de Vatican II*, 163–76. Originally published in *Les
Églises après Vatican II: Dynamisme et prospective*, Actes du Colloque international
de Bologne, 1980, ed. Giuseppe Alberigo (Paris: Beauchesne, 1982), 117–30.
"Nouveaux regards sur la christologie de Luther." Reprinted in Congar, *Martin Luther*,
105–34. Originally published under the same title in *RSPhTh* 62 (1982): 180–97.
"Pneumatologie dogmatique." In *Initiation à la pratique de la théologie*, edited by Ber-
nard Lauret and François Refoulé, 2:485–516. Paris: Cerf, 1982.
"Théologie de l'eucharistie." Reprinted in Congar, *Martin Luther*, 85–103. Originally
published under the same title in *RSPhTh* 66 (1982): 169–80.
"Théologie historique." In *Initiation à la pratique de la théologie*, edited by Bernard
Lauret and François Refoulé, 1:233–62. Paris: Cerf, 1982.
"Actualité de la pneumatologie." In *Credo in Spiritum Sanctum*, edited by P. José Sar-
aiva Martins, 15–28. Vatican City: Libreria Editrice Vaticana, 1983.
"Luther réformateur. Retour sur une étude ancienne." In Congar, *Martin Luther*
(1983), 15–83.
"Christ-Eucharistie-Église." In *In necessariis unitas: Mélanges offerts à J.-L. Leuba*, edited
by R. Stauffer, 69–80. Paris: Cerf, 1984.
"Moving towards a Pilgrim Church." In *Vatican II Revisited by Those Who Were There*,
edited by Alberic Stacpoole, 129–52. Minneapolis, MN: Winston Press, 1986.
Originally published as "Situation ecclésiologique au moment de *Ecclesiam Suam*
et passage à une Église dans l'itinéraire des hommes," in Congar, *Le Concile de
Vatican II* (1984), 7–32.
"Letter from Father Yves Congar, O.P." *TheoDgst* 32 (1985): 213–16.
"Le Troisième article du symbole. L'Impact de la pneumatologie dans la vie de
l'Église." In *Dieu, Église, Société*, edited by J. Doré, 287–309. Paris: Cerf, 1985.

WORKS ABOUT YVES CONGAR

Biographical Works

Beauchesne, Richard. "Yves Congar Leaves Rich Legacy." *NatCathRep* 31 (14 July
1995): 2.
Bosch, Juan. "Una aproximación a la vida y obra del Padre Congar." *CT* 123 (1996):
7–26.
———. "El rostro de una teología tolerante." *CT* 123 (1996): 99–114.
Dulles, Avery. "Yves Congar: In Appreciation." *America* 173 (15 July 1995): 6–7.
Duval, André. "Yves Congar: A Life for the Truth." *Thom* 48 (1984): 505–11.
Egan, Keith. "Yves Congar: 1904–1995." *Christian Spirituality Bulletin* 3 (1995): 22–24.
Fouilloux, Étienne. "Comment devient-on expert à Vatican II? Le cas du Père Yves

Congar." In *Le Deuxième Concile du Vatican II (1959–1965)*, 307–31. Rome: Ecole française de Rome, 1989.

———. "Frère Yves, Cardinal Congar, Dominicain. Itinéraire d'un théologien." *RSPhTh* 79 (1995): 379–404. Translated by Chris Dupont under the title "Friar Yves, Cardinal Congar, Dominican: Itinerary of a Theologian," *U.S. Catholic Historian* 17 (1999): 63–90.

Heath, Mark. "Yves Congar: Shining Star at Vatican II." *National Catholic Register* 70 (28 August 1994): 1ff.

Henn, William. "Yves Congar, O.P. (1904–95)." *America* (12 August 1995): 23–25.

Jossua, Jean-Pierre. *Yves Congar: Theology in Service of God's People.* Chicago: Priory Press, 1968.

———. "L'Oeuvre oecuménique du Père Congar." *Études* 357 (1982): 543–55.

———. "Yves Congar: La Vie et l'oeuvre d'un théologien." *Cristianesimo nella storia* 17 (1996): 1–12.

Kerr, Fergus. "Cardinal Yves Congar, O.P." *NewBlckfrs* 76 (July/August 1995): 314–16.

Komonchak, Joseph. "The Return of Yves Congar." *Comm* 110 (15 July 1983): 402–5.

———. "A Hero of Vatican II: Yves Congar." *Comm* 15 (1 December 1995): 15–17.

Lago Alba, Luis. "Y. Congar Ecumenista." *CT* 123 (1996): 149–86.

Le Guillou, Jean-Marie. "Yves Congar." In *Bilan de la théologie du XXᵉ siècle*, 2:791–805. Edited by Robert Vander Gucht and Herbert Vorgrimler. Paris: Casterman, 1970.

McBrien, Richard. "The Long-Overdue Elevation of an Extraordinary Theologian." *NatCathRep* 31 (9 December 1994): 2.

O'Meara, Thomas F., O.P. "Ecumenist of Our Time: Yves Congar." *Mid-Stream* 28 (1988): 67–76.

———. "'Raid on the Dominicans': The Repression of 1954." *America* 170 (4 February 1994): 8–16.

Philibert, Paul J., O.P. "Yves Congar: Theologian, Ecumenist, and Visionary." *U.S. Catholic Historian* 17 (1999): 116–20.

Puyo, Jean. *Une vie pour la vérité. Jean Puyo interroge le Père Congar.* Paris: Centurion, 1975.

Radcliffe, Timothy, O.P. "Church of God, My Mother." *Priests and People* 9 (1995): 340–42.

Saxon, Wolfgang. "Congar, Yves M. J., Cardinal, d. 1995." *New York Times* 144 (25 June 1995): I17.

Torvend, Samuel. "A Tribute to Yves Congar." *TheoDgst* 31 (1984): 102.

Wedig, Mark. "The Fraternal Context of Congar's Achievement: The Platform for a Renewed Catholicism at *Les Éditions du Cerf* (1927–1954)." *U.S. Catholic Historian* 17 (1999): 106–115.

Willebrands, Johannes Cardinal. "Cher frère Yves Congar." *CT* 123 (1996): 5–6.

Bibliographies of Congar's Writings

Nichols, Aidan. "An Yves Congar Bibliography 1967–1987." *Ang* 66 (1989): 422–66.

Quattrocchi, Pietro. "General Bibliography of Yves Congar." In *Yves Congar*, by Jean-Pierre Jossua, 189–241. Chicago: Priory, 1968.

Monographs and Essays

Areeplackal, Joseph. *Spirit and Ministries: Perspectives of East and West.* Bangalore, India: Dharmaram Publications, 1990.

Beauchesne, R. J. "Heeding the Early Congar Today, and Two Recent Roman Catholic Issues: Seeking Hope on the Road Back." *JEcSt* 27 (1990): 535–60.

Blakebrough, Denise S. *El Cardenal Congar o la libertad teológica: Ensayo sobre su comprensión del Espíritu Santo.* Salamanca: Varona, 1995.

Bunnenberg, Johannes. *Lebendige Treue zum Ursprung. Das Traditionverständnis Yves Congars.* Mainz: Matthias-Grünewald, 1989.

Canavaris, Iakovos John. *The Ecclesiology of Yves M.-J. Congar: An Orthodox Evaluation.* Athens, Greece: P. Klissiounis Society Press, 1968.

Dietrich, Wendell Sanford. "Yves Congar: The Church as Structured Communion." In *The New Day: Catholic Theologians of the Renewal,* 21–33. Edited by William Jerry Boney and Lawrence E. Molumby. Richmond, VA: John Knox Press, 1968.

Doyle, Dennis M. "Journet, Congar, and the Roots of Communion Ecclesiology." *TS* 58 (1997): 461–79.

Dunne, Victor. *Prophecy in the Church: The Vision of Yves Congar.* New York: P. Lang, 2000.

Dupuy, Bernard. "Aux sources de l'oeuvre du Père Congar." *Istina* 41 (1996): 117–135.

Espeja, Jesús. "¿Misericordia y no sacrificios?" *CT* 123 (1996): 55–76.

Famerée, Joseph. "*Chrétiens désunis* du P. Congar: 50 ans après." *NRT* 110 (1988): 666–86.

———. *L'Ecclésiologie d'Yves Congar avant Vatican II: Histoire et Église. Analyse et reprise critique.* Leuven: Leuven University Press, 1992.

———. "L'Ecclésiologie du Père Yves Congar. Essai de synthèse critique." *RSPhTh* 76 (1992): 377–419.

———. "Aux origines de Vatican II. La Démarche théologique d'Yves Congar." *EphThL* 71 (1995): 121–38.

———. "Orthodox Influence on the Roman Catholic Theologian Yves Congar, O.P.: A Sketch." *SVTQ* 39 (1995): 409–16.

———. "Y. M.-J. Congar. Un théologien de la catholicité." In *Le Christianisme nuée des témoins,* Cahiers oecuméniques no. 33, 15–31. Edited by Guido Vergauwen. Fribourg, Switzerland: Editiones Universitaries, 1998.

Fierens, M. "L'Esprit Saint et la liturgie dans la pneumatologie de Congar." *Questions liturgiques* 66 (1985): 221–27.

Finnegan, Gerald F. "Ministerial Priesthood in Yves Congar." *RRel* 46 (1987): 523–32.

Fuster, Sebastián. "Aportación a la teología del seglar." *CT* 123 (1996): 77–98.

Galeano, A. "La Eclesiología de Yves Congar." *Fran* 22 (1980): 141–204.

———. "La Reforma en la Iglesia según Yves Congar." *Fran* 24 (1981): 117–70.

———. "La Reforma protestante y el ecumenismo según Yves Congar." *Fran* 24 (1982): 149–84.

Gianazza, Pier Giorgio. *Lo Spirito Santo: Summa pneumatologica di Yves Congar.* Biblioteca di Scienze Religiose, no. 139. Rome: Libreria Ateneo Salesiano, 1988.

Ginter, Mark. "An Ecumenical Colloquium on Yves Congar: His Pneumatology." *CTSAP* 51 (1996): 163–87.

———. "Ecumenical Colloquium on Yves Congar: Congar and Christian Worship." *CTSAP* 52 (1997): 113–14.

———. "Congar's Theological Anthropology and His Doctrine of Salvation." *CTSAP* 53 (1998): 107–8.

———. "Yves Congar Ecumenical Colloquium." [Topic: Authentic Expressions of Apostolic Faith] *CTSAP* 54 (1999): 174–76.

———. "Yves Congar Ecumenical Colloquium." [Topic: Congar's Developing Understanding of the Mission of the Laity] *CTSAP* 55 (2000): 181–82.

Hausman, N., S.C.M. "Le Père Yves Congar au Concile Vatican II." *NRT* 120 (1998): 267–81.

Henn, William. *The Hierarchy of Truths According to Yves Congar, O.P.* Analecta Gregoriana, no. 246. Rome: Editrice Pontificia Università Gregoriana, 1987.

Jelly, Frederick M. "Congar's Theological Anthropology and Doctrine of Salvation." *The Josephinum Journal of Theology* 6 n.s. (1999): 80–87.

Kembe, Kitengie. *Conciliarité et unité à la lumière de l'ecclésiologie de Yves Congar: Étude pour une ecclésialité de communion.* Rome: Pontifical University, 1989.

Kizhakkeparampil, Isaac. *The Invocation of the Holy Spirit as Constitutive of the Sacraments According to Cardinal Yves Congar.* Rome: Gregorian University Press, 1995.

Komonchak, Joseph. "Vatican II as Ecumenical Council: Yves Congar's Vision Realized." *Comm* 129 (2002): 12–14.

MacDonald, Charles. *Church and World in the Plan of God. Aspects of History and Eschatology in the Thought of Yves Congar.* Frankfurt am Main: P. Lang, 1982.

MacDonald, Timothy I. *The Ecclesiology of Yves Congar: Foundational Themes.* Lanham, MD: University Press of America, 1984.

McBrien, Richard. "Church and Ministry: The Achievement of Yves Congar." *Theo-Dgst* 32 (1985): 203–11.

Meaken, Christopher. *"The Same but Different?" The Relationship between Unity and Diversity in the Theological Ecumenism of Yves Congar.* Lund, Sweden: Lund University Press.

Muñoz Duran, Maximo. "La concepción de la teología en Congar." *CT* 123 (1996): 27–54.

Nichols, Aidan. *Yves Congar.* Wilton, CT: Morehouse-Barlow, 1989.

O'Meara, Thomas F., O.P. "Revelation and History: Schelling, Möhler, and Congar." *ITQ* 55 (1987): 17–35.

———. "Beyond 'Hierarchology': Johann Adam Möhler and Yves Congar." In *The Legacy of the Tübingen School: The Relevance of Nineteenth-Century Theology for the Twenty-First Century,* 173–91. Edited by Donald J. Dietrich and Michael J. Himes. New York: Crossroad, 1997.

———. "Reflections on Yves Congar and Theology in the United States." *U.S. Catholic Historian* 17 (1999): 91–105.

Osuna-Fernández-Largo, Antonio. "La 'Viva traditio.'" *CT* 123 (1996): 115–48.

Pellitero, Ramiro. *La teología del laicado en la obra de Yves Congar.* Pamplona: Universidad de Navarra, 1996.

———. "Congar's Developing Understanding of the Laity and Their Mission." *Thom* 65 (2001): 327–59.

Prunières, J. "L'ecclésiologie du P. Congar: Oeuvre témoin d'une crise." *Études francis-caines* 16 (1966): 253–83.

Rigal, J. "Trois approaches de l'ecclésiologie de communion: Congar, Zizioulas, Molt-mann." *NRT* 120 (1998): 605–19.

Sicouly, Pablo. "Yves Congar und Johann Adam Möhler: Ein theologisches Gespräch zwischen den Zeiten." *Catholica* 45 (1991): 36–43.

Steger, Carlos Alfredo. *Apostolic Succession in the Writings of Yves Congar and Oscar Cullman.* Andrews University Seminary Doctoral Dissertation Series, no. 20. Berrien Springs, MI: Andrews University Press, 1993.

Torrell, Jean-Pierre. "Yves Congar et l'écclésiologie de Saint Thomas d'Aquin." *RSPhTh* 82 (1998): 201–42.

Untener, Kenneth. *The Church-World Relationship According to the Writings of Yves Congar, O.P.* Rome: Gregorian University, 1976.

Van Vliet, Cornelis Th. M. *Communio sacramentalis: Das Kirchenverständis von Yves Congar—genetisch und systematisch betrachtet.* Mainz: Matthias-Grünewald, 1995.

Vauchez, André, ed. *Cardinal Yves Congar: 1904–1995.* Paris: Cerf, 1999.

Wolff, Maria-Monika. *Gott und Mensch. Ein Beitrag Yves Congars zum ökumenischen Dialog.* Frankfurt: Joseph Knecht, 1990.

Dissertations

Beauchesne, R. J. "Laity and Ministry in Yves M.-J. Congar, O.P.: Evolution, Evaluation and Ecumenical Perspectives." Ph.D. diss., Boston University, 1975.

Brown, Susan Mader. "Faith and History: The Perspective of Yves Congar." Ph.D. diss., University of St. Michael's College, 1995.

Cameron-Mowat, Andrew. "Yves Congar as Liturgical Theologian: The Significance of His Writings for Christian Liturgy and Church Architecture." Ph.D. diss., Graduate Theological Union, 1998.

Czyz, P. "Il rapporto tra la dimensione cristologica e pneumatolgica dell'ecclesiologia nel pensiero di Y. Congar." Diss., Gregorian University, 1986.

Dobryznski, Andrzej. "The Pneumatology in the Ecumenical Ecclesiology of Cardinal Yves Congar." D.Th. diss., Universidad de Navarra (Spain), 1999.

Eckley, Richard Kevin. "Pneumatology in the Wesleyan Tradition and Yves Congar: A Comparative Ecumenical Study." Ph.D. diss., Duquesne University, 1998.

Gottemoeller, Doris A. "The Theory of Development of Dogma in the Ecclesiology of Yves Congar." Ph.D. diss., Fordham University, 1976.

Harnett, A. "The Role of the Holy Spirit in Revelation and its Transmission. The Interpretation of Yves Congar." Ph.D. diss., Catholic University of America, 1989.

Jagdeo, Diane. "Holiness and Reform of the Church in the Writings of Yves Congar, O.P." Ph.D. diss., Catholic University of America, 1987.

Kallarangatt, J. "The Holy Spirit, Bond of Communion of the Churches. A Comparative Study of the Ecclesiology of Yves Congar and Nikos A. Nissiotis." S.T.D. diss., Gregorian University, 1989.

Lara Barbosa, Dimas. "Apostolicidade da Igreja e seu Fundamento Teologico segundo Yves Congar, O.P." Th.D. diss., Gregorian University, 1994.

Lehning, Thomas Joseph. "The Foundations, Functions and Authority of the Magisterium in the Theology of Yves Congar." Ph.D. diss., Catholic University of America, 1985.

Louch, David. "The Contribution of Yves Congar to a Renewed Understanding of Teaching Authority in the Catholic Church." Th.D. diss., University of St. Michael's College, 1979.

Mallon, Colleen Mary. "Traditioning Disciples (Clifford Geertz, Victor Turner, Mary Douglas, Yves Congar)." Ph.D. diss., Graduate Theological Union, 2002.

McDonnell, John J. "Communio, Collegiality, Conciliarity: A Comparative Analysis of These Concepts Drawn from Certain Catholic and Orthodox Theologians." S.T.D. diss., Gregorian University, 1990.

McHenry, Stephen Patrick. "Three Significant Moments in the Theological Development of the Sacramental 'Character' of Orders. Its Origin, Standardization, and New Direction in Augustine, Aquinas, and Congar." Ph.D. diss., Fordham University, 1982–1983.

Meini, M. "Lo Spirito Santo nell'ecclesiologia di Yves Congar." S.T.D. diss., Gregorian University Rome, 1979.

Meredith, Richard. "Themes of Thomistic Eschatology in the Ecumenical Theology of Yves Congar." Ph.D. diss., Catholic University of America, 1993.

Muñoz Duran, Maximo. "Mysteriorum intelligentiam quaerere e nexu inter se et cum fine hominis ultimo. Estudio sobre el concepto y significado de theología y teologo en Y. M. Congar." Th.D. diss., Gregorian University, 1993.

Osner, M. "L'Action du Saint-Esprit dans la communion ecclésiale: Étude sur l'oeuvre de Yves Congar." Ph.D. diss., Strassbourg Faculté de Théologie catholique, 1980.

Pietropaoli, David. "Visible Ecclesial Communion: Authority and Primacy in the Conciliar Church. Roman Catholic and Orthodox Theologians in Dialogue (John Meyendorff, John D. Zizioulas, Yves Congar, Jean-Marie Roger Tillard)." Th.D. diss., Gregorian University, 1997.

Stoneburner, J. H. "The Doctrine of the Church in the Theology of Yves Congar." Ph.D. diss., Drew University, 1961.

Venstermans, M. Gibaud. "Sacerdocio común y sacerdocio ministerial en Yves Congar y en Vatican II." Ph.D. diss., Angelicum, 1983.

ADDITIONAL SECONDARY SOURCES

Blunt, Hugh Francis. *Life with the Holy Ghost: Thoughts on the Gifts of the Holy Ghost.* Milwaukee: Bruce Publishing Company, 1943.

Bourassa, François. "Adoptive Sonship: Our Union with the Divine Persons." *TS* 13 (1952): 309–34.

Carroll, James. *God the Holy Ghost.* New York: P. J. Kenedy & Sons, 1940.

Chenu, Marie-Dominique. *Une école de théologie: Le Saulchoir.* Kain-lez-Tournai, Belgium: Le Saulchoir, 1937.

Chirico, Petro F. *The Divine Indwelling and Distinct Relations to the Indwelling Persons in Modern Theological Discussion.* Rome: Pontificiae Universitatis Gregoriana, 1960.

de Letter, P. "Sanctifying Grace and Our Union with the Holy Trinity." *TS* 13 (1952): 33–58.

———. "Sanctifying Grace and the Divine Indwelling." *TS* 14 (1953): 242–72.

————. "Grace, Incorporation, Inhabitation." *TS* 19 (1958): 1–31.

de Lubac, Henri. *Catholicism: A Study of Dogma in Relation to the Corporate Destiny of Mankind*. Translated by Lancelot Sheppard. New York: Sheed and Ward, 1950. Originally published as *Catholicisme: Les Aspects sociaux du dogme* (Paris: Cerf, 1938).

————. *Surnaturel: Études Historiques*. Paris: Aubier, 1946.

Donnelly, Malachi. "The Indwelling of the Holy Spirit According to M. J. Scheeben." *TS* 7 (1946): 244–80.

————. "The Inhabitation of the Holy Spirit: A Solution According to de la Taille." *TS* 8 (1947): 445–70.

————. "Sanctifying Grace and Our Union with the Holy Trinity: A Reply." *TS* 13 (1952): 190–204.

Doyle, Dennis M. "Möhler, Schleiermacher, and the Roots of Communion Ecclesiology." *TS* 57 (1996): 467–80.

Froget, Barthélemy. *The Indwelling of the Holy Spirit in the Souls of the Just*. Translated by Sydney Raemers. Baltimore, MD: Carroll Press, 1950. Originally published as *De l'inhabitation du S. Esprit dans les âmes justes*. Paris: Leithielleux, 1890.

Galtier, P. "Temples du Saint-Esprit." Parts 1–3. *RAM* 7 (1926): 365–413; 8 (1927), 40–76, 170–79.

————. *Le Saint-Esprit en nous d'après les Pères Grecs*, Annalecta Gregoriana 35. Rome: Pontificia Universita Gregoriana, 1946.

Gustafson, James. *Treasure in Earthen Vessels: The Church as a Human Community*. Chicago: University of Chicago Press, 1961.

Hamer, Jerome. *The Church Is a Communion*. New York: Sheed and Ward, 1964.

Hasenhüttl, G. *Charisma, Ordnungsprinzip der Kirche*. Freiburg: Herder, 1969. Summarized in the French study "Les Charismes dans la vie de l'Église," in *Vatican II: L'Apostolat des laïcs*, Unam Sanctam, no. 75 (Paris: Cerf, 1970), 203–14.

Hilberath, Bernd. *Der Personbegriff der Trinitätstheologie in Rückfrage von Karl Rahner zu Tertullians "Adversus Praxean."* Innsbruck: Tyrolia, 1986.

Hill, William. *The Three-Personed God: The Trinity as a Mystery of Salvation*. Washington, DC: Catholic University of America Press, 1982.

Himes, Michael J. " 'A Great Theologian of our Time': Möhler on Schleiermacher." *Heythrop* 37 (1996): 24–46.

————. *Ongoing Incarnation: Johann Adam Möhler and the Beginnings of Modern Ecclesiology*. New York: Crossroad, 1997.

Hinze, Bradford. "The Holy Spirit and the Catholic Tradition: The Legacy of Johann Adam Möhler." In *The Legacy of the Tübingen School: The Relevance of Nineteenth-Century Theology for the Twenty-First Century*, 75–94. Edited by Donald J. Dietrich and Michael J. Himes. New York: Crossroad, 1997.

Holden, G. F. *The Holy Ghost the Comforter*. London: Longmans, Green and Co., 1907.

Kasper, Walter. "Church as *Communio*." *Communio* 13 (1986): 100–117.

————. "The Church as Sacrament of Unity." *Communio* 14 (1987): 4–11.

LaCugna, Catherine Mowry. *God for Us: The Trinity and Christian Life*. San Francisco: HarperCollins, 1991.

————. "Response to John R. Sachs." *CTSAP* 51 (1996): 39–44.

Leen, Edward. *The Holy Ghost and His Work in Souls*. New York: Sheed and Ward, 1937.

Legrand, O.P., Hervé-Marie. "Theology and the Election of Bishops in the Early
Church." In *Election and Consensus in the Church*, 31–42. Edited by Giuseppe Alberigo and Anton Weiler. New York: Herder and Herder, 1972.

Manning, Cardinal Henry Edward. *The Internal Mission of the Holy Ghost*. London:
Burns and Oates, 1895.

——. *The Temporal Mission of the Holy Ghost*. London: Burns and Oates, 1909.

Martínez, Luis M. *The Sanctifier*. Translated by M. Aquinas. Paterson, NJ: St. Anthony
Guild Press, 1957.

Martins, J. Saraiva, ed. *Credo in Spiritum Sanctum: Atti del Congresso Teologico Internazionale di Pneumatologia in occasione del 1600 anniversario del I Concilio de Con-
stantinopoli e del 1550 anniversario del Concilio de Efeso*. Vatican City: Libreria Ed.
Vaticana, 1983.

McDonnell, Kilian. "The Determinative Doctrine of the Holy Spirit." *ThToday* 39
(1982): 142–61.

——. "A Trinitarian Theology of the Holy Spirit?" *TS* 46 (1985): 191–227.

Möhler, Johann Adam. *Unity in the Church or the Principle of Catholicism Presented in
the Spirit of the Church Fathers of the First Three Centuries*. Translated by Peter C.
Erb. Washington, DC: Catholic University of America Press, 1996. Originally
published as *Die Einheit in der Kirche Oder das Prinzip des Katholizismus dargestellt im Geiste der Kirchenväter der ersten drei Jahrhunderte* (Tübingen: Heinrich
Laupp, 1825).

——. *Symbolism or Exposition of the Doctrinal Differences between Catholics and Protestants as Evidenced by Their Symbolical Writings*. Translated by James Burton Robertson. London: Gibbings and Company, 1894. Originally published as *Symbolik
oder Darstellung der dogmatischen Gegensätze der Katholiken und Protestanten nach
ihren öffentlichen Bekenntnisschriften* (Mainz: Kupferberg, 1832).

Moltmann, Jürgen. *The Spirit of Life*. Minneapolis: Fortress Press, 1992.

Mühlen, Heribert. *Der Heilige Geist als Person. Beitrag zur Frage nach der dem Heiligen
Geiste eigentümlichen Funktion in der Trinität, bei der Inkarnation und im Gnadenbund*. Münster: Aschendorff, 1963.

——. *Una Mystica Persona. Die Kirche als das Mysterium der heilsgeschictlichen Identi-
tät des Heiligen Geistes in Christus und den Christen: Ein Person in vielen Personen*.
Munich: Schoningh, 1964.

——. "Person und Appropriation." *MThZ* 16 (1965): 37–57.

Nichols, Terence. *That All May Be One: Hierarchy and Participation in the Church*. Collegeville, MN: Liturgical Press, 1977.

Nissiotis, Nikos A. "The Main Ecclesiological Problem of the Second Vatican Council
and the Position of the Non-Roman Churches Facing It." *JEcSt* 6 (1965): 31–62.

——. "A Pneumatological Christology as a Presupposition of Ecclesiology." In *Oecumenica: K. E. Skydsgaard*, 235–52. Edited by F. Kantzenback and Vilmos Vajta.
Minneapolis, MN: Augsburg, 1967.

——. "La Pneumatologie ecclésiologique au service de l'unité de l'Église." *Istina* 3
and 4 (1967): 323–40.

O'Connor, William. "The Inhabitation of the Holy Spirit." 2 Parts. *CTSAP* 4 (1949):
39–89.

Pedrini, Arnaldo. *Bibliografia Tomistica sulla Pneumatologie*. Vatican City: Libreria Editrice Vaticana, 1994.

Rahner, Karl. "History of the World and Salvation History." *TI.* 5:97–114. Baltimore: Helicon Press, 1966.

———. *Hearers of the Word.* New York: Herder and Herder, 1969.

———. "Concerning the Relationship between Nature and Grace." *TI.* 1:297–317. Baltimore: Helicon, 1961.

———. "Some Implications of the Scholastic Concept of Uncreated Grace." *TI.* 1:345–46. Baltimore: Helicon, 1961.

———. *The Trinity.* Translated by Joseph Donceel. Introduction by Catherine Mowry LaCugna. New York: Herder and Herder, 1970; New York: Crossroad, 1997.

Ratzinger, Joseph Cardinal. "The Ecclesiology of the Second Vatican Council." *Communio* 13 (1986): 239–52.

———. *Called to Communion: Understanding the Church Today.* Trans. Adrian Walker. San Francisco: Ignatius Press, 1996. Originally published as *Zur Gemeinschaft gerufen: Kirche heute verstehen* (Freiburg: Herder, 1991).

Rodriguez, Victorino. "Inhabitación de la SS. Trinidad en el alma en gracia." *CT* 86 (1959): 65–115.

Schillebeeckx, Edward. *Church: The Human Story of God.* New York: Crossroad, 1990.

Schindler, David. *Heart of the World, Center of the Church: Communio Ecclesiology, Liberalism, and Liberation.* Grand Rapids, MI: Eerdmans, 1996.

Schüssler Fiorenza, Elisabeth. *Discipleship of Equals: A Critical Feminist Ekklesia-logy of Liberation.* New York: Crossroad, 1994.

Tanquerey, Adolphe. *Brevior synopsis theologiae dogmaticae,* 9th ed. Paris: Desclée, 1952. The original edition was published in 1931.

Torrance, Alan. *Persons in Communion: An Essay on Trinitarian Description and Human Participation.* Edinburgh: T & T Clark, 1996.

Von Balthasar, Hans Urs. "Der Unbekannte jenseits des Wortes." In *Interpretation der Welt; Festschrift R. Guardini,* 638–45. Edited by Helmut Kuhn. Würzburg: Echter, 1965.

———. "Christology and Ecclesial Obedience." In *Explorations in Theology IV: Spirit and Institution,* 139–68. Translated by Edward Oakes. San Francisco: Ignatius Press, 1995. Originally published as "Christologie und kirchlicher Gehorsam," *Geist und Leben* 42 (1969): 185–203.

Zizioulas, John D. "Human Capacity and Human Incapacity." *ScotJTh* 28 (1975): 401–48.

———. *Being as Communion: Studies in Personhood and the Church.* Crestwood, NY: Saint Vladimir's Seminary Press, 1985.

———. "On Being a Person. Towards an Ontology of Personhood." In *Persons, Divine and Human,* 33–46. Edited by Christoph Schwöbel and Colin E. Gunton. Edinburgh: T & T Clark, 1991.

———. "The Doctrine of the Holy Trinity: The Significance of the Cappadocian Contribution." In *Trinitarian Theology Today: Essays on Divine Being and Act,* 44–60. Edited by Christoph Schwöbel. Edinburgh: T & T Clark, 1995.

Index